CIMA
PRACTICE & REVISION KIT

Intermediate Paper 8

Management Accounting –
Performance Management

BPP Professional Education
January 2003

First edition 2001
Third edition January 2003

ISBN 0 7517 0282 X (previous edition 0 7517 3814 X)

British Library Cataloguing-in-Publication Data
A catalogue record for this book
is available from the British Library

Published by

BPP Professional Education
Aldine House, Aldine Place
London W12 8AW

www.bpp.com

Printed in Great Britain by Ashford Colour Press

We are grateful to the Chartered Institute of Management Accountants for permission to reproduce past examination questions. The answers to past examination questions have been prepared by BPP Professional Education.

CONTENTS

BPP
PROFESSIONAL EDUCATION

Question and answer checklist/index

The headings in this checklist/index indicate the main topics of questions, but questions often cover several different topics.

Preparation questions, listed in italics, provide you with a firm foundation for attempts at exam-standard questions.

Questions set under the old syllabus *Operational Cost Accounting* (OCA), *Management Science Applications* (MSA) and *Management Accounting Applications* (MAA) papers are included because their style and content are similar to those in the Paper 8 exam.

BPP PROFESSIONAL EDUCATION

Question and answer checklist/index

OBJECTIVE TEST QUESTIONS

MOCK EXAM 1 (MAY 2002)

Questions 92 – 97

MOCK EXAM 2 (NOVEMBER 2002)

Questions 98 – 103 Q5 + Q6 TQM

TOPIC INDEX

Listed below are the key Paper 8 syllabus topics and the numbers of the questions in the main bank of questions in this Kit covering those topics.

If you need to concentrate your practice and revision on certain topics or if you want to attempt all available questions that refer to a particular subject you will find this index useful.

Syllabus topic	Question numbers
Absorption costing	19, 55, 56, 57, 58, 65, 66, 91
Activity based budgeting	28, 51, 61, 67
Activity based costing	4, 7, 9, 16, 17, 19, 28, 49, 61, 62, 63, 64, 65, 67, 68, 89, 91
Balanced scorecard	36, 43, 89
Behavioural implications	36, 37, 42, 45, 51, 90
Benchmarking	2, 20
Budget preparation	18, 20, 22, 23, 24, 25, 26, 28, 35, 44, 89
Controllable and uncontrollable costs	36
Cost reduction programmes	47, 51, 52, 53
Criticisms of standard costing	1, 3, 52
Fixed budgeting	39
Fixed overhead variances	1, 2, 4, 5, 6, 7, 8, 9, 12, 13, 14, 16, 17, 18, 90, 91
Flexible budgeting	4, 5, 36, 37, 38, 39, 40, 41, 46, 89, 90
Incremental budgeting	27, 51, 89
Interpretation of variances	2, 8, 10, 12
Just-in-time	47, 48, 49, 53, 66, 91
Labour mix and yield variances (total)	2
Limiting factor analysis	69, 73, 75, 76, 77, 90, 91
Linear programming (graphical)	78, 79, 80, 81, 82, 83
Marginal costing	55, 56, 57, 91
Materials mix and yield variances (total)	1, 13, 15, 16
Multi-product CVP analysis	78, 84, 85, 86, 87, 88, 89, 90, 91
Planning	20, 21, 27
Process costing	55, 58, 59, 60
Regression	29, 30, 31, 33, 89, 90, 91
Relevant costs and revenues	69, 70, 71, 72, 74
Rolling budgets	27
Sales price and volume variances	1, 2, 5, 7, 8, 12, 13, 14, 90, 91
Significance of variances	10
Standard costing	2, 3, 4, 5, 11, 18, 40
Throughput accounting	55, 73
Time series	29, 30, 32, 33, 89, 90, 91
Total Quality Management	47, 49, 50, 66, 89
Value and functional cost analysis	47, 51, 52, 54
Variable cost variances	1, 2, 4, 5, 6, 7, 8, 9, 10, 11, 12, 13, 14, 15, 16, 17, 18
'What if' analysis	34
Zero base budgeting (ZBB)	27, 45, 51, 52

EFFECTIVE REVISION

What you must remember

Effective use of time as you approach the exam is very important. You must remember:

> **Believe in yourself**
> **Use time sensibly**

Believe in yourself

Are you cultivating the right attitude of mind? There is absolutely no reason why you should not pass this exam if you adopt the correct approach.

- **Be confident** – you've passed exams before, you can pass them again
- **Be calm** – plenty of adrenaline but no panicking
- **Be focused** – commit yourself to passing the exam

Use time sensibly

1. **How much study time do you have?** Remember that you must **eat, sleep**, and of course, **relax**.

2. **How will you split that available time between each subject?** A **revision timetable**, covering **what** and **how** you will revise, will help you organise your revision effectively.

3. **What is your learning style?** AM/PM? Little and often/long sessions? Evenings/weekends?

4. **Do you have quality study time?** Unplug the phone. Let everybody know that you're studying and shouldn't be disturbed.

5. **Are you taking regular breaks?** Most people absorb more if they do not attempt to study for long uninterrupted periods of time. A five minute break every hour (to make coffee, watch the news headlines) can make all the difference.

6. Are you **rewarding yourself** for your hard work? Are you leading a **healthy lifestyle**?

What to revise

Key topics

You need to spend most time on, and practise full questions on, **key topics**.

> Key topics
>
> - Recur regularly
> - Underpin whole paper
> - Appear often in compulsory questions
> - Discussed currently in press
> - Covered in recent articles by examiner
> - Shown as high priority in study material
> - Tipped by lecturer

Difficult areas

You may also still find certain areas of the syllabus difficult.

Difficult areas

- Areas you find dull or pointless
- Subjects you highlighted as difficult when taking notes
- Topics that gave you problems when you answered questions or reviewed the material

---

DON'T become depressed about these areas; instead do something about them.

- Build up your knowledge by **quick tests** such as the quick quizzes in your BPP Study Text.

- Work carefully through **numerical examples** and **questions** in the Text, and refer back to the Text if you struggle with computations in the Kit.

- **Note down weaknesses** that your answers to questions contained; you are less likely to make the same mistakes if you highlight where you went wrong.

Breadth of revision

Make sure your revision has sufficient **breadth**. You need to be able to answer all the compulsory questions and enough optional questions on the paper. On certain papers all major topics in the syllabus will be tested, through objective test questions or longer questions. On other papers it will be impossible to predict which topics will be examined in compulsory questions, which topics in optional questions.

Paper 8

In this paper do not spend all your revision practising the numerical techniques. In each of the exams to date you would have been forced to answer one entirely discursive question.

How to revise

There are four main ways that you can revise a topic area.

Write it!
Read it!
Teach it!
Do it!

Write it!

The Course Notes and the Study Text are too bulky for revision. You need a slimmed down set of notes that summarise the key points. Writing important points down will help you recall them, particularly if your notes are presented in a way that makes it easy for you to remember them.

> ## Read it!

You should read your notes or BPP Passcards actively, testing yourself by doing quick quizzes or writing summaries of what you have just read.

> ## Teach it!

Exams require you to show your understanding. Teaching what you are revising to another person helps you practise explaining topics. Teaching someone who will challenge your understanding, someone for example who will be taking the same exam as you, can help both of you.

> ## Do it!

Remember that you are revising in order to be able to answer questions in the exam. Answering questions will help you practise **technique** and **discipline**, which examiners emphasise over and over again can be crucial in passing or failing exams.

1   A bank of **objective text questions** is included for each syllabus area. Attempt all of these banks and use them as a **diagnostic tool**: if you get lots of them wrong go back to your BPP Study Text or look through the Paper 8 Passcards and do some revision. Additional guidance on how to tackle objective test questions is given on page (xxiv). If you get the majority of the objective test questions correct, move on to any **preparation questions** included for the syllabus area. These provide you with a firm foundation from which to attempt exam-standard questions.

2   The more exam-standard questions you do, the more likely you are to pass the exam. At the very least, you should attempt the **key questions** that are highlighted from page (xii) onwards.

3   You should produce **full answers** under **timed conditions,** and don't cheat by looking at the answer! Look back at your notes or at your BPP Study Text instead if you are really struggling. Produce answer plans if you are running short of time.

4   Always read the **Pass marks** in the answers. They are there to help you, and will show you which points in the answer are the most important.

5   **Don't get despondent** if you didn't do very well. Refer to the **topic index** and try another question that covers the same subject.

6   When you think you can successfully answer questions on the whole syllabus, attempt the **two mock exams** at the end of the Kit. You will get the most benefit by sitting them under strict exam conditions, so that you gain experience of the four vital exam processes.

- Selecting questions
- Deciding on the order in which to attempt them
- Managing your time
- Producing answers

BPP's *Learning to Learn Accountancy* book gives further invaluable advice on how to approach revision.

BPP has also produced other vital revision aids.

- **Passcards** – Provide you with clear topic summaries and exam tips
- **Success tapes** – Help you revise on the move
- **Videos** – Show you an overview of key topics and how they are related
- **MCQ cards** – Give you lots of practice in answering MCQs
- **i-Pass CDs** – Offer you tests of knowledge to be completed against the clock

You can purchase these products by completing the order form at the back of this Kit or by visiting www.bpp.com/cima.

BPP
PROFESSIONAL EDUCATION

DETAILED REVISION PLAN

The table below gives you **one possible approach** to your revision for *Management Accounting – Performance Management*. There are of course many ways in which you can tackle the final stages of your study for this paper and this is just a **suggestion**: simply following it is no guarantee of success. You or your college may prefer an alternative but equally valid approach.

The BPP plan below, requires you to devote a **minimum of 25 hours** to revision of Paper 8. Any time you can spend over and above this should only increase your chances of success.

Suggested approach

1   For each section of the syllabus, **review** your **notes** and the relevant chapter summaries in the Paper 8 **Passcards**.

2   Then do the **key questions** for that section. These are **shaded** in the table below. As we Even if you are short of time you must attempt these questions if you want to pass the exam. Try to complete your answers without referring to our solutions.

3   For some questions we have suggested that you prepare **answer plans** rather than full solutions. This means that you should spend about 30% of the full time allowance on brainstorming the question and drawing up a list of points to be included in the answer.

4   Once you have worked through all of the syllabus sections attempt **mock exam 1** (the May 2002 paper) under strict exam conditions. Then, if you've got enough time, have a go at **mock exam 2** (the November 2002 paper), again under strict exam conditions.

Syllabus section	2003 Passcards chapters	Key questions in this Kit	Comments	Done ☑
Standard costing	1 – 4	1	Answer all of these OT questions.	☐
		2	Answer all of these OT questions.	☐
		3	Answer in full.	☐
			This question looks at a topical area popular with examiners – the relevance of standard costing in the modern business environment.	
		10	Answer in full.	☐
			The examiner has confirmed that a question like this is possible. (Indeed a similar question appeared in the May 2002 paper.)	
		5 & 11	Answer in full.	☐
			These are 'working backwards' questions – a favourite with the examiner under the old syllabus and an approach he has confirmed he could adopt in Paper 8. The questions also give you the chance to go over the more straightforward variances covered at Foundation level.	
		13	Answer part (a) in full.	☐
			This part of a pilot paper question gives you the opportunity to calculate a wide range of variances, including the more complex total mix and yield variances introduced in Paper 8.	

Syllabus section	2003 Passcards chapters	Key questions in this Kit	Comments	Done ☑
		16	Answer in full.	☐
			As well as needing practice in calculating the variances introduced in Paper 8, the examiner's reports make it clear that students need to practice calculating the more straightforward variances too. This question gives you the opportunity to do both.	
Budgets	5	20	Answer all of these OT questions.	☐
		21	Answer in full.	☐
			This question checks your understanding of the budgeting process. You need to be concise (make as many points as possible in a minimum amount of time and writing), a key exam skill.	
		28	Answer in full.	☐
			This is a useful question incorporating budget preparation and ABC. Given that straightforward budgeting is covered at Foundation level, adding ABC to the topic is one way in which the examiner can make budgeting questions that bit more complicated.	
Forecasting	6	29	Answer all of these OT questions.	☐
		30	Answer in full.	☐
			This question from the 11/01 paper is a very important one to try as it integrates the key forecasting techniques in the syllabus in one question.	
		34	Do an answer plan only.	☐
			This question require both the calculation of figures for a sensitivity analysis and an explanation of its use – areas yet to be examined.	
Budgetary control and performance measurement	7	36	Answer all of these OT questions.	☐
		37	Answer in full.	☐
			This pilot paper question gives an indication of the type of budgetary control questions you could face.	

BPP
PROFESSIONAL EDUCATION

Syllabus section	2003 Passcards chapters	Key questions in this Kit	Comments	Done ☑
		44	Answer in full.	☐
			This question covers budget preparation in a service environment, which at Intermediate level is perhaps a more probable question scenario than a manufacturing environment.	
			Note that although Paper 8 will not have a number of questions based on a long scenario (such as questions 44, 45 and 46 in this Kit), you may be required to work with a short scenario.	
		45	Do an answer plan only.	☐
			This question covers two important topics – the behavioural aspects of budgeting and ZBB. You will need to apply theoretical concepts to the given scenario.	
Modern business environment and cost reduction	8 & 12	47	Answer all of these OT questions.	☐
		51	Do an answer plan only.	☐
			This 11/01 question covers a range of syllabus topics which inevitably will be examined using this style of question.	
		52	Answer in full.	☐
			Like question 51, attempting this question will give you practice in providing an answer about a variety of topics to a typical Paper 8 style discursive question.	
Costing systems	9 & 11	55	Answer all of these OT questions.	☐
		57	Answer in full.	☐
			Absorption costing and marginal costing are specifically mentioned in the revised Paper 8 syllabus which applies with effect from the 5/03 exam and so it is worth having a go at this question, which asks you to contrast the two systems.	
		58	Answer in full.	☐
			Process costing is another topic specifically mentioned in the revised Paper 8 syllabus. You must be able to deal with the easier aspects of the topic covered at Foundation level and the more complex areas introduced at Intermediate level, a number of which are covered in this question.	

Syllabus section	2003 Passcards chapters	Key questions in this Kit	Comments	Done ☑
		59	Do an answer plan only.	☐
			Another of the more complex areas of process costing which could be examined is covered in this question – that of joint and by-products. As process costing is new to the syllabus the examiner could well include it in one of the 2003 papers.	
		60	Do an answer plan only.	☐
			If the examiner wants you to demonstrate real understanding of aspects of a particular technique, he could well pose a discursive question like this one on a topic traditionally associated with calculation questions.	
ABC	10	61	Answer all of these OT questions.	☐
		64	Answer in full.	☐
			Answering this question will give you invaluable practice at calculating ABC costs.	
		67	Do an answer plan only.	☐
			The subject of this question, ABC, is a popular exam topic.	
Relevant costs and limiting factors	13 & 14	69	Answer all of these OT questions.	☐
		70	Answer in full.	☐
			This is a good question to attempt for practice at the newly-introduced syllabus area of 'Relevant costs and revenues for short-term decision making'.	
		73	Do an answer plan only.	☐
			Although you are unlikely to face a complete question on throughput accounting, it has been specifically mentioned in the revised Paper 8 syllabus and so you should have a go at drawing up an answer plan to this question.	
		74	Answer in full.	☐
			This pilot paper question is worth attempting as it looks at a wide range of topics including information analysis, profit maximisation and production scheduling.	
		76	Answer in full.	☐
			This question is a good example of the syllabus area 'limiting factors with restricted freedom of action'.	

Detailed revision plan

Syllabus section	2003 Passcards chapters	Key questions in this Kit	Comments	Done ☑
Linear programming and CVP analysis	15 & 16	78	Answer all of these OT questions.	☐
		79	Answer in full.	☐
			This 11/01 exam question is a particularly useful question on linear programming as it incorporates computer package output.	
		80	Do an answer plan only.	☐
			Preparation of a plan will ensure that you are able to draw up those all-important steps required in the formulation of a linear programming problem.	
Final revision		89	Answer all of these OT questions.	☐
		90	Answer all of these OT questions.	☐
		91	Answer all of these OT questions.	☐

THE EXAM PAPER

Format of the paper

		Number of marks
Section A	Objective test questions	20
Section B	One compulsory question	30
Section C	One question from two	25
Section D	One question from two	25
		100

Time allowed : 3 hours

Analysis of past papers

The analysis below shows the topics which have been examined under the current syllabus and included in the Pilot paper for *Management Accounting – Performance Management*.

Note that because of the syllabus changes effective from the May 2003 exam, some topics in past Paper 8 exams are no longer examinable.

November 2002

Section A

1.1   Breakeven analysis
1.2   Variance analysis
1.3   Variance analysis
1.4   Limiting factor analysis
1.5   Absorption costing
1.6   Marginal costing
1.7   Breakeven analysis
1.8   Variance analysis
1.9   Variance analysis

Section B

2   Budgetary control and ABC; behavioural issues; forecasting

Section C

3   Variance analysis
4   Transfer pricing

Section D

5   TQM
6   JIT and cost reduction

This paper forms mock exam 2 at the end of the Kit.

BPP
PROFESSIONAL EDUCATION

The exam paper

May 2002

Section A

1.1   Breakeven analysis
1.2   Budgeting
1.3   Breakeven analysis
1.4   Forecasting
1.5   ABC
1.6   Variance analysis
1.7   Budgeting
1.8   Budgeting

Section B

2   Limiting factor analysis; profit statements; graphical approach to linear programming; shadow prices

Section C

3   Variance analysis; variance charts; variance investigation
4   Learning curves and standard costs; planning and operational variances

Section D

5   Balanced scorecard; benchmarking
6   Budgets, including behavioural aspects; transfer pricing

This paper forms mock exam 1 at the end of the Kit.

Examiner's comments

Many of the common errors noted by the examiner have been mentioned on previous occasions.

- In limiting factor analysis, not ranking by contribution per unit of limiting factor (Question 2)
- Not indicating whether variances are adverse or favourable (Question 3)
- Inability to deal with material losses, multiplying by 1.05 instead of by 100/95 (Question 4)
- Not considering the question scenario when discussing the balanced scorecard (Question 5)
- Not answering the question in sufficient depth to earn all of the marks (Question 6)

Question number in this Kit

November 2001

Section A

1.1	Variances	91
1.2	Variances	
1.3	Learning curve	
1.4	Variances	
1.5	Variances	
1.6	Activity based costing	
1.7	Transfer pricing	
1.8	Breakeven analysis	
1.9	Limiting factor analysis	

Section B

2	Mix and yield variances; planning and operational variances	Topics no longer in syllabus

Section C

3	Linear programming (graphical and simplex); learning curves	79
4	Forecasting; performance measurement	30

Section D

5	Budgeting; cost reduction and value analysis	51
6	JIT; transfer pricing	JIT - included in ME1. Transfer pricing - no longer in syllabus

---

Examiner's comments

Key comments made by the examiner include:

- Too many candidates were unable to calculate variances which are actually part of the Foundation level Paper 2 syllabus.

- Candidates should state whether variances are adverse or favourable, rather than use brackets, which can be unclear.

- Some candidates had no idea of the meaning of planning and operating variances.

- Many candidates had no idea how to present a graph.

- Some candidates did not answer the question set but instead regurgitated notes and/or wrote all that they knew about a topic.

- Inability to allocate time in proportion to the marks available and failure to apply understanding of a topic to the scenario in the question were evident in scripts.

May 2001

Question number in this Kit

Section A

1.1	Variances	90
1.2	Forecasting	
1.3	Breakeven analysis	
1.4	Flexible budgets	
1.5	Behavioural aspects of budgeting	
1.6	Limiting factor analysis	
1.7	Breakeven analysis	
1.8	Variances	
1.9	Variances	

Section B

2	Limiting factor analysis; learning curves; profit statements	73 (part of)

Section C

3	Activity based costing; pricing; modern business environment	63
4	Cost reduction; value analysis; ZBB; relevance of standard costing	52

Section D

5	Planning and operational variances; mix and yield variances	No longer in syllabus. See mock exam 1
6	Activity based costing	

Examiner's comments

Candidates' inability to be able to apply knowledge to the context of the question was noted by the examiner in relation to all of the non-OT questions.

Many candidates were unable to deal with the learning curve aspects of question 2 and few candidates could deal with question 5 part (e), which required the calculation of percentage variance values to determine the trend and significance of variances.

Too many candidates made assumptions about the requirements of various parts of question 6, and answered the question they would have like to have been set.

The examiner

The examiner for Paper 8 was the examiner of Paper 6 *Operational Cost Accounting* under the old syllabus and so questions taken from that paper give some guidance as to the type of question that you might encounter.

Formula to learn

You will be provided with certain formulae and mathematical tables in the exam paper but the following formula is not provided and you may need to use it in the exam.

LEARN IT.

Coefficient of correlation

(Also known as the Pearsonian coefficient of correlation and the product moment correlation coefficient)

$$r = \frac{n\Sigma xy - \Sigma x \Sigma y}{\sqrt{(n\Sigma x^2 - (\Sigma x)^2)(n\Sigma y^2 - (\Sigma y)^2)}}$$

EXAM TECHNIQUE

Passing professional examinations is half about having the knowledge, and half about doing yourself full justice in the examination. You must have the right approach at the following times.

> **Before the exam**
> **Your time in the exam hall**

Before the exam

1 Set at least one **alarm** (or get an alarm call) for a morning exam.

2 Have **something to eat** but beware of eating too much; you may feel sleepy if your system is digesting a large meal.

3 Allow plenty of **time to get to the exam hall**; have your route worked out in advance and listen to news bulletins to check for potential travel problems.

4 **Don't forget** pens, pencils, rulers, erasers, watch. Also make sure you remember **entrance documentation** and **evidence of identity**.

5 Put **new batteries** into your calculator and take a spare set (or a spare calculator).

6 **Avoid discussion** about the exam with other candidates outside the exam hall.

Your time in the exam hall

1 *Read the instructions (the 'rubric') on the front of the exam paper carefully*

   Check that the exam format hasn't changed. Examiners' reports often remark on the number of students who attempt too few – or too many – questions, or who attempt the wrong number of questions from different parts of the paper.

2 *Select questions carefully*

   Read through the paper once, underlining the key words in the question and jotting down the most important points.   Select the optional questions that you feel you can answer best. You should base your selection on:

   - The **topics** covered
   - The **requirements of the whole question** (see page (xxv) for the guidance on what the examiner means)
   - How easy it will be to **apply the requirements** to the details you are given
   - The availability of **easy marks**

   Make sure that you are planning to answer the **right number of questions,** all the compulsory questions plus the correct number of optional questions.

3 *Plan your attack carefully*

   Consider the **order** in which you are going to tackle questions. It is a good idea to start with your best question to boost your morale and get some easy marks 'in the bag'.

4   *Check the time allocation for each question*

Each mark carries with it a **time allocation** of 1.8 minutes (including time for selecting and reading questions, and checking answers). A 25 mark question therefore should be selected, completed and checked in 45 minutes. When time is up, you **must** go on to the next question or part. Going even one minute over the time allowed brings you a lot closer to failure.

5   *Read the question carefully and plan your answer*

Read through the question again very carefully when you come to answer it. Plan your answer taking into account how the answer should be **structured**, what the **format** should be and **how long** it should take.

Confirm before you start writing that your plan makes **sense**, covers **all relevant points** and does not include **irrelevant material**. Two minutes of planning plus eight minutes of writing is virtually certain to earn you more marks than ten minutes of writing.

6   *Answer the question set*

Particularly with written answers, make sure you **answer the question set**, and not the question you would have preferred to have been set.

7   *Gain the easy marks*

Include the obvious if it answers the question and don't try to produce the perfect answer.

Don't get bogged down in small parts of questions. If you find a part of a question difficult, get on with the rest of the question. If you are having problems with something, the chances are that everyone else is too.

8   *Produce an answer in the correct format*

The examiner will **state in the requirements** the format in which the question should be answered, for example in a report or memorandum.

9   *Follow the examiner's instructions*

You will **annoy** the examiner if you ignore him or her.

10   *Lay out your numerical computations and use workings correctly*

Make sure the layout fits the **type of question** and is in a style the examiner likes. Show all your **workings** clearly and explain what they mean. **Cross reference** them to your solution. This will help the examiner to follow your method (this is of particular importance where there may be several possible answers).

11   *Present a tidy paper*

You are a professional, and it should show in the **presentation of your work**. Students are penalised for poor presentation and so you should make sure that you write legibly, label diagrams clearly and lay out your work neatly. Markers of scripts each have hundreds of papers to mark; a badly written scrawl is unlikely to receive the same attention as a neat and well laid out paper.

12   *Stay until the end of the exam*

Use any spare time **checking and rechecking** your script. This includes checking:

- You have **filled out** the **candidate details correctly**
- Question parts and workings are **labelled clearly**
- Aids to navigation such as **headers and underlining** are used effectively
- **Spelling, grammar** and **arithmetic** are correct

13 **Don't discuss an exam with other candidates afterwards**

There's nothing more you can do about it so why discuss it?

14 **Don't worry if you feel you have performed badly in the exam**

It is more than likely that the other candidates will have found the exam difficult too. Don't forget that there is a competitive element in these exams. As soon as you get up to leave the exam hall, *forget* **that exam** and think about the next – or, if it is the last one, celebrate!

BPP's *Learning to Learn Accountancy* book gives further invaluable advice on how to approach the day of the exam.

TACKLING OBJECTIVE TEST QUESTIONS

Of the total marks available for this paper, objective test questions comprise 20 per cent.

The objective test questions (OTs) in your exam contain four possible answers. You have to **choose the option that best answers the question**. The three incorrect options are called distracters. There is a skill in answering OTs quickly and correctly. By practising OTs you can develop this skill, giving you a better chance of passing the exam.

You may wish to follow the approach outlined below, or you may prefer to adapt it.

Step 1. Skim read all the OTs and identify what appear to be the easier questions.

Step 2. Attempt each question – **starting with the easier questions** identified in Step 1. Read the question thoroughly. You may prefer to work out the answer before looking at the options, or you may prefer to look at the options at the beginning. Adopt the method that works best for you.

Step 3. Read the four options and see if one matches your own answer. Be careful with numerical questions, as the distracters are designed to match answers that incorporate common errors. Check that your calculation is correct. Have you followed the requirement exactly? Have you included every stage of the calculation?

Step 4. You may find that none of the options matches your answer.

- Re-read the question to ensure that you understand it and are answering the requirement

- Eliminate any obviously wrong answers

- Consider which of the remaining answers is the most likely to be correct and select the option

Step 5. If you are still unsure make a note and continue to the next question.

Step 6. Revisit unanswered questions. When you come back to a question after a break you often find you are able to answer it correctly straight away. If you are still unsure have a guess. You are not penalised for incorrect answers, so **never leave a question unanswered!**

After extensive practice and revision of OT, you may find that you recognise a question when you sit the exam. Be aware that the detail and/or requirement may be different. If the question seems familiar read the requirement and options carefully – do not assume that it is identical.

WHAT THE EXAMINER MEANS

The table below has been prepared by CIMA to help you interpret exam questions.

The verbs used in questions indicate which key skills you will be using to answer them, and therefore the depth your answer should have, and how you should use the information you are given in the question.

Learning objective	Verbs used	Definition	Examples in the Kit
1 Knowledge What you are expected to know	• List • State • Define	• Make a list of • Express, fully or clearly, the details of/facts of • Give the exact meaning of	Q 48
2 Comprehension What you are expected to understand	• Describe • Distinguish • Explain • Identify • Illustrate	• Communicate the key features of • Highlight the differences between • Make clear or intelligible/state the meaning of • Recognise, establish or select after consideration • Use an example to describe or explain something	Q 79 Q 4 Q 30 Q 28
3 Application Can you apply your knowledge?	• Apply • Calculate/ compute • Demonstrate • Prepare • Reconcile • Solve • Tabulate	• To put to practical use • To ascertain or reckon mathematically • To prove the certainty or to exhibit by practical means • To make or get ready for use • To make or prove consistent/ compatible • Find an answer to • Arrange in a table	Q 79 Q 14 Q 30 Q 14
4 Analysis Can you analyse the detail of what you have learned?	• Analyse • Categorise • Compare and contrast • Construct • Discuss • Interpret • Produce	• Examine in detail the structure of • Place into a defined class or division • Show the similarities and/or differences between • To build up or complete • To examine in detail by argument • To translate into intelligible or familiar terms • To create or bring into existence	Q 14 Q 18 Q 63
5 Evaluation Can you use your learning to evaluate, make decisions or recommendations?	• Advise • Evaluate • Recommend	• To counsel, inform or notify • To appraise or assess the value of • To advise on a course of action	Q 59 Q 35

BPP)))
PROFESSIONAL EDUCATION

USEFUL WEBSITES

The websites below provide additional sources of information of relevance to your studies for *Management Accounting – Performance Management.*

- BPP   www.bpp.com
- CIMA   www.cimaglobal.com
- *Financial Times*   www.ft.com
- *The Economist*   www.economist.com
- *Wall Street Journal*   www.wsj.com

SYLLABUS MINDMAP

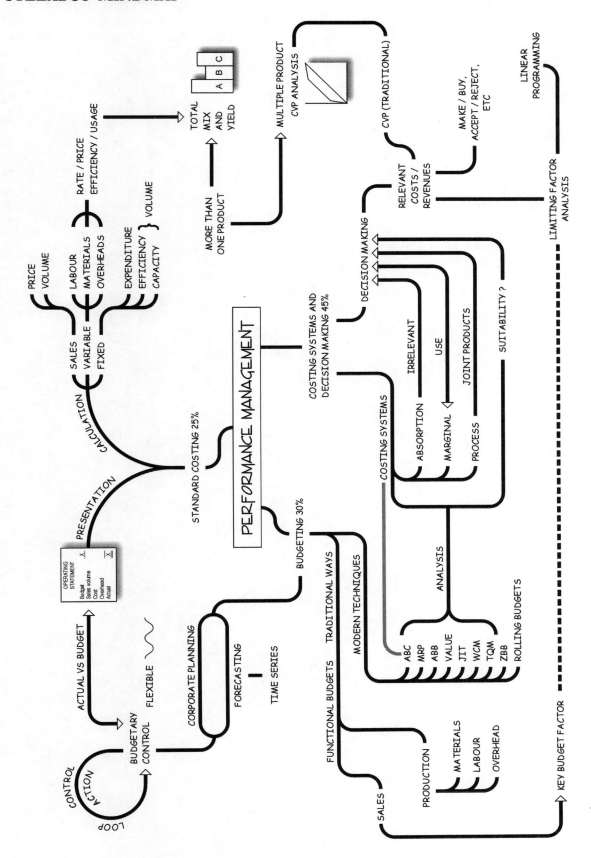

BPP
PROFESSIONAL EDUCATION

Questions

STANDARD COSTING

Questions 1 to 19 cover standard costing, the subject of Part A of the BPP Study Text for Paper 8.

1   OBJECTIVE TEST QUESTIONS: STANDARD COSTING   *36 mins*

The following information relates to questions 1 to 4.

JF Ltd manufactures a single product. An extract from a variance control report together with relevant standard cost data is shown below.

Standard selling price per unit	£70
Standard direct material cost (5kg × £2 per kg)	£10 per unit
Budgeted total material cost of sales	£2,300 per month
Budgeted profit margin	£6,900 per month

Actual results for February

Sales revenue	£15,200
Total direct material cost	£2,400
Direct material price variance	£800 adverse
Direct material usage variance	£400 favourable

There was no change in stock levels during the month.

1   What was the actual production in February?

    A   200 units
    B   217 units
    C   240 units
    D   280 units   **2 Marks**

2   What was the actual usage of direct material during February?

    A   800 kg
    B   1,000 kg
    C   1,200 kg
    D   None of the above   **2 Marks**

3   What was the selling price variance for February?

    A   £120 Favourable
    B   £900 Adverse
    C   £1,200 Adverse
    D   £1,200 Favourable   **2 Marks**

4   What was the sales volume variance for February?

    A   £900 Favourable
    B   £1,200 Favourable
    C   £900 Adverse
    D   £2,100 Adverse   **2 Marks**

The following information relates to questions 5 and 6.

A company manufactures a single product, and relevant data for December is as follows.

	Budget/standard	*Actual*
Production units	1,800	1,900
Labour hours	9,000	9,400
Fixed production overhead	£36,000	£39,480

5   The fixed production overhead capacity variance for December is

    A   £1,600 (F)
    B   £1,600 (A)
    C   £1,680 (F)
    D   £2,000 (F)   **2 Marks**

6   The fixed production overhead efficiency variance for December is

    A   £400 (F)
    B   £400 (A)
    C   £420 (F)
    D   £1,600 (F)   **2 Marks**

7   Which of the following criticisms of standard costing apply in all circumstances?

    (i)   Standard costing can only be used where all operations are repetitive and output is homogeneous.

    (ii)   Standard costing systems cannot be used in environments which are prone to change. They assume stable conditions.

    (iii)   Standard costing systems assume that performance to standard is acceptable. They do not encourage continuous improvement.

    A   Criticism (i)
    B   Criticism (ii)
    C   Criticism (iii)
    D   None of them   **2 Marks**

The following information relates to questions 8 and 9.

The standard material cost of one unit of product F is as follows.

		£ per unit
Material G	9 litres × £4 per litre	36
Material H	6 litres × £2 per litre	12
	15	48

During March, 2,800 units of product F were produced, using 24,500 litres of material G and 20,500 litres of material H.

8   What mix variance arose in March?

    A   £5,000 (A)
    B   £ nil
    C   Impossible to tell from the information provided
    D   £5,000 (F)   **3 Marks**

9   What is the material yield variance which arose in March?

    A   £640 (A)
    B   £4,600 (A)
    C   £9,600 (A)
    D   £9,600 (F)   **3 Marks**

                                   Total Marks = 20

2   OBJECTIVE TEST QUESTIONS: STANDARD COSTING AGAIN   *36 mins*

1   During October 50,820 direct labour hours were worked, for which the standard labour cost was £264,264. The direct labour efficiency variance was £130 adverse.

How many standard hours were produced during October?

A   50,690
B   50,795
C   50,820
D   50,845   **2 Marks**

2   W Limited uses a standard costing system and absorbs fixed production overhead using a predetermined standard rate per labour hour. The following is an extract from the overhead variance report for March.

Fixed production overhead variances (extract):

total variance	£8,000 favourable
expenditure variance	£9,500 favourable
efficiency variance	£1,500 adverse

Which of the following statements is/are true for March?

1   The fixed production overhead was under absorbed by £8,000.
2   Production output was equal to the original budget.
3   Production overhead expenditure was £9,500 lower than in the original budget.
4   Labour hours worked were equal to the original budget.

A   Statements 1 and 2 only
B   Statements 2, 3 and 4 only
C   Statements 2 and 3 only
D   Statements 3 and 4 only   **2 Marks**

3   Which of the following is likely to be a consequence of switching from labour intensive operations to automated production systems in manufacturing industries?

A   Ideal and attainable standards should now be the same.
B   Any reported variances are likely to be due to uncontrollable causes.
C   The significance of any direct labour cost variances will be reduced.
D   It will not be possible to establish standard costing systems properly.   **2 Marks**

4   The manager responsible for grounds maintenance of the area surrounding E Limited's factory premises is engaged in a benchmarking exercise. He is comparing his operations with those of grounds maintenance operations in a nearby hospital and a school. He hopes to improve the performance of his operations by adopting the best practices of the other operations. This type of benchmarking is known as

A   Internal benchmarking
B   Functional benchmarking
C   Competitive benchmarking
D   Strategic benchmarking   **2 Marks**

5   In order to indicate to managers the trend and materiality of variances, B plc expresses them as percentages as in the following examples.

	July	*August*	*September*	*October*	*November*
Material usage variance as a percentage of standard total production cost	3% (F)	2% (A)	6% (A)	10%(A)	12%(A)
Material price variance as a percentage of standard cost of material used	1%(A)	2%(A)	7% (F)	8% (F)	9%(F)

5

(A) donates an adverse variance; (F) denotes a favourable variance

The following statements relate to recent operational events.

Statement

1   In September the buyer located a new supplier who charged a lower price than the previous supplier. The material was found to be of low quality, however, leading to a high level of waste.

2   The general trend is that all direct material variances are becoming more significant and are likely to be worthy of management attention.

3   A change in the bonus payment scheme has improved the productivity of labour, who are now processing material more effectively.

Which of the statements is or are consistent with the results shown?

A   Statements 1 and 2 only
B   Statements 1 and 3 only
C   Statements 2 and 3 only
D   Statement 2 only   **2 Marks**

The following information relates to questions 6 and 7.

Two grades of labour work together in teams to produce product W. The standard labour cost of product W is shown below.

Labour grade		£ per unit
1	3 hours × £8	24
2	5 hours × £6	30
		54

During February, 800 units of product W were produced using 2,550 hours of grade 1 labour and 4,090 hours of grade 2 labour.

6   What labour mix variance arose in February?

A   £60 (A)
B   £60 (F)
C   £120 (A)
D   £nil   **3 Marks**

7   What is the labour yield variance which arose in February?

A   £202.5 (A)
B   £1,620 (A)
C   £1,620 (F)
D   £1,740 (A)   **3 Marks**

8   Which of the following situations would help to explain a favourable sales volume variance?

(i)   Increased competitor activity led to a reduction in the number of units sold.

(ii)   Customers were given discounts at a higher level than standard in order to encourage increased sales volume.

(iii) The unit cost of production was lower than standard and selling prices were maintained at the standard level, so that a higher profit was achieved per unit sold.

(iv)   Higher quality material supplies led to improvements in the quality of the final output, which customers found attractive.

A (i), (ii) and (iv) only
B (ii), (iii) and (iv) only
C (ii) and (iv) only
D (ii) only **2 Marks**

9 PQ Limited currently uses a standard absorption costing system. The fixed overhead variances extracted from the operating statement for November are:

	£
Fixed production overhead expenditure variance	5,800 adverse
Fixed production overhead capacity variance	4,200 favourable
Fixed production overhead efficiency variance	1,400 adverse

PQ Limited is considering using standard marginal costing as the basis for variance reporting in future. What variance for fixed production overhead would be shown in a marginal costing operating statement for November?

A No variance would be shown for fixed production overhead
B Expenditure variance: £5,800 adverse
C Volume variance: £2,800 favourable
D Total variance: £3,000 adverse **2 Marks**

Total Marks = 20

If you struggled with these objective test questions, go back to your BPP Study Text for Paper 8 and revise Chapters 1 to 4 before you tackle the exam-standard questions on standard costing.

If you would like a bank of objective test questions which covers a range of syllabus topics, order our MCQ cards using the order form at the back of this Kit.

---

3 **RELEVANCE OF STANDARD COSTING AND VARIANCE ANALYSIS (MAA, 5/99, AMENDED)** *45 mins*

In recent years, writers have argued that standard costing and variance analysis should not be used for cost control and performance evaluation purposes in today's manufacturing world. Its use, they argue, is likely to induce behaviour which is inconsistent with the strategic manufacturing objectives that companies need to achieve in order to survive in today's intensively competitive international economic environment.

Required

(a) Explain the arguments referred to in the above paragraph concerning the relevance of standard costing and variance analysis. **11 Marks**

(b) Explain the arguments in favour of the relevance of standard costing and variance analysis in the modern manufacturing environment. **10 Marks**

(c) Suggest methods that might be used by management accountants to control costs and evaluate efficiency as alternatives or complements to standard costing and variance analysis. **4 Marks**

Total Marks = 25

4 **DL HOSPITAL TRUST (OCA, Specimen paper)** *45 mins*

You have been appointed as the management accountant of the DL Hospital Trust, a newly-formed organisation with specific responsibility for providing hospital services to its local community. The hospital trust is divided into a number of specialist units: one of these, unit H, specialises in the provision of a particular surgical operation.

Although the trust does not have profit maximisation as its objective, it is concerned to control its costs and to provide a value-for-money service. To achieve this, it engages teams of specialist staff on a sub-contract basis and pays them an hourly rate based upon the direct hours attributable to the surgical operation being carried out.

Surgical team fees (ie labour costs) are collected and attributed to each surgical operation, whereas overhead costs are collected and attributed to surgical operations using absorption rates. These absorption rates are based on the surgical team fees. For the year ended 31 December 20X3, these rates were as follows:

Variable overhead	62.5% of surgical team fees
Fixed overhead	87.5% of surgical team fees

Each surgical operation is expected to take ten hours to complete, and the total fees of the team for each operation are expected to be £2,000.

The budget for the year ended 31 December 20X3 indicated that a total of 20 such surgical operations were expected to be performed each month, and that the overhead costs were expected to accrue evenly throughout the year.

During November 20X3 there were 22 operations of this type completed. These took a total of 235 hours and the total surgical team fees amounted to £44,400.

Overhead costs incurred in unit H in November 20X3 amounted to the following:

Variable overhead	£28,650
Fixed overhead	£36,950

Required

(a) Prepare a statement which reconciles the original budget cost and the actual cost for this type of operation within unit H for the month of November 20X3, showing the analysis of variances in as much detail as possible from the information given.

15 Marks

(b) Distinguish between the use of budgetary control and standard costing as a means of cost control in service-based organisations.

Explain clearly the arguments in favour of using both of these methods simultaneously.

5 Marks

(c) The DL Hospital Trust has been preparing its budgets for 20X4, and the finance director has questioned the appropriateness of using surgical team fees as the basis of attributing overhead costs to operations.

Write a brief report to her explaining the arguments for and against the use of this method.

5 Marks

Total Marks = 25

5   WORKING BACKWARDS (OCA, 5/95)   *45 mins*

The following profit reconciliation statement has been prepared by the management accountant of ABC Ltd for March 20X5.

		£	
Budgeted profit		30,000	
Sales volume profit variance		5,250	A
Selling price variance		6,375	F
		31,125	

Cost variances		*A*	*F*		
		£	£		
Material:	price	1,985			
	usage		400		
Labour:	rate		9,800		
	efficiency	4,000			
Variable overhead:	expenditure		1,000		
	efficiency	1,500			
Fixed overhead:	expenditure		500		
	volume	24,500			
		31,985	11,700		
				20,285	A
Actual profit				10,840	

The standard cost card for the company's only product is as follows.

			£
Materials	5 litres @ £0.20		1.00
Labour	4 hours @ £4.00		16.00
Variable overhead	4 hours @ £1.50		6.00
Fixed overhead	4 hours @ £3.50		14.00
			37.00
Standard profit			3.00
Standard selling price			40.00

The following information is also available.

(a)   There was no change in the level of finished goods stock during the month.

(b)   Budgeted production and sales volumes for March 20X5 were equal.

(c)   Stocks of materials, which are valued at standard price, decreased by 800 litres during the month.

(d)   The actual labour rate was £0.28 lower than the standard hourly rate.

Required

(a)   Calculate the following.

(i)	The actual production/sales volume	**4 Marks**
(ii)	The actual number of hours worked	**4 Marks**
(iii)	The actual quantity of materials purchased	**4 Marks**
(iv)	The actual variable overhead cost incurred	**2 Marks**
(v)	The actual fixed overhead cost incurred	**2 Marks**

(b)   ABC Ltd uses a standard costing system whereas other organisations use a system of budgetary control.

Required

Explain the reasons why a system of budgetary control is often preferred to the use of standard costing in non-manufacturing environments.   **9 Marks**

Total Marks = 25

6   TUR PLC (OCA, 11/95/5/96, AMENDED)   *54 mins*

(a)   TUR plc uses an integrated standard costing system, with stocks being valued at standard cost. The standard cost card of one of its products, K, is shown below. This product is the only one of TUR plc's products which uses raw material F.

Standard cost card of product K
Year ended 31 October 20X5

			£
Raw material F	5 kilos	@ £3.50 per kilo	17.50
Direct labour	4 hours	@ £4.50 per hour	18.00
Overhead			
Variable	4 hours	@ £1.50 per hour	6.00
Fixed	4 hours	@ £2.50 per hour	10.00
			51.50

TUR plc prepares its annual accounts to 31 October each year. The trial balance at 30 September 20X5 shows that the stock of raw material F at that date was valued at £8,750.

Raw material F is added to the process continuously at a constant flow rate until the final product K is complete. Any price variances which arise are calculated and recorded in the material stock account at the time of purchase.

Company policy is to enter actual labour and overhead costs into the work in progress account, from which appropriate variances are extracted at the month end.

The budgeted production of product K during October 20X5 was 1,000 units. There was no opening or closing work in progress, and 965 units were transferred into finished goods stocks during October 20X5.

The following transactions occurred during October 20X5.

Purchased raw material F on credit	4,800 kilos costing £18,240
Issued raw material F to production	4,840 kilos
Direct wages	4,000 hours @ £4.60
Variable overhead incurred	£5,950
Fixed overhead incurred	£9,900

Required

Calculate the following variances for the month of October 20X5.

(i)   Material price variance - raw material F
(ii)   Material usage variance - raw material F
(iii) Direct labour rate variance
(iv)   Direct labour efficiency variance
(v)   Variable overhead expenditure variance
(vi)   Variable overhead efficiency variance
(vii) Fixed overhead expenditure variance
(viii) Fixed overhead volume variance

17 Marks

(b)   Q plc uses a standard absorption costing system which it developed five years ago. Three years ago, the specification of Q plc's material requirements changed and its standard costs were revised. Apart from this, the only change made to Q plc's material standards is to update its standard prices each year when preparing its annual budgets. Q plc calculates its material price variances at the time of purchase.

One of Q plc's products - product 2258 - uses material R. It is the only product made by Q plc which uses this material. According to the standard cost card, 5.00 kgs of material R are required per unit of product 2258, and the standard price of material R during the year ending 30 June 20X6 is £3.00 per kg.

During April 20X6, seven hundred units of product 2258 were manufactured. There was no opening stock of material R on 1 April 20X6. During April 20X6, 4,000 kgs of material R were purchased at a cost of £12,800. At the end of the month, on 30 April 20X6, there were 320 kgs of material R in stock.

Required

(i)   Calculate the material price and usage variances for April 20X6 using the standard cost data shown on the standard cost card.   **4 Marks**

(ii)   Explain the advantages and disadvantages of calculating the material price variance at the time of purchase.   **5 Marks**

(iii) The standard shown on the standard cost card assumes 0% material wastage, though 5% wastage is considered normal.

       Recalculate the material usage variance using a more appropriate standard, *and* explain why this is more useful to management than the usage variance calculated in your answer to (i) above.   **4 Marks**

Total Marks = 30

7   **S PLC (OCA, 11/96)**   *54 mins*

You have been provided with the following data for S plc for September 20X6.

Accounting method:	Absorption	Marginal
Variances	£	£
Selling price	1,900 (A)	1,900 (A)
Sales volume	4,500 (A)	7,500 (A)
Fixed overhead expenditure	2,500 (F)	2,500 (F)
Fixed overhead volume	1,800 (A)	not applicable

During September 20X6 production and sales volumes were as follows.

	Sales	*Production*
Budget	10,000	10,000
Actual	9,500	9,700

Required

(a) Calculate the following.

     (i)   The standard contribution per unit
     (ii)   The standard profit per unit
     (iii) The actual fixed overhead cost total   **9 Marks**

(b) Using the information presented above, explain why different variances are calculated depending upon the choice of marginal or absorption costing.   **8 Marks**

(c) Explain the meaning of the fixed overhead volume variance and its usefulness to management.   **5 Marks**

(d) Fixed overhead absorption rates are often calculated using a single measure of activity. It is suggested that fixed overhead costs should be attributed to cost units using multiple measures of activity (activity based costing).

BPP
PROFESSIONAL EDUCATION

Explain 'activity based costing' and how it may provide useful information to managers.

(Your answer should refer to both the setting of cost driver rates and subsequent overhead cost control.)   **8 Marks**

Total Marks = 30

8   **SEW (OCA, 5/97)**   *45 mins*

The following profit reconciliation statement summarises the performance of one of SEW's products for March 20X7.

	£
Budgeted profit	4,250
Sales volume variance	850 (A)
Standard profit on actual sales	3,400
Selling price variance	4,000 (A)
	(600)

Cost variances	Adverse £	Favourable £	
Direct material price		1,000	
Direct material usage	150		
Direct labour rate	200		
Direct labour efficiency	150		
Variable overhead expenditure	600		
Variable overhead efficiency	75		
Fixed overhead expenditure		2,500	
Fixed overhead volume		150	
	1,175	3,650	2,475 (F)
Actual profit			1,875

The budget for the same period contained the following data.

Sales volume		1,500 units
Sales revenue	£20,000	
Production volume		1,500 units
Direct materials purchased		750 kgs
Direct materials used		750 kgs
Direct material cost	£4,500	
Direct labour hours		1,125
Direct labour cost	£4,500	
Variable overhead cost	£2,250	
Fixed overhead cost	£4,500	

Additional information

(a)   Stocks of raw materials and finished goods are valued at standard cost.

(b)   During the month the actual number of units produced was 1,550.

(c)   The actual sales revenue was £12,000.

(d)   The direct materials purchased were 1,000 kgs.

Required

(a)   Calculate the following.

    (i)   The actual sales volume
    (ii)   The actual quantity of materials used
    (iii)   The actual direct material cost
    (iv)   The actual direct labour hours
    (v)   The actual direct labour cost
    (vi)   The actual variable overhead cost
    (vii)   The actual fixed overhead cost   **19 Marks**

(b) Explain the possible causes of the direct materials usage variance, direct labour rate variance, and sales volume variance. **6 Marks**

Total Marks = 25

9 OVERHEAD COST VARIANCES (OCA, 11/97) *45 mins*

The following details have been extracted from the standard cost card for product X.

	£/unit
Variable overhead	
4 machine hours @ £8.00/hour	32.00
2 labour hours @ £4.00/hour	8.00
Fixed overhead	20.00

During October 20X7, 5,450 units of the product were made compared to a budgeted production target of 5,500 units. The actual overhead costs incurred were:

Machine-related variable overhead	£176,000
Labour-related variable overhead	£42,000
Fixed overhead	£109,000

The actual number of machine hours was 22,000 and the actual number of labour hours was 10,800.

Required

(a) Calculate the overhead cost variances in as much detail as possible from the data provided. **12 Marks**

(b) Explain the meaning of, and give possible causes for, the variable overhead variances which you have calculated. **8 Marks**

(c) Explain the benefits of using multiple activity bases for variable overhead absorption. **5 Marks**

Total Marks = 25

10 E PLC *54 mins*

E plc has a semi-automated machine process in which a number of tasks are performed. A system of standard costing and budgetary control is in operation. The process is controlled by machine minders who are paid a fixed rate per hour of process time. The process has recently been reorganised as part of an ongoing total quality management programme in the company. The nature of the process is such that the machines incur variable costs even during non-productive (idle time) hours. Non-productive hours include time spent on the rework of products. *Note that gross machine hours = productive hours + non-productive (idle time) hours*.

The standard date for the machine process are as follows.

(a) Standard non-productive (idle time) hours as a percentage of gross machine hours is 10%.

(b) Standard variable machine cost per gross hour is £270.

(c) Standard output productivity is 100% ie one standard hour of work is expected in each productive machine hour.

(d) Machine costs are charged to production output at a rate per standard hour sufficient to absorb the cost of the standard level of non-productive time.

13

Actual data for the period August to November has been summarised as follows:

	Aug	Sept	Oct	Nov
Standard hours of output achieved	3,437	3,437	4,061	3,980
Machine hours (gross)	4,000	3,800	4,200	4,100
Non-productive machine hours	420	430	440	450
Variable machine costs (£'000)	1,100	1,070	1,247	1,218
Variance analysis	£	£	£	£
Productivity	42,900 (A)	?	?	99,000 (F)
Excess idle time	6,000 (A)	?	?	12,000 (A)
Expenditure	20,000 (A)	?	?	111,000 (A)
Variance analysis (in % terms)	%	%	%	%
Productivity	4.2 (A)	?	7.4 (F)	?
Excess idle time	5.0 (A)	?	4.8 (A)	?
Expenditure	1.9 (A)	?	10.0 (A)	?

Required

(a) Calculate the machine variances for productivity, excess idle time and expenditure for each of the months September and October.   **14 Marks**

(b) In order to highlight the trend of the variances in the August to November period, express each variance in percentage terms as follows:

Productivity variance: as a percentage of the standard cost of production achieved.

Excess idle time variance: as a percentage of the cost of expected idle time.

Expenditure variance: as a percentage of hours paid for at standard machine cost per hour.

(Note that the August and October calculations are given in the question.)   **7 Marks**

(c) Comment on the trend of the variances in the August to November period and possible inter-relationships, particularly in the context of the total quality management programme which is being implemented.   **9 Marks**

                           Total Marks = 30

11   RBF TRANSPORT LTD (OCA, 5/99)   *45 mins*

RBF Transport Ltd, a haulage contractor, operates a standard costing system and has prepared the following report for April 20X9.

Operating statement

		£	£	£
Budgeted profit				8,000
Sales volume profit variance				880 (A)
				7,120
Selling price variance				3,560 (F)
				10,680
Cost variances		A	F	
Direct labour	- rate		1,086	
	- efficiency	240		
Fuel	- price	420		
	- usage	1,280		
Variable overhead	- expenditure		280	
	- efficiency	180		
Fixed overhead	- expenditure		400	
	- volume	1,760		
		3,880	1,766	2,114 (A)
Actual profit				8,566

The company uses delivery miles as its cost unit, and the following details have been taken from the budget working papers for April 20X9.

- Expected activity   200,000 delivery miles
- Charge to customers   £0.30 per delivery mile
- Expected variable cost per delivery mile:

Direct labour (0.02 hours)	£0.08
Fuel (0.1 litres)	£0.04
Variable overhead (0.02 hours)	£0.06

The following additional information has been determined from the actual accounting records for April 20X9.

- Fixed overhead cost   £15,600
- Fuel price   £0.42 per litre
- Direct labour hours   3,620

Required

(a) Calculate the following for April 20X9.

    (i) The actual number of delivery miles
    (ii) The actual direct labour rate per hour
    (iii) The actual number of litres of fuel consumed
    (iv) The actual variable overhead expenditure   **16 Marks**

(b) Prepare a report, addressed to the transport operations manager, explaining the different types of standard which may be set, and the importance of keeping standards meaningful and relevant.   **9 Marks**

Total Marks = 25

12   WYE NOT (OCA, 11/99)   *45 mins*

Data from the October 20X9 standard cost card of product Wye, the only product of Exe plc, is as follows.

			£
Direct materials	4 kg	@ £2.50 per kg	10.00
Direct labour	3 hours	@ £6.00 per hour	18.00
Variable overhead	3 hours	@ £4.00 per hour	12.00
Fixed overhead			20.00
			60.00
Standard profit			15.00
Standard selling price			75.00

Budgeted fixed overhead cost for October 20X9 was £25,000.

The operating statement for October 20X9, when raw material stock levels remained unchanged, was as follows.

		£ Adverse	£ Favourable	£
Budgeted profit				17,250
Sales volume profit variance				750 (Adverse)
				16,500
Selling price variance				5,500 (Favourable)
				22,000
Cost variances:				
Direct materials	- price	535		
	- usage	375		
Direct labour	- rate	410		
	- efficiency	1,200		
Variable overhead	- expenditure		820	
	- efficiency	800		
Fixed overhead	- expenditure		1,000	
	- volume		1,000	
		3,320	2,820	500 (Adverse)
				21,500

Required

(a) Calculate the following.

(i)	Actual sales units	**3 Marks**
(ii)	Actual production units	**3 Marks**
(iii)	Actual selling price per unit	**2 Marks**
(iv)	Actual material price per kg	**2 Marks**
(v)	Actual labour hours	**2 Marks**
(vi)	Actual variable overhead cost	**3 Marks**
(vii)	Actual fixed overhead cost	**3 Marks**

(b) Prepare a report addressed to the operations manager which explains the meaning and possible causes of the two most significant variances which occurred in October 20X9.

7 Marks

Total Marks = 25

13 **M LTD (PILOT PAPER, AMENDED)** *45 mins*

(a) M Ltd operates a standard absorption costing system in respect of its only product. The standard cost card of this product for the budget year ending 31 December 2000 is as follows.

	£	£
Selling price		120.00
Direct material A (5 kgs)	12.50	
Direct material B (10 kgs)	40.00	
Direct wages (3 hours)	18.00	
Variable overhead (3 hours)	9.00	
Fixed overhead★ (3 hours)	15.00	
		94.50
Profit/unit		25.50

★Fixed overhead is absorbed on the basis of direct labour hours. Budgeted fixed overhead costs are £180,000 for the year. Cost and activity levels are budgeted to be constant each month.

During January 2000, when budgeted sales and production were 1,000 units, the following actual results were achieved.

		£
Sales (900 units)		118,800
Production costs (1,050 units)		
Direct material A (5,670 kg)		14,742
Direct material B (10,460 kg)		38,179
Direct wages (3,215 hours)		19,933
Variable overhead		10,288
Fixed overhead		15,432

Direct material and direct labour variances have already been calculated as follows.

		£
Direct material A	price variance	567 (A)
	usage variance	1,050 (A)
Direct material B	price variance	3,661 (F)
	usage variance	160 (F)
Direct labour	rate variance	643 (A)
	efficiency variance	390 (A)

You have confirmed with the production manager that the nature of the production method is such that direct materials A and B are mixed together to produce the final product.

All materials were purchased and used during January.

Required

Prepare for the production manager a statement that reconciles the budgeted and actual profits for January 2000 using the following variances.

(i)   Sales volume profit
(ii)   Sales price
(iii)   Direct material price
(iv)   Total direct material mix (valued using standard prices)
(v)   Total direct material yield
(vi)   Direct labour rate
(vii)   Direct labour efficiency
(viii) Variable production overhead expenditure
(ix)   Variable production overhead efficiency
(x)   Fixed production overhead expenditure
(xi)   Fixed production overhead capacity
(xii)   Fixed production overhead efficiency

Variances should be calculated so as to provide useful information to the production manager.   **15 Marks**

(b) Variance analysis involves the separation of individual cost variances into component parts. The benefit that may be derived from variance analysis depends on the interpretation and investigation of the component variances.

Required

Explain, with the aid of a simple numeric example, the logic, purpose and limitation of the separation of the fixed overhead volume variance into capacity utilisation and efficiency components, and describe how the management accountant should go about investigating the component variances disclosed.   **10 Marks**

Total Marks = 25

14 SEMI-AUTOMATED PLANTS

45 mins

(a) A UK site of B Ltd, a chemical company, has a number of semi-automated plants which specialise in individual products. One product, A, has an annual budgeted volume of 240,000kg for which equal amounts of production and sales are planned in each of 12 reporting periods. The budgeted/standard manufacturing and selling costs for period 1 (P1) are shown below.

	Per kg	*Total P1*
Manufacturing		
Material	3.50	70,000
Labour and variable overhead	2.50	50,000
Fixed overhead		100,000
Total manufacturing cost		220,000
Variable selling overhead	1.50	30,000
Fixed selling overhead		40,000
		70,000

- The standard selling price is £17 per kg.
- Variable selling overheads are incurred in proportion to units sold.
- Manufacturing overheads are recovered based on the budgeted volume levels.

For reporting purposes and identifying stock values the company operates a standard absorption costing system. For P1 the production was 18,400 kg, however sales amounted to only 12,400 kg.

In order to undertake some basic sales and marketing planning the accountant analyses costs into variable and fixed elements in order to compute the breakeven point and profits at various sales volume. The sales manager had calculated the breakeven point as 14,737 kg and for 12,400 kg sales he predicts a loss. He was mildly surprised therefore to see the profit statement which was produced for the period to reveal a small profit as follows.

PRODUCT A
PROFIT STATEMENT P1

Production   18,400 kg
Sales   12,400 kg

	£	£
Sales		208,800
Manufacturing costs		
Standard cost of sales (12,400 × £11)	136,400	
Add Manufacturing variances		
Volume	8,000	
All other expenditure	5,500	
	149,900	
Actual selling overheads		
Variable	17,500	
Fixed	38,300	
		205,700
Actual net profit		3,100

Required

(i) Analyse the budgeted costs into fixed and variable elements and calculate both the breakeven point and the budgeted profit/loss based on the actual kg sold where a marginal cost system is in use. **3 Marks**

(ii) (1) Demonstrate how the value of the manufacturing volume variance has been computed and briefly explain its significance. **5 Marks**

(2) Calculate the variances which apply to the variable and fixed selling overheads.   **3 Marks**

(iii) Reconcile the profit/loss from (i) above with the actual net profit given in the question showing all relevant variances. Briefly explain how a profit is revealed when a loss was anticipated by the sales manager.   **9 Marks**

(b) You are provided with the following information about product B.

	Budget	*Actual*
Sales (units)	72,000	64,000
Selling price	£10 per unit	£8.40 per unit
Variable cost	£6 per unit	£6.20 per unit

Using a contribution approach, calculate appropriate variances and comment briefly on the possible causes of those variances.   **5 Marks**

Total Marks = 25

15   **POC LTD**   *45 mins*

POC Ltd has one product which requires inputs from three types of material to produce batches of product S. Standard cost details for a single batch are shown below.

| | *Materials* | | *Labour* | |
Material type	Standard input Kgs	Standard price per kg £	Standard input Hrs	Standard rate per hour £
S1	8	0.3	1	5.00
S2	5	0.5		
S3	3	0.4		

Standard loss of 10% of input is expected. Actual production was 15,408 kgs for the previous week. Details of the materials used are as follows.

Actual material used (kg)

S1   8,284
S2   7,535
S3   3,334

Total labour cost for the week was £6,916 for 1,235 hours worked.

Required

(a) Calculate the following.

(i)   Total material mix, yield and usage variances   **9 Marks**
(ii)   Labour rate and efficiency variances   **2 Marks**

(b) Explain why the sum of the mix variances for materials measured in kg should be zero.   **3 Marks**

(c) Write a report to management which explains and interprets your results in part (a). The report should pay particular attention to the following.

(i)   Explaining what is meant by mix and yield variances in respect of materials
(ii)   Possible reasons for all the results you have derived   **11 Marks**

Total Marks = 25

16   FC LTD (MAA, 5/98, AMENDED)   *54 mins*

FC Ltd produces FDN. The standard ingredients of 1 kg of FDN are as follows.

0.65 kg of ingredient F @ £4.00 per kg
0.30 kg of ingredient D @ £6.00 per kg
0.20 kg of ingredient N @ £2.50 per kg
1.15 kg

Production of 4,000 kg of FDN was budgeted for April 20X8. The production of FDN is entirely automated and production costs attributed to FDN production comprise only direct materials and overheads. The FDN production operation works on a JIT basis and no ingredient or FDN inventories are held.

Overheads were budgeted for April 20X8 for the FDN production operation as follows.

Activity		*Total amount*
		£
Receipt of deliveries from suppliers	(standard delivery quantity is 460 kg)	4,000
Despatch of goods to customers	(standard despatch quantity is 100kg)	8,000
		12,000

In April 20X8, 4,200 kg of FDN were produced and cost details were as follows.

- **Materials used**

  2,840 kg of F, 1,210 kg of D and 860 kg of N at a total cost of £20,380

- **Actual overhead costs**

  12 supplier deliveries (cost £4,800) were made, and 38 customer despatches (cost £7,800) were processed

FC Ltd's budget committee met recently to discuss the preparation of the financial control report for April 20X8, and the following discussion occurred.

Chief Accountant	'The overheads do not vary directly with output and are therefore by definition "fixed". They should be analysed and reported accordingly.'
Management Accountant	'The overheads do not vary with output, but they are certainly not fixed. They should be analysed and reported on an activity basis.'

Required

Having regard to this discussion:

(a) Prepare a variance analysis for FDN production costs in April 20X8. Separate the material cost variance into price, mixture and yield components. Separate the overhead cost variance into expenditure, capacity and efficiency components using consumption of ingredient F as the overhead absorption base.   **13 Marks**

(b) Prepare a variance analysis for FDN production overhead costs in April 20X8 on an activity basis.   **11 Marks**

(c) Explain how, in the design of an activity based costing system, you would identify and select the most appropriate activities and cost drivers.   **6 Marks**

       Total Marks = 30

17   THE X, THE Y AND THE Z (MAA, 5/97, AMENDED)   *54 mins*

XYZ Ltd produces three products – the X, the Y and the Z. Relevant details are as follows.

		X	Y	Z
Standard direct labour hours per unit		4	2	3
Quarter 1 budget output	('000 units)	30	45	8
Quarter 1 actual output	('000 units)	25	60	9
Standard size of production run	('000 units)	5	15	1
Standard size of customer order	('000) units	1	3	0.1
Standard component orders per '000 units		0.2	0.1	2

In recent years, XYZ Ltd's production operation has become increasingly automated and the majority of its production costs are now overheads. Details of the overheads (budget and actual) for quarter 1 and the activities to which they relate have been identified as follows.

	Budget	*Actual*
	£'000	£'000
Component receiving and handling	120	134
Setting up equipment for production runs	200	178
Consignment of orders to customers	75	82

In the control of costs, XYZ Ltd's management accountant has previously absorbed overheads using a conventional cost accounting system and a direct labour hour overhead absorption base. For management accounting purposes it is always assumed that 80% of overheads are fixed and 20% are variable. In quarter 1 a total of 266,000 direct labour hours were worked, 26 component orders were processed, 18 production runs were carried out and 145 customer orders were processed.

XYZ Ltd's managing director has now made the following comment to you.

'I will be very interested to see what the overhead cost variances would look like if we were to adopt an activity based costing system. Try treating the activity costs as if they are variable. I realise that this will require a little imagination - but see what you can do.'

Required

As XYZ Ltd's management accountant:

(a) Prepare XYZ Ltd's overhead cost variance analysis for quarter 1, using the existing conventional system. The fixed overhead volume variance should be split into the following components:

(i)   Capacity utilisation variance

(ii) Efficiency variance   **12 Marks**

(b) Undertake XYZ Ltd's overhead cost variance analysis for quarter 1, using an activity based approach in a manner you consider most informative.   **12 Marks**

(c) Appraise the relative merits of the two alternative approaches used in (a) and (b) above.
                                                                         6 Marks

                                                          Total Marks = 30

18   WCL LTD (MAA, 11/99, AMENDED)   *54 mins*

WCL Ltd is a manufacturer of components.

At one of its factories, three components (X, Y and Z) are in continuous mass production. The standard direct costs associated with each of the three components are as follows.

	Component X	Component Y	Component Z
	£	£	£
Labour (at £15 per hour)	3.00	1.50	2.50
Materials	1.80	2.40	1.60

Fixed manufacturing overheads at the factory are budgeted at £40,000 per month. For management accounting purposes, fixed overheads are absorbed into product costs on a direct labour hour basis. Variable manufacturing overheads are budgeted at £23,760 for the month of November. For management accounting purposes, variable overheads at the factory are considered to vary with material quantity usage.

Details of production in November at the site are as follows.

	Component X	Component Y	Component Z
	Units	Units	Units
Budget	4,000	6,800	5,100
Actual	4,400	6,100	4,900

Costs in November at the site are as follows.

Labour	£31,000 (1,980 direct labour hours worked)
Materials	£33,800
Fixed manufacturing overheads	£40,800
Variable manufacturing overheads	£24,800

It is reported that material quantity usage was 98.5% of standard, with the variance spread evenly across the different value items.

Manufacturing costs incurred by WCL Ltd are reported in monthly operating statements using a conventional variance analysis.

Required

(a) Construct the November manufacturing costs budget for WCL Ltd's factory. Construct the standard cost for the output achieved at the factory during November. Explain why the budget and standard you have calculated differ, and explain how the two relate to each other.
         8 Marks

(b) Construct the November operating statement for the factory. This statement should reconcile standard and actual manufacturing costs for the month through calculation of the following cost variances.

- Labour rate
- Labour efficiency
- Materials usage
- Materials price
- Fixed overhead expenditure
- Fixed overhead capacity
- Fixed overhead efficiency
- Variable overhead efficiency
- Variable overhead expenditure

         11 Marks

22

(c) 'I have serious doubts about just how meaningful WCL Ltd's monthly operating statements are. The methods used to calculate the cost variances include a whole range of approximations and assumptions that are not immediately apparent to users of the statements. It is easy to misinterpret these statements.'   *Comment by a consultant*

Critically appraise the treatment of manufacturing overhead costs (fixed and variable) in the construction of WCL Ltd's operating statements. Explain how a statement user might be misled or confused by this treatment.   **11 Marks**

Total Marks = 30

19   BENCHMARKING   *54 mins*

(a) Within a diversified group, one division, which operates many similar branches in a service industry, has used internal benchmarking and regards it as very useful.

Group central management is now considering the wider use of benchmarking.

Required

Explain the aims, operation, and limitations of internal benchmarking, and explain how external benchmarking differs in these respects.   **15 Marks**

(b) A multinational group wishes to internally benchmark the production of identical components made in several plants in different countries. Investments have been made in some plants in installing new Advanced Manufacturing Technology (AMT) and supporting this with new manufacturing management systems such as Just in Time (JIT) and Total Quality Management (TQM). Preliminary comparisons suggest that the standard cost in plants using new technology is no lower than that in plants using older technology.

Required

Explain possible reasons for the similar standard costs in plants with differing technology. Recommend appropriate benchmarking measures, recognising that total standard costs may not provide the most useful measurement of performance.

15 Marks

Total Marks = 30

BUDGETING

Questions 20 to 46 cover budgeting, the subject of Part B of the BPP Study Text for Paper 8.

---

20   OBJECTIVE TEST QUESTIONS: BUDGETS   *36 mins*

1   What is another name for tactical planning?

A   Strategic planning
B   Budgetary planning
C   Operation planning
D   Corporate planning   **2 Marks**

2   Which of the following are functional budgets?

I   Purchasing budget
II   Cash budget
III   Sales budget
IV   Marketing cost budget

A   I and II
B   None of the above
C   All of the above
D   I, III and IV   **2 Marks**

3   BDL plc is currently preparing its cash budget for the year to 31 March 20X8. An extract from its sales budget for the same year shows the following sales values.

	£
March	60,000
April	70,000
May	55,000
June	65,000

40% of its sales are expected to be for cash. Of its credit sales, 70% are expected to pay in the month after sale and take a 2% discount; 27% are expected to pay in the second month after the sale, and the remaining 3% are expected to be bad debts.

The value of sales receipts to be shown in the cash budget for May 20X7 is

A   £38,532
B   £39,120
C   £60,532
D   £61,120   **3 Marks**

4   An extract from J Limited's sales budget is as follows.

	£
January	18,000
February	22,000
March	24,000
April	21,000

J Limited offers a 2 per cent cash discount to customers who pay during the month of sale. Five per cent of customers are expected to take advantage of the discount. The payment pattern of the remaining customers is expected to be as follows.

•   60 per cent in the month after sale
•   25 per cent in the month two months after sale
•   8 per cent in the month three months after sale

The remainder is budgeted to be bad debts.

The amount budgeted to be received from customers in April is:

A   £21,302
B   £21,323
C   £22,369
D   £20,672   **3 Marks**

5   When preparing a material purchases budget, what is the quantity to be purchased?

A   Materials required for production – opening stock of materials – closing stock of materials

B   Materials required for production – opening stock of materials + closing stock of materials

C   Opening stock of materials – materials required for production – closing stock of materials

D   Opening stock of materials + closing stock of materials – materials required for production   **2 Marks**

6   The following details have been extracted from the debtor collection records of L Ltd.

Invoices paid in the month after sale	70%
Invoices paid in the second month after sale	20%
Invoices paid in the third month after sale	8%
Bad debts	2%

Invoices are issued on the last day of each month.

Customers paying in the month after sale are entitled to deduct a 3% settlement discount.

Credit sales values for June to September 20X9 are budgeted as follows:

June	*July*	*August*	*September*
£52,500	£60,000	£90,000	£67,500

What is the amount budgeted to be received in September 20X9 from credit sales?

A   £79,200
B   £75,764
C   £77,310
D   £76,824   **3 Marks**

7   Of what does the master budget comprise?

A   The budgeted profit and loss account

B   The budgeted cash flow, budgeted profit and loss account and budgeted balance sheet

C   The entire set of budgets prepared

D   The budgeted cash flow   **2 Marks**

8   Each unit of product B uses 6 kg of raw material. The production budget and stock budgets for December are as follows.

Opening stocks	– raw materials	21,000 kg
	– finished goods	15,000 units
Closing stocks	– raw materials	24,400 kg
	– finished goods	11,400 units

Budgeted sales of B for December are 18,000 units. During the production process it is usually found that 10% of production units are scrapped as defective. This loss occurs after the raw materials have been input.

What are the budgeted raw materials purchases for December?

A   89,800 kg
B   96,000 kg
C   98,440 kg
D   99,400 kg

3 Marks

Total Marks = 20

If you struggled with these objective test questions, go back to your BPP Study Text for Paper 8 and revise Chapter 5 before you tackle the preparation and exam-standard questions on budgeting.

If you would like a bank of objective test questions which covers a range of syllabus topics, order our MCQ cards using the order form at the back of this Kit.

---

21   BUDGET PLANNING

54 mins

The newly appointed group finance director of a medium-sized quoted company has expressed considerable dissatisfaction with the budget prepared before his appointment. He considered that the comparisons of the budget with the results of the first quarter of the current financial year, which he had recently reviewed, were far from helpful in understanding changes in the business environment. He has asked you to suggest possible changes in the process of budget preparation for next year.

In the past, budgets have been prepared after the third quarter's results were known and the fourth quarter forecast prepared. This timetable left finance staff very little time to prepare the budgets before the end of the financial year and the start of the new year. You believe that the preparation of the budget for the next financial year should be commenced after the half-year results for the current financial year have been completed.

You think that the change should be implemented in the current year, preparing the budget for the next financial year, but there are three problems.

(a) Division A has no managing director. He resigned after very poor results for the first quarter followed disappointing results for the last financial year. A search is being made for a new managing director, almost certainly an external appointment, but this could take several months. In the meantime, the divisional financial director is acting as managing director as well as carrying out his own duties.

(b) Division B has launched in the first quarter of this year a new product range aiming at a new group of customers. This is effectively a new marketing strategy.

(c) Division C is installing new plant which will not be fully operational until the third quarter. There are some doubts whether the plant will produce, without modification, products of acceptable quality, as customer requirements have changed since the plant was ordered.

Required

Prepare a report for the group finance director, explaining the reasons for the proposed changes in budget preparation and planning for next year.

Discuss the three specific problems and any other anticipated difficulties, and advise how they could be dealt with in the new proposed system.

30 Marks

22   **ZED PLC (OCA, 11/97, AMENDED)**   *54 mins*

(a)   Sales are often considered to be the principal budget factor of an organisation.

Explain the meaning of the 'principal budget factor' and, assuming that it is sales, explain how sales may be forecast, making appropriate reference to the use of statistical techniques and the use of microcomputers.   **8 Marks**

(b)   You are the assistant management accountant of ZED plc. Preliminary discussions concerning the company budgets of the year ended 30 June 20X9 have already taken place, and the sales and production directors have produced the following forecasts.

Sales Director:

'I forecast that the total sales for the year will be 24,000 units of product A if we continue to sell them at £10.00 per unit for the first six months of the year and increase the price to £11.00 per unit thereafter. I estimate the quarterly sales to be as follows.

July – September	7,200 units
October – December	3,000 units
January – March	4,800 units
April – June	9,000 units

This represents a 20% increase over our present quarterly sales targets, and I expect that within each quarter the monthly demand will be equal. We can also sell up to 2,000 units of product B per month at a selling price of £8.00 per unit. This is a less profitable product, so we should concentrate on product A.'

Production Director:

'Our maximum capacity is at present limited by the available machine hours. Each unit of product A requires 2 machine hours, and on this basis we can usually produce 2,000 units per month. However, because of employee holidays in August, the number of machine operators is reduced, and in that month we can produce only 1,000 units. We have placed an order for new semi-automatic machines which are being installed in August 20X8. These should be capable of producing a further 2,000 units per month starting on 1 September 20X8.

Product B requires 4 machine hours per unit. The quantity that we can produce is limited because of the demands on the available machine time by making product A.'

You have predicted the costs per unit of the two products for the 20X9 budget year as follows.

	A	*B*
	£/unit	£/unit
Direct materials	1.50	1.60
Direct labour	2.50	3.00
Variable overhead	1.50	3.00
	5.50	7.60

Required

(i)   Use the above information to calculate the extent of the limiting factor during the budget period.   **5 Marks**

(ii)   Prepare monthly sales and production budgets, expressed in units, for the period *July to December 20X8*, based upon the limiting factor you determined in (a)

above. Assume that stocks of products A and B cannot be held, and that ZED plc wishes to concentrate on production of product A.   **6 Marks**

(iii) Prepare monthly sales and production budgets, expressed in units, for the period *July to December 20X8*, based upon the limiting factor you determined in (a) above. Assume that stocks of products A and B can now be held, and assume that ZED plc decided to sell equal quantities of product A and product B each month.   **9 Marks**

(iv) Determine the effect on profits of the change in sales mix proposed in part (c) above.   **2 Marks**

Total Marks = 30

---

23   LMN LTD   *45 mins*

LMN Ltd is preparing budgets for the first quarter of 20X1. The company makes a single product, the details of which are as follows.

Budgeted variable costs per unit	£
Materials	12
Labour (4 hours at £6)	24
Production overhead	8
Selling price per unit	90

Administration overhead is £23,000 per month and the fixed production overhead is £15,000 per month, including £3,500 depreciation.

Finished goods stocks are valued at full actual production cost and the budgeted opening stock at 1 January 20X1 is 1,200 units valued at £66,500. It is company policy to keep finished stocks at a constant ratio to the budgeted unit sales of the following month. Extra production over 1,500 units per month can be achieved by working overtime which means paying labour double time for the overtime.

Expected sales

	Units
December 20X0	1,300
January 20X1	1,000
February 20X1	1,400
March 20X1	1,600
April 20X1	1,800
May 20X1	1,550

Materials are paid for in the month following delivery and enough stock is kept to cover the next month's budgeted production. Sales are on credit with 30% of debts collected in the month of sale and 67% in the following month, the balance being bad debts. All other costs are paid for in the month they are incurred and no capital expenditure is expected.

Required

(a) Prepare a single budgeted profit and loss account for the quarter (January, February, March).   **9 Marks**

(b) Prepare cash budgets for each month of the quarter.   **10 Marks**

(c) Reconcile the net cash movement for the quarter to the budgeted profit.   **6 Marks**

Total Marks = 25

24   **AZ LTD (OCA, 5/96)**   *45 mins*

The following budgeted sales values have been extracted from the budget of AZ Limited for the year ending 31 December 20X7.

	£
April	400,000
May	450,000
June	520,000
July	420,000
August	480,000

The contribution/sales ratio is 40%. Fixed costs are budgeted to be £1,200,000 for the year arising at a constant rate per month and including depreciation of £300,000 per annum.

40% of each month's sales are produced in the month prior to sale, and 60% are produced in the month of sale. 50% of the direct materials required for production are purchased in the month prior to their being used in production.

30% of the variable costs are labour costs, which are paid in the month they are incurred.

60% of the variable costs are direct material costs. Suppliers of direct materials are paid in the month after purchase.

The remaining variable costs are variable overhead costs. 40% of the variable overhead costs are paid in the month they are incurred, the balance being paid in the month after they are incurred.

Fixed costs are paid in the month they are incurred.

Capital expenditure expected in June is £190,000.

Sales receipts for the three months of May, June and July are budgeted as follows:

	£
May	401,700
June	450,280
July	425,880

The bank balance on 1 May 20X7 is expected to be £40,000.

Required

Prepare a cash budget for AZ Limited.

Your budget should be in columnar format showing separately the receipts, payments and balances for each of the months of May, June and July 20X7.

25 Marks

25   **LIST PRICE (OCA, 5/95)**   *45 mins*

XYZ Ltd has the following forecast sales at list price for the nine months to 29 February 20X6.

June	£40,000	September	£48,000	December	£44,000
July	£44,000	October	£40,000	January	£42,000
August	£50,000	November	£45,000	February	£50,000

60% of the company's sales are on credit, payable in the month after sale. Cash sales attract a 5% discount off list price.

Purchases amount to 40% of selling price, and these are paid for two months after delivery.

BPP
PROFESSIONAL EDUCATION

Stock is maintained at a level equal to 50% of the following month's sales except that in November stock is to be increased by £2,000 (at cost prices) to ensure that XYZ Ltd has a safety stock during the period when its major supplier shuts down. This safety stock will be released in March.

Wages comprise a fixed sum of £2,000 per month plus a variable element equal to 10% of sales; these are payable in the month they are incurred.

Fixed costs amount to £7,500 per month, payable one month in arrears, of which £1,500 is depreciation.

XYZ Ltd has capital expenditure/receipts scheduled as follows.

	£
Acquisitions	
September	15,000
November	10,000
February	4,000
Disposal	
October	8,000

Corporation tax, payable in November, amounts to £44,000.

The bank balance on 1 September 20X5 is expected to be £5,000.

Required

(a) Prepare a cashflow forecast for XYZ Ltd for each of the six months from September 20X5 to February 20X6, using a row and column format.   **10 Marks**

(b) Explain clearly, using your answer to (a) above, how a spreadsheet may be used to assist in the preparation of cash forecasts.   **10 Marks**

(c) Explain how a cash forecast is an example of both feedforward and feedback control mechanisms.   **5 Marks**

Total Marks = 25

26   **Q PLC (OCA, 5/98)**   *45 mins*

The following budgeted profit and loss account has been prepared for Q plc for the four months January to April 20X9.

	January	*February*	*March*	*April*
	£'000	£'000	£'000	£'000
Sales	60	50	70	60
Production cost	50	55	32.5	50
Stock adjustment	(5)	(17.5)	20	(5)
Cost of sales	45	37.5	52.5	45
Gross profit	15	12.5	17.5	15
Admin/selling overhead	8	7.5	8.5	8
Net profit before interest	7	5	9	7

The working papers provide the following additional information.

(a) 40% of the production cost relates to direct materials. Materials are bought in the month prior to the month in which they are used, and 50% of them are paid for in the month of purchase. The remainder are paid for one month later.

(b) 30% of the production cost relates to direct labour which is paid for when it is used.

(c) The remainder of the production cost is production overhead. £5,000 per month is a fixed cost which includes £3,000 depreciation. Fixed production overhead costs are paid monthly in arrears. The variable production overhead is paid 40% in the month of usage and the balance one month later.

(d) The administration and selling costs are paid quarterly in advance on 1 January, 1 April, 1 July and 1 October. The amount payable is £15,000 per quarter.

(e) Creditors on 1 January 20X9 are expected to be:

Direct materials	£10,000
Production overheads	£11,000

(f) The amounts expected to be received from customers during January to March are:

	£
January	69,600
February	56,944
March	56,470

(g) The company intends to purchase capital equipment costing £30,000 in February which will be payable in March.

(h) The bank balance on 1 January 20X9 is expected to be £5,000 overdrawn. The bank balance on 1 December 20X8 is expected to be £5,000 (positive).

(i) Interest is payable/receivable on average monthly bank balances ($\frac{opening + closing}{2}$) at the following rates.

Positive balances	interest receivable	1% per month
Overdrawn balances	interest payable	2% per month

Interest is payable/receivable in the following month.

Required

(a) Prepare a cash budget for each of the months January to March 20X9 for Q plc, showing clearly the bank balance at the beginning and end of each month.   **17 Marks**

(b) Explain how cash budgets are used in both feedforward and feedback control mechanisms. Use your answer to (a) above to assist in your explanation.   **8 Marks**

Total Marks = 25

27   PREPARATION QUESTION: BUDGETS ETC

(a) Outline the difference between budgets for **planning** and budgets for **control**, citing an example of each.

(b) Briefly describe the differences between an incremental budget and a zero base budget, outlining the advantages and disadvantages of each.

(c) Discuss the use of rolling budgets as an aid to planning **and** control and describe the extent to which the incidence of budgetary slack is likely to be affected by the use of rolling budgets.

28   H PLC

54 mins

The budget for the production, planning and development department of H plc is currently prepared as part of a traditional budgetary planning and control system. The analysis of costs by expense type for the period ended 30 November 20X6 where this system is in use is as follows.

BPP
PROFESSIONAL EDUCATION

Expense type	Budget	Actual
	%	%
Salaries	60	63
Supplies	6	5
Travel cost	12	12
Technology cost	10	7
Occupancy cost	12	13

The total budget and actual costs for the department for the period ended 30 November 20X6 are £1,000,000 and £1,060,000 respectively.

The company now feels that an activity based budgeting approach should be used. A number of activities have been identified for the production, planning and development department. An investigation has indicated that total budget and actual costs should be attributed to the activities on the following basis.

	Activities	Budget	Actual
		%	%
1	Routing/scheduling – new products	20	16
2	Routing/scheduling – existing products	40	34
3	Remedial re-routing/scheduling	5	12
4	Special studies – specific orders	10	8
5	Training	10	15
6	Management and administration	15	15

Required

(a) (i) Prepare *two* budget control statements for the production, planning and development department for the period ended 30 November 20X6 which compare budget with actual cost and show variances using the following.

     1   A traditional expense based analysis

     2   An activity based analysis   **7 Marks**

  (ii) Identify and comment on *four* advantages claimed for the use of activity based budgeting over traditional budgeting using the production, planning and development example to illustrate your answer.   **8 Marks**

  (iii) Comment on the use of the information provided in the activity based statement which you prepared in (i) in activity based performance measurement and suggest additional information which would assist in such performance measurement.   **6 Marks**

(b) Other activities have been identified and the budget quantified for the three months ended 31 March as follows.

Activities	Cost driver unit basis	Units of cost driver	Cost
			£'000
Product design	design hours	8,000	2,000 (Note 1)
Purchasing	purchase orders	4,000	200
Production	machine hours	12,000	1,500 (Note 2)
Packing	volume (m³)	20,000	400
Distribution	weight (kg)	120,000	600

Notes

1   This includes all design costs for new products released this period.

2   This includes a depreciation provision of £300,000 of which £8,000 applies to three month's depreciation on a straight line basis for a new product (NPD). The remainder applies to other products.

New product NPD is included in the above budget. The following additional information applies to NPD.

(i)   Estimated total output over the product life cycle: 5,000 units (4 years life cycle)

(ii)   Product design requirement: 400 design hours

(iii)   Output in quarter ended 31 March 20X7: 250 units

(iv)   Equivalent batch size per purchase order: 50 units

(v)   Other product unit data: production time 0.75 machine hours; volume 0.4 m³; weight 3 kg

Required

Prepare a unit overhead cost for product NPD using an activity based approach which includes an appropriate share of life cycle costs using the information provided in (b) above.   **9 Marks**

Total Marks = 30

29   **OBJECTIVE TEST QUESTIONS: FORECASTING**   *36 mins*

1   Based on the last 15 periods, the underlying trend of sales is $y = 345.12 - 1.35x$, where y is the number of items sold and x represents the period number. If the 16th period has a seasonal factor of -23.62, assuming an additive forecasting model, then the sales forecast for that period, to the nearest whole unit, is:

   A   247 units
   B   300 units
   C   324 units
   D   347 units   **3 Marks**

2   A regression equation $y = a + bx$ is used to forecast the value of y for a given value of x. Which of the following increase the reliability of the forecast?

   A   A large sample used to calculate the regression equation

   B   Forecasting for values of x outside the range of those in the sample used to calculate the equation

   C   Working to a higher number of decimal places of accuracy

   D   A correlation coefficient numerically close to 0   **2 Marks**

3   Over an 18-month period, sales have been found to have an underlying linear trend of $y = 7.112 + 3.949x$, where y is the number of items sold and x represents the month. Monthly deviations from trend have been calculated and month 19 is expected to be 1.12 times the trend value.

   The forecast number of items to be sold in month 19 is approximately

   A   82
   B   83
   C   72
   D   92   **3 Marks**

4   The value of the correlation coefficient between x and y is 0.95. Which of the following is correct?

A   There is a strong relationship between x and y.

B   There is a weak relationship between x and y.

C   x is 95%.

D   If the values of x and y were plotted on a graph, the line relating them would have a slope of 0.95.   **2 Marks**

5   A time series for sales volumes has been analysed into trend and seasonal variations, using the multiplicative model and assuming a twelve-month period for the seasonal variations. The trend value for January 20X9 was 452 units, and the trend is increasing by 16 units each month. The average seasonal variation for May is 103%. What is the predicted actual sales volume figure for May 20X9?

A   501 units
B   516 units
C   531 units
D   548 units   **3 Marks**

6   A company has established the following transport costs for the last two periods.

	Period 4	Period 5
Miles travelled	20,000	28,000
Transport cost per mile	£1.90	£1.70

The estimated transport cost per mile for period 6, when 24,000 miles will be travelled is

A   £0.58
B   £1.20
C   £1.78
D   £1.80   **3 Marks**

7   Which of the following is *not* one of the four components of a time series?

A   Random variations
B   Cyclical variations
C   Four-quarter totals
D   Seasonal variations   **2 Marks**

8   A time series has been compiled of the number of calls to a sales enquiry telephone number each day. The series has been analysed into the following four components. Which one would be designated the seasonal variation?

A   A basic level which was 1,000 calls per day thirty years ago and has increased by 25 to 30 calls per day each year since then.

B   Variations of up to 50 calls per day which occur at unpredictable times, but on average four times each year.

C   An extra 64 to 85 calls per day in the first six months of each year.

D   An extra 50 to 60 calls per day in the first half of each decade.   **2 Marks**

Total Marks = 20

If you struggled with these objective test questions, go back to your BPP Study Text for Paper 8 and revise Chapter 6 before you tackle the exam-standard questions on forecasting.

If you would like a bank of objective test questions which covers a range of syllabus topics, order our MCQ cards using the order form at the back of this Kit.

30   PMF PLC (11/01)   *45 mins*

PMF plc is a long-established public transport operator that provides a commuter transit link between an airport and the centre of a large city.

The following data has been taken from the sales records of PMF plc for the past two years.

Quarter	Number of passengers carried	
	Year 1	Year 2
1	15,620	34,100
2	15,640	29,920
3	16,950	29,550
4	34,840	56,680

The trend equation for the number of passengers carried has been found to be

$$x = 10,000 + 4,200q$$

where x =   number of passengers carried per quarter
and q =   time period (year 1 quarter 1: $q = 1$)
                                (year 1 quarter 2: $q = 2$)
                                (year 2 quarter 1: $q = 5$)

Based on data collected over the last two years, PMF plc has found that its quarterly costs have the following relationships with the number of passengers carried.

Cost item	Relationship		
Premises costs	y	$=$	$260,000$
Premises staff	y	$=$	$65,000 + 0.5x$
Power	y	$=$	$13,000 + 4x$
Transit staff	y	$=$	$32,000 + 3x$
Other	y	$=$	$9,100 + x$

where y =   the cost per quarter (£)
           x =   number of passengers per quarter

Required

(a) Using the trend equation for the number of passengers carried and the multiplicative (proportional) time series model, determine the expected number of passengers to be carried in the third quarter of year 3.   **7 Marks**

(b) Explain why you think that the equation for the Transit staff cost is in the form $y = 32,000 + 3x$.   **3 Marks**

(c) Using your answer to part *(a)* and the cost relationships equations, calculate for each cost item and in total, the costs expected to be incurred in the third quarter of year 3.
                                                                              3 Marks

(d) Explain briefly why there may be differences between the actual data for the third quarter of year 3 and the values you have predicted.   **5 Marks**

(e) Prepare a report, addressed to the board of directors of PMF plc, that briefly explains the following in the context of measuring the **effectiveness** of the transport service.

   (i)   Why the company should consider the use of non-financial performance measures

   (ii)   Three non-financial performance measures that could be used   **7 Marks**

                                                              Total Marks = 25

31   FGH HOLIDAYS (MSA, 11/95, AMENDED)   *45 mins*

FGH Holidays sells guided walking holidays for adults, from leisurely countryside rambles to strenuous mountain walks.

The holidays are advertised in specialist walking magazines and are only sold direct from the head office in Manchester. Anyone who has bought an FGH holiday in the last three years is automatically sent the new brochures. The number of brochures mailed in response to (new) enquiries and the number of weekly holidays bought by new customers are shown below.

	20X4 Dec	20X5 Jan	Feb	Mar	April	May	June	July	Aug	Sept	Oct
Brochures mailed to new enquirers (hundreds)	10	31	27	15	22	13	7	12	4	2	1
Holidays bought by new customers	29	156	293	232	137	184	120	95	111	68	15

Required

(a) Calculate the regression of holidays (at time t) on brochures [at time (t − 1)] for new buyers and the correlation coefficient.

$$\sum X = 143 \quad \sum X^2 = 2,881 \quad \sum Y = 1,411 \quad \sum Y^2 = 257,229 \quad \sum XY = 26,869 \quad n = 10$$

15 Marks

(b) Compare your answer with the regression of holidays on brochures for new buyers, both at time t, which is $Y = 56.8 + 5.66X$ (r = 0.68), and explain any implications for forecasting.   **10 Marks**

Total Marks = 25

32   MOC (MSA, 5/97, AMENDED)   *45 mins*

MOC is a small mail-order company, which sells direct to established customers on its mailing list (using catalogues and leaflets), and to new customers via newspaper advertising.

One of the company's products is a patchwork real leather holdall which it sells for £19.99. The management accountant has reported recently that the trend in unit sales has shown a steady increase every quarter – the trend equation is given by the computer as $Y = 300 + 20X$, where X denotes the quarter (X increases by one for each new quarter), and Y is unit sales. The unit sales for the first quarter of 20X7 were 520 units. The average seasonal variations in demand are shown in the table below.

	Q_1	Q_2	Q_3	Q_4
Average seasonal variation	none	−20%	−20%	+40%

The marketing manager believes that 20X7's seasonal variations will be 'of the order of double the average seasonal variation to date'. The contribution per holdall is £5.

Required

(a) Calculate forecasts for sales of holdalls for the second, third and fourth quarters of 20X7, assuming the following.

   (i)   The average seasonal variations apply

   (ii)   The marketing manager's assumption applies   **15 Marks**

(b) Calculate **two** estimates of the 20X7 contribution from sales of holdalls, assuming (i) and (ii) above, **and** comment on the results.   **5 Marks**

(c) Explain how the equation for the trend in sales would have been obtained by computer.

5 Marks

Total Marks = 25

33   **FURNITURE STORE**   *45 mins*

In June 20X3 the managing director of a large furniture store engaged a management consultant to devise a simple and practical method of forecasting the store's quarterly sales levels for a period of six months ahead. On taking up the task the consultant felt that a forecasting method appropriate for the purpose would first require him to determine the trend in the store's gross quarterly sales over the last 30 months. The time series obtained could then be plotted, and a line of best fit established and extrapolated over the next two quarters. By applying an appropriate seasonal index to these figures, sales for the two periods ahead could be estimated.

Gross sales data

Sales period		*Value of retail sales*
		£'000
Jan-Mar	20X1	285
Apr-Jun	20X1	310
Jul-Sep	20X1	315
Oct-Dec	20X1	385
Jan-Mar	20X2	340
Apr-Jun	20X2	370
Jul-Sep	20X2	375
Oct-Dec	20X2	460
Jan-Mar	20X3	395
Apr-Jun	20X3	425

The management consultant also gave some thought to how he could avoid getting the store to compute its own seasonal indices, an operation he felt inappropriate considering the small amount of past data he had available. He decided to use a national quarterly seasonal index as published in a national journal. He thought that his client's furniture store had a product mix not too different from the aggregate mix on which the index was based.

National quarterly seasonal index (multiplicative) for furniture

Jan-Mar	94
Apr-Jun	98
Jul-Sept	96
Oct-Dec	112

Required

(a) Plot the actual quarterly sales figures on a graph and explain which model of time series may be more appropriate for this data, the additive or the multiplicative.

6 Marks

(b) Calculate the trend in the actual data and plot this data on your graph.

5 Marks

(c) Use the method of least squares to determine the equation of the trend in the sales. Explain the meaning of the variables and figures in this trend line.   **6 Marks**

37

(d) Estimate the gross sales figures for quarters 3 and 4 in 20X3.   **4 Marks**

(e) Comment on the likely accuracy of your estimates.   **4 Marks**

Total Marks = 25

34   KDF LTD (MAA, 5/99, AMENDED)   *54 mins*

KDF Ltd manufactures a wide variety of components used in the electronics sector. It is forecast that in 20Y0, customers will demand components corresponding to 120,000 standard hours' work. There is no opening stock at the start of 20Y0. Sales revenue is forecast to average £28 per standard hour of work sold. Demand in 20Y0 is forecast to follow a seasonal pattern as follows.

	Standard hours
Quarter 1	18,000
Quarter 2	24,000
Quarter 3	30,000
Quarter 4	48,000

Incremental variable production costs per standard hour worked are forecast to be as follows in each quarter.

Output level		*Labour*	*Material*
		£	£
1	– 12,000	6	4
12,001	– 24,000	8	4
24,001	– 36,000	14	6
36,001	– 48,000	28	8

Fixed production overheads are forecast at £300,000 per quarter. Inventory holding costs for any one quarter (finance, insurance and security) are forecast to be £3 per standard hour's work held at the end of that quarter, but there is some uncertainty about this holding cost figure. Agreements with labour unions and component suppliers mean that production must take place at the same rate throughout quarters 1 to 3, but production in quarter 4 can be at a different rate.

Required

(a) Identify the minimum quarterly production rate in quarters 1 to 3 required to ensure that all demand is satisfied. Calculate annual costs (quarters 1 to 4) at this minimum rate and at four 4,000 standard hours per quarter increments above this rate. Identify the profit-maximising rate of production in quarters 1 to 3.   **13 Marks**

(b) Draw a diagram to illustrate the sensitivity of KDF Ltd's annual profit (at both the minimum and profit-maximising quarters 1 to 3 production rates) to the quarterly inventory holding cost. Use this diagram to identify the inventory holding cost at which both options give an equal profit.   **13 Marks**

(c) Explain what sensitivity analysis is, and the role that it plays in budgeting.   **4 Marks**

Total Marks = 30

35   **PQR AND PRODUCTS A, B, C (OCA, 11/99)**   *45 mins*

PQR plc is preparing its budgets for next year. It has already prepared forecasts of demand levels for its product range. These are as follows.

	Forecast 1		*Forecast 2*	
	Price	*Quantity*	*Price*	*Quantity*
	£		£	
Product A	10.00	500	15.00	350
Product B	20.00	800	25.00	700
Product C	30.00	2,200	40.00	1,000

You are to assume that *only one of either* forecast 1 *or* forecast 2 can be accepted.

The expected variable unit costs of each product are as follows:

	Product A	*Product B*	*Product C*
	£	£	£
Direct materials (50p per kg)	2.00	3.50	7.00
Direct labour	3.00	5.00	7.40
Variable overhead	1.50	2.50	3.70
	6.50	11.00	18.10

No specific fixed costs are expected for any product.

General fixed costs are budgeted as £20,000 for the year.

All three products use the same direct material which is expected to be limited in supply to a maximum of 22,020 kgs in the budget year.

Required

(a)   Recommend, with supporting calculations, whether forecast 1 *or* forecast 2 should be adopted for the budget period.   **15 Marks**

(b)   Prepare a report, addressed to the Managing Director, to explain the budget preparation process, with particular reference to:

   (i)   the principal budget factor;
   (ii)   the budget manual; and
   (iii) the role of the budget committee.   **10 Marks**

Total Marks = 25

36   **OBJECTIVE TEST QUESTIONS: OTHER ASPECTS OF BUDGETING**   *36 mins*

1   In which of the following circumstances are participative budgets likely to be effective?

   I   In very large organisations
   II   During periods of economic affluence
   III   When an organisation's different units act autonomously
   IV   In newly-formed organisations

   A   All of the above
   B   None of the above
   C   III and IV
   D   I, II and III   **2 Marks**

2   The following extract is taken from the production cost budget for K Ltd.

Production (units)	1,650	2,400
Production cost	£20,770	£23,170

PROFESSIONAL EDUCATION

What is the budget cost allowance for an activity level of 1,980 units?

A   £21,826
B   £24,924
C   £19,115
D   £15,490   **3 Marks**

3   A Limited uses a variety of computer models in its budgetary planning and control process. Three of these models are described below.

Model

1   An exponential smoothing model is used to prepare a forecast of sales volumes each month. If these forecasts indicate that budgeted sales levels will not be achieved, the marketing department is required to take appropriate control action.

2   A stock control model is used to determine minimum and maximum levels for each stock item. The model produces an exception report whenever the actual stock level reaches minimum level or maximum level, so that control action can be taken if necessary.

3   A target is set for month-end cash balances. A spreadsheet model is used to forecast the net cash flow and the resulting cash balance for each month. Control action is taken if necessary to achieve the desired cash balance.

Which of these is a feedforward control model?

A   Models 1 and 2 only
B   Models 1 and 3 only
C   Models 2 and 3 only
D   Model 2 only   **2 Marks**

4   In the context of a balanced scorecard approach to the provision of management information, which of the following measures would be appropriate for monitoring the innovation and learning perspective?

(i)   Training days per employee
(ii)   Percentage of revenue generated by new products and services
(iii)   Labour turnover rate

A   (i) and (ii)
B   (i) and (iii) only
C   (ii) and (iii) only
D   (i), (ii) and (iii)   **2 Marks**

5   What is the purpose of a flexible budget?

A   To ensure the efficient control of resources
B   To provide a revised forecast once actual costs are known
C   To provide a limit to discretionary expenditure
D   To provide targets for employee motivation purposes   **2 Marks**

6   What does the term 'goal congruence' mean in relation to budget preparation?

A   The alignment of managerial and organisational goals
B   The coordination of budgets
C   The setting of targets for individual managers
D   The use of feedback control to set organisational objectives   **2 Marks**

7   Which of the following statements is/are true?

I   Discretionary fixed costs are uncontrollable costs.
II   Committed fixed costs are controllable in the short term.
III   All costs are controllable by an organisation's management team.
IV   Advertising expenditure is a sunk fixed cost.

A   All of the above
B   II and III
C   I, II and IV
D   None of the above   **2 Marks**

8   BW Ltd recorded the following total costs over the last three years.

Year	Volume of production	Total cost	Average price level index
	Units	£	
0	160,000	2,770,000	100
1	140,000	2,551,500	105
2	110,000	2,092,800	109

What are the expected costs (to the nearest £'000) in year 3 when output is 120,000 units and the average price level index is 112?

A   £2,090,000
B   £2,341,000
C   £2,340,000
D   £2,040,000   **3 Marks**

9   What is budgetary slack?

A   An increased expenditure allowance which is determined for control purposes when activity levels are higher than budgeted

B   The excess of budgeted resources available above the amount needed to achieve the approved budget

C   The deficit of budgeted resources available below the amount needed to achieve the approved budget

D   The intentional overestimation of expenses and/or underestimation of revenues in the budgeting process   **2 Marks**

Total Marks = 20

If you struggled with these objective test questions, go back to your BPP Study Text for Paper 8 and revise Chapter 7 before you tackle the preparation and exam-standard questions on other aspects of budgeting.

If you would like a bank of objective test questions which covers a range of syllabus topics, order our MCQ cards using the order form at the back of this Kit.

---

37   **MPL LTD (PILOT PAPER)**   *45 mins*

MPL Ltd is a company specialising in providing consultancy services to the catering industry. MPL Ltd prepared its operating statement for period 5 of the year ending 31 August 2000. This was as follows.

BPP PROFESSIONAL EDUCATION

	Budget	*Actual*	*Variance*
Chargeable consultancy hours	2,400	2,500	100
	£	£	£
Administration staff salaries – fixed	15,000	15,750	750
Consultants' salaries – fixed	80,000	84,000	4,000
Casual wages – variable	960	600	360
Motor and travel costs – fixed	4,400	4,400	-
Telephone – fixed	600	800	200
Telephone – variable	2,000	2,150	150
Printing, postage & stationery – variable	2,640	2,590	50
Premises and equipment costs – fixed	3,200	3,580	380
Total costs	110,400	116,480	6,080
Fees charged	180,000	200,000	20,000
Profit	69,600	83,520	13,920

While the directors are pleased that the actual profit exceeded their budget expectations they are interested to now how this has been achieved. After the budgets had been issued to them, the consultants expressed concern at the apparent simplicity of assuming that costs could be classified as being either fixed or varying in direct proportion to chargeable consultancy hours.

Required

(a)   As the newly appointed management accountant, prepare a report addressed to the board of directors of MPL Ltd which:

   (i)   explains the present approach to budgeting adopted in MPL Ltd and discusses the advantages and disadvantages of involving consultants in the preparation of future budgets;   **10 Marks**

   (ii)   critically discusses the format of the operating statement for period 5.   **5 Marks**

(b)   Explain how a spreadsheet could be set up so that a flexed budget and variance calculations could be rapidly produced by inserting only the actual data, assuming that variable costs are thought to vary in line with chargeable consultancy hours. **10 Marks**

Total Marks = 25

38   **TJ LTD**   *45 mins*

TJ Ltd is in an industry sector which is recovering from the recent recession. The directors of the company hope next year to be operating at 85% of capacity, although currently the company is operating at only 65% of capacity. 65% of capacity represents output of 10,000 units of the single product which is produced and sold. One hundred direct workers are employed on production for 200,000 hours in the current year.

The flexed budgets for the current year are as follows.

Capacity level	55%	65%	75%
	£	£	£
Direct materials	846,200	1,000,000	1,153,800
Direct wages	1,480,850	1,750,000	2,019,150
Production overhead	596,170	650,000	703,830
Selling and distribution overhead	192,310	200,000	207,690
Administration overhead	120,000	120,000	120,000
Total costs	3,235,530	3,720,000	4,204,470

Profit in any year is budgeted to be $16^2/_3\%$ of sales.

The following percentage increases in costs are expected for next year.

	Increase %
Direct materials	6.0
Direct wages	3.0
Variable production overhead	7.0
Variable selling and distribution overhead	7.0
Fixed production overhead	10.0
Fixed selling and distribution overhead	7.5
Administration overhead	10.0

Required

(a) Prepare for next year a flexible budget statement on the assumption that the company operates at 85% of capacity; your statement should show both contribution and profit.

14 Marks

(b) Discuss briefly *three* problems which may arise from the change in capacity level.

6 Marks

(c) State who is likely to serve on a budget committee operated by TJ Ltd and explain the purposes of such a committee.   **5 Marks**

Total Marks = 25

---

39   FIXED AND FLEXIBLE (OCA, 11/96)   *45 mins*

(a) Explain briefly the differences between fixed and flexible budgets.   **5 Marks**

(b) Prepare a report, addressed to the Board of Directors, clearly explaining the advantages/disadvantages of using fixed/flexible budgets as part of a budgetary control system.   **10 Marks**

(c) Spreadsheets are often used by accountants to assist in the preparation of budgets.

Describe how a spreadsheet may be used to prepare a sales budget *and* explain the advantages of using spreadsheets to assist in this task.   **10 Marks**

(Your answer should refer to input, use of formulae, and output reports.)

Total Marks = 25

---

40   PDC LTD (OCA, 5/97, AMENDED)   *45 mins*

(a) The following report has been prepared, relating to one product for March 20X7. This has been sent to the appropriate product manager as part of PDC Ltd's monitoring procedures.

Monthly variance report: March 20X7

	Actual	Budget	Variance	%
Production volume (units)	9,905	10,000	95 A	0.95 A
Sales volume (units)	9,500	10,000	500 A	5.00 A
Sales revenue (£)	27,700	30,000	2,300 A	7.67 A
Direct material (kgs)	9,800	10,000	200 F	2.00 F
Direct material (£)	9,600	10,000	400 F	4.00 F
Direct labour (hours)	2,500	2,400	100 A	4.17 A
Direct labour (£)	8,500	8,400	100 A	1.19 A
Contribution (£)	9,600	11,600	2,000 A	17.24 A

The product manager has complained that the report ignores the principle of flexible budgeting and is unfair.

Required

Prepare a report addressed to the management team which comments critically on the monthly variance report.

Include as an appendix to your report the layout of a revised monthly variance report which will be more useful to the product manager.

Include row and column headings, but do *not* calculate the contents of the report.

15 Marks

(b) Explain the differences between budgetary control and standard costing/variance analysis. Describe the circumstances in which an organisation would find it beneficial to operate both of these cost control systems. **5 Marks**

(c) It has been said that we live in an age of discontinuity and that the only thing we know for certain about the future is that it will not be the same as the past.

In spite of this, many statistical and accounting techniques are based on extrapolations of past performance into the future in order to provide information for planning and decision making.

Required

Discuss the problems of extrapolating past performance into the future. **5 Marks**

Total Marks = 25

41 B LTD *45 mins*

Extracts from the budgets of B Ltd are given below.

	Period 1	Period 2	Period 3	Period 4	Period 5
Opening stock (units)	4,000	2,500	3,300	2,500	3,000
Sales (units)	15,000	20,000	16,500	21,000	18,000

	Period 1	Period 2	Period 3
	£'000	£'000	£'000
Direct labour	270.0	444.0	314.0
Direct materials	108.0	166.4	125.6
Production overhead (excluding depreciation)	117.5	154.0	128.5
Depreciation	40.0	40.0	40.0
Administration overhead	92.0	106.6	96.4
Selling overhead	60.0	65.0	61.5

The following information is also available.

(a) Production above 18,000 units incurs a bonus in addition to normal wage rates.

(b) Any variable costs contained in selling overhead are assumed to vary with sales. All other variable costs are assumed to vary with production.

Required

(a) Calculate the budgeted production for periods 1 to 4. **3 Marks**

(b) Prepare a suitable cost budget for period 4. **11 marks**

(c) In period 4 the stock and sales budgets were achieved and the following actual costs recorded.

	£'000
Direct labour	458
Direct material	176
Production overhead	181
Depreciation	40
Administration overhead	128
Selling overhead	62
	1,045

Show the budget variances from actual. **4 Marks**

(d) Criticise the assumptions on which the cost budgets have been prepared. **7 Marks**

Total Marks = 25

42   RELUCTANCE   *45 mins*

'Managers may be reluctant to participate in the setting of budgets but when they do, it should lead to better performance.'

Required

Discuss the above statement, suggesting reasons for the reluctance expressed, how such reservations may be overcome and some of the benefits which may arise from participation in the budgeting process. **25 Marks**

43   PREPARATION QUESTION: BALANCED SCORECARD

Performance measurement in companies has traditionally been based on feedback on the budget, expressed in financial terms. There is now much discussion about alternative methods of performance measurement to ensure that a company achieves its overall goals.

Required

Briefly outline what you understand by the balanced scorecard as a performance measure.

> Although you will not face scenario-based questions in the Paper 8 exam, we have included the following old syllabus *Management Accounting Applications* scenario and three questions based on it as they cover topics central to the Paper 8 syllabus.

SMALLTOWN COLLEGE: SCENARIO (MAA, 5/96, AMENDED)

Candidates should read the following scenario carefully before answering questions 44, 45 and 46.

For many years Smalltown College provided a range of one-year courses (which run from January to December) to local students in a town in the north of England. In 20X6 the College gained university status and changed its name to University of the North West (UNW). A new Chief Executive has been appointed to manage UNW.

For financial years prior to 20X7, Smalltown College/UNW organised its budget under functional headings such as teaching staff, support staff, building maintenance etc. Budgets were prepared by a committee of senior teaching and administrative staff. The new Chief Executive has issued the following policy statement in regard to budgeting for 20X7.

'For management purposes I have divided UNW into five departments – three teaching (Business, Engineering and Social Sciences) and two support (Reprographics and Services). Each of these departments is to be a profit centre. The two support departments will invoice teaching departments for work done at full cost plus 5%. The structure of the budget should match this new organisation. The 20X7 budget should essentially be a plan to maximise UNW's profit.'

After your appointment as UNW's finance officer, you are given the following forecast data for the financial year to 31 December 20X7.

	Business £'000	Engineering £'000	Social Sciences £'000	Repro-graphics £'000	Services £'000
Fixed costs (Note 1)	3,126	2,580	890	800	680
Variable costs per student (Note 2)	4	5	3	-	0.25
Variable costs per study manual	-	-	-	0.03	-
Tuition fee per student (Note 3)	6	7	3	-	-
Subsidy per student (Note 4)	5	7	5	-	-

Notes

1   Includes most of the teaching and other staff salaries.

2   Excludes the cost of study manuals produced in the Reprographics department and supplied free to students.

3   Fee paid by students or their sponsoring body on enrolment, complying with government guidelines.

4   A government subsidy paid (in addition to normal fees) for a limited number of students.

Non-financial data

	Business	Engineering	Social Sciences
Staff teaching capacity, students	760	520	200
Maximum number of students the government will subsidise	420	340	100
Demand for enrolment at present fees	800	460	350
Study manuals per student	30	40	8

44   SMALLTOWN COLLEGE I   *45 mins*

(Read the scenario above before answering this question.)

Prepare UNW's 20X7 budget having regard to the Chief Executive's policy statement *and* the information with which you have been supplied.

25 Marks

45   SMALLTOWN COLLEGE II   *45 mins*

(Read the scenario above before answering this question.)

'The budgetary process provides a means for reconciling the conflicts between the components of an organisation.'

'Frequently, a new top management group will use budgeting procedures, installed or changed for the purpose, as a means of conveying power.'

Required

(a)   Explain the relevance of the above statements to the current situation at UNW.

13 Marks

(b)   Explain the purpose of zero base budgeting (ZBB), having regard to the above statements.   **12 Marks**

Total Marks = 25

46   SMALLTOWN COLLEGE III   *45 mins*

(Read the scenario above before answering this question.)

The Chief Executive of UNW gives you the following instruction.

'We must have a rigorous system of budgetary control in order to make both teaching staff and departmental management aware of the need for performance and efficiency. I want monthly budgetary control reports for each department which should include a full variance analysis and appropriate performance indicators linked to the achievement of budget.

Also, the support departments should have to compete for business with outside contractors. People have had things too easy for too long around here.'

After hearing of this instruction to you, a lecturer in management accounting at UNW comments as follows.

'One of the most important things to understand about financial controls is that they are not neutral. They can distort the whole management process.'

Required

(a) Write a memorandum to the Chief Executive detailing your design for a budgetary control report – specifying variances and performance indicators consistent with his instruction.   **15 Marks**

(b) Explain and discuss the lecturer's comments having regard to the Chief Executive's instruction.   **10 Marks**

Total Marks = 25

47   OBJECTIVE TEST QUESTIONS: MODERN BUSINESS ENVIRONMENT AND COST REDUCTION   *36 mins*

1   Which of the following would not hinder the introduction of a cost reduction programme in an organisation?

   A   A divisional focus
   B   A lack of planning
   C   Staff resistance
   D   Market resistance   **2 Marks**

2   Which of the following are key success factors for successful organisations in the current business environment?

   I   Quality product/service
   II   Innovative management
   III   Profit maximisation
   IV   Timely response to market

   A   I, II and III
   B   All of the above
   C   II and III only
   D   I, II and IV   **2 Marks**

3   Which of the following are approaches to cost reduction?

   I   Functional analysis
   II   Function analysis
   III   Valuation analysis
   IV   O & M
   V   Method measurement
   VI   Work study
   VII   Value engineering

   A   All of the above
   B   I and III
   C   I, IV, VI and VII
   D   VI and VII   **2 Marks**

4   Which of the following aspects of 'value' should be considered in a value analysis exercise?

   I   Sales value
   II   Replacement value
   III   Exchange value
   IV   Disposal value

   A   None of the above
   B   All of the above
   C   III only
   D   I and IV   **2 Marks**

5   A World Class Manufacturing manufacturer will have a clear manufacturing strategy aimed at which of the following issues?

   I   Customer satisfaction
   II   Flexibility
   III   Quality and reliability
   IV   Overhead recovery

   A   IV only
   B   I only
   C   II and III
   D   I, II and III   **2 Marks**

6   In a TQM environment, which of the following would be classified as an external failure cost?

   I   Cost of repairing products returned from customers
   II   Cost of customer service section
   III   Product liability costs
   IV   Cost of providing replacement items due to marketing errors

   A   None of the above
   B   All of the above
   C   I only
   D   III only   **2 Marks**

7   Which of the following are methods of cost reduction?

   I   Using a better quality of materials
   II   Cutting rates of pay
   III   Giving pay incentives for better productivity
   IV   Using a cheaper material

   A   I and IV
   B   I and III
   C   All of the above
   D   None of the above   **2 Marks**

8   Why might it be argued that, in a total quality environment, variance analysis from a standard costing system is redundant?

   I   The control aspect of standard costing systems is achieved by making individual managers responsible for the variances relating to their part of the organisation's activities.

   II   For standard costing to be useful for control purposes, it requires a reasonably stable environment.

   III   Ideal standards are usually set.

   IV   The ethos behind a system of standard costing is that performance is satisfactory if it meets predetermined standards.

   A   All of the above
   B   III only
   C   I, II and IV
   D   II and IV   **2 Marks**

9   Which of the following is a particular problem of JIT?

I   JIT makes the organisation far more vulnerable to disruptions in the supply chain.

II   Wide geographical spread makes JIT difficult.

III   It is not always easy to predict patterns of demand.

IV   There is a risk that stock might become obsolete.

A   All of the above
B   None of the above
C   I, II and III
D   I and III   **2 Marks**

10 Which of the following is an aspect of JIT?

I   The use of small frequent deliveries against bulk contracts

II   The grouping of machines or workers by product or component instead of by type of work performed

III   A reduction in machine set-up time

IV   Production driven by demand

A   None of the above
B   All of the above
C   I only
D   III and IV   **2 Marks**

Total Marks = 20

If you struggled with these objective test questions, go back to your BPP Study Text for Paper 8 and revise Chapters 8 and 12 before you tackle the preparation and exam-standard questions on the modern business environment and cost reduction.

If you would like a bank of objective test questions which covers a range of syllabus topics, order our MCQ cards using the order form at the back of this Kit.

---

48   JIT (PILOT PAPER)   *45 mins*

Many organisations believe that a key element of just-in-time (JIT) systems is JIT production.

Required

(a) Discuss five main features of a JIT production system.   **20 Marks**
(b) State the financial benefits of JIT.   **5 Marks**

Total Marks = 25

49   WORLD CLASS MANUFACTURING   *45 mins*

The implementation of budgeting in a world class manufacturing environment may be affected by the impact of the following.

• A total quality ethos
• A just-in-time philosophy
• An activity based focus

Required

Briefly describe the principles incorporated in *each* of the above and discuss ways in which each may result in changes in the ways in which budgets are prepared as compared to a traditional incremental budgeting system.

25 Marks

50   PREPARATION QUESTION: QUALITY COSTS

A Total Quality Management (TQM) programme has been introduced in a large manufacturing company, and is regarded as useful by senior managers. They are now planning to extend the TQM programme from manufacturing to the whole of the company. You have been asked to devise a TQM programme, including appropriate quality measures and calculations of quality cost, in the management accounting section of the finance department.

Required

Briefly explain each of the four categories of quality cost (prevention cost, appraisal cost, internal failure cost, and external failure cost). Give examples of each category appropriate to a manufacturing environment, and examples relevant to management accounting.

51   ML PLC (11/01)   *45 mins*

ML plc was formed three years ago to develop e-commerce systems and design web sites for clients. The company has expanded rapidly since then and now has a multi-site operation with bases in the UK and overseas.

ML plc has recognised the need to formalise its planning and budgeting procedures and one of its divisional managers has been assigned to co-ordinate the budgets for the year to 31 March 20X3. He recently attended a course on Financial Planning and Budgeting and has been puzzled by some of the concepts. In particular, he would like you to explain the following.

- The differences and similarities between zero based budgeting and activity based budgeting

- The reasons why budget holders should prepare their own budgets

- The reasons why incremental budgeting may not be appropriate as a basis of budgeting if budget bias is to be minimised

Required

(a) Prepare a report, addressed to the divisional manager, that explains the issues he has identified above.   **15 Marks**

(b) Techniques that are used in order to improve an organisation's performance include cost reduction and value analysis.

    Required

    Explain these techniques and how they may be used by ML plc as part of its planning activities.   **10 Marks**

Total Marks = 25

52 WYE HOTEL GROUP (5/01) *45 mins*

(a) The WYE hotel group operates a chain of 50 hotels. The size of each hotel varies, as do the services that each hotel provides. However, all of the hotels operated by the group provide a restaurant, swimming pool, lounge bar, guest laundry service and accommodation. Some of the hotels also provide guest entertainment, travel bureaux and shopping facilities. The managing director of the group is concerned about the high level of running costs being incurred by the hotels.

Required

Explain how cost reduction, value analysis and zero based budgeting techniques could be used by the WYE hotel group to improve the profitability of its hotels. **15 Marks**

(b) M plc is a food manufacturer. It operates a just-in-time (JIT) system with computer-controlled, automated processing and packaging equipment. The focus of M plc's weekly management reports is on the variance analysis that is generated from a standard absorption costing system that uses labour hours as the basis of overhead absorption.

Required

Explain why standard costing systems based upon absorption costing principles may be inappropriate in the modern manufacturing environment of companies such as M plc. **10 Marks**

Total Marks = 25

53 BWR PLC (MAA, 5/95, AMENDED) *45 mins*

BWR plc has acquired the franchise (operating rights) to operate freight services on a main line railway connecting Lindon with Fristol. In order to operate this franchise BWR plc has had to acquire the use of freight depots (in both Lindon and Fristol), locomotives, container wagons and maintenance facilities.

Each freight depot receives loaded containers by lorry from factories around the locality, transfers loaded containers from lorries to rail wagons and reloads the lorries with empty containers. Road hauliers prefer to use freight depots where the expected queueing time is low.

The demand for rail transport falls into two categories.

- Category A: explosives, petroleum products, nuclear products and hazardous chemicals which cannot be carried by road

- Category B: products that can equally easily be carried by road or rail

There is a linear relationship between demand for rail transport and price per container journey for each category of transport and for each direction of travel.

Required

As BWR plc's management accountant, do the following.

(a) Explain how you would design and implement a cost reduction programme; identify those features of BWR plc's operation which would give particular difficulty in this regard. **15 Marks**

(b) Explain how the adoption of modern management practices such as JIT (just-in-time) and synchronous manufacturing by BWR plc's customers would impact on the operations of BWR plc itself. **10 Marks**

Total Marks = 25

54   PREPARATION QUESTION: VALUE ANALYSIS

Clifton plc manufactures video recorders/players. In recent years increased competition and technological developments have caused the company's profit margins to be reduced. In an attempt to improve profitability, management has adopted two major policies.

The first of these is to invest in research and development of new products. The second is to improve factory efficiency and thereby increase output.

The video recorders/players are assembled by the assembly department which, in addition to using its own components, requires parts from the circuit boards and the plastic moulding departments. To increase production levels the circuit boards and plastic moulding departments have begun to cut corners. Preventative maintenance in these departments has been postponed and only essential repair work is taking place in order to increase production.

The assembly manager has persuaded the maintenance section to prioritise maintenance on machines in his department. This has resulted in increased machine downtime in the other two departments, and more rejects have occurred as a result of this.

Required

As management accountant you have been asked to produce a value analysis report for Clifton plc. Explain what this is and indicate the areas on which you would concentrate when producing such a value analysis report for an organisation of this type.

55   OBJECTIVE TEST QUESTIONS: COSTING SYSTEMS   *36 mins*

1   B Ltd manufactures a single product, the budgeted selling price and variable cost details of which are as follows.

		£
Selling price		79.21
Variable costs per unit	Direct materials	12.35
	Direct labour	10.22
	Variable overhead	8.74

Budgeted fixed overhead costs are £195,000 per annum incurred evenly throughout the year, which is divided into 13 control periods. Budgeted production is 24,375 units per annum. In a period when budgeted production was 1,220 units, which was 150 less than the budgeted number of units sold, the budgeted profit reported under absorption costing was:

A   £50,623 profit
B   £51,823 profit
C   £128,177 loss
D   £47,423 profit   **2 Marks**

2   When comparing the profits reported under absorption costing and marginal costing during a period when the level of stock increased:

A   Absorption costing profits will be higher and closing stock valuations lower than those under marginal costing.

B   Absorption costing profits will be higher and closing stock valuations higher than those under marginal costing.

C   Marginal costing profits will be higher and closing stock valuations lower than those under absorption costing.

D   Marginal costing profits will be higher and closing stock valuations higher than those under absorption costing.   **2 Marks**

3   Which of the following features distinguish throughput accounting from other costing systems?

I   Work in progress is valued at labour cost only.
II   It does not attempt to maximise profit.
III   Work in progress is valued at material cost only.
IV   Costs are allocated to products when they are completed or sold.
V   Only labour cost is treated as a variable cost.

A   None of the above
B   I and II only
C   II, III, IV and V
D   II and III only   **2 Marks**

4   W Ltd operates a system of throughput accounting and manufactures four products, details of which are as follows.

	Product Alpha	Product Beta	Product Gamma	Product Delta
	£ per hour	£ per hour	£ per hour	£ per hour
Sales price	35.20	72.10	237.61	67.25
Material cost	3.41	15.90	192.15	12.22
Conversion cost	3.62	21.10	14.52	29.53
Profit	28.17	35.10	30.94	25.50

Given unlimited demand for the four products, which should W Ltd manufacture to maximise profits?

A   Alpha
B   Beta
C   Gamma
D   Delta   **2 Marks**

5   L Ltd operates a process which produces three joint products: M, N and P. The costs of operating this process during control period 4 totalled £210,600. During the period the output of the three products was:

M   3,600 kgs
N   8,100 kgs
P   5,850 kgs

N is further processed at a cost of £16.20 per kg. The actual loss in the second process was 10% of input, which is normal. Products M and P are sold without further processing.

The final selling prices of each product are:

M   £36 per kg
N   £45 per kg
P   £32.40 per kg

Joint costs are attributed to products on the basis of output volume.

What profit is attributable to product N?

A   £34,776
B   £104,976
C   £7,776
D   £34,020   **3 Marks**

6   When deciding, purely on financial grounds, whether or not to process a joint product further, the information required is:

(i)   The value of the common process costs
(ii)   The method of apportioning the common costs between the joint products
(iii)   The sales value of the joint product at the separation point
(iv)   The final sales value of the joint product
(v)   The further processing cost of the joint product

Which of the above statements is/are correct?

A   All of them
B   (i), (ii) and (iii) only
C   (iii), (iv) and (v) only
D   (i), (iii), (iv) and (v) only   **2 Marks**

7   ABC Ltd manufactures its product through a series of processes. The FIFO method of valuing opening work in progress is used, and the following details relate to control period 2.

Opening work in progress was 1,080 units, each 70% processed as to materials and 80% processed as to conversion costs.

Normal loss was 900 units, fully completed.

Finished output was 26,100 units. There were no abnormal losses or gains.

Closing work in progress was 1,440 units, each 60% processed as to materials and 55% processed on to conversion costs.

When calculating the costs per equivalent unit, the number of equivalent units to be used are:

	Materials	*Conversion*
A	26,208	25,956
B	26,100	26,100
C	26,964	26,820
D	27,108	26,856

2 Marks

8   The following details relate to process A of C Ltd, a chemical manufacturer.

Opening WIP	3,500 units, 30% complete as to materials and 90% complete as to conversion
Material input	29,120 units
Normal loss	5% of input
Output to process B	21,950 units
Closing WIP	2,220 units, 10% complete as to materials and 15% complete as to conversion

The number of equivalent units to be included in C Ltd's calculation of the cost per equivalent unit, using a weighted average basis of valuation are:

	Materials	*Conversion*
A	23,628	23,739
B	21,122	19,133
C	21,950	21,950
D	22,172	22,283

3 Marks

9   In process costing, the value attributed to any abnormal gain units is:

A   Debited to the abnormal gain account and credited to the process account

B   Debited to the process account and credited to the abnormal gain account

C   Debited to the normal loss account and credited to the abnormal gain account

D   Debited to the scrap sales account and credited to the abnormal gain account

2 Marks

Total Marks = 20

> If you struggled with these objective test questions, go back to your BPP Study Text for Paper 8 and revise Chapters 9 and 11 before you tackle the exam-standard questions on costing systems.
>
> If you would like a bank of objective test questions which covers a range of syllabus topics, order our MCQ cards using the order form at the back of this Kit.

56   MARGINAL AND ABSORPTION RECONCILIATION (OCA, 5/96)   *45 mins*

The following budgeted profit statement has been prepared using absorption costing principles.

	January to June 20X7 £'000	January to June 20X7 £'000	July to December 20X7 £'000	July to December 20X7 £'000
Sales		540		360
Opening stock	100		160	
Production costs:				
Direct materials	108		36	
Direct labour	162		54	
Overhead	90		30	
	460		280	
Closing stock	160		80	
		300		200
Gross profit		240		160
Production overhead:				
(Over)/under absorption	(12)		12	
Selling costs	50		50	
Distribution costs	45		40	
Administration costs	80		80	
		163		182
Net profit		77		(22)
Sales units		15,000		10,000
Production units		18,000		6,000

The members of the management team are concerned by the significant change in profitability between the two six-month periods. As management accountant, you have analysed the data upon which the above budget statement has been produced, with the following results.

(a)   The production overhead cost comprises both a fixed and a variable element, the latter appears to be dependent on the number of units produced. The fixed element of the cost is expected to be incurred at a constant rate throughout the year.

(b)   The selling costs are fixed.

(c)   The distribution cost comprises both fixed and variable elements, the latter appears to be dependent on the number of units sold. The fixed element of the cost is expected to be incurred at a constant rate throughout the year.

(d)   The administration costs are fixed.

Required

(a)   Present the above budgeted profit statement in marginal costing format.   **10 Marks**

(b)   Reconcile *each* of the six-monthly profit/loss values reported respectively under marginal and absorption costing.   **4 Marks**

(c)   Reconcile the six-monthly profit for January to June 20X7 from the absorption costing statement with the six-monthly loss for July to December 20X7 from the absorption costing statement.   **4 Marks**

(d)   Calculate the annual number of units required to break even.   **3 Marks**

(e)   Explain briefly the advantages of using marginal costing as the basis of providing managers with information for decision making.   **4 Marks**

Total Marks = 25

57   **CA PLC**   *45 mins*

The following budget and actual data relates to CA plc for the past three periods.

Budget	Period 1	Period 2	Period 3
Sales (units)	10,000	14,000	12,200
Production (units)	8,000	14,200	12,400
Fixed overheads	£10,400	£19,170	£17,360
Actual			
Sales (units)	9,600	12,400	10,200
Production (units)	8,400	13,600	9,200
Fixed overheads	£11,200	£18,320	£16,740

The value of the opening and closing stock of the units produced is arrived at by using FIFO. The budgeted and actual opening stock for period 1 was 2,600 units and its valuation included £3,315 of fixed overheads. The company absorbs its fixed overheads via a predetermined fixed overhead rate per unit which is the same for each period. It is assumed that variable costs per unit and selling prices per unit remained the same for each of the periods.

Required

(a)   Calculate the under or over recovery of fixed overhead for each period and indicate how it will affect the profit or loss.   **7 Marks**

(b)   'Absorption costing will produce a higher profit than marginal costing'. Explain why you agree or disagree with this statement, making reference to the data provided above as appropriate.   **8 Marks**

(c)   Explain briefly why absorption costing is usually considered to be unsuitable as an aid for decision making. Justify your answer.   **10 Marks**

Total Marks = 25

58   **PROCESS AND P&L (OCA, 11/98, AMENDED)**   *45 mins*

ABC plc has a financial year which ends on 30 September. It operates in a processing industry in which a single product is produced by passing inputs through two sequential processes. A normal loss of 10% of input is expected in each process.

The following account balances have been extracted from its ledger at 31 August 20X8.

	Debit	Credit
	£	£
Process 1 (Materials £4,400; Conversion costs £3,744)	8,144	
Process 2 (Process 1 £4,431; Conversion costs £5,250)	9,681	
Abnormal loss	1,400	
Abnormal gain		300
Overhead control account		250
Sales		585,000
Cost of sales	442,500	
Finished goods stock	65,000	

ABC plc uses the weighted average method of accounting work in process.

During September 20X8 the following transactions occurred.

Process 1	Materials input	4,000 kg costing	£22,000
	Labour cost		£12,000
	Transfer to process 2	2,400 kg	
Process 2	Transfer from process 1	2,400 kg	
	Labour cost		£15,000
	Transfer to finished goods	2,500 kg	

Overhead costs incurred	£54,000
Sales to customers	£52,000

Overhead costs are absorbed into process costs on the basis of 150% of labour cost.

The losses which arise in process 1 have no scrap value: those arising in process 2 can be sold for £2 per kg.

Details of opening and closing work in process for the month of September 20X8 are as follows.

	Opening	*Closing*
Process 1	3,000 kg	3,400 kg
Process 2	2,250 kg	2,600 kg

In both processes closing work in process is fully complete as to material cost and 40% complete as to conversion cost.

Stocks of finished goods at 30 September 20X8 were valued at cost of £60,000.

Required

Prepare the profit and loss account of ABC plc for the year to 30 September 20X8.

25 Marks

59 P AND Q (OCA, 5/95) *54 mins*

PQR Ltd produces two joint products – P and Q – together with a by-product R, from a single main process (process 1). Product P is sold at the point of separation for £5 per kg whereas product Q is sold for £7 per kg after further processing into product Q2. By-product R is sold without further processing for £1.75 per kg.

Process 1 is closely monitored by a team of chemists who planned the output per 1,000 kg of input materials to be as follows.

Product P	500 kg
Product Q	350 kg
Product R	100 kg
Toxic waste	50 kg

The toxic waste is disposed of at a cost of £1.50 per kg and arises at the end of processing.

Process 2, which is used for further processing of product Q into product Q2, has the following cost structure.

Fixed costs	£6,000 per week
Variable costs	£1.50 per kg processed

The following actual data relate to the first week of accounting period 10.

Process 1

Opening work in process		Nil
Materials input	10,000 kg costing	£15,000
Direct labour		£10,000
Variable overhead		£4,000
Fixed overhead		£6,000

Outputs

Product P	4,800 kg
Product Q	3,600 kg
Product R	1,000 kg
Toxic waste	600 kg
Closing work in process	Nil

Process 2

Opening work in process	Nil
Input of product Q	3,600 kg
Output of product Q2	3,300 kg
Closing work in process	300 kg, 50% converted

Conversion costs were incurred in accordance with the planned cost structure.

Required

(a) Prepare the main process account for the first week of period 10 using the final sales value method to attribute pre-separation costs to joint products.   **12 Marks**

(b) Prepare the toxic waste accounts and process 2 account for the first week of period 10.   **9 Marks**

(c) Comment on the method used by PQR Ltd to attribute pre-separation costs to its joint products.   **4 Marks**

(d) Advise the management of PQR Ltd whether or not, on purely financial grounds, it should continue to process product Q into product Q2:

   (i) If product Q could be sold at the point of separation for £4.30 per kg; *and*

   (ii) If 60% of the weekly fixed costs of process 2 were avoided by not processing product Q further.   **5 Marks**

Total Marks = 30

60   NUMBER OF PROCESSES   *45 mins*

(a) Your company will shortly be completing its acquisition of a small manufacturing company which is engaged in producing a range of products via a number of processes. The production side of that company is well established. However, its cost and management accounting function is not so well developed. This type of multi-process production system is new to your company.

Required

Prepare a report for management which clearly explains the problems associated with process costing, and which looks particularly at the following.

- The treatment of overheads
- Valuation problems
- Normal and abnormal gains and losses   **20 Marks**

(b) Discuss the problems associated with joint cost apportionments in relation to:

(i)   Planning
(ii)   Control
(iii) Decision making   **5 Marks**

Total Marks = 25

61   **OBJECTIVE TEST QUESTIONS: ABC**   *36 mins*

The following information relates to questions 1 and 2.

DEF Ltd publishes three newspapers, *The Post*, *The Gazette* and *The News*. The following information has been obtained from the accounting system for period 6.

	The Post	*The Gazette*	*The News*
Number published	60,000	80,000	90,000
Direct labour hours per unit	0.2	0.3	0.1
Machine hours per unit	0.4	0.5	0.3
Set-ups	4	3	3
Distribution outlets	15	18	12

Overheads are related to the following activities.

Activities	*Cost of activities*
	£
Distribution	22,500
Machine maintenance	24,570
Machine set-up	25,730
	72,800

1   What is the traditional overhead absorption rate for period 6?

    A   £0.32 per publication
    B   £1.62 per labour hour
    C   £0.80 per machine hour
    D   None of the above   **2 Marks**

2   What is the overhead attributable to each *Post* using ABC?

    A   £0.40
    B   £24,272
    C   £0.80
    D   £0.32   **3 Marks**

3   For which of the following reasons is activity based costing regarded as an improvement on traditional absorption costing?

    I   Recognises the factors which drive costs
    II   Addresses all overheads
    III   Improves the quality of the costing process

A   I and III only
B   I, II and III
C   II and III only
D   None of the above   **2 Marks**

4   Which of the following statements about activity based costing is / are correct?

I   Short-term variable overhead costs should be traced to products using volume-related cost drivers, such as machine hours or direct labour hours.

II   Long-term variable production overhead costs are driven partly by the complexity and diversity of production work, as well as by the volume of output.

III   Transactions undertaken by support department personnel are the appropriate cost drivers for long-term variable overhead costs.

IV   Overheads should be charged to products on the basis of their usage of an activity. A product's usage of an activity is measured by the number of the activity's cost driver it generates.

A   All of the above
B   I only
C   II only
D   I, III and IV   **2 Marks**

5   Using activity based costing and the information below, what is the budgeted overhead cost per unit of Product Y?

	Product X	*Product Y*
Budgeted production (units)	1,000	4,000
Machine hours per unit	10	10
Production runs required	10	4
Inspections during production (for budgeted production level)	12	12
Production set-up costs	£84,000	
Quality control costs	£48,000	

A   £12
B   £9.43
C   £16.50
D   £26.40   **3 Marks**

6   Which of the following is not a feature of activity based costing?

I   It recognises that a single factor such as machine hours cannot be the driver of all overhead costs.

II   It seeks to recognise the causes of the costs of activities through the use of cost drivers.

III   It allocates the costs associated with cost drivers into cost pools.

IV   It uses a basis such as labour hours to incorporate overheads into product costs.

A   None of the above
B   All of the above
C   IV only
D   II only   **2 Marks**

7   In activity based costing (ABC), what is a cost driver?

A   A mechanism for accumulating the costs of an activity
B   An overhead cost that is incurred as a direct consequence of an activity
C   A factor which causes the costs of an activity
D   A cost relating to more than one product or service   **2 Marks**

61

8   Which of the following would you not consider to be a strength of activity based costing?

    I   Particularly appropriate for an AMT environment
    II   Identifies the driver of the overhead cost
    III   Particularly fashionable technique
    IV   Recognises the complexity of the production process

    A   All of the above
    B   III only
    C   II, III and IV
    D   IV only   **2 Marks**

9   Which of the following could be used to describe activity based budgeting?

    I   A method of budgeting based on an activity framework and utilising cost driver data in the budget-setting and variance feedback processes

    II   The use of costs determined using ABC as a basis for preparing budgets

    III   The definition of the activities that underlie the financial figures in each function and the use of the level of activity to decide how much resource should be allocated, how well it is being managed and to explain variances from budget

    A   All of the above
    B   None of the above
    C   II and III
    D   II only   **2 Marks**

Total Marks = 20

If you struggled with these objective test questions, go back to your BPP Study Text for Paper 8 and revise Chapter 10 before you tackle the preparation and exam-standard questions on ABC.

If you would like a bank of objective test questions which covers a range of syllabus topics, order our MCQ cards using the order form at the back of this Kit.

---

62   PREPARATION QUESTION: ACTIVITY BASED COSTING

XYZ plc manufactures four products, namely A, B, C and D, using the same plant and processes.

The following information relates to a production period.

Product	Volume in units	Material cost per unit	Direct labour per unit	Machine time per unit	Labour cost per unit
A	500	£5	$^{1}/_{2}$ hour	$^{1}/_{4}$ hour	£3
B	5,000	£5	$^{1}/_{2}$ hour	$^{1}/_{4}$ hour	£3
C	600	£16	2 hours	1 hour	£12
D	7,000	£17	$1^{1}/_{2}$ hours	$1^{1}/_{2}$ hours	£9

Total production overhead recorded by the cost accounting system is analysed under the following headings.

	£
Factory overhead applicable to machine-orientated activity	37,424
Set-up costs	4,355
Cost of ordering materials	1,920
Handling materials	7,580
Administration for spare parts	8,600

These overhead costs are absorbed by products on a machine hour rate of £4.80 per hour, giving the following overhead costs per product.

A £1.20   B £1.20   C £4.80   D £7.20

Investigation into the production overhead activities for the period reveals the following totals.

Product	Number of set-ups	Number of material orders	Number of times material was handled	Number of spare parts
A	1	1	2	2
B	6	4	10	5
C	2	1	3	1
D	8	4	12	4

Required

(a) Compute an overhead cost per product using activity based costing, tracing overheads to production units by means of cost drivers.

(b) Comment briefly on the differences disclosed between overheads traced by the present system and those traced by activity based costing.

Although you will not face scenario-based questions in the Paper 8 exam, we have included the following old syllabus *Management Accounting Applications* scenario and three questions based on it as they cover topics central to the Paper 8 syllabus.

---

63   EXE PLC (5/01)   *45 mins*

Exe plc is a motor car manufacturer. Exe plc has been in business for many years, and it has recently invested heavily in automated processes. It continues to use a total costing system for pricing, based on recovering overheads by a labour hour absorption rate.

Exe plc is currently experiencing difficulties in maintaining its market share. It is therefore considering various options to improve the quality of its motor cars, and the quality of its service to its customers. It is also investigating its present pricing policy, which is based on the costs attributed to each motor car.

Required

(a) Discuss the significance to Exe plc of developing and maintaining communications with suppliers and customers.   **15 Marks**

(b) Explain the benefits (or otherwise) that an activity based costing system would give Exe plc.   **10 Marks**

Total Marks = 25

KL: SCENARIO (MAA, 5/99, AMENDED)

Candidates should read the following scenario carefully before answering questions 64, 65 and 66.

During the last 20 years, KL's manufacturing operation has become increasingly automated with computer-controlled robots replacing operatives. KL currently manufactures over 100 products of varying levels of design complexity. A single, plant-wide overhead absorption rate (OAR), based on direct labour hours, is used to absorb overhead costs.

In the quarter ended March 20X9, KL's manufacturing overhead costs were as follows.

BPP
PROFESSIONAL EDUCATION

	£'000
Equipment operation expenses	125
Equipment maintenance expenses	25
Wages paid to technicians	85
Wages paid to storemen	35
Wages paid to dispatch staff	40
	310

During the quarter, RAPIER Management Consultants were engaged to conduct a review of KL's cost accounting system. RAPIER's report includes the following statement.

'In KL's circumstances, absorbing overhead costs in individual products on a labour hour absorption basis is meaningless. Overhead costs should be attributed to products using an activity based costing (ABC) system. We have identified the following as being the most significant activities.

(a) Receiving component consignments from suppliers

(b) Setting up equipment for production runs

(c) Quality inspections

(d) Dispatching goods orders to customers

Our research has indicated that, in the short term, KL's overheads are 40% fixed and 60% variable. Approximately half the variable overheads vary in relation to direct labour hours worked and half vary in relation to the number of quality inspections. This model applies only to relatively small changes in the level of output during a period of two years or less.'

Equipment operation and maintenance expenses are apportionable as follows.

• Component stores (15%), manufacturing (70%) and goods dispatch (15%)

Technician wages are apportionable as follows.

• Equipment maintenance (30%), setting up equipment for production runs (40%) and quality inspections (30%)

The following details relate to the quarter ended March 20X9.

• A total of 2,000 direct labour hours were worked (paid at £12 per hour)

• 980 component consignments were received from suppliers

• 1,020 production runs were set up

• 640 quality inspections were carried out

• 420 goods orders were dispatched to customers

64   KL I   *54 mins*

(Read the scenario above before answering this question.)

KL's production during the quarter included components r, s and t. The following information is available.

	Component r	*Component s*	*Component t*
Direct labour hours worked	25	480	50
Direct material costs	£1,200	£2,900	£1,800
Component consignments received	42	24	28
Production runs	16	18	12
Quality inspections	10	8	18
Goods orders dispatched	22	85	46
Quantity produced	560	12,800	2,400

In April 20X9 a potential customer asked KL to quote for the supply of a new component (z) to a given specification. 1,000 units of z are to be supplied each quarter for a two-year period. They will be paid for in equal instalments on the last day of each quarter. The job will involve an initial design cost of £40,000 and production will involve 80 direct labour hours, £2,000 materials, 20 component consignments, 15 production runs, 30 quality inspections and 4 goods dispatches per quarter.

KL's sales director comments:

'Now we have a modern ABC system, we can quote selling prices with confidence. The quarterly charge we quote should be the forecast ABC production cost of the units plus the design cost of the z depreciated on a straight-line basis over the two years of the job – to which we should add a 25% mark-up for profit. We can base our forecast on costs experienced in the quarter ended March 20X9.'

Required

(a) Calculate the unit cost of components r, s and t, using KL's existing cost accounting system (single factory labour hour OAR).   **6 Marks**

(b) Explain how an ABC system would be developed using the information given. Calculate the unit cost of components r, s and t, using this ABC system.   **13 Marks**

(c) Calculate the charge per quarter that should be quoted for supply of component z in a manner consistent with the sales director's comments. Advise KL's management on the merits of this selling price, having regard to factors you consider relevant. **11 Marks**

Total Marks = 30

65   **KL II**   *45 mins*

(Read the scenario above before answering this question.)

'It is often claimed that ABC provides better information concerning product costs than traditional management accounting techniques. It is also sometimes claimed that ABC provides better information as a guide to decision making. However, one should treat these claims with caution. ABC may give a different impression of product costs but it is not necessarily a better impression. It may be wiser to try improving the use of traditional techniques before moving to ABC.'

Comment by KL's management accountant on the RAPIER report

Required

(a) Explain the ideas concerning cost behaviour which underpin ABC. Explain why ABC may be better attuned to the modern manufacturing environment than traditional techniques. Explain why KL might or might not obtain a more meaningful impression of product costs through the use of ABC.   **10 Marks**

(b) Explain how the traditional cost accounting system being used by KL might be improved to provide more meaningful product costs.   **6 Marks**

(c) Critically appraise the reported claim that ABC gives better information as a guide to decision making than do traditional product costing techniques.   **9 Marks**

Total Marks = 25

66   KL III   *45 mins*

(Read the scenario above before answering this question.)

'The *lean enterprise* [characterised by just-in-time (JIT), total quality management (TQM) and supportive supplier relations] is widely considered a better approach to manufacturing. Some have suggested, however, that ABC hinders the spread of the lean enterprise by making apparent the cost of small batch sizes.'

Comment by an academic accountant

Required

(a) Explain the roles that JIT, TQM and supportive supplier relations play in modern manufacturing management. How might the adoption of such practices improve KL's performance?   **13 Marks**

(b) Explain what the writer of the above statement means by 'the cost of small batch sizes'. Critically appraise the manner in which this cost is treated by KL's existing (single OAR-based) cost accounting system. Explain the benefits that KL might obtain through a full knowledge and understanding of this cost.   **12 Marks**

Total Marks = 25

67   ABC AND ABB   *45 mins*

The basic ideas justifying the use of activity based costing (ABC) and activity based budgeting (ABB) are well publicised, and the number of applications has increased. However, there are apparently still significant problems in changing from existing systems.

Required

(a) Explain which characteristics of an organisation, such as its structure, product range, or environment, may make the use of activity based techniques particularly useful.

13 Marks

(b) Explain the problems that may cause an organisation to decide not to use, or to abandon use of, activity based techniques.   **12 Marks**

Total Marks = 25

68   R PLC   *54 mins*

R plc makes and sells a range of products. Management has carried out an analysis of the total cost of production. The information in the appendix below reflects this analysis of budgeted costs for the six-month period to 30 June 20X9. The analysis has identified that the factory is organised in order to permit the operation of three production lines X, Y and Z. Each production line facilitates the production of two or more products. Production line X is only used for the production of products A and B. The products are manufactured in batches on a just-in-time basis in order to fulfil orders from customers. Only one product can be manufactured on the production line at any one time. Materials are purchased and received on a just-in-time basis. Actual information is available for production line X as follows.

(a) Production line machine costs including labour, power, etc vary in proportion to machine hours.

(b) Costs incurred for production scheduling, WIP movement, purchasing and receipt of materials are assumed to be incurred in proportion to the number of batches of product which are manufactured. Machine set-up costs vary in proportion to the number of set-ups required and are linked to a batch costing system.

(c)   Costs for material scheduling systems and design/testing routines (product sustaining activities) are assumed to be incurred by each product in proportion to the total quantity of components purchased and the total number of types of component used respectively. The number of different components designed/tested for products A and B are 12 and 8 respectively.

(d)   Product line development cost is identified with changes in product design and production method. At present such costs for production line X are apportioned 80%:20% to products A and B respectively. Production line maintenance costs are assumed to vary in proportion to the maintenance hours required for each product. These are both production line-sustaining activities.

(e)   General factory costs are apportioned to each of production lines X, Y and Z in the ratio 25%:30%:45% respectively. Such costs are absorbed by product units at an average rate per unit through each production line.

Required

(a)   Prepare an activity based budget for production line X for the six-month period to 30 June 20X9 analysed into sub-sets for activities which are product unit based, batch based, product sustaining, production line sustaining and factory sustaining.

The budget should show the following.

(i)   Total cost for each activity sub-set grouped to reflect the differing operational levels at which each sub-set is incurred/controlled

(ii)   Average cost per unit for each of products A and B analysed by activity sub-set
22 Marks

(b)   Discuss the incidence and use of each of the following terms in relation to R plc, giving examples from the question to illustrate your answer.

(i)   Cost pools
(ii)   Cost drivers   **4 Marks**

(c)   Prepare a sequential set of steps which may be included in an investigation of activities in order to improve company profitability.

This should be a general list of steps and *not* specifically relating to R plc.   **4 Marks**

Total Marks = 30

Appendix

R PLC
BUDGET DATA SIX MONTHS TO 30 JUNE 20X9

	Product A	*Product B*
Material cost per product unit	£60	£45
Production line X – machine hours per unit	0.8	0.5
Production batch size (units)	100	200
Total production (units)	9,000	15,000
Components per product unit (quantity)	20	12
Number of customers	5	10
Number of production line set-ups	15	25
Production line X – maintenance hours	300	150

Cost category	Production line X £	Factory total £
Labour, power, etc	294,000	
Set-up of machines	40,000	
Production scheduling	29,600	
WIP movement	36,400	
Purchasing and receipt of material	49,500	
Material scheduling system	18,000	
Design/testing routine	16,000	
Product line development	25,000	
Production line maintenance	9,000	
General factory administration		500,000
General factory occupancy		268,000

69   OBJECTIVE TEST QUESTIONS: RELEVANT COSTS AND LIMITING FACTOR ANALYSIS   *36 mins*

1   Z plc manufactures three products which have the following selling prices and costs per unit.

	Z1 £	Z2 £	Z3 £
Selling price	15.00	18.00	17.00
Costs per unit: Direct materials	4.00	5.00	10.00
Direct labour	2.00	4.00	1.80
Overhead: Variable	1.00	2.00	0.90
Fixed	4.50	3.00	1.35
	11.50	14.00	14.05
Profit per unit	3.50	4.00	2.95

All three products use the same type of labour.

In a period in which labour is in short supply, the rank order of production is:

	Z1	Z2	Z3	
A	First	Second	Third	
B	Third	Second	First	
C	Second	First	Third	
D	First	Third	Second	**3 Marks**

2   HF Ltd has contracted to buy a replacement piece of machinery costing £572,000 and will receive a trade-in value of £29,200 for the old machine, which has a book value of £57,100. To maintain the machine HF Ltd must either recruit three new members of staff at an estimated annual salary of £21,000 each, or retrain three of the existing workforce at a total cost of £18,290. If existing staff are used, four new recruits would need to be hired at a cost of £11,100 each. The factory manager, whose annual salary is £40,700, estimates that 12% of her time would be spend supervising the four new recruits and 7% of her time would be spent supervising the new maintenance staff, whether they are newly hired or internally trained.

What is the total relevant cost of this decision?

A   £62,690

B   £63,000

C   £65,849

D   £44,400   **3 Marks**

3   Z Ltd manufactures three products, the selling price and cost details of which are given below.

	Product X £	Product Y £	Product Z £
Selling price per unit	75	95	96
Costs per unit			
Direct materials (£5/kg)	10	5	15
Direct labour (£4/hour)	16	24	20
Variable overhead	8	12	10
Fixed overhead	24	36	30

In a period when direct materials are restricted in supply, the most and the least profitable uses of direct materials are

	Most profitable	*Least profitable*
A	Y	X
B	Y	Z
C	Z	X
D	Z	Y

3 Marks

4   AP Ltd has been asked to quote a price for a special contract which will take four days to complete. Labour requirements are 20 hours of skilled labour (£12 per hour), 23 hours of semi-skilled labour (£8 per hour) and 12 hours of unskilled labour (£5 per hour).

A shortage of skilled labour means that the relevant staff would have to be moved from other work which currently earns a contribution of £15 per hour, net of wages cost. Semi-skilled labour are being paid semi-skilled rates to do unskilled work. If the semi-skilled labour are moved from this work to the contract, unskilled labour would be taken on to replace them.

What is the relevant cost of labour for this contract?

A   £475
B   £484
C   £415
D   £715

4 Marks

5   MW Ltd have just received an order for a particular product which will require 27.5 units of a component which, though used regularly by the company, is in short supply.

The company currently has a stock of 1,120 units of these components that it bought for £11.10 per unit, but has since written them down in its books to a net realisable value of £8.70 per unit. A new supplier has contacted the company to say that is has secured a supply of the component and is offering a bulk discount of 5% on the current market price of £13.75 for orders of 400 units and above.

Surplus units could be sold for £12.15 per unit.

What is the relevant cost per unit of the components for this order?

A   £11.10
B   £13.06
C   £13.75
D   £8.70

3 Marks

6   SW Ltd produces four products, A, B, C and D, and production capacity is limited. If product A has a C/S ratio of 27%, product B a C/S ratio of 22%, product C a C/S ratio of 19% and product D one of 11%, given unlimited demand for the four products, which product should SW Ltd concentrate on producing?

A   Product A

B   Product B

C   Product C

D   Product D   **2 Marks**

7   Which of the following statements is correct about a company that has to subcontract work to make up a shortfall in its own in-house capabilities?

A   Its total costs will be minimised if those units made have the lowest extra variable cost of making per unit of scarce resource used

B   Its total costs will be minimised if those units bought have the lowest extra variable cost of buying per unit of scarce resource saved

C   Its total costs will be minimised if those units bought have the highest extra variable cost of buying per unit of scarce resource saved

D   Its total costs will be minimised if those units made have the highest extra variable cost of making per unit of scarce resource used   **2 Marks**

Total Marks = 20

If you struggled with these objective test questions, go back to your BPP Study Text for Paper 8 and revise Chapters 13 and 14 before you tackle the exam-standard questions on relevant costs and limiting factor analysis.

---

70   CIVIL ENGINEERING INDUSTRY   *45 mins*

A company in the civil engineering industry with headquarters located 22 miles from London undertakes contracts anywhere in the United Kingdom.

The company has had its tender for a job in north-east England accepted at £288,000 and work is due to begin in March 20X3. However, the company has also been asked to undertake a contract on the south coast of England. The price offered for this contract is £352,000. Both of the contracts cannot be taken simultaneously because of constraints on staff site management personnel and on plant available. An escape clause enables the company to withdraw from the contract in the north-east, provided notice is given before the end of November and an agreed penalty of £28,000 is paid.

The following estimates have been submitted by the company's quantity surveyor.

COST ESTIMATES

		North-east £	South Coast £
Materials:	In stock at original cost, Material X	21,600	
	In stock at original cost, Material Y		24,800
	Firm orders placed at original cost, Material X	30,400	
	Not yet ordered – current cost, Material X	60,000	
	Not yet ordered – current cost, Material Z		71,200
Labour – hired locally		86,000	110,000
Site management		34,000	34,000
Staff accommodation and travel for site management		6,800	5,600
Plant on site – depreciation		9,600	12,800
Interest on capital, 8%		5,120	6,400
Total local contract costs		253,520	264,800
Headquarters costs allocated at rate of 5% on total contract costs		12,676	13,240
		266,196	278,040
Contract price		288,000	352,000
Estimated profit		21,804	73,960

Notes

(a) X, Y and Z are three building materials. Material X is not in common use and would not realise much money if re-sold; however, it could be used on other contracts but only as a substitute for another material currently quoted at 10% less than the original cost of X. The price of Y, a material in common use, has doubled since it was purchased; its net realisable value if re-sold would be its new price less 15% to cover disposal costs. Alternatively it could be kept for use on other contracts in the following financial year.

(b) With the construction industry not yet recovered from a recent recession, the company is confident that manual labour, both skilled and unskilled, could be hired locally on a sub-contracting basis to meet the needs of each of the contracts.

(c) The plant which would be needed for the south coast contract has been owned for some years and £12,800 is the year's depreciation on a straight-line basis. If the north-east contract is undertaken, less plant will be required but the surplus plant will be hired out for the period of the contract at a rental of £6,000.

(d) It is the company's policy to charge all contracts with notional interest at 8% on the estimated working capital involved in contracts. Progress payments would be receivable from the contractee.

(e) Salaries and general costs of operating the small headquarters amount to about £108,000 each year. There are usually ten contracts being supervised at the same time.

(f) Each of the two contracts is expected to last from March 20X3 to February 20X4 which, coincidentally, is the company's financial year.

(g) Site management is treated as a fixed cost.

Required

As the management accountant to the company, do the following.

(a) Present comparative statements to show the net benefit to the company of undertaking the more advantageous of the two contracts.   **12 Marks**

(b) Explain the reasoning behind the inclusion in (or omission from) your comparative financial statements of each item given in the cost estimates and the notes relating thereto.   **13 Marks**

Total Marks = 25

71   ANOTHER PRODUCT   *54 mins*

(a) EM Ltd currently produces P1 and is considering the addition of another product, P2, to its sales mix. A market has been identified for P2 with a three-year cycle to 30 June 20Y1.

Additional information is as follows.

    (i) Production constraints will only permit the manufacture of a mix of 10,000 units of P1 and P2. Each product will use the same amount of production capacity per unit.

    (ii) An advertising campaign for P1 is expected to considerably increase the level of demand for the product in the three-year period to 30 June 20Y1. The maximum sales estimates of the products are as follows.

Year to 30 June	P1	P2
	Units	Units
20X9	8,000	8,000
20Y0	6,000	8,000
20Y1	4,000	6,000

Each product will be produced and sold at the maximum level of demand.

(iii)   Advertising expenditure for P1 and P2 will be £100,000 and £60,000 respectively for each of three years payable on 1 July each year.

(iv)   The production of P2 could be sub-contracted each year where a shortfall of production capacity exists. The price paid to the supplier of each sub-contracted unit would be £80.

(v)   Components for P2 can be obtained at a cost of £30 per unit of P2 with no penalty clauses in the agreement.

(vi)   P2 will require expenditure of £100,000 per year on computer software related to its production process. This is not payable in any year to 30 June in which the production of P2 is totally sub-contracted.

(vii)   Sundry additional variable costs of £40 per unit are payable in respect of P2. This amount will be reduced to £15 per unit for which production is sub-contracted.

(viii)   It is estimated that the selling price of P1 will be maintained at £100 per unit and that P2 will be sold at £120 per unit over the three-year period.

Required

(i)   Determine for *each* of the years to 30 June 20X9, 20Y0 and 20Y1 whether EM Ltd should sub-contract production of *all* of P2 or whether it should only sub-contract that part of its production which cannot be achieved with its own production capacity. P1 will be produced and sold at its maximum demand forecast level. You should make the decision on financial grounds and show all relevant workings.   **13 Marks**

(ii)   Name and comment on additional factors which may influence the decision to sub-contract the production of part or all of P2.   **5 Marks**

(b)   Explain the relevance (if any) of each of the undernoted cost classifications in decisions relating to the following.

(i)   Acceptance of a contract
(ii)   Make or buy decisions

Your answers should include specific examples of each cost classification for each decision situation.

Cost classifications

Directly attributable fixed costs
Opportunity cost
Sunk cost
Incremental cost   **12 Marks**

Total Marks = 30

B/E Analys

72   ICE RINK   NB Question   Q70,   *45 mins*

A sports complex includes an ice rink and a swimming pool in its facilities. The ice rink is used for skating and for curling which became more popular after the 20X8 Winter Olympics. The swimming pool is used for leisure purposes and as a venue for swimming competitions. The sports complex management is concerned at falling profit levels which are due to falling revenue and rising costs.

A proposal to change, and hence improve, the method used for heating the water in the swimming pool is currently being investigated as part of a quality improvement programme. A survey of the complex has been carried out at a cost of £30,000 to check energy usage. This has shown that the heat removed from the ice rink in keeping the ice temperature regulated to the required level for good ice conditions could be used to heat the swimming pool. At present the heat removed in the regulation of ice temperature is not utilised and is simply vented into the atmosphere outside the complex.

The following additional information is available.

(a)   The expected costs for the ice rink heat extraction for the year ended 31 May 20X9 are £120,000. It is estimated that due to rising prices, this cost will increase by 10% during the year to 31 May 20Y0. Heat extracted totalled 500,000 units of heat during the year to 31 May 20X9 and this figure is expected to apply for the year to 31 May 20Y0.

(b)   The water in the swimming pool is currently heated by a separate system which is also used for a range of other heating purposes in the sports complex. In the year ended 31 May 20X9 the swimming pool share of the system had operating costs of £150,000 using 200,000 units of heat. This was made up of 70% variable avoidable cost and 30% which is a share of general fixed overhead. On average all such costs will increase by 10% through price changes in the year to 31 May 20Y0.

(c)   In order to utilise the heat extracted from the ice rink for heating the water in the swimming pool, equipment would be hired at a cost of £75,000 per annum. This equipment would be supervised by an employee who is currently paid a salary of £15,000 for another post in the year ended 31 May 20X9 and who would be retiring if not given this post. His salary for the year to 31 May 20Y0 would be £17,500. His previous post would not be filled on his retirement. It is anticipated that this system would help to improve the ice quality on the rink.

(d)   Only part of the heat extracted from the ice rink could be recovered for use in heating the water in the swimming pool using the new equipment. The current most likely estimate of the recovery level is 25% of the heat extracted from the ice rink. If the quantity of heat available was insufficient for the heating of the swimming pool, any balance could continue to be obtained from the existing system.

Required

(a)   Prepare an analysis for the year to 31 May 20Y0 to show whether the sports complex should proceed with the heat recovery proposal on financial grounds where a 25% level of recovery applies. Explain any assumptions made and give reasons for the figures used in or omitted from your calculations.   **15 Marks**

(b)   Calculate the percentage level of heat recovery from the ice rink at which the sports complex management will be indifferent to the proposed changes on financial grounds for the year ended 31 May 20Y0.   **10 Marks**

Breakeven Situation

Total Marks = 25

73   PR PLC (5/01, AMENDED)   *45 mins*

(a)   PR plc is a marketing consultancy company that offers three different types of service. It is preparing the budget for the year ending 31 December 20X2. The details of each type of service are as follows.

	Service A	Service B	Service C
Estimated demand (number of services)	150	800	200
	£ per service	£ per service	£ per service
Fee income	2,500	2,000	3,200
Consultant (£300 per day)	900	750	1,500
Specialists' report	400	200	500
Variable overhead	200	160	300

It has been estimated that the consultants will be able to work for a total of 2,400 days during the year. PR plc estimates that the fixed overhead for the year will be £600,000.

Required

(i)   Prepare calculations that show how many of each type of service should be undertaken in order for PR plc to maximise its profits.

(ii)   Prepare a statement that shows the budgeted profit for the year 20X2 based on your answer to (i) above.   **8 Marks**

(b)   Watlis Developments Ltd (WDL) has acquired a 600-hectare site. The site comprises the following land groups.

(1)   Agricultural land in current use   280 hectares
(2)   Derelict land formerly occupied by factories   250 hectares
(3)   Contaminated land formerly used for chemical storage   70 hectares

It is possible for WDL to develop this site with a combination of houses, apartments and shops.

WDL's planning consent for the development specifies that no more than 40 hectares of the development should be occupied by shops and no less than 200 hectares should be occupied by houses. Land developed for houses in excess of the minimum specified by the planning consent will qualify for a government subsidy in the form of an interest-free loan repayable in four annual instalments.

Required

(i)   Explain what a limiting (or 'key') factor is and what sorts of things can become limiting factors in a business situation. Describe the factors which would become limiting factors for WDL in relation to the acquisition.   **7 Marks**

(ii)   Explain the management idea known as throughput accounting. State and justify your opinion on whether or not throughput accounting and limiting factor analysis are the same thing. Briefly comment on whether throughput accounting is likely to be of relevance to WDL.   **10 Marks**

Total Marks = 25

74   ABC LTD (PILOT PAPER)   *45 mins*

ABC Ltd manufactures one product in each of its three factories in Anytown. Each factory makes the same complete product. One factory is located to the north of the town, another is in the central area, and a third is located in the south of the town. ABC Ltd owns a warehouse to the east of the town which it uses as a distribution centre and also to store finished goods. These locations are illustrated below.

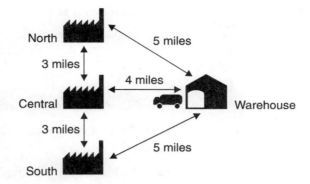

The company is now preparing its budgets for the year to 31 December 20X3 and has recognised that demand for its product will be 30 per cent less than its activity during the year ended 31 December 20X1. ABC Ltd is therefore considering the resources that it has available and seeks to identify the most profitable way of reducing its activity level. Factory closure is being considered, provided that at least one of the remaining factories is utilised at maximum capacity. All units to be sold in the year ending 31 December 20X3 will have to be made in that year because the company has no spare capacity in the year ending 31 December 20X2. This is due to its acceptance of some subcontracting work. This contract will be completed on 31 December 20X2 and it is not expected to be renewed.

Cost statements for the three factories for the year ended 31 December 20X1 are set out below.

	North	Central	South
Number of units produced	100,000	200,000	150,000
	£'000	£'000	£'000
Direct materials	500	1,000	750
Direct wages	800	1,600	1,200
Indirect materials	375	800	530
Indirect wages	250	1,000	750
Indirect expenses	1,000	2,000	750
Administration	300	550	350
Transport	500	800	750
Total cost	3,725	7,750	5,080

Additional information

1   Direct costs are totally variable, and are dependent on the number of units produced.

2   Indirect production costs are semi-variable. The variable element varies in relation to the number of units produced. Analysis has revealed that the variable element in each factory is as follows:

	North	Central	South
	%	%	%
Indirect materials	80	75	85
Indirect wages	20	15	20
Indirect expenses	35	30	40

The fixed cost element of the indirect production costs is avoidable if the factory is closed.

3   The administration costs include £900,000 for head-office costs. These costs have been apportioned to the factories based on the number of units produced. The balance of administration costs are fixed costs specific to each factory.

4   Transport costs represent the costs of transporting finished goods from the factory to the warehouse. The transport costs are variable and were allocated using 'unit mile' as the cost unit.

BPP
PROFESSIONAL EDUCATION

5   The annual production capacity of the factories is as follows:

	Units
North	160,000
Central	250,000
South	180,000

Based on trade/industry averages, the following estimates have been made.

- If production levels exceed 85 per cent of capacity, then there is a 40 per cent increase in specific fixed cost.

- If more than 95 per cent of available capacity is used, then specific fixed cost doubles from its original level.

Required

(a) (i)   Prepare a cost statement analysing the cost information provided by behaviour.

6 Marks

(ii)   Calculate how the production should be scheduled for the factories of ABC Ltd so as to maximise its profit for the year ended 31 December 20X3.

Show all workings.   **14 Marks**

(b)   Prepare a memorandum to the production controller that states other factors which should be considered before making a final decision about how to schedule the production.   **5 Marks**

Total Marks = 25

75   X LTD (OCA, 11/95, AMENDED)   *45 mins*

(a)   X Ltd manufactures four liquids – A, B, C and D. The selling price and unit cost details for these products are as follows.

	A	B	C	D
	£/litre	£/litre	£/litre	£/litre
Selling price	100	110	120	120
Direct materials	24	30	16	21
Direct labour (£6/hour)	18	15	24	27
Direct expenses	–	–	3	–
Variable overhead	12	10	16	18
Fixed overhead (note 1)	24	20	32	36
Profit	22	35	29	18

Note 1. Fixed overhead is absorbed on the basis of labour hours, based on a budget of 1,600 hours per quarter.

During the next three months the number of direct labour hours is expected to be limited to 1,345. The same labour is used for all products.

The marketing director has identified the maximum demand for each of the four products during the next three months as follows.

A	200 litres
B	150 litres
C	100 litres
D	120 litres

These maximum demand levels include the effects of a contract already made between X Ltd and one of its customers, Y Ltd, to supply 20 litres of each of A, B, C and D during the next three months.

Required

Determine the number of litres of products A, B, C and D to be produced/sold in the next three months in order to maximise profits, and calculate the profit that this would yield.

Assume that no stock is held at the beginning of the three months which may be used to satisfy demand in the period.   **15 Marks**

(b)   After completing the production plan in (i) above, you receive two memos.

The first is from the research director.

'New environmental controls on pollution must be introduced with effect from the start of next month to reduce pollution from the manufacture of product D. These will incur fixed costs of £6,000 per annum.'

The second memo is from the sales director.

'An overseas supplier has developed a capacity to manufacture products C and D on a sub-contract basis, and has quoted the following prices to X Ltd.

C   £105/litre
D   £100/litre'

Required

Using the information from *both* of these memos, state and quantify the effect (if any) on X Ltd's plans.   **10 Marks**

Total Marks = 25

76   **PQR LTD (OCA, SPECIMEN PAPER)**   *45 mins*

PQR Ltd is an engineering company engaged in the manufacture of components and finished products.

The company is highly mechanised and each of the components and finished products requires the use of one or more types of machine in its machining department. The following costs and revenues (where appropriate) relate to a single component or unit of the finished product.

	Components		Finished products	
	A	B	C	D
	£	£	£	£
Selling price			127	161
Direct materials	8	29	33	38
Direct wages	10	30	20	25
Variable overhead				
Drilling	6	3	9	12
Grinding	8	16	4	12
Fixed overhead				
Drilling	12	6	18	24
Grinding	10	20	5	15
Total cost	54	104	89	126

Notes

(a)   The labour hour rate is £5 per hour.

(b)   Overhead absorption rates per machine hour are as follows.

PROFESSIONAL EDUCATION

	Variable	Fixed
	£	£
Drilling (per hour)	3	6
Grinding (per hour)	4	5

(c)   Components A and B are *not* used in finished products C and D. They are used in the company's other products, none of which use the drilling or grinding machines. The company does not manufacture any other components.

(d)   The number of machine drilling hours available is limited to 1,650 per week. There are 2,500 machine grinding hours available per week. These numbers of hours have been used to calculate the absorption rates stated above.

(e)   The maximum demand in units per week for each of the finished products has been estimated by the marketing director as:

Product C	250 units
Product D	500 units

(f)   The internal demand for components A and B each week is as follows.

Component A	50 units
Component B	100 units

(g)   There is no external market for components A and B.

(h)   PQR Ltd has a contract to supply 50 units of each of its finished products to a major customer each week. These quantities are included in the maximum units of demand given in (e) above.

Required

(a)   Calculate the number of units of *each* finished product that PQR Ltd should produce in order to maximise its profits, and the profit per week that this should yield.

12 Marks

(b)   (i)   The production director has now discovered that he can obtain unlimited quantities of components identical to A and B for £50 and £96 per unit respectively.

State whether this information changes the production plan of the company if it wishes to continue to maximise its profits per week. If appropriate, state the revised production plan and the net benefit per week caused by the change to the production plan.   **7 Marks**

   (ii)   The solution of problems involving more than one limiting factor requires the use of linear programming.

Explain why this technique must be used in such circumstances, and the steps used to solve such a problem when using the graphical linear programming technique.   **6 Marks**

Total Marks = 25

77   **FULLY AUTOMATED**   *45 mins*

T Ltd has two fully automated machine groups X and Y through which lengths of timber are passed in order to produce decorative lampstand centres. There are production capacity constraints and T Ltd has decided to produce only one of the two lampstand models, T or M, in the year to 31 March 20X2.

The following forecast information is available for the year to 31 March 20X2.

		Model T	Model M
(a)	Maximum sales potential (units)	7,400	10,000

(b) Lampstand unit data:

		Model T	Model M
Selling price		£45	£40
Machine time:	Group X (hours)	0.25	0.150
	Group Y (hours)	0.20	0.225

(c) Machine groups X and Y have maximum operating hours of 1,700 and 1,920 hours respectively. Lampstand production is the sole use available for production capacity.

(d) The maximum quantity of timber available is 17,000 metres. Each lampstand requires a two metre length of timber. Timber may be purchased in lengths as required at £2.50 per metre.

(e) Variable machine overhead for machine groups X and Y is estimated at £25 and £30 per machine hour respectively.

(f) All units are sold in the year in which they are produced.

Required

(a) Use the above information to determine which of the lampstand models, T or M, should be produced and sold in the year to 31 March 20X2 in order to maximise profit. Your answer should state the number of units to be produced and sold and the resulting contribution.   **7 Marks**

(b) T Ltd wish to consider additional sales outlets which would earn contribution at the rate of £20 and £30 per machine hour for machine groups X and Y respectively. Such additional sales outlets would be taken up only to utilise any surplus hours not required for lampstand production.

Prepare figures which show whether T or M lampstands should now be produced in order to maximise total contribution in the year to 31 March 20X2 and state what that contribution would be.   **6 Marks**

(c) A linear programming model which incorporates the data given in parts (a) and (b) of the question has shown that where T Ltd is willing to produce and sell both T and M lampstands and use any spare capacity for the additional sales outlets detailed in (b) above, the profit-maximising mix is the production and sale of 4,250 units of each type of lampstand in the year to 31 March 20X2.

Prepare a budget analysis showing the total machine hours and timber (metres) required for each lampstand type and in total for the above production/sales mix, the budgeted contribution for each type of lampstand and the total budgeted contribution for T Ltd in the year to 31 March 20X2.   **6 Marks**

(d) Suggest ways in which T Ltd may overcome the capacity constraints which limit the opportunities available to it in the year to 31 March 20X2 and indicate the types of costs which may be incurred in overcoming each constraint.   **6 Marks**

                                              Total Marks = 25

78   OBJECTIVE TEST QUESTIONS: LINEAR PROGRAMMING AND MULTI-PRODUCT CVP ANALYSIS
36 mins

1   A company produces two types of orange juice, ordinary (X cartons per year) and premium (Y cartons per year). Which of the following inequalities represents the fact that the amount of ordinary orange juice produced must be no more than twice the amount of premium orange juice produced.

  A $X \geq 2Y$

  B $2X \geq Y$

  C $2X \leq Y$

  D $X \leq 2Y$ **2 Marks**

2   In a linear programming problem, the constraints are $X \leq 41$ and $Y \geq 19$. Describe the feasible region, assuming where appropriate that the axes also constitute boundaries.

  A   A rectangle to the left of X = 41 and below Y = 19

  B   An infinite rectangle to the right of X = 41 and below Y = 19

  C   An infinite region above Y = 19 and to the right of X = 41

  D   An infinite rectangle to the left of X = 41 and above Y = 19   **2 Marks**

3   In a linear programming problem the objective function is to maximise contribution given by $50X + 250Y$. If the feasible region has vertices (0, 160), (40, 140), (80, 120) and (140, 0), find the vertex representing the optimal solution.

  A   (140, 0)

  B   (0, 160)

  C   (40, 140)

  D   (80, 120)   **3 Marks**

4   In a linear programming problem, contribution is $4X + 2Y$ and the vertices of the feasible region are P (0, 250), Q (50, 200) and R (100, 100). Which of the following statements is the full, correct statement about maximising contribution?

  A   Contribution is maximised at point P.

  B   Contribution is maximised at point Q.

  C   Contribution is maximised at point R.

  D   Contribution is maximised at point Q and R and all points on the straight line joining them.   **2 Marks**

5   Z plc currently sells products Aye, Bee and Cee in equal quantities and at the same selling price per unit. The contribution to sales ratio for product Aye is 40%, for product Bee it is 50% and the total is 48%. If fixed costs are unaffected by mix and are currently 20% of sales, the effect of changing the product mix to

               Aye 40%   Bee 25%   Cee 35%

is that the total contribution/total sales ratio changes to:

  A   40%

  B   54%

  C   47.4%

  D   32%   **3 Marks**

6   By convention, how are multiple products shown on a P/V chart?

    A   Individually, from left to right, in order of increasing size of C/S ratio

    B   Individually, from left to right, in order of decreasing size of C/S ratio

    C   Individually, from right to left, in order of increasing size of margin of safety

    D   A P/V chart cannot be drawn for a multiple product situation   **2 Marks**

7   J Ltd produces and sells two products. The O sells for £12 per unit and has a total variable cost of £7.90, while the H sells for £17 per unit and has a total variable cost of £11.20. For every four units of O sold, three of H are sold. J Ltd's fixed costs are £131,820 per period. Budgeted sales revenue for the next period is £398,500.

What is the margin of safety?

    A   £386,100

    B   £254,280

    C   £266,680

    D   £12,400   **3 Marks**

8   A company makes and sells three products A, B and C. The products are sold in the proportions A: B: C = 1:1:4.

Monthly fixed costs are £55,100 and product details are as follows.

Product	Selling price £ per unit	Variable cost £ per unit
A	47	25
B	39	20
C	28	11

The company wishes to earn a profit of £43,000 next month. What is the required sales value of product A in order to achieve this target profit?

    A   £22,500

    B   £42,300

    C   £100,800

    D   £900   **3 Marks**

Total Marks = 20

If you struggled with these objective test questions, go back to your BPP Study Text for Paper 8 and revise Chapters 15 and 16 before you tackle the preparation and exam-standard questions on linear programming and multi-product CVP analysis.

If you would like a bank of objective test questions which covers a range of syllabus topics, order our MCQ cards using the order form at the back of this Kit.

---

79   **DP PLC (11/01)**   *45 mins*

DP plc assembles computers from bought-in components, using a computer-controlled robotic assembly line. The assembled computers are then tested by highly qualified computer engineers before they are packaged for despatch to customers.

DP plc currently assembles two different types of computer from different combinations of the same components.

The following budgeted details relate to the computers.

		Computer X	Computer Y
Selling price/unit		£800	£1,200
Component costs per unit		£150	£310
		Minutes per unit	*Minutes per unit*
Assembly time	(S1)	80	130
Testing time	(S2)	120	180
Packaging time	(S3)	60	30

The following costs are derived from DP plc's budget for the year to 31 December 20X1.

Assembly	£180/hour
Testing	£60/hour
Packaging	£20/hour

No cost increases are expected until July 20X2.

DP plc is now preparing its detailed plans for the six-month period to 30 June 20X2. During this period, it expects that the assembly time available will be limited to 1,000 hours and the testing time available will be limited to 875 hours. The packaging is carried out by part-time workers, and the company believes that there are a number of local residents who would be pleased to undertake this work if the existing packaging staff were unable to complete the level of activity needed. The maximum levels of demand for each computer will be as follows.

300 units of X (S4)
800 units of Y (S5)

Required

(a) Calculate the contribution per unit for each type of computer. **2 Marks**

(b) Determine the mix of computers that will maximise DP plc's profits for six months ending 30 June 20X2, using a graphical linear programming solution, and calculate the contribution that will be earned. **8 Marks**

(c) DP plc now realises that there may be a limit on the number of packaging hours available. A computer package for linear programming has been used and the following solution determined.

Variables		
X	268.75	
Y	112.50	
Constraints		
S1	23,875.00	
S2		1.46
S3		4.75
S4	31.25	
S5	687.50	
Contribution	£107,437.50	

Required

Write a report to the management team that interprets the solution produced by the computer package and makes appropriate recommendations.

(*Note.* Do not formulate, or explain the basis of, the computer model.) **7 Marks**

(d) Describe briefly four possible management accounting uses of linear programming.

8 Marks

Total Marks = 25

80   RAB CONSULTING (PILOT PAPER)   *45 mins*

RAB Consulting Ltd specialises in two types of consultancy project.

• Each Type A project requires twenty hours of work from qualified researchers and eight hours of work from junior researchers.

• Each Type B project requires twelve hours of work from qualified researchers and fifteen hours of work from junior researchers.

Researchers are paid on an hourly basis at the following rates:

Qualified researchers   £30/hour
Junior researchers   £14/hour

Other data relating to the projects:

Project type	A	B
	£	£
Revenue per project	1,700	1,500
Direct project expenses	408	310
Administration*	280	270

* Administration costs are attributed to projects using a rate per project hour. Total administration costs are £28,000 per four-week period.

During the four-week period ending on 30 June 20X0, owing to holidays and other staffing difficulties the number of working hours available are:

Qualified researchers   1,344
Junior researchers   1,120

An agreement has already been made for twenty type A projects with XYZ group. RAB Consulting Ltd must start and complete these projects in the four-week period ending 30 June 20X0.

A maximum of 60 type B projects may be undertaken during the four-week period ending 30 June 20X0.

RAB Consulting Ltd is preparing its detailed budget for the four-week period ending 30 June 20X0 and needs to identify the most profitable use of the resources it has available.

Required

(a) (i)   Calculate the contribution from each type of project.   **4 Marks**

     (ii) Formulate the linear programming model for the four-week period ending 30 June 20X0.   **4 Marks**

     (iii) Calculate, using a graph, the mix of projects that will maximise profit for RAB Consulting Ltd for the four-week period ending 30 June 20X0.

           (Note: projects are not divisible.)   **9 Marks**

(b) Calculate the profit that RAB Consulting Ltd would earn from the optimal plan.
                                                                          3 Marks

(c) Explain the importance of identifying scarce resources when preparing budgets and the use of linear programming to determine the optimum use of resources.   **5 Marks**

                                                          Total Marks = 25

81   **HJK LTD (MSA, 5/96, AMENDED)**   *45 mins*

HJK Ltd is a light engineering company which produces a range of components, machine tools and electronic devices for the motor and aircraft industry.

HJK Ltd produces two types of alarm system, one for offices and homes (X) and the other for motor vehicles (Y), on the same equipment. For financial reasons, it is important to minimise the costs of production. To match the current stock and demand position at least 100 alarm systems in total are required each week, but the quantity of one type must not exceed twice that of the other. The inputs necessary for the manufacture of one alarm system are given below, together with the availability of resources each week.

Type	Plating	Circuitry	Assembly
X	3 feet	4 units	20 minutes
Y	2 feet	8 units	8 minutes
Totals available each week	420 feet	800 units	34 hours

The management accountant estimates that the unit costs of production are £100 for X and £80 for Y. Past experience suggests that all alarms can be sold. At present, 75 of each alarm system are produced each week.

Required

(a)   State the objective function and the constraints for the production of alarm systems *and* use a graphical method of linear programming to find the optimal product mix.

17 Marks

(b)   Explain briefly any points of significance for management.   **8 Marks**

Total Marks = 25

82   **WOODEN TABLES AND CHAIRS (MSA, 5/98, AMENDED)**   *45 mins*

FM Ltd is a furniture manufacturer. In one of its factories, the company manufactures wooden tables and chairs for schools, colleges, local authorities etc. Four production stages are involved – cutting, machining, assembly and finishing – and there is a workshop for each stage. Within each workshop the equipment can be used for either the production of tables or chairs or any combination of the two. The numbers of tables and chairs, or their equivalent in parts, that can be made at each stage, per day, are shown below. (For example, if only chairs are processed by the Cutting Shop, 120 could be dealt with in 8 hours; similarly, 60 tables could be processed in the Cutting Shop in 8 hours.)

Maximum daily capacities in production units are as follows.

	Cutting	Machining	Assembly	Finishing
Chairs	120	96	60	56
Tables	60	96	80	96

Each workshop works an 8-hour day. Current company policy is to make equal numbers of tables and chairs each day because they both make the same contribution to profit, ie £4 per unit. One immediate problem is to identify the optimal production mix of tables and chairs, given that the demand for them exceeds production capacity.

Required

(a)   Formulate the linear programme of the problem of the optimal production mix of tables and chairs. Solve the problem *graphically*, given that FM Ltd wishes to maximise contribution to profit.   **17 Marks**

(b)   Write a short management report, setting out your recommendations and any other points of significance for management.   **8 Marks**

Total Marks = 25

83 G LTD   *45 mins*

G Ltd, a manufacturer of superior garden ornaments, is preparing its production budget for the coming period. The company makes four types of ornament, the data for which is as follows.

Product	Pixie	Elf	Queen	King
	£ per unit	£ per unit	£ per unit	£ per unit
Direct materials	25	35	22	25
Variable overheads	17	18	15	16
Selling price	111	98	122	326

Direct labour hours	Hours per unit	Hours per unit	Hours per unit	Hours per unit
Type 1	8	6	–	–
Type 2	–	–	10	10
Type 3	–	–	5	25

Fixed overhead amounts to £15,000 per period.

Each type of labour is paid £5 per hour but because of the skills involved, an employee of one type cannot be used for work normally done by another type.

The maximum hours available for each type of labour are as follows.

Type 1	8,000 hours
Type 2	20,000 hours
Type 3	25,000 hours

The marketing department judges that, at the present selling prices, the demand for the products is likely to be as follows.

Pixie	Unlimited demand
Elf	Unlimited demand
Queen	1,500 units
King	1,000 units

Required

(a) Calculate the product mix that will maximise profit, and the amount of that profit.

16 Marks

(b) Determine whether it would be worthwhile paying Type 1 labour for overtime working at time and a half and, if so, calculate the extra profit for each 1,000 hours of overtime.

2 Marks

(c) Comment on the principles used to find the optimum product mix in part (a), pointing out any possible limitations.   **3 Marks**

(d) Explain how a computer could assist in providing a solution for the data shown above.

4 Marks

Total Marks = 25

84 PREPARATION QUESTION: BREAKEVEN POINT

PE Ltd produces and sells two products, P and E. Budgets prepared for the next six months give the following information.

	Product P per unit £	Product E per unit £
Selling price	10.00	12.00
Variable costs: production and selling	5.00	10.00

Common fixed costs for six months: production and selling £561,600

Required

In respect of the forthcoming six months, do the following.

(a) State the breakeven point in £s and the number of each product this figure represents if the two products are sold in the ratio 4P to 3E.

(b) State the breakeven point in £s and the number of each product this figure represents if the sales mix changes to 4P to 4E. (Ignore fractions of products).

(c) Advise the sales manager which product mix should be better, that in (a) above or that in (b) above, and why.

(d) Advise the sales manager which of the two products should be concentrated on and the reason(s) for your recommendation. Assume that whatever can be made can be sold, that both products go through a machining process and that there are only 32,000 machine hours available, with product P requiring 0.40 hours per unit and product E requiring 0.10 hours per unit.

85 PREPARATION QUESTIONS: CVP ANALYSIS

JK Ltd has prepared a budget for the next twelve months when it intends to make and sell four products, details of which are shown below.

Product	Sales in units (thousands)	Selling price per unit £	Variable cost per unit £
J	10	20	14.00
K	10	40	8.00
L	50	4	4.20
M	20	10	7.00

Budgeted fixed costs are £240,000 per annum.

Required

(a) Calculate the total contribution earned by each product and their combined total contributions.

(b) Plot the data of your answer to (a) above in the form of a contribution to sales graph (sometimes referred to as a profit-volume graph).

(c) Explain your graph to management, comment on the results shown and state the breakeven point.

86 POD LTD

45 mins

(a) POD Ltd makes and sells three products, X, Y and Z. The selling price per unit and costs are as follows.

	X	Y	Z
Selling price per unit	£80	£50	£70
Variable cost per unit	£50	£10	£20
Fixed costs per month	£160,000		

The maximum sales demand per month is 2,000 units of each product and the minimum sales demand is 1,000 of each.

Required

(i) Comment on the potential profitability of the company. **4 Marks**

(ii)   Suppose that there is a fixed demand for X and Y of 1,500 units per month, which will not be exceeded, but for which firm orders have been received. Calculate the number of units of Z that would have to be sold to achieve a profit of at least £25,000 per month.   **5 Marks**

(b)   L Ltd achieved the following results in 20X1.

	£'000	£'000
Sales (200,000 units)		2,000
Cost of sales		
Direct materials	800	
Direct labour	400	
Overheads	600	
		1,800
Profit		200

Throughout 20X1, sales were £10 per unit, and variable overheads, which vary with the number of units produced, amount to £1 per unit.

Required

Using CVP analysis, calculate the sales volume necessary to achieve a profit of £330,000 in 20X2 if, at beginning of the year, the sales price is increased by £0.50 per unit, while the increases in costs above 20X1 levels are expected to be as follows. Comment on the result obtained.

Direct material	10%
Direct labour	15%
Variable overhead	10%
Fixed overhead	20% **7 Marks**

(c)   The following statistics have been taken from the information system of PZ Ltd for the last five years.

	20X0	*20X1*	*20X2*	*20X3*	*20X4*
Activity index	100	98	101	103	106
Cost index	100	105	109	113	115
Total costs (£)	70,000	73,080	76,518	79,778	81,880
Sales (£)	100,000				
Profit	30,000				

Notes

1   The activity index measures the volume of sales/production.

2   The cost index is representative of the costs incurred by PZ Ltd and measures the effects of inflation on costs over the five-year period.

3   The activity index for 20X5 is forecast as 110.

4   The cost index for 20X5 is forecast as 117.

Required

(i)   Calculate, using the high and low points method, the forecast fixed and variable costs of PZ Ltd for 20X5.   **4 Marks**

(ii)   Prepare a breakeven chart for 20X5, assuming that selling prices will be 20% higher than those of 20X0.   **5 Marks**

Total Marks = 25

87   **ZED LTD**   *45 mins*

The Bigtown branch of Zed Ltd manufactures a single product, B10, which is normally sold to external customers at a selling price of £70 per unit. The branch is expected to have a minimum operating level of 15,000 units and maximum output of 25,000 units in the coming year and the following unit variable costs and annual fixed costs are to be used for the preparation of budgets.

	Variable cost £	*Annual fixed cost* £
Direct wages	20	20,000
Direct materials	15	-
Purchased components	4	-
Production overhead	8	30,000
Administration overhead	2	80,000
Selling and distribution overhead	6	10,000
Depreciation	-	60,000

The branch has contracts to manufacture 22,000 units in the coming year to be sold at the standard price.

The Newtown branch of Zed Ltd is about to market a new product which requires a supply of B10 and the management of Newtown has offered to purchase 2,000 units per annum at a price of £52 per unit. If sales are made internally the variable selling and distribution costs are avoided.

Bigtown's net assets are £400,000.

The sales manager has suggested that, if the price to external customers were reduced to £68 per unit, the whole of the output of 25,000 units could be sold to external customers.

Required

(a)   Prepare budgets for the following.

  (i)   22,000 units of external sales only
  (ii)   24,000 units assuming that 2,000 units are sold to the Newtown branch   **7 Marks**

(b)   Calculate the sales value required to achieve a 10 per cent return on capital employed for the Bigtown branch assuming that all sales are made at the standard price of £70 per unit.   **7 Marks**

(c)   Give calculations to show whether or not the sales manager's proposal should be adopted.   **7 Marks**

(d)   Comment on the results in (a), (b) and (c).   **4 Marks**

                                                                        Total Marks = 25

88   **STANDARD AND DE LUXE**   *45 mins*

A manufacturer is considering a new product which could be produced in one of two qualities – standard or de luxe. The following estimates have been made.

	Standard £	*De Luxe* £
Unit labour cost	2.00	2.50
Unit material cost	1.50	2.00
Unit packaging cost	1.00	2.00
Proposed selling price per unit	7.00	10.00

Budgeted fixed costs per period are as follows.

0 – 99,999 units	200,000	250,000
100,000 and above	350,000	400,000

At the proposed selling prices, market research indicates the following demand.

Standard

Quantity	Probability
172,000	0.1
160,000	0.7
148,000	0.2

De luxe

Quantity	Probability
195,500	0.3
156,500	0.5
109,500	0.2

Required

(a)   Draw separate breakeven charts for each quality, showing the breakeven points.

10 Marks

(b)   Comment on the position shown by the charts and what guidance they provide for management.   **6 Marks**

(c)   Calculate, for each quality, the expected unit sales, expected profits and the margin of safety.   **9 Marks**

Total Marks = 25

89   OBJECTIVE TEST QUESTIONS: MIXED BANK 1 (PILOT PAPER, AMENDED)

36 mins

1   W plc is preparing its budgets for next year.

The following regression equation has been found to be a reliable estimate of W plc's deseasonalised sales in units:

y = 10x + 420

where y is the total sales units and x refers to the accountancy period. Quarterly seasonal variations have been found to be as follows.

Q1	Q2	Q3	Q4
+ 10%	+ 25%	− 5%	− 30%

In accounting period 33 (which is quarter 4), the seasonally-adjusted sales units are expected to be:

A   525
B   589
C   750
D   975   **3 Marks**

2   P Ltd is preparing its cash budget for the year ended 31 December 20X0. An extract of its sales budget is as follows.

January	£50,000
February	£45,000
March	£60,000
April	£55,000
May	£48,000
June	£60,000

Twenty per cent of the monthly sales are for cash. The payment pattern of the credit sales is expected to be as follows.

- 50 per cent in the month after sale
- 25 per cent in the month two months after sale
- 20 per cent in the month three months after sale

The remainder is expected to be bad debts. The amount budgeted to be received from customers in May 20X0 is:

A   £41,200
B   £50,800
C   £51,500
D   £61,100   **3 Marks**

3   An incremental budgeting system is:

A   a system which budgets only for the extra costs associated with a particular plan.

B   a system which budgets for the variable manufacturing costs only.

C   a system which prepares budgets only after the manager responsible has justified the continuation of the relevant activity.

D   a system which prepares budgets by adjusting the previous year's values by expected changes in volumes of activity and price/inflation effects.   **2 Marks**

4   The following cost per unit details have been extracted from the production overhead cost budget of E Ltd.

Output (units)	5,000	8,000
Production overhead (£/unit)	2.78	2.60

The budget cost allowance for production overhead for an activity level of 6,250 units is:

A   £1,125
B   £14,375
C   £15,000
D   £16,775   **3 Marks**

5   Which of the following perspectives are encompassed in a balanced scorecard?

(i)   Customer perspective
(ii)   Financial perspective
(iii) Supplier perspective

A   (i) and (ii) only
B   (i) and (iii) only
C   (ii) and (iii) only
D   (i), (ii) and (iii)   **2 Marks**

6   Activity-based costing is:

A   a method of total costing which attributes costs to cost units using multiple activity drivers.

B   a method of costing which is used to recognise the effects of changes in output activity and their effect on total costs.

C   a method of costing which is used to calculate the cost per unit in organisations which have only one single activity.

D   a method of cost accounting which derives unit costs according to planned outputs.   **2 Marks**

7   In the context of quality costs, training costs and reworking costs are classified as:

	Training costs	*Reworking costs*
A	prevention costs	internal failure costs
B	prevention costs	internal failure costs
C	internal failure costs	external failure costs
D	prevention costs	external failure costs

2 Marks

8   KEM Ltd produces and sells two products, the L and the E. The company expects to sell 2 L for every 5 E and have monthly sales revenue of £320,000. The L has a C/S ratio of 25% whereas the E has a C/S ratio of 35%. Budgeted monthly fixed costs are £90,000.

What is the budgeted breakeven sales revenue?

A   £300,000
B   £28,800
C   £1,050,000
D   £281,250   **3 Marks**

Total Marks = 20

BPP
PROFESSIONAL EDUCATION

90   OBJECTIVE TEST QUSTIONS: MIXED BANK 2 (5/01)   *36 mins*

1   XY plc uses a standard absorption costing system. Details for period 5 are as follows.

	Budget	*Actual*
Sales units	5,600	5,940
Selling price per unit	£18.00	£18.75
Profit per unit	£4.60	£5.20

The sales price and volume variances for period 5 were:

	Price	*Volume*
A	£4,455 (A)	£1,564 (F)
B	£4,555 (F)	£1,564 (F)
C	£4,455 (A)	£1,768 (F)
D	£4,455 (F)	£1,768 (F)

2 Marks

2   The trend of a company's sales in units has been found to be represented by

$$Y = 1.8x + 250$$

where   Y = sales units

x = an accounting period reference

In accounting period 35, the seasonal variation will have an index value of 110. The expected sales for period 35, to the nearest unit, are

A   285 units

B   313 units

C   319 units

D   344 units

2 Marks

3   PER plc sells three products. The budgeted fixed cost for the period is £648,000. The budgeted contribution to sales ratio (C/S ratio) and sales mix are as follows.

Product	C/S ratio	Mix
P	27%	30%
E	56%	20%
R	38%	50%

The breakeven sales revenue is nearest to

A   £248,000

B   £1,606,700

C   £1,692,000

D   £1,522,700

2 Marks

4   A purpose of a flexible budget is

A   to cap discretionary expenditure

B   to produce a revised forecast by changing the original budget when actual costs are known

C   to control resource efficiency

D   to communicate target activity levels within an organisation by setting a budget in advance of the period to which it relates   **2 Marks**

5   In the context of budget preparation the term 'goal congruence' is

A   the alignment of budgets with objectives using feed-forward control

B   the setting of a budget which does not include budget bias

C   the alignment of corporate objectives with the personal objectives of a manager

D   the use of aspiration levels to set efficiency targets   **2 Marks**

6   MNP plc produces three products from a single raw material that is limited in supply. Product details for period 6 are as follows.

	Product M	Product N	Product P
Maximum demand (units)	1,000	2,400	2,800
Optimum planned production	720	nil	2,800
Unit contribution	£4.50	£4.80	£2.95
Raw material cost per unit (£0.50 per kg)	£1.25	£1.50	£0.75

The planned production optimises the use of the 6,000 kgs of raw material that is available from MNP plc's normal supplier at the price of £0.50 kg. However, a new supplier has been found that is prepared to supply a further 1,000 kgs of the material.

What is the maximum price that MNP plc should be prepared to pay for the additional 1,000 kgs of the material?

A   £2,100
B   £2,240
C   £2,300
D   £2,465   **3 Marks**

7   PQR plc manufactures three products which have the following cost and demand data.

	Product P	Product Q	Product R
Contribution to sales ratio	20%	25%	30%
Maximum sales value (£'000)	800	1,000	1,500
Minimum sales value (£'000)	100	100	100

There are fixed costs of £700,000 per period.

The lowest breakeven sales value per period, subject to meeting the minimum sales value constraints, is nearest to

A   £2,320,000
B   £2,380,000
C   £2,520,000
D   £2,620,000   **3 Marks**

The following information is to be used for questions 1.8 and 1.9.

DEF plc uses an absorption costing system in which machine hours are used as the basis of recovering overhead costs. Its accounting year is divided into 13 four-week accounting periods, with fixed production overhead costs budgeted to be incurred at a constant rate of £266,000 per four-week period. Budgeted machine hours per four-week period are 38,000 hours.

In a recent accounting period, actual hours worked were 36,925 and output was 37,240 standard hours.

8   The fixed overhead efficiency variance was

A   £7,525 (F)
B   £2,205 (F)
C   £2,205 (A)
D   £7,525 (A)   **2 Marks**

9   The fixed overhead capacity variance was

A   £7,525 (A)
B   £2,205 (A)
C   £2,205 (F)
D   £7,525 (F)   **2 Marks**

Total Marks = 20

91   OBJECTIVE TEST QUESTIONS: MIXED BANK 3 (11/01, AMENDED)   *36 mins*

The following data is to be used for questions 1 and 2.

M plc sells televisions that it purchases through a regional distributor. An extract from its budget for the 4-week period ended 28 October 20X1 shows that it planned to sell 500 televisions at a unit price of £300, which would give a contribution to sales ratio of 30%.

Actual sales were 521 televisions at an average selling price of £287. The actual contribution to sales ratio averaged 26%.

1   The sales price variance (to the nearest £1) was

    A   £6,773 (A)
    B   £6,500 (A)
    C   £6,500 (F)
    D   £6,773 (F)   **2 Marks**

2   The sales volume contribution variance (to the nearest £1) was

    A   £1,890 (F)
    B   £1,808 (F)
    C   £1,638 (F)
    D   £1,567 (F)   **2 Marks**

The following data is to be used for questions 3 and 4.

The following details have been taken from the budget of R Limited for the 4-week period ended 28 October 2001.

Fixed production overhead   £120,000
Standard hours, assuming 100% efficiency   8,000

Actual data for the same period includes the following.

Fixed production overhead   £117,350
Standard hours produced   8,215
Actual hours worked   8,850

3   The fixed overhead capacity variance (to the nearest £1) is

    A   £12,750 (F)
    B   £3,225 (F)
    C   £3,225 (A)
    D   £12,750 (A)   **2 Marks**

4   The fixed overhead efficiency variance (to the nearest £1) is

    A   £9,525 (A)
    B   £9,071 (A)
    C   £9,071 (F)
    D   £9,525 (F)   **2 Marks**

5   Z plc operates an activity based costing (ABC) system to attribute its overhead costs to cost objects.

In its budget for the year ending 31 December 20X1, the company expected to place a total of 2,785 purchase orders at a total cost of £94,690. This activity and its related costs were budgeted to occur at a constant rate throughout the budget year, which is divided into 13 four-week periods.

During the four-week period ended 27 October 20X1, a total of 202 purchase orders was placed at a cost of £7,318.

The under recovery of these costs for the four-week period (to the nearest £1) was

A   £34
B   £416
C   £443
D   £450   **2 Marks**

6   Which of the following are required to determine the breakeven sales value in a multi-product manufacturing environment?

(i)   Individual product gross contribution to sales ratios
(ii)   The general fixed cost
(iii)   The product-specific fixed cost
(iv)   The product mix ratio
(v)   The method of apportionment of general fixed costs

A   (i), (ii), (iii) and (iv) only
B   (i), (iii) and (iv) only
C   (i), (ii) and (iv) only
D   All of them   **2 Marks**

7   Which of the following is not a feature of JIT?

A   Functional factory layout
B   Pull system
C   Uniform loading
D   Employee involvement   **2 Marks**

8   The trend in the number of units sold (y) is given by the equation $y = 350 + 45/x$, where x is the year, with 20X1 denoted by $x = 1$. What is the forecast for the number of units to be sold in 20X9 if, due to cyclical factors, the forecast is expected to be 7% below the trend in that year?

A   755
B   380
C   355
D   330   **2 Marks**

9   CM Ltd reported an absorption costing profit of £132,500 for the year to 30 April 20X2. Opening stock was 3,800 units higher than the closing stock of 14,950 units. The marginal costing profit for the period was £167,460. What was the fixed overhead absorption rate per unit?

A   £2.34
B   £1.86
C   £9.20
D   £34,960

                                                            2 Marks

10   M Limited manufactures four products from different quantities of the same material which is in short supply. The following budgeted data relates to the products.

	Product M1 £/unit	Product M2 £/unit	Product M3 £/unit	Product M4 £/unit
Selling price	70	92	113	83
Materials (£4 per kg)	16	22	34	20
Conversion costs	39	52	57	43
	55	74	91	63
Profit	15	18	22	20
Machine time per unit in **minutes**	40	40	37.5	45

The conversion costs include general fixed costs that have been absorbed using a rate of £24 per machine hour.

The most profitable use of the raw materials is to make

A   product M1
B   product M2
C   product M3
D   product M4

2 Marks

Total Marks = 20

Answers

1   OBJECTIVE TEST QUESTIONS: STANDARD COSTING

1   A

	£
Total actual direct material cost	2,400
Add back variances: direct material price	(800)
direct material usage	400
Standard direct material cost of production	2,000
Standard material cost per unit	£10
Number of units produced (2,000 ÷ £10)	200

Option B is the actual sales revenue divided by the standard selling price. This does not lead to a *production* figure, and it does not allow for any selling price variance which may have arisen.

If you selected **option C** you divided the actual material cost by £10 without adjusting first for the material cost variances.

If you selected **option D** you had the right idea about adjusting the variances, but you got the additions and subtractions the wrong way round. An adverse variance must be deducted from the actual cost to derive the standard cost, and vice versa with a favourable variance.

2   A   Saving in material used compared with standard $= \dfrac{\pounds 400(\text{F})}{\pounds 2 \text{ per kg}} = 200 \text{ kg}$

Standard material usage for actual production (200 units × 5kg)	1,000 kg
Usage variance in kg	200 kg (F)
Actual usage of material	800 kg

Option B is the standard usage for the output of 200 units.

If you selected **option C** you added the 200 kg usage variance instead of subtracting it.

3   D   Since there was no change in stocks, the number of units sold is equal to the number of units produced.

	£
200 units should sell for (× £70)	14,000
but did sell for	15,200
Selling price variance	1,200 (F)

Option A is 1/10 of the correct value – did you miss off a zero?

Option B is the sales volume variance.

If you selected **option C** you calculated the correct value for the variance, but misinterpreted it as adverse.

4   C   Budgeted sales volume per month $= \dfrac{\text{Budgeted material cost of sales}}{\text{Standard material cost per unit}}$

$= \dfrac{\pounds 2,300}{\pounds 10} = 230 \text{ units}$

Budgeted profit margin per unit $= \dfrac{\text{Budgeted monthly profit margin}}{\text{Budgeted monthly sales volume}}$

$= \dfrac{\pounds 6,900}{230} = \pounds 30 \text{ per unit}$

Budgeted sales volume	230 units
Actual sales volume	200 units
Sales volume variance in units	30 units adverse
Standard profit per unit	× £30
Sales volume variance in £	£900 adverse

If you selected **option A** you calculated the correct value for the variance, but misinterpreted it as favourable.

Option B is the selling price variance.

If you selected **option D** you evaluated the sales volume variance in units at the standard selling price per unit, instead of using the standard profit per unit. Remember that the volume variance highlights the margin lost or gained as a result of achieving a lower or higher sales volume than budgeted.

5   A

Budgeted hours of work	9,000 hours
Actual hours of work	9,400 hours
Capacity variance in hours	400 hours (F)
× standard fixed overhead absorption rate per hour *	× £4
Fixed production overhead capacity variance	£1,600 (F)

* £36,000/9,000 = £4 per hour

If you selected **option B** you performed the calculations correctly but misinterpreted the variance as adverse. Since the labour force worked 400 hours longer than budgeted, there is the potential for output to be 400 standard hours (or 80 units of production) higher than budgeted and hence the variance is favourable.

If you selected **option C** you evaluated the variance in hours at the actual hourly rate for fixed overhead, instead of at the standard rate per hour.

If you selected **option D** you have calculated the fixed production overhead volume variance, of which the capacity variance is a sub-component.

6   A

1,900 units of product should take (× 9,000/1,800 hrs)	9,500 hours
but did take	9,400 hours
Efficiency variance in hours	100 hours (F)
× standard fixed overhead absorption rate per hour *	× £4
Fixed production overhead efficiency variance in £	£400 (F)

* £36,000/9,000 = £4 per hour

If you selected **option B** you performed the calculations correctly but misinterpreted the variance as adverse. Time was saved compared to the standard time allowed for 1,900 units and so the efficiency variance is favourable.

If you selected **option C** you evaluated the 100 hours time saved at the actual hourly rate for fixed overhead, instead of at the standard rate per hour.

If you selected **option D** you calculated the fixed production overhead capacity variance, which together with the fixed production overhead efficiency variance make up the fixed production overhead volume variance.

7   D   None of the criticisms apply in *all* circumstances.

Criticism (i) has some validity but even where output is not standardised it may be possible to identify a number of standard components and activities whose costs may be controlled effectively by the use of standard costs.

Criticism (ii) also has some validity but the use of information technology means that standards can be updated rapidly and more frequently, so that they may be useful for the purposes of control by comparison.

Criticism (iii) can also be addressed in some circumstances. The use of ideal standards and more demanding performance levels can combine the benefits of continuous improvement and standard costing control.

8   D   Standard mix: $^3/_5$ G, $^2/_5$ H

Material	Actual input Litres	Standard mix of actual input Litres	Variance Litres	× standard price £	Variance £
G	24,500	27,000	2,500 (F)	4	10,000 (F)
H	20,500	18,000	2,500 (A)	2	5,000 (A)
	45,000	45,000	–		5,000 (F)

> **Alternative approach**
>
> Standard weighted average price of materials $= \dfrac{£48}{15\,\text{litres}} = £3.20$ per litre
>
> | Material | Actual input Litres | Standard mix of actual input Litres | Difference Litres | × difference between weighted average price and standard price £ | Mix variance £ |
> |---|---|---|---|---|---|
> | G | 24,500 | 27,000 (45,000 × 0.6) | (2,500) | (£3.20 – £4) (0.80) | 2,000 (F) |
> | H | 20,500 | 18,000 (45,000 × 0.4) | 2,500 | (£3.20 – £2) 1.20 | 3,000 (F) |
> | | 45,000 | 45,000 | – | | 5,000 (F) |

If you selected **option A**, you calculated the correct absolute value for the variance, but did not correctly interpret whether it was adverse or favourable.

Option B is incorrect – it is the mix variance in quantity that is nil.

9   C

Total input of 45,000 litres should have yielded (÷ 15 litres)	3,000 units
but did yield	2,800 units
Yield variance in units	200 units (A)
× standard material cost per unit of output	× £48
Yield variance in £	£9,600 (A)

If you selected **option A**, you calculated the correct yield variance in units but you evaluated it at the standard cost per litre of input (£3.20).

Option B is the usage variance, which you could check is the total of the correct variances for mix and yield.

If you selected **option D**, you calculated the variance correctly but misinterpreted it as favourable.

2   OBJECTIVE TEST QUESTIONS: STANDARD COSTING AGAIN

1   B

Standard labour rate per hour	= £264,264/50,820
	= £5.20
Excess hours worked, above standard	= £130/£5.20
	= 25 hours
∴ Standard hours produced	= 50,820 – 25
	= 50,795

If you selected **option A** you subtracted the monetary value of the variance from the actual hours worked. You were correct to subtract the variance, but you should have first converted it to a number of hours.

Option C is the actual hours worked. This would only be equal to the standard hours produced if there was no efficiency variance.

If you selected **option D** you added the excess 25 hours to the actual hours instead of subtracting them. The standard hours produced must be less than the actual hours worked because the efficiency variance is adverse.

2   D   **Statement 1** is incorrect because under-absorbed fixed overhead is represented by an adverse total overhead variance.

Statement 2 is incorrect because if production output was equal to the original budget the volume variance would be zero. The volume variance can be calculated as total variance – expenditure variance = £8,000 (F) – £9,500 (F) = £1,500 (A).

Statement 3 is correct because lower expenditure is represented by a favourable expenditure variance.

Statement 4 is correct because the capacity variance is zero: total variance = capacity variance + efficiency variance + expenditure variance and so £8,000 (F) = capacity variance + £1,500 (A) + £9,500 (F).

3   C   Direct labour costs will become a smaller proportion of total costs and so the significance of any direct labour cost variances will be less than in non-automated systems or systems with a bigger labour cost element.

Option A is not correct because there may still be inefficiencies in an automated system, for example slow setting-up of the machines. These inefficiencies may be allowed for in an attainable standard so that there will be a difference between an ideal standard and an attainable standard.

Option B is not correct because variances might identify controllable causes, for example inefficient maintenance, where management control action would be worthwhile.

Option D is not correct because standard costing systems can be established in an automated manufacturing environment.

4   B   Functional benchmarking involves comparing internal functions with those of the best external practitioners of those functions, from all types of industry. Three different industries are involved in this comparison.

Internal benchmarking, **option A**, involves comparisons within the same industry.

Competitive benchmarking (**option C**) and strategic benchmarking (**option D**) both involve comparisons with competitors. E Limited does not compete with a hospital or a school.

5   A   **Statement 1** is consistent with the variances because a fairly large favourable price variance arose at the same time as an adverse usage variance, which could have been caused by the higher wastage.

Statement 2 is consistent with the variances because the trend is towards higher percentage variances. Even if these variances are still within any control limits set by management, the persistent trend is probably worthy of investigation.

Statement 3 is not consistent with the variances, because more effective use of material should produce a favourable usage variance.

6   C   Standard mix is $^3/_8$ grade 1, $^5/_8$ grade 2.

Labour grade	Actual input Hours	Standard mix of actual input Hours	Variance Hours	×standard rate £	Variance £
1	2,550	2,490	60 (A)	8	480 (A)
2	4,090	4,150	60 (F)	6	360 (F)
	6,640	6,640	–		120 (A)

> **Alternative approach**
>
> | Labour grade | Actual input Hours | Standard mix of actual input Hours | Difference Hours | ×difference between weighted average rate and standard rate £ | Mix variance £ |
> |---|---|---|---|---|---|
> | 1 | 2,550 | 2,490 | 60 | (£6.75* – £8) (1.25) | 75 (A) |
> | 2 | 4,090 | 4,150 | (60) | (£6.75 – £6) 0.75 | 45 (A) |
> | | 6,640 | 6,640 | – | | 120 (A) |
>
> * £54/8

Options A and B are incorrectly based on the variances for 1 and 2 in hours.

Option D is incorrect – it is the mix variance in hours that is nil.

7   B

6,640 hours of labour should yield (÷ 8 hours)	830 units
but did yield	800 units
Yield variance in units	30 units (A)
× standard labour cost per unit of output	× £54
Yield variance in £	£1,620 (A)

If you selected **option A** you calculated the correct yield variance in units but you evaluated it at the average standard rate per labour hour (£6.75).

If you selected **option C** you calculated the variance correctly but misinterpreted it as favourable.

Option D is the efficiency variance, which you could check is the total of the correct variances for labour mix and yield.

8   C   **Situation (i)** would result in an adverse sales volume variance because volumes were reduced.

Situation (ii) would result in a favourable sales volume variance, evaluated at the standard profit or contribution achievable on the extra sales volume above standard.

A higher profit per unit (**situation (iii)**) would not affect the sales volume variance because the variance is evaluated at the *standard* profit per unit.

Situation (iv) would lead to an increased sales volume and hence a favourable sales volume variance.

9   B   The only fixed overhead variance in a marginal costing statement is the fixed overhead expenditure variance. This is the difference between budgeted and actual overhead expenditure, calculated in the same way as for an absorption costing system.

There is no volume variance with marginal costing, because under or over absorption due to volume changes cannot arise.

3 RELEVANCE OF STANDARD COSTING AND VARIANCE ANALYSIS

> **Pass marks.** Make sure that you didn't answer the question that you wanted to be set: 'Explain the techniques of standard costing and variance analysis' or 'Explain how variances are calculated'. It is all too easy to catch onto a few key words and launch into a previously-prepared answer.
>
> Part (c) was an invitation to discuss newer management accounting practices which have been developed in recent years. If you have begun your Paper 9 studies you might have mentioned target costing, life cycle costing, throughput accounting and so on.

(a) **Introduction**

Standard costing was developed between World War I and World War II, during the era in which scientific management was popular. Its use is intended to promote the efficient use of resources – materials, labour and capacity.

When to use standard costing

The greatest benefit from its use can be gained if there is a **degree of repetition in the production process.** It is therefore most appropriate in a stable, standardised and repetitive environment and hence is ideally suited to mass production and repetitive assembly work. One of its main aims is to **ensure that processes conform to standard, that they do not vary, and that variances are eliminated.** But this may seem **restrictive and inhibiting** in the current business environment.

The current business environment

Because of technological improvement, customer demands and increased competition, **the rate of change in product type and design has rapidly increased,** having an enormous effect on how businesses operate.

(i) The implementation of **just-in-time systems** reduces stock levels and maintains them at **fairly constant levels.**

(ii) High levels of automation, multi-skilling and teamworking **reduce levels of direct labour** and maintain them at fairly constant levels.

(iii) The rise in **support activities** such as setting-up, inspection and so on **increases the level of overhead costs.**

The importance of variable costs is therefore reducing. **Standard costing,** however, is of most value when applied to **variable costs.**

Quantity versus quality

Standard costing concentrates on quantity and ignores other factors contributing to effectiveness. In the **total quality environment** of the modern manufacturing organisation, however, quantity is no longer the issue: quality is.

(i) **Predetermined standards** are at odds with the philosophy of **continual improvement** inherent in a total quality management programme, as continual improvements are likely to alter methods of working, prices, quantities of inputs and so on.

(ii) Material standards often incorporate a **planned level of scrap,** but this is at odds with the TQM aim of **zero defects** and there is no motivation to '**get it right first time**'.

(iii) The use of **attainable standards,** which make some allowance for wastage and inefficiencies, conflicts with the **elimination of waste** which is such a vital ingredient of a TQM programme.

(iv) Standard costing systems make **individual managers responsible** for the variances relating to their part of the organisation's activities. A TQM programme, on the other hand, aims to make **all personnel** aware of, and responsible for, the importance of supplying the customer with a quality product.

(v) Effectiveness in a TQM environment centres on high quality output (produced as a result of high quality input and the elimination of non-value-adding activities). And the cost of failing to achieve the required level of effectiveness is measured not in variances but in terms of **internal and external failure costs**, which would not be identified by a traditional standard costing analysis.

Standard costing – the wrong focus

The use of standard costing in the modern manufacturing environment can make managers **focus their attention on the wrong issues**.

(i) **Adverse efficiency variances** are meant to be avoided, which means that managers need to prevent idle time and keep up production. In **a just-in-time environment**, however, action to **eliminate idle time** could result in the **manufacture of unwanted products** that would need to be held in store and might eventually be scrapped, which is totally at odds with the aims of JIT.

(ii) In a **JIT environment**, the key issues with materials purchasing are **supplier reliability, materials quality, and delivery in small order quantities**. Purchasing managers should not be shopping around each month looking for the cheapest price. Many JIT systems depend on long-term **contractual links with suppliers**, which means that material price variances are not relevant for control purposes.

(iii) The use of standard costing encourages the production of **large batches** as these permit more effective use of labour and materials and hence minimise adverse efficiency and utilisation variances. This **conflicts with JIT and flexible manufacturing strategies**, however.

It could therefore be argued that standard costing and variance analysis are irrelevant in today's manufacturing world.

(b) **Standard costing can be relevant**

Despite the arguments set out in (a) above, standard costing and variance analysis can be relevant in the modern manufacturing environment.

They are **suited** to organisations with the following **features**.

- Large or fluctuating stock levels held to meet seasonal or unpredictable demand
- Variable and significant direct labour cost
- Relatively large batch sizes

In such organisations a full standard costing system can used, although it is best **supplemented by a range of management accounting measures**, including non-financial indicators.

Standard costing for materials and variable overheads

In 'Standard costing: a technique at variance with modern management?' (*Management Accounting*, November 1999), Colin Drury reported that 'It is claimed that overhead costs have become the dominant factory costs, direct labour costs have diminished in importance and that most of a firm's costs have become fixed in the short-term. Given that standard costing is a mechanism that is most suited to the control of direct and variable costs, but not fixed or indirect costs, its usefulness has been questioned.

However, **recent surveys** in many different countries have reported remarkably similar results in terms of cost structures. They all report that **direct costs and overheads averaged approximately 75% and 25%** respectively of total manufacturing costs with average direct labour costs ranging from 10% – 15% of total manufacturing cost'.

Standard costing and variance analysis for control purposes would still therefore appear to be appropriate for direct materials and variable overheads.

Uses of standard costing and variance analysis

Standard costing and variance analysis can also be usefully **employed by modern manufacturing organisations as follows.**

(i) **Planning**. Even in a TQM environment, budgets will still need to be quantified. For example, the planned level of prevention and appraisal costs needs to be determined. Standards, such as 'returns of a particular product should not exceed 1% of deliveries during a budget period', can be set.

(ii) **Control**. Cost and mix changes from plan will still be relevant in many processing situations.

(iii) **Decision making**. Existing standards can be used as the starting point in the construction of a cost for a new product.

(iv) **Performance measurement**. If the product mix is relatively stable, performance measurement may be enhanced by the use of a system of planning and operational variances.

(v) **Improvement and change**. Variance trends can be monitored over time to assess whether a situation is in control or out of control.

(vi) **With ABC**. Standard costing can be used to control the costs of unit-level activities (which consume resources in proportion to the number of units produced) and to manage those overhead costs that are fixed in the short term, but variable in the longer term.

(c) There are a number of methods that might be used by management accountants to control costs and evaluate efficiency as **alternatives or complements to standard costing and variance analysis.**

Activity based costing

This is particularly well suited to an AMT environment in which there is high capital investment, low material and labour costs and high levels of the costs associated with support activities. ABC helps with the identification of the activities which cause costs to be incurred and the understanding of such cost behaviour assists with cost reduction action and allows managers to assess product profitability realistically.

Non-financial indicators

The use of a wide range of such measures can help to prevent production managers from concentrating on achieving standard production efficiencies without taking into consideration associated effects on quality and delivery performance. NFIs tend to be available quickly and allow for a rapid response to problems.

The method or methods adopted will, of course, **depend very much on the environment** in which the organisation operates.

4   DL HOSPITAL TRUST

> **Pass marks**. In (b) the examples given are of service organisations, as required by the question. The key point in (c) is the **objectives** the information system is designed to fulfil – is it primarily meant to be easy to use or to provide clear management information for decision making? A further important consideration is whether labour and overheads are influenced by the same factors.

(a)   We begin by calculating variances.

Surgical team (ie labour) rate variance

	£
235 hours should cost ($\times$ £200 (£2,000 $\div$ 10))	47,000
but did cost	44,400
	2,600 (F)

Surgical team efficiency variance

22 operations should take ($\times$ 10hrs)	220 hrs
but did take	235 hrs
Variance in hours	15 hrs (A)
$\times$ standard rate per hour	$\times$ £200
	£3,000 (A)

Variable overhead expenditure variance

	£
235 hours should cost ($\times$ 0.625 $\times$ £200)	29,375
but did cost	28,650
	725 (F)

Variable overhead efficiency variance

Variance in hours (as labour efficiency variance)	15 hrs (A)
$\times$ standard rate per hour (0.625 $\times$ £200)	$\times$ £125
	£1,875 (A)

Fixed overhead expenditure variance

	£
Budgeted expenditure (0.875 $\times$ £2,000 $\times$ 20)	35,000
Actual expenditure	36,950
	1,950 (A)

Fixed overhead volume variance

	£
Actual number of operations at standard rate (0.875 $\times$ £2,000 $\times$ 22)	38,500
Budgeted expenditure	35,000
	3,500 (F)

DL HOSPITAL TRUST – UNIT H
BUDGET COST – ACTUAL COST RECONCILIATION
NOVEMBER 20X3

Budgeted cost for 20 operations	£
Labour (20 × £2,000)	40,000
Variable overhead (20 × £2,000 × 0.625)	25,000
Fixed overhead (20 × £2,000 × 0.875)	35,000
	100,000

Flexed budgeted cost for 22 operations (£100,000 × 22/20)	110,000

	£	£	
Variances	(F)	(A)	
Surgical team rate	2,600		
Surgical team efficiency		3,000	
Variable overhead expenditure	725		
Variable overhead efficiency		1,875	
Fixed overhead expenditure		1,950	
Fixed overhead volume	3,500		
	6,825	6,825	–
Actual cost			110,000

(b) **Uses of budgetary control**

A budgetary control system is concerned with **cost and revenue totals,** those totals representing **future expectations** of departments or the organisation as a whole. The major uses are as follows. A labour budget may therefore be set for a unit within a hospital or a fixed overhead budget may be set for the restaurant within a hotel.

(i)   The totals are used as **yardsticks** against which actual performances are measured.

(ii)   They also represent **expenditure allowances**. Management must maintain their expenditure within the allowance and can only exceed it if a case is made.

Uses of standard costing

Standard costing, on the other hand, represents **cost control** on a **units basis,** that is to say particular products or services. A labour standard may be set, therefore, for an operation in a hospital and a variable overhead standard may be set for each passenger/kilometre in a passenger transport organisation. The main use of standard costings are as follows.

(i)   Standards are set as means of controlling activities.

(ii)   Standards enable the principles of management by exception to be practised by highlighting variances that appear to be significant.

Why both methods should be used simultaneously

Standard costing and budgetary control should be used in conjunction with each other since together they can encompass the whole organisation. In fact, budgets and standards are **interrelated**. For example, a **standard labour operation cost** can act as the basis for the **budget of a unit** within a hospital. The **standard cost** is **multiplied** by the **budgeted activity level** to arrive at the **budgeted expenditure** on labour in the hospital unit.

It is well nigh impossible to set realistic budgets without considering the **operational level standards** and it makes little sense to plan or control at an operational level without planning and controlling at a department or organisation-wide level.

(c)

REPORT

To: Finance director
From: Management accountant   Date: 1 November 20X3
Subject: **Absorbing overheads on a labour basis**

1   Advantages of using labour costs as the basis for attributing overhead costs to operations in the context of the hospital

1.1   The method is cheap.

1.2   It is easily understood (both by management accountants and non-management accountants).

1.3   It will be fair if the mix of staff involved in the operation does not vary too much, thereby ensuring that the labour cost for each similar operation is approximately the same.

2   Disadvantages associated with such an attribution method

2.1   One operation might be performed by a highly paid consultant. On another occasion the operation might be performed by the consultant's assistant and hence the labour cost of the operation will be less. It is likely, however, that the overheads associated with the two operations would actually be the same but the operations would be attributed with different amounts because of the different labour costs.

2.2   The method assumes that labour costs and overheads are related. This may not be true. Overheads may be driven by another factor such as time or there may be a number of different drivers of different elements of the total overhead cost.

3   Conclusion

3.1   **Labour costs** will be an **adequate basis** to use for apportionment of overheads if it is important that the system of apportionment is **simple** and **straightforward** to understand.

3.2   On the other hand the information may be of **limited use** for **management** and **control purposes** if labour and overheads are **not related**. In these circumstances some form of **activity based costing** focusing on the identification of the causes of different elements of the total cost may well be appropriate.

If I can provide any further information, please do not hesitate to contact me.

Signed: Management accountant

5   WORKING BACKWARDS

Pass marks. This question requires you to work 'backwards' to calculate actual data from standard costs and variances. This type of question is a very searching test of your understanding of variance analysis and you will need to adopt a logical and methodical approach.

There is more than one way of arriving at the correct solution. If you have used a different method to derive the same answer, well done! (We have included some alternative answers below.)

(a)   (i)

	£
Budgeted profit	30,000
Sales volume profit variance	5,250 (A)
Standard profit from actual sales	24,750
Standard profit per unit	÷ £3
Actual units produced and sold	8,250

Alternative approach

Budgeted production/sales volume $= \dfrac{\text{Budgeted profit}}{\text{Budgeted profit per unit}}$

$= \dfrac{£30,000}{£3 \text{ per unit}}$

$= 10,000$ units

Sales volume profit variance in £ $= £5,250$ (A)

Sales volume profit variance in units $= \dfrac{£5,250 \text{ (A)}}{£\,3 \text{ per unit}} = 1,750$ (A) units

This means that actual production/sales volume was 1,750 less than budgeted, ie $10,000 - 1,750 = 8,250$ units.

(ii)

	Hours
Standard hours for actual production ($8,250 \times 4$)	33,000
Labour efficiency variance ($£4,000 \div £4$)	1,000 (A)
Actual hours worked	34,000

Alternative approach

Let x = the actual number of hours worked
Let y = labour efficiency variance in hours

8,250 units should have taken ($\times$ 4 hours)	33,000	hours
but did take	x	hours
Labour efficiency variance (in hours)	y	hours
$\times$ standard rate per hour	$\times £4$	
Labour efficiency variance (in £)	£4,000	(A)

$\therefore$ Labour efficiency variance (in hours) $= y = \dfrac{£4,000 \text{ (A)}}{£4} = 1,000$ hrs (A)

If the labour efficiency variance in hours was 1,000 (A), then it took 1,000 hours more than expected to produce 8,250 units, ie $33,000 + 1,000 = 34,000$ hours.

(iii)

	Litres
Standard material usage for actual production ($8,250 \times 5$)	41,250
Material usage variance ($£400 \div £0.20$)	2,000 (F)
Actual material usage	39,250
Less decrease in stock	800
Actual material purchases	38,450

Alternative approach

Let x = actual quantity of materials used

Let y = materials usage variance (in litres)

Actual units produced and sold = 8,250

8,250 units should have used (× 5 litres)	41,250	litres
but did use	x	litres
Materials usage variance (in litres)	y	litres
× standard cost per litre	× £0.20	
Materials usage variance (in £)	400	(F)

$\therefore$ y, materials usage variance (in litres) $= \dfrac{£400 \text{ (F)}}{£0.20} = 2{,}000$ (F)

$\therefore$ 2,000 litres less than expected were **used** to make 8,250 units, ie 41,250 – 2,000 = 39,250 litres.

However, the question asks for the actual quantity of materials **purchased** = 39,250 litres – decrease in stock = 39,250 litres – 800 litres = 38,450 litres.

(iv)

	£
Standard variable overhead cost for actual production (8,250 × £6)	49,500
Variable overhead expenditure variance	(1,000)
Variable overhead efficiency variance	1,500
Actual variable overhead cost incurred	50,000

Alternative approach

Variable production overhead total variance = expenditure variance + efficiency variance = £1,000 (F) – £1,500 (A) = £500 (A).

Let x = actual variable overhead cost incurred.

	£
8,250 units should have cost (× £1.50 × 4 hrs)	49,500
but did cost	x
Variable production overhead total variance	500 (A)

$\therefore$ The actual variable overhead cost incurred was £500 more than expected, ie £49,500 + £500 = £50,000.

(v) Budgeted production volume = budgeted profit ÷ standard profit per unit = £30,000 ÷ £3 = 10,000 units

	£
Budgeted fixed overhead (10,000 × £14)	140,000
Fixed overhead expenditure variance	500 (F)
Actual fixed overhead cost incurred	139,500

Alternative approach

Fixed overhead total variance = expenditure variance + volume variance = £500 (F) – £24,500 (A) = £24,000 (A).

Let x = the actual fixed overhead cost incurred.

	£
8,250 units should have cost (× 4 hrs × £3.50)	115,500
but did cost	x
Fixed overhead total variance	24,000 (A)

$\therefore$ The actual fixed overhead cost incurred was £24,000 more than expected, ie £115,500 + £24,000 = £139,500.

BPP PROFESSIONAL EDUCATION

(b) **Reasons why a budgetary control system is often preferred to a standard costing system in non-manufacturing organisations** include the following.

(i) **A standard costing system controls costs at a unit level, with actual units being compared with a standard unit cost.**

A **large proportion** of the **costs** however in a non-manufacturing environment tend to be **fixed** and **indirect**. This means that the **proportion** of costs that can be **directly attributed** to individual service units is **small**; it also means that a **significant proportion** of costs may have to be **allocated** on an **arbitrary basis**. Therefore variances from standard may be of **limited use** for control purposes since they may not be due to factors affecting direct unit costs.

Budgetary control monitors **total costs** and **revenue, comparing actual** expenditure and revenue with **expected**. A non-manufacturing organisation can prepare budgeted levels of expenditure for each type of expenditure; the classification of expenditure should be what is most appropriate for the business. This will mean that **relevant comparisons** can be made.

(ii) Under **standard costing** the **units** of output must be **homogenous**. In non-manufacturing organisations the units of service may contain a number of standard operations; however as a whole they may not be homogenous.

Under **budgeting control** comparisons are made using the **consistent** measure of £ rather than dissimilar units of output.

6 TUR PLC

> **Pass marks**. Remember that the budgeted production figure is used only when you come to calculate the fixed overhead variances. All of the other variances should be based on the actual volume because you are monitoring the actual costs against a realistic target for the actual activity level.

(a) (i)

	£
4,800 kgs should cost (× £3.50)	16,800
but did cost	18,240
Material price variance	1,440 (A)

(ii)

965 units should have used (× 5 kgs)	4,825 kgs
but did use	4,840 kgs
Variance in kgs	15 kgs (A)
× standard cost per kg	× £3.50
Material usage variance	£52.50 (A)

(iii)

	£	£
4,000 hours should have cost (× £4.50)		18,000
but did cost (× £4.60)		18,400
Direct labour rate variance		400 (A)

(iv)

965 units should have taken (× 4 hrs)	3,860 hrs
but did take	4,000 hrs
Variance in hours	140 hrs (A)
× standard rate per hour	× £4.50
Direct labour efficiency variance	£630 (A)

(v)

	£
4,000 hours should have cost (× £1.50)	6,000
but did cost	5,950
Variable overhead expenditure variance	50 (F)

(vi)   Labour efficiency variance in hours   140 hrs (A)
       × standard rate per hour   × £1.50
       Variable overhead efficiency variance   £210 (A)

                                                          £
(vii) Budgeted expenditure (1,000 × £10)   10,000
       Actual expenditure   9,900
       Fixed overhead expenditure variance   100 (F)

(viii) Budgeted production   1,000 units
       Actual production   965 units
       Variance in units   35 units (A)
       × rate per unit   × £10.00
       Fixed overhead volume variance   £350 (A)

(b) (i)   £
       4,000 kg should have cost × £3   12,000
       but did cost   12,800
       Price variance   800 (A)

       700 units should have used (× 5 kg)   3,500 kg
       but did use (4,000 – 320)   3,680 kg
       Usage variance in kg   180 kg (A)
       × standard cost of R   × £3.00
       Usage variance in £   £540 (A)

(ii)   **Advantages of calculating the price variances at the time of purchase**

   (1)   The variance is **reported promptly,** and hence any necessary management action can be taken more quickly.

   (2)   The raw materials stock account is maintained at standard cost. This means that all **issues** can be made at a **standard price.** If the raw materials account is maintained at actual price, it will be necessary to calculate a separate variance on every issue.

   (3)   Prompt reporting means the **effect** of any purchase variance can be seen **immediately,** rather than being carried over the periods of usage.

   (4)   Reporting the price variance on usage requires decisions to be made concerning **issue pricing** (FIFO, LIFO etc) before the conversion to standard cost. The problem is avoided if the price variance is calculated on purchase.

   Disadvantages

   (1)   The **timing** of the reporting of price variances is **arbitrary,** and may cause difficulties in comparing period performances or extracting trends.

   (2)   If stock is slow-moving the price variance may be based on prices which are **out-of-date** when the stock is actually used.

(iii) 700 units should have used (× 5kg × (100/95))   3,684 kg
       but did use   3,680 kg
       Usage variance in kg   4 kg (F)
       × standard cost of R   ×   £3
       Usage variance in £   £12 (F)

   This variance may be **more useful** for the following reasons.

   (1)   The direction of the variance can be used to judge whether the transformation process has operated at a level of efficiency greater than what could realistically have been expected.

(2) Since the standard is more realistic, the amount of the variance gives a better idea of the loss/gain due to differences between standard and actual usage.

7 S PLC

> **Pass marks**. Part (a) provides a test of your understanding of variances; the unknown figures are not the variances. You should note therefore how the answers to part (a) are arrived at. In part (b) the differences in the variances calculated should be used to illustrate your answer. In part (d) you should, as the question requires, give sufficient detail about cost drivers and cost control. The question does appear to require that other aspects of ABC, notably its use in decision making, are also mentioned briefly.
>
> Beware of answering your own questions rather than the ones set in parts (b) and (c). You might be tempted to write pages on the differences between marginal and absorption costing, making up examples to illustrate your answer. This is simply a waste of time and will earn you no marks.

(a) (i) **Sales volume variance under marginal costing**

Budgeted sales volume	10,000 units
Actual sales volume	9,500 units
Sales volume variance in units	500 units (A)
× standard contribution per unit	× £ x
Sales volume variance	£7,500 (A)

$$\therefore \text{Standard contribution per unit, x} = \frac{7,500}{500} = £15$$

(ii) **Sales volume variance under absorption costing**

Budgeted sales volume	10,000 units
Actual sales volume	9,500 units
Sales volume variance in units	500 units (A)
× standard profit per unit	× £ y
Sales volume variance	£4,500 (A)

$$\therefore \text{Standard profit per unit, y} = \frac{4,500}{500} = £9$$

(iii) **Fixed overhead volume variance**

Let z = fixed overhead absorption rate per unit

	£
Actual production at standard rate	9,700 z
Budgeted production at standard rate	10,000 z
Fixed overhead volume variance	1,800 (A)

$$\therefore \quad 300 z = 1,800$$
$$\therefore \quad z = £6$$

Fixed overhead expenditure variance

	£
Budgeted fixed overhead expenditure (10,000 × £6)	60,000
Actual fixed overhead expenditure	a
Fixed overhead expenditure variance	2,500 (F)

$$\text{Actual fixed overhead expenditure, a} = £(60,000 - 2,500)$$
$$= £57,500$$

(b) The main reason why **different variances** are calculated under marginal and absorption costing is the differing **treatment of overheads**.

Treatment of overheads – absorption costing

In absorption costing **fixed overheads are absorbed into the cost of products.** **Variances** will **arise** not only if **actual** fixed cost expenditure **differs** from **budgeted** fixed cost expenditure, (the **expenditure variance**), but also if actual activity levels differ from those expected. If there is a **difference** between **actual and budgeted activity level**, there will be **over** or **under absorption of overheads** as a result, and hence a **volume variance**.

Treatment of overheads – marginal costing

By contrast **fixed overheads are not absorbed into the cost of products** under marginal costing. Hence no volume variance can arise, and the **only** variance that is therefore relevant will be the **fixed overhead expenditure variance**. This will be the same as the expenditure variance arising in absorption costing (as demonstrated in the question).

Differences due to sales volume variance

The other significant variance where differences arise is the sales volume variance. Under both marginal and absorption costing the variance will be calculated on the basis of the **difference** between **expected sales** and **actual sales**. However the difference in units will be **priced differently** under the two costing methods. Under **marginal costing** the difference in units will be priced at **contribution per unit**. Under **absorption costing** the difference in units will be priced at **standard profit per unit**. The standard profit figure will equal contribution less fixed overhead absorbed per unit.

In the question the difference of £3,000 between the two volume variances is the amount of fixed overhead absorbed per unit (£6) multiplied by the volume variance in units (500 units).

(c) **The fixed overhead volume variance is the difference between actual and budgeted levels of activity multiplied by the standard absorption rate per unit.**

Meaning

The variance **indicates** to management whether **levels of activity have been more or less than expected**. A favourable variance means more has been produced than expected; an adverse variance means less has been produced than expected.

Use

However **by itself the volume variance is of limited use to management**, since there are a number of different reasons why it could have arisen.

(i)   Expectations of activity levels were unrealistic.
(ii) Production was more or less efficient than expected.
(iii) Resources were used at more or less than expected capacity.

Even if management can be sure a favourable volume variance is due to more efficient production, there may be problems if increased production is not matched by more sales.

(d) CIMA *Official Terminology* defines **activity based costing (ABC)** as an approach to costing that 'involves tracing resource consumption and costing final outputs. Resources are assigned to activities and activities to cost objects based on consumption estimates'.

Stages of ABC

Activity based costing involves four major stages.

(i)   Identification of an organisation's major activities

(ii)   Identification of **cost drivers**, factors which determine the size of costs of an activity

Costs that vary with production volume such as power costs should be traced to products using production volume-related cost drivers such as direct labour hours. Overheads that do not vary with output but with some other activity should be traced using transaction-based cost drivers, such as number of production runs or number of orders received.

(iii) Collection of the costs of activity into **cost pools**

(iv)   Charging of the costs of activity to products on the basis of their usage of the activity

Focus of ABC

ABC thus focuses on **cost behaviour**. It is also concerned with all overhead costs, including non-factory floor activities such as product design, quality control and customer service.

Benefits of ABC

The principal benefits of ABC are as follows.

(i)   It produces information based on activities; this will be useful for management control purposes as management is seeking to **manage activities**.

The activity **information** itself is useful, as it **represents a (non-financial) measure** of the performance of service departments which may otherwise be difficult to cost. It also can indicate what activities do not add value to the product.

In addition ABC gives management **better information about cost behaviour**, particularly about those costs which do not vary with production but with other activities. Thus ABC leads to **better monitoring of those costs.**

(ii)   Use of ABC should mean **product costs** are **more meaningful**, with more overheads being able to be traced to products on a fair basis. Hence **profitability** and **performance measurement** will be more **realistic**.

(iii) ABC provides realistic **indicators of long-run variable costs**, which will **aid decision making**.

8   SEW

> **Pass marks**. Yet another 'working backwards' question. In part (a) you need to take account of whether you are dealing with favourable or adverse variances. If you adopt the approach we have taken you will need to insert minus signs for adverse variances when performing the algebraic manipulation to calculate the actual data.

(a)   Budgeted profit = £4,250

∴ Budgeted profit per unit = £4,250 ÷ 1,500 = £17/6

(i)	Budgeted sales volume	1,500 units
	Sales volume variance in units (£850 ÷ £17/6)	300 units (A)
	Actual sales volume	1,200 units

(ii)

1,550 units should have used ($\times$ (750 ÷ 1,500) kgs)	775	kgs
but did use	X	kgs
Material usage variance in kgs	(775 – X)	kgs (A)
$\times$ standard cost per kg (£4,500 ÷ 750 kgs)	$\times$ £6	
Material usage variances in £	£150	(A)

Because the variance is adverse, X must be greater than 775 and hence 775 – X is negative.

$$\therefore \quad -(775 - X) \times 6 = 150$$
$$-775 + X = 25$$
$$X = 800$$

$\therefore$ **Actual material usage** = 800 kgs

(iii)

	£
1,000 kgs should have cost ($\times$ £6)	6,000
but did cost	X
Material price variance	1,000 (F)

$\therefore (6,000 - X) = £1,000$

$\therefore 5,000 = X$

$\therefore$ **Actual direct material cost** = £5,000

(iv)

1,550 units should have taken ($\times$ (1,125 ÷ 1,500) hours)	1,162.5	hrs
but did take	X	hrs
Labour efficiency variance in hrs	(1,162.5 – X)	hrs (A)
$\times$ standard rate per hour (4,500 ÷ 1,125)	$\times$ £4	
Labour efficiency variance	£150	(A)

Because the variance is **adverse**, 1,162.5 is less than X and so (1,162.5 – X) is **negative**.

$$\therefore \quad -(1,162.5 - X) \times 4 = 150$$
$$-(1,162.5 - X) = 37.5$$
$$X = 37.5 + 1,162.5 = 1,200 = \textbf{actual direct labour hours}$$

(v)

	£
1,200 hours should have cost ($\times$ £4)	4,800
but did cost	X
Direct labour rate variance	200 (A)

$\therefore \quad -(4,800 - X) = 200$
$X = 200 + 4,800 = £5,000$

Actual direct labour cost = £5,000

(vi)

	£
1,200 hrs should have cost ($\times$ £(2,250 ÷ 1,125))	2,400
but did cost	X
Variable overhead expenditure variance	600 (A)

$\therefore \quad -(2,400 - X) = 600$
$X = 600 + 2,400 = 3,000$

Actual variable overhead cost = £3,000

(vii)

	£
Budgeted fixed overhead expenditure	4,500
Actual fixed overhead expenditure	X
Fixed overhead expenditure variance	2,500 (F)

$$\therefore \quad 4{,}500 - X = 2{,}500$$
$$X = 2{,}000$$

Actual fixed overhead cost = £2,000

(b) **Adverse direct materials usage variance**

This may have been caused by any of the following.

- Defective material
- Excessive waste
- Theft of material
- Stricter quality control (so that units had to be reworked)
- Errors in allocating material to jobs

Adverse direct labour rate variance

This may have been caused by any of the following.

- A wage rate increase
- The use of a higher grade labour than expected

Adverse sales volume variance

This may have been caused by any of the following.

- The activities of competitors
- A general downturn in consumer spending
- Adverse reports about the product

9   OVERHEAD COST VARIANCES

> **Pass marks**. In order to calculate the variable overhead cost variances in part (a), you need to calculate the machine-related variances and the labour-related variances separately and then add them together.

(a) **Variable overhead expenditure variances**

	£	£
22,000 machine hours should have cost (× £8)	176,000	
but did cost	176,000	
Machine-related variance		–
10,800 labour hours should have cost (× £4)	43,200	
but did cost	42,000	
Labour-related variance		1,200 (F)
Total variance		1,200 (F)

Variable overhead efficiency variances

5,450 units should have taken (× 4 machine hours)	21,800 hrs	
but did take	22,000 hrs	
Machine-related variance in hrs	200 hrs (A)	
× standard rate per hr	× £8	
Machine-related variance		£1,600 (A)
5,450 units should have taken (× 2 labour hours)	10,900 hrs	
but did take	10,800 hrs	
Labour-related variance in hrs	100 hrs (F)	
× standard rate per hr	× £4	
Labour-related variance		£400 (F)
Total variance		£1,200 (A)

Fixed overhead expenditure variance

	£
Budgeted expenditure (£20 × 5,500)	110,000
Actual expenditure	109,000
	1,000 (F)

Fixed overhead volume variance

	£
Absorbed overhead (5,450 × £20)	109,000
Budgeted overhead	110,000
	1,000 (A)

(b) **Machine-related expenditure**

Meaning The variable overhead costs incurred were exactly in line with those which would have been expected for the machine hours actually worked.

Cause No variance.

Machine-related efficiency

Meaning It took longer in terms of machine hours to produce the actual output than expected and so spending on machine-related variable overhead was higher that it should have been.

Cause Machines had not been properly maintained and so were not working as efficiently as anticipated.

Labour-related expenditure

Meaning The variable overhead costs incurred were lower than would have been expected, given the number of hours worked by employees.

Cause The hourly rate for the overhead was less than expected, possibly because a different type of service was used or savings in costs were made.

Labour-related efficiency

Meaning It took less time in terms of labour hours to produce the actual output than expected and so the spending on labour-related variable overhead was lower than it should have been.

Cause The labour force worked efficiently and produced the actual output more quickly than anticipated, perhaps because they were well motivated or they were using better quality equipment, materials or methods.

(c) There are a number of **benefits of using multiple activity bases** for overhead absorption.

(i) The link between activities and the costs they cause will be more apparent. A greater understanding of what causes costs should lead to **successful cost reduction exercises.** For example, it may become evident that significant variable overheads are caused by the number of industrial accidents within a production department. Attempts can then be made to lower the number of accidents and hence the level of overheads.

(ii) More meaningful product costs will be obtained which will result in **improved pricing decisions** and decision making in general. For example, it may become evident that Product X has been overcharged with variable overhead and so has been significantly overpriced.

(iii) The use of overhead absorption bases other than output volume, labour hours or machine hours should **broaden the focus of management's outlook** and give them the opportunity to look beyond the traditional factory floor boundaries of the organisation.

(iv) The use of multiple activity bases **reflects the complexity** of the modern manufacturing environment.

10 E PLC

> **Pass marks.** You are given a lot of the data that you need and you are told how to calculate the numbers required in (a) and (b). This question ought not to have been too difficult, but the presentation of the data is slightly unusual. If you can't remember how to calculate the variances required in (a), use the August variances provided to work them out. Expenditure variances are always easier to calculate than productivity variances, so do these first. You should have been able to make some comments on the trend even if you couldn't do parts (a) and (b). For example, you should have been able to see that expenditure gets worse as productivity improves.

(a) **Productivity**

September

Standard hours of output achieved	3,437	hrs
Productive hours worked (3,800 − 430)	3,370	hrs
Variance	67	hrs (F)
× standard charge rate (W1)	× £300	
Productivity variance	£20,100	

October

Standard hours of work achieved	4,061	hrs
Productive hours worked (4,200 − 440)	3,760	hrs
Variance	301	hrs (F)
× standard rate	× £300	(F)
Productivity variance	£90,300	(F)

Excess idle time

September

Excess time should have been (3,800 × 10%)	380	hrs
but was	430	hrs
Variance	(50)	hrs (A)
× standard rate (W1)	× £300	
Variance in £	£(15,000)	(A)

October

Excess time should have been (4,200 × 10%)	420	hrs
but was	440	hrs
Variance	(20)	hrs (A)
× standard rate	× £300	(A)
Variance in £	£(6,000)	(A)

Expenditure

September

	£	
Expenditure should have been (3,800 × £270)	1,026,000	
but was	1,070,000	
Variance	(44,000)	(A)

October

Expenditure should have been (£4,200 × £270)	1,134,000	
but was	1,247,000	
Variance	(113,000)	(A)

(b)

Variances	*Aug*	*Sept* (W3)	*Oct*	*Nov*
Productivity	(4.2)	1.9	7.4	8.3
Excess idle time	(5.0)	(13.2)	(4.8)	(9.8)
Expenditure	(1.9)	(4.3)	(10.0)	(10.0)

Workings

1   *Standard charge rate*

Standard variable machine cost per gross hour is £270 divided by $(100 - 10)\% = £300$.

2   *Standard costs*

	Aug	*Sept*	*Oct*	*Nov*
Standard hours of output (given)	3,437	3,437	4,061	3,980
Standard cost (× £300)(W1)	1,031,100	1,031,100	1,218,300	1,194,000
Expected idle time				
(10% × 4,000 etc)	400	380	420	410
Expected cost (× £300)	120,000	114,000	126,000	123,000
Gross machine hours (given)	4,000	3,800	4,200	4,100
Standard cost (× £270)	1,080,000	1,026,000	1,134,000	1,107,000

3   *Variances as percentages*

These are calculated as instructed in the question. For example, for September:

$$\text{Productivity} = \frac{\text{Productivity variance (part (a))}}{\text{Standard cost of output (W2)}} \times 100\%$$

$$= \frac{20,100}{1,031,100}$$

$$= 1.9\%$$

$$\text{Excess idle time} = \frac{\text{Variance (part (a))}}{\text{Expected cost (W2)}}$$

$$= \frac{(15,000)}{114,000} \times 100\%$$

$$= (13.2\%)$$

$$\text{Expenditure} = \frac{\text{Variance (part (a))}}{\text{Standard machine cost (W2)}}$$

$$= \frac{(44,000)}{1,026,000}$$

$$= (4.3)\%$$

(c) **Trends exhibited**

The following comments may be made.

(i)   **Productivity has improved** in each month, suggesting that the extra attention to *quality* is having a positive effect.

(ii)   **Excess idle time has fluctuated** in the period: it is higher (more adverse) in October and November.

(iii) **Expenditure has been increasing**, notably between September and October, but seems to have held steady in November.

121

In the absence of other information we can suggest the following possible **interdependencies**.

(i) The **productivity improvement** may have been brought about by means of **increased expenditure**, perhaps on better quality materials, machine maintenance or supervision. The fact that improvements continue may be due to a learning curve effect, however.

(ii) The fluctuating levels of **idle time do not have a clear cause**, though they do suggest that the quality improvement process is not yet fully under control.

11   RBF TRANSPORT LTD

> **Pass marks.** Part (a) really tests your understanding of variances. It is likely that the examiner will provide information about variances from which you have to 'work backwards' to determine the actual results. You need to take an algebraic approach. A common mistake often made by candidates is to think that the sales volume profit variance is calculated using the standard selling price per unit rather than the standard profit per unit. If you made the same mistake in part (a)(i) this would have had a direct effect on the answers that you calculated for parts (a)(iii) and (iv).

(a) (i)   Standard profit per delivery mile $= \dfrac{\text{budgeted profit}}{\text{budgeted activity}}$

$$= \frac{£8,000}{200,000} = £0.04$$

Sales volume profit variance

Budgeted activity	200,000	delivery miles
Actual activity	x	delivery miles
Sales volume variance in delivery miles	22,000 *	delivery miles (A)
× standard profit per delivery mile	× £0.04	
Sales volume profit variance (given)	£880 (A)	

* This figure is calculated by working backwards from the sales volume profit variance which is given in the question. £880 ÷ £0.04 = 22,000.

We can therefore deduce that the **actual number of delivery miles** was 22,000 less than expected (since the sales volume variance was adverse) ie (200,000 − 22,000) delivery miles = 178,000 delivery miles.

(ii)   Let x = the cost of 3,620 direct labour hours.

	£
3,620 direct labour hours cost	x
but should have cost (× £4 *)	14,480
Direct labour rate variance (given)	1,086 (F)

* Standard direct labour rate per hour $= \dfrac{£0.08}{0.02 \text{ hrs}} = £4$

∴ x = £14,480 − £1,086 = £13,394

$$\frac{£13,394}{3,620 \text{ hrs}} = £3.70$$

∴ The **actual direct labour rate per hour** = £3.70.

(iii)   Let x = the number of litres of fuel that 178,000 delivery miles actually used.

178,000 delivery miles did use		x L
but should have used ($\times$ 0.1 litres)		17,800 L
Fuel usage variance in litres		3,200 L$\star$ (A)
$\times$ standard rate per litre	$\times$	£0.4 $\star\star$
Fuel usage variance (given)		£1,280 (A)

$\star$ This figure is calculated by working backwards (£1,280 ÷ £0.4 = 3,200 litres)

$\star\star$ £0.04 ÷ 0.1 litres = £0.4 per litre

$\therefore$ x = (17,800 + 3,200) litres = 21,000 litres

$\therefore$ The actual number of litres of fuel consumed = 21,000

(iv)

	£
Variable overhead cost of 178,000 delivery miles should have been ($\times$ £0.06)	10,680
but was	y
Variable overhead variance (£280 (F) + £180 (A))	100 (F)

$\therefore$ **Actual variable overhead cost** = £(10,680 – 100) = **£10,580**

(b)   REPORT

To:	Transport operations manager
From:	Management accountant
Subject:	**Operating standards**

Date: xx.xx.xx

1   Introduction

1.1   This report explains the different types of standard that may be set and the importance of keeping standards meaningful and relevant.

2   Types of standard

2.1   When standards are set, it raises the problem of **how demanding** the standard should be. There are four types of standard.

2.2   **Ideal standard**

These standards are based on **perfect operating conditions** where there is no wastage, no spoilage, no inefficiencies, no idle time and no breakdowns. Such variances are likely to have an **unfavourable motivational impact** because reported variances will always be **adverse**. Employees will often feel that the goals are **unattainable** and not work so hard.

2.3   **Attainable standard**

These standards are based on the hope that a standard amount of work will be carried out **efficiently**, machines **properly operated** or materials **properly used**. Some **allowance** is made for **wastage** or **inefficiencies**. If such standards are well set, they provide a useful psychological incentive by giving employees a **realistic** but **challenging** target of efficiency.

2.4   **Current standard**

These standards are based on current working conditions (**current wastage, current inefficiencies**). The disadvantage of such standards is that they **do not attempt to improve on current levels of efficiency**.

2.5   **Basic standard**

These standards are kept **unaltered** over a long period of time and may therefore be **out-of-date**. They are used to show changes in efficiency or performance over time. Such standards are perhaps the **least useful** and **least common** type of standard in use.

3 The importance of keeping standards meaningful and relevant

3.1 Standards may be **used as a control device**. If standards which are irrelevant are used, they cannot usefully be used as such a device – they **need to be relevant**.

3.2 Standards must be determined in a way that is understood by the **employees** whose actual **performance** will be compared with standards, ie they **must be meaningful**. If they are not meaningful, the employees who are being assessed will have no reason to have any faith in the system operating.

3.3 If **out-of-date** standards are in use, they are not relevant to conditions that are currently operating within a system. Such standards may **encourage slack** and **waste** to be built into the system.

3.4 **Motivation and morale of employees** is affected by the control system operating within the workplace. If such a system has been poorly implemented, employees may react adversely. For example, if standards are set which even the most conscientious employee fails to reach, he will be demotivated and may give up working as hard as he can as there 'doesn't seem to be any point'.

3.5 If standards are to be meaningful and relevant then they should set out to **focus on the controllability of costs**.

Signed: Management accountant

12 WYE NOT

> **Pass marks.** In part (b) it is not obvious what is meant by the most 'significant variances'. A small absolute variance can be significant and therefore worthy of management attention if, for example, it recurs on a regular basis. In circumstances such as these, where you feel there may be a different interpretation of the question, you should make an assumption and state it clearly in your answer. Incidentally, note that the seven marks for part (b) can be earned even if you have made a total mess of part (a). Remember to keep going on each question until you have used up your time allowance.

(a) (i) **Actual sales units** $= \dfrac{\text{Standard profit from actual sales}}{\text{Standard profit per unit}}$

$= \dfrac{£16,500}{£15}$

$= \underline{\underline{1,100 \text{ units}}}$

(ii) Production volume in excess of budget $= \dfrac{\text{Fixed overhead volume variance}}{\text{Fixed overhead per unit}}$

$= \dfrac{£1,000}{£20}$

$= \underline{50 \text{ units}}$

Budgeted production volume $= \dfrac{\text{Budgeted fixed overhead}}{\text{Fixed overhead per unit}}$ $= \dfrac{£25,000}{£20}$

$= \underline{1,250 \text{ units}}$

∴ **Actual production volume** = 50 + 1,250 $= \underline{\underline{1,300 \text{ units}}}$

(iii)

	£
Standard selling price per unit	75
Selling price variance per unit sold (£5,500 ÷ 1,100)	5
Actual selling price per unit	80

(iv)

Excess material used above standard (£375 ÷ £2.50)	150 kg
Standard material usage (1,300 units × 4 kg)	5,200 kg
Actual material usage	5,350 kg

Since raw material stock levels remained unchanged, raw material purchases were equal to raw material usage.

$$\text{Material price variance per kg purchased} = \frac{£535}{5,350}$$
$$= £0.10$$
$$\therefore \textbf{Actual material price per kg} = £0.10 + £2.50$$
$$= £2.60$$

(v)

Excess labour hours above standard (£1,200 ÷ £6)	200
Standard labour hours (1,300 units × 3 hours)	3,900
Actual labour hours	4,100

(vi)

	£
Standard variable overhead for actual hours worked (4,100 × £4)	16,400
Variable overhead expenditure variance	820 (F)
Actual variable overhead cost	15,580

(vii)

	£
Budgeted fixed overhead cost	25,000
Fixed overhead expenditure variance	1,000 (F)
Actual fixed overhead cost	24,000

(b) *Assumption.* The two most **significant** variances for October 20X9 are the **largest** variances, ie the selling price variance and the direct labour efficiency variance.

REPORT

To: Operations manager
From: Management accountant
Subject: **Variances for October 20X9**   Date: XX.XX.XX

1   Introduction

1.1   This report considers the meaning and possible causes of the two most significant variances which occurred in October 20X9.

2   Selling price variance: meaning

2.1   The **favourable** selling price variance of £5,500 means that the **actual** selling price during October 20X9 was **higher than the standard** selling price.

3   Selling price variance: causes

3.1   There was an unplanned price increase during October 20X9.

3.2   The original standard selling price was set too low.

3.3   Competition in the market was not as fierce as had been expected when the standard selling price was determined, therefore a higher price could be charged.

4   Direct labour efficiency variance: meaning

4.1   The **adverse** labour efficiency variance of £1,200 means that **more** labour hours were **used than the standard allowed** for the output achieved.

5   Direct labour efficiency variance: causes

5.1   Lost time was in excess of the standard allowed.

5.2   Production was slow due to difficulties in processing sub-standard materials.

5.3   The original standard time allowance was set too low.

If I can be of any further assistance please do not hesitate to contact me.

Signed: Management accountant

13   M LTD

> **Pass marks.** Part (a) of this question has been amended to reflect the syllabus changes announced in 2002, with the result that it is now more straightforward, the only complication being the calculation of the mix and yield variances.
>
> Part (b) (which was not a part of the original pilot paper question) specified the use of a **simple** generic example. But it would have been all to easy to get caught up in an extremely complicated example, wasting time and obscuring the issues you were meant to be explaining.
>
> You would have lost marks if you had ignored the requirement to provide an example and had instead provided a wholly discursive answer.

(a)   *Workings*

(i)

Budgeted sales volume		1,000 units
Actual sales volume		900 units
Variance in units		100 units (A)
× standard profit per unit		× £25.50
Sales volume variance		£2,550 (A)

(ii)

	£
900 units should have sold for (× £120)	108,000
but did sell for	118,800
Sales price variance	10,800 (F)

(iii)   Material A – provided in question – £567 (A)
Material B – provided in question – £3,661 (F)

(iv)   Actual input = (5,670 + 10,460) kgs = 16,130 kgs

Standard mix of actual input

A =	16,130 × 5/15 =	5,376.67 kgs
B =	16,130 × 10/15 =	10,753.33 kgs
		16,130.00 kgs

	Actual input Kgs	Standard mix of actual input Kgs	Variance Kgs	× standard price £	Variance £
A	5,670	5,376.67	293.33 (A)	2.50	733.33 (A)
B	10,460	10,753.33	293.33 (F)	4.00	1,173.33 (F)
	16,130	16,130.00	–		440.00 (F)

Alternative approach

Standard weighted average cost = standard cost/standard quantity
= £(40 + 12.50)/(5 + 10) kgs
= £3.50 per kg

	Actual input Kgs	Standard mix of actual input Kgs	Difference Kgs	×difference between w. av. price and standard price	£	Variance £
A	5,670	5,376.67	293.33	£(3.50 − 2.50)	1.00	293.33 (F)
B	10,460	10,753.33	(293.33)	£(3.50 − 4.00)	(0.50)	146.67 (F)
	16,130	16,130.00	–			440.00 (F)

(v)   Yield variance = (actual total quantity used – quantity that should have been used for actual output) × standard weighted average cost per unit input.

= ((5,670 + 10,460) − (1,050 × 15)) × £3.50 = £1,330 (A)

(vi)

	£
3,215 hours should have cost (× £6)	19,290
but did cost	19,933
Labour rate variance	643 (A)

(vii)

1,050 units should have taken (× 3hrs)	3,150 hrs
but did take	3,215 hrs
Variance in hrs	65 hrs (A)
× standard rate per hr (× £6)	× £6
Labour efficiency variance	£390 (A)

(viii)

	£
3,215 hours of variable overhead should have cost (× £3)	9,645
but did cost	10,288
Variable production overhead expenditure variance	643 (A)

(ix)

1,050 units should have taken (× 3hrs)	3,150 hrs
but did take	3,215 hrs
Variance in hrs	65 hrs (A)
× standard rate per hr	× £3
Variable production overhead efficiency variance	£195 (A)

(x)

	£
Budgeted expenditure (£180,000/12)	15,000
Actual expenditure	15,432
Fixed production overhead expenditure variance	432 (A)

(xi)

Budgeted labour hours	3,000 hrs
Actual labour hours	3,215 hrs
Variance in hrs	215 hrs (F)
× standard absorption rate per hr	× £5
Fixed production overhead capacity variance	£1,075 (F)

(xii)

Variable overhead efficiency variance in hrs	65hrs (A)
× standard absorption rate per hr	× £5
Fixed production overhead efficiency variance	£325 (A)

PROFIT RECONCILIATION STATEMENT (BUDGET TO ACTUAL) JANUARY 20X0

	£	£	£
Budgeted profit (1,000 units × £25.50)			25,500
Sales volume variance			2,550 (A)
Standard profit from sales achieved			22,950
Operating variances	£	£	
	(F)	(A)	
Sales price	10,800.00		
Material price – A		567	
– B	3,661.00		
Material mix	440.00		
Material yield		1,330	
Labour rate		643	
Labour efficiency		390	
Variance production overhead expenditure		643	
Variable production overhead efficiency		195	
Fixed production overhead expenditure		432	
Fixed production overhead capacity	1,075.00		
Fixed production overhead efficiency		325	
	15,976.00	4,525	11,451 (F)
Actual profit			34,401

We can do a check on the actual profit figure in the reconciliation statement by calculating actual profit based on the figures given in the question.

(Pass marks. Only do this if you have time in the exam – perhaps at the very end if you have a few minutes to spare.)

Check	£	£
Sales		118,800
Costs incurred	98,574	
Closing stock (150 × £94.50)	(14,175)	
		84,399
Actual profit		34,401

(b) **Logic, purpose and limitations of fixed overhead variances**

(i) **Volume variance**

The **fixed production overhead volume variance** generated in an absorption costing system is 'a measure of over- or under-absorption of overhead cost caused by actual production volume differing from that budgeted' (CIMA *Official Terminology*). It is calculated as the **difference between the budgeted and actual production levels, valued at the standard absorption rate per unit**.

(ii) **Capacity utilisation variation**

The **fixed production overhead capacity utilisation variance** 'measures the over- or under-absorption of fixed production overhead costs caused by the actual hours worked differing from the hours originally budgeted to be worked' (CIMA *Official Terminology*). It is calculated as the **difference between actual hours of work and budgeted hours of work, valued at the standard absorption rate per hour**.

(iii) **Efficiency variance**

The **fixed production overhead efficiency variance** 'measures the over- or under-absorption of fixed production overhead costs caused by actual labour efficiency differing from the standard level of labour efficiency' (CIMA *Official Terminology*). It is calculated as the **difference between the number of hours**

that actual production should have taken and the number of hours taken, valued at the standard absorption cost per hour.

Example

Let's consider a simple **example**. Suppose that the budgeted fixed overhead for a month is £500,000 and the budgeted output is 2,000 units, each unit requiring 10 labour hours. The overhead absorption rate is therefore £250 per unit or £25 per hour. If the actual output in a month is 1,600 units and the actual hours worked are 16,400 then the variances are calculated as follows.

Fixed production overhead volume variance = (2,000 – 1,600) units × £250 = £100,000 (A)

Fixed production overhead capacity utilisation variance = (20,000 – 16,400) hours × £25 = £90,000 (A)

Fixed production overhead efficiency variance = (16,000 – 16,400) hours × £25 = £10,000 (A)

Dividing the volume variance

The fixed overhead variance is divided into capacity and efficiency variances because the actual production volume used to calculate the fixed production overhead **volume variance** is a **function of the labour hours worked (i.e. capacity) and the efficiency with which the labour hours are used.** The two sub-variances are meant to **highlight** variations from budget in terms of both the **availability** and the **efficiency** of direct labour.

Limitations of dividing the volume variance

The volume variances can only be calculated in an absorption costing system and the **limitations** of dividing it into the sub-variances are those which are inherent in absorption costing.

(i)   Fixed overhead costs are treated as if they are variable (in relation to labour hours).

(ii)   The analysis concentrates on the effect of only one input (labour) when others, such as machine hours, may have a significant impact.

(iii)   The measures may encourage managers to over-produce in order to achieve favourable volume variances. For example, labour may be used to produce output for stock (which may never be required) rather than being left idle. This could waste both materials and power.

Investigating the component variances

(i)   **Capacity variance**

The management accountant, when investigating **capacity variances,** needs to find out **why more (or less) labour was available than budgeted.** Was it due to budgeting error, to non-standard sickness or absence or labour turnover, to under– or over-recruitment, to excessive overtime, to a fall or increase in demand or perhaps to a strike? Hence, investigation of both the payroll and production records is required, along with discussions with the HR department and production supervisors.

(ii)   **Efficiency variance**

If the organisation operates in a jobbing or batch production environment, the **efficiency variance** may be isolated on a job-by-job basis. Jobs which have a significantly higher or lower efficiency variance can be investigated in collaboration with **production supervisors. Production records** can also be used to identify whether **idle time** levels were significantly different from standard. The management accountant should check whether the **mix of labour** (between experienced and less experienced staff) differs from standard. S/he should also check with production supervisors whether factors such as poor quality material, machine failures or excessive reworking may have contributed to the efficiency variance.

14   SEMI-AUTOMATED PLANTS

> **Pass marks.** Did you notice that you were asked to use marginal costing in part (a)(i) and so you simply had to calculate contribution (sales revenue minus marginal costs) and then deduct fixed costs?
>
> Part (a)(iii) was particularly tricky. Because you are performing a reconciliation between budgeted marginal costing profit and actual absorption costing profit, your reconciling items are variances *and* stock value adjustments. Don't worry if you didn't get all the reconciling items. Each one would have only been worth a couple of marks.
>
> Here are some key reasons why you might have failed to gain marks.
>
> •   Using actual contribution or actual fixed costs to calculate the breakeven point (part (a)(i))
>
> •   Failing to use actual sales volume to calculate budgeted profit (part (a)(i))
>
> •   Failing to comment about the volume variance (part (a)(ii))
>
> •   Attempting to flex the fixed overhead when calculating the expenditure variance (part (a)(ii))
>
> •   Omitting the stock adjustment (part (a)(iii))
>
> •   Failing to explain the reason for the profit difference (part (a)(iii))

(a)   (i)

Cost	Total	Variable cost per unit	Total variable cost (W1)	Fixed cost (W2)
	£	£	£	£
Material	70,000	3.50	70,000	–
Labour and variable overhead	50,000	2.50	50,000	–
Fixed overhead	100,000	–	–	100,000
Variable selling overhead	30,000	1.50	30,000	–
Fixed selling overhead	40,000	–	–	40,000
	290,000	7.50	150,000	140,000

Workings

1   Variable cost per unit × 240,000/12 kgs

2   Total cost – total variable cost

Breakeven point   =   Fixed costs/contribution per unit

=   £140,000/£(17 – 7.50)

=   14,737 kgs

Budgeted profit/loss (based on actual kgs sold)

	£
Sales (12,400 kg × £17)	210,800
less: marginal costs (12,400 kg × £7.50)	93,000
Contribution	117,800
less: fixed costs	140,000
Loss	22,200

(ii) (1) The **volume variance** has been calculated as follows.

Budgeted manufacturing volume (240,000/12)	20,000	kgs
Actual manufacturing volume	18,400	kgs
Volume variance in kgs	1,600	kgs (A)
× manufacturing overhead recovery rate*	× £5	
	£8,000	(A)

* £100,000 ÷ 240,000/12 kgs = £5 per kg

The manufacturing volume variance has arisen because the **actual production level in period 1 was below the budgeted production level** used to compute the fixed manufacturing overheads recovery rate. It is therefore **part of the under-absorbed fixed manufacturing overhead** for the period, the total of which will be charged against the periods' profit/loss. The variance does not actually represent an additional cost or loss to the company but it does provide some measure of the difference between budgeted production volume and actual production volume.

(2)

	£	
Variable selling overheads for 12,400 kg should have cost (× £1.50)	18,600	
but did cost	17,500	
Variable selling overhead expenditure variance	1,100	(F)

	£	
Budgeted fixed selling overhead	40,000	
Actual fixed selling overhead	38,300	
Fixed selling overhead expenditure variance	1,700	(F)

Budgeted sales	20,000	kgs
Actual sales	12,400	kgs
Volume variance in kgs	7,600	kgs (A)
× standard rate per kg*	× £2	
Fixed selling overhead volume variance	£15,200	(A)

* £40,000 ÷ 20,000 kgs = £2 per kg

(iii)

		£	£	
Budgeted (marginal costing) loss			(22,200)	
Variances				
Expenditure	- variable manufacturing	5,500 (A)		
	- variable selling	1,100 (F)		
	- fixed selling	1,700 (F)		
Selling price variance (W1)		2,000 (A)		
Stock value adjustment				
Fixed overhead carried forward in closing stock (W2)		30,000 (F)		
			25,300	(F)
Actual absorption costing profit			3,100	

Workings

1

	£	
12,400 kg should have sold for (× £17)	210,800	
but did sell for	208,800	
	2,000	(A)

2 There were (18,400 − 12,400) kgs = 6,000 kgs in closing stock. The fixed overhead carried forward under absorption costing in this stock = 6,000 × £5 = £30,000.

The statement above is a **reconciliation** between **budgeted marginal costing profit** and **actual absorption costing profit** and hence accounts for all differences between the two profit statements.

(1) These differences include **expenditure variances** which formed part of the profit statement provided but did not appear in the statement in (a)(i).

(2) There are **no volume variances** because both the actual profit and the budgeted marginal costing profit are based on the same sales/production levels.

(3) **A selling price variance** needs to be calculated because the actual sales level should have resulted in revenue of £210,800 but only produced revenue of £208,800.

(4) Fixed manufacturing overheads are written off during the period to arrive at the marginal costing profit whereas some fixed overheads are carried forward in closing stock when absorption costing is used. Stocks increased by 6,000 kgs (difference between production level and sales level) and so £5 **of fixed manufacturing overheads was carried forward in each kilogram when absorption costing is used,** thereby increasing the absorption costing profit by £30,000.

By taking account of these differences it is therefore possible to show how a profit is revealed in absorption costing terms when a marginal costing loss was anticipated by the sales manager.

(b) **Calculation of variances**

	£	
64,000 units should have sold for (× £10)	640,000	
but did sell for (× £8.40)	537,600	
Selling price variance	102,400	(A)

Budgeted sales volume	72,000	units
Actual sales volume	64,000	units
Sales volume variance in units	8,000	units (A)
× standard contribution per unit	× £4	
Sales volume contribution variance	£32,000	(A)

	£	
Variable cost of 64,000 units should have been (× £6)	384,000	
but was (× £6.20)	396,800	
Variable cost variance	12,800	(A)

Possible causes of variances

(i) Stronger than anticipated **competition** forced prices down.

(ii) A **reduction** in the overall levels of **demand** resulted in a downward pressure on prices.

(iii) The **costs** of labour and raw materials (variable costs) **could have risen** more than anticipated, resulting in an adverse variable cost variance.

(iv) The **actual mix** of labour and raw materials used could have resulted in the use of a **higher proportion of more skilled labour and/or more expensive materials** than those included in the standard, thereby increasing the actual variable cost per unit.

(v) **Assumptions** upon which the budgeted figures were based **could have changed** during the control period but the budget figures were not revised.

15   **POC LTD**

> **Pass marks.** The only difficulty with this question is taking account of the wastage rate. This impacts on the usage and yield variances.
>
> We valued the mix variance using standard input prices. If you had used the weighted average approach (using a weighted average price of £0.38125), you should have got the following individual variances:
>
> S1   £105.02 (A)   S2   £184.03 (A)   S3   £4.82 (F)

(a) (i)   **Usage variance**

Output of 15,408 kgs should have used input of 15,408/90% = 17,120 kgs.

∴ Standard input should have been as follows.

		Kgs
S1	$8/16 \times 17,120$ =	8,560
S2	$5/16 \times 17,120$ =	5,350
S3	$3/16 \times 17,120$ =	3,210
		17,120

	S1	S2	S3
Output 15,408 kgs should have used	8,560 kgs	5,350 kgs	3,210 kgs
but did use	8,284 kgs	7,535 kgs	3,334 kgs
Usage variance in kgs	276 kgs (F)	2,185 kgs (A)	124 kgs (A)
× standard cost per kg	× £0.30	× £0.50	× £0.40
Usage variance	£82.80 (F)	£1,092.50 (A)	£49.60 (A)

∴ Total variance = £(82.80 (F) + 1,092.50 (A) + 49.60 (A))
= £1,059.30 (A)

Mix variance

Actual usage = (8,284 + 7,535 + 3,334) kgs
= 19,153 kgs

Standard mix of actual usage

		Kgs
S1	$8/16 \times 19,153$ =	9,576.5
S2	$5/16 \times 19,153$ =	5,985.3
S3	$3/16 \times 19,153$ =	3,591.2
		19,153.0

	Actual input Kgs	Sandard mix of actual input Kgs	Variance Kgs	× std cost per kg £	Variance £
S1	8,284	9,576.5	1,292.5 (F)	0.30	387.75 (F)
S2	7,535	5,985.3	1,549.7 (A)	0.50	774.85 (A)
S3	3,334	3,591.2	257.2 (F)	0.40	102.88 (F)
	19,153	19,153.0	-		284.22 (A)

Yield variance

Each batch of S requires

		£
8 kg	of S1, costing (× £0.30)	2.40
5 kg	of S2, costing (× £0.50)	2.50
3 kg	of S3, costing (× £0.40)	1.20
16 kg		6.10

This will produce 16 × 90% = 14.4 kgs of output.

∴ Standard cost per kg of output = £6.10/14.4 = £0.4236

19,153 kg should have yielded (× 90%)	17,237.70 kgs
but did yield	15,408.00 kgs
Yield variance in kgs	1,829.70 kgs (A)
× standard cost per unit of output	× £0.4236
Yield variance	£775.08 (A)

(ii)

	£
1,235 hrs should have cost (× £5)	6,175
but did cost	6,916
Labour rate variance	741 (A)

Standard input per batch = (8 + 5 + 3) = 16 kgs

Standard output = 16 × 90% = 14.4 kgs

∴ 14.4 kgs of output are processed in 1 standard hour

15,408 kgs should have taken (÷ 14.4)	1,070 hrs
but did take	1,235 hrs
Efficiency variance in hrs	165 hrs (A)
× standard rate per hour	× £5
Labour efficiency variance	£825 (A)

(b) The total mix variance in quantity must be zero since the **expected mix is based on the total quantity actually used** and hence the difference between the total expected mix (total actual quantity) and the total actual mix (total actual quantity) is zero.

(c) REPORT

To: Management of POC Ltd
From: Management accountant
Date: 17 January 20X1
Subject: **Analysis of material and labour variances, week number 2**

1 Introduction

1.1 This report explains and interprets the variance analysis carried out on material and labour for week 2 (set out in the Appendix to this report). It will consider in detail the materials mix and yield variances and will suggest reasons for the results of the variance analysis.

2 Materials variances

2.1 The total materials variance (the difference between what week 2 output should have cost in terms of material, and what it did cost) can be divided two variances, price and usage. Product S uses three types of material and so the usage can then be divided into mix and yield components.

2.2 Mix variance

2.2.1 Although there is a standard mix of the three input materials to produce a batch of product S, this standard mix is not always used as it is possible to use a range of different proportions of the input materials without affecting the quality of S too adversely. If the **proportions of the input materials used differ from the standard proportions** a mix variance will occur. The effect of a mix variance on profit will depend on whether the particular mix used is **cheaper than the standard mix** (if the proportion of the cheaper materials in the mix has increased) or **more expensive**.

2.2.2 The mix variance for week 2 was £284 adverse as S2, the **most expensive input material, comprised a greater proportion of the actual mix** than standard (the proportions of the two cheaper input materials being less than standard). There may have been a **shortage** of S1 and S3 so that S2 had to be used as a replacement.

2.3 Yield variance

2.3.1 By changing the proportions in the mix, the **efficiency of the combined material usage may change**. The yield variance shows the **effect** on profit of **any difference between the actual input materials used and the amounts that should have been used given the actual output** of S.

2.3.2 In week 2, more input material was required than expected given actual production of 15,408 kgs of S. It may be that the **actual mix** of input materials was **unstable** or **difficult to use** and so **wastage levels were higher**. This had an adverse effect on profit of £775.

3 Labour variance

3.1 The total labour variance (the difference between what week 2 output should have cost in terms of labour and what it did cost) can be split into a rate variance and an efficiency variance.

3.2 Rate variance

3.2.1 The **actual hours** worked during week 2 **cost more than anticipated** as the labour rate variance for the period was £741 adverse. The variance was caused by payment of a rate of £5.60 compare with a standard rate of £5. There are a number of possible **reasons** for this.

    (i)   Overtime working may have been required, resulting in the payment of an overtime premium.

    (ii) The standard rate may not have been updated to reflect a pay increase.

    (iii) The mix of workers used may have differed from standard and incorporated a larger proportion of more skilled, and hence more expensive, workers.

3.3 Efficiency variance

3.3.1 The efficiency variance of £825 adverse reflects the fact that it **took longer to produce the given output than the standard time allowed,** at an additional cost of £825. This may be because the materials were difficult to work with (see comments on yield variance above), the introduction of new machinery or processes or possibly the use of new (and hence untrained) workers.

4 Conclusion

4.1 Management should carry out **investigative action** to determine the reasons for the occurrence of these variances. The standards used may no longer be appropriate and may need amending or additional control procedures may need adopting over, for example, wastage levels.

4.2 Analyses carried out over the last few weeks should also be reviewed to assess whether these poor results are part of a **trend** or a simply a one-off occurrence.

4.3 If I can provide any further information please do not hesitate to contact me.

16 FC LTD

> **Pass marks**. Although the usage variance is not required by the question, it is easy to calculate (total variance less price variance) and as it is made up of the mix and yield variances, it can be used as a check on your calculations. A summary of the variances is another useful check.
>
> You might have been slightly mystified as to how to deal with the overhead absorption rate in part (a). The standard overhead absorption rate is calculated as budgeted overheads divided by budgeted consumption of material F. Overhead absorbed is based on material F usage instead of the usual labour or machine hours. So instead of basing the efficiency variance on how long production should have taken, in terms of labour hours, you base it on how much material F should have been used. Don't worry if you were unsure how to approach this. The material variances and the overhead expenditure variance were straightforward and so you should have picked up marks there.
>
> You may not have known how to start part (b) but basically you had to find a standard cost per activity and the standard and actual number of activities per month so that you could calculate activity and expenditure variances.

(a) **Materials variances**

Standard cost per kg of output = $(0.65 \times £4) + (0.3 \times £6) + (0.2 \times £2.50) = £4.90$.

Total variance

	£
4,200 kgs of FDN should have cost ($\times £4.90$)	20,580
but did cost	20,380
	200 (F)

Price variance

	£	£
2,840 kg of F should have cost ($\times £4$)	11,360	
1,210 kg of D should have cost ($\times £6$)	7,260	
860 kg of N should have cost ($\times £2.50$)	2,150	
		20,770
but did cost		20,380
		390 (F)

Mix variance

Material	Actual input Kgs	Standard mix of actual input Kgs		Variance Kgs	$\times$ standard price £	Variance £
F	2,840	($4,910 \times 0.65/1.15$)	2,775	65 (A)	4.00	260 (A)
D	1,210	($4,910 \times 0.3/1.15$)	1,281	71 (F)	6.00	426 (F)
N	860	($4,910 \times 0.2/1.15$)	854	6 (A)	2.50	15 (A)
	4,910		4,910	–		151 (F)

> **Alternative approach**
>
> Standard weighted average price of input materials = £4.90/1.15 = £4.26
>
> | Material | Difference Kgs | $\times$ difference between w. av. price and standard price | £ | Variance £ |
> |---|---|---|---|---|
> | F | 65 | £(4.26 – 4) | 0.26 | 16.90 (F) |
> | D | (71) | £(4.26 – 6) | (1.74) | 123.54 (F) |
> | N | 6 | £(4.26 – 2.50) | 1.76 | 10.56 (F) |
> | | – | | | 151.00 (F) |

Yield variance

4,910 kgs of input should yield ($\times$ 1/1.15)	4,269.57 kgs
but did yield	4,200.00 kgs
Variance in kgs	69.57 kgs (A)
$\times$ standard price per kg of output	$\times$ £4.90
	£341 (A)

Summary

	£	£
Standard cost		20,580
Price variance	390 (F)	
Mix variance	151 (F)	
Yield variance	341 (A)	
Total variance		200 (F)
Actual cost		20,380

Overhead cost variances

Standard overhead absorption rate = budgeted overheads ÷ budgeted consumption of ingredient F = £12,000 ÷ (0. 65 $\times$ 4,000) = £12,000 ÷ 2,600 = £4.6154 per kg.

Total variance

	£
Total overhead incurred	12,600
Total overhead absorbed (£4.6154 $\times$ (4,200 kg $\times$ 0.65))	12,600
	–

Expenditure variance

	£
Budgeted expenditure	12,000
Actual expenditure	12,600
	600 (A)

Capacity variance

Budgeted use of material F (4,000 $\times$ 0.65)	2,600 kgs
Actual use of material F	2,840 kgs
Capacity variance in kgs	240 kgs (F)
$\times$ standard absorption rate per kg	$\times$ £4.6154
Capacity variance in £	£1,108 (F)

Efficiency variance

Output of 4,200 kgs should have used ($\times$ 0.65)	2,730 kgs
but did use	2,840 kgs
Efficiency variance in kgs	110 kgs (A)
$\times$ standard absorption rate per kg	$\times$ £4.6154 kgs
Efficiency variance in £	£508 kgs (A)

Summary

	£	£
Standard cost (4,200 $\times$ 0.65 $\times$ £4.6154)		12,600
Expenditure variance	600 (A)	
Capacity variance	1,108 (F)	
Efficiency variance	508 (A)	
Total variance		–
Actual cost		12,600

(b) (i) **Receipts of deliveries from suppliers**

Budgeted overhead for the month	£4,000
Budgeted kgs required in the month (4,000 kgs × 1.15)	4,600 kgs
Standard delivery quantity	460 kgs
Budgeted number of deliveries in the month	10
Standard activity-based cost per delivery (£4,000 ÷ 10)	£400
Actual overhead in the month	£4,800
Standard kgs required in the month (4,200 kg × 1.15)	4,830 kgs
Standard number of deliveries in the month (4,830 kgs ÷ 460 kgs)	10.5
Actual number of deliveries in the month	12

Activity variance

Actual output should have needed	10.5 deliveries
but did need	12.0 deliveries
Variance in deliveries	1.5 deliveries (A)
× standard activity-based cost per delivery	× £400
	£600 (A)

Expenditure variance

	£
12 deliveries should have cost (× £400)	4,800
but did cost	4,800
	–

(ii) **Despatch of goods to customers**

Budgeted despatch overhead for the month	=	£8,000
Budgeted despatches in month (4,000 kg ÷ 100 kg)	=	40
Standard activity-based cost per despatch	=	£200
Actual despatch overhead in month	=	£7,800
Standard number of despatches in month (4,200 kg ÷ 100kg)	=	42
Actual number of despatches in month	=	38

Activity variance

4,200 kgs should have needed	42 despatches
but did need	38 despatches
Variance in despatches	4 despatches (F)
× standard activity-based cost per despatch	× £200
	£800 (F)

Expenditure variance

	£
38 despatches should have cost (× £200)	7,600
but did cost	7,800
	200 (A)

(c) **Designing on ABC system – costs versus benefits**

As with the introduction and implementation of any system, a **balance** should be achieved between the **benefits** obtainable from the system and the **cost** of operating it. Consequently, when designing an activity based costing system, the **activities** selected and subjected to an activity-based appraisal should be those **from which the most significant cost saving can be obtained** as a result of effective cost management and/or those activities which **produce a very significant proportion of total overheads**.

Identifying activities

The first step in identifying and selecting the most appropriate activities and cost drivers should therefore be to carry out an **analysis of the entire production/service provision process,** from (for example) receipt of materials to despatch of finished goods with the aim of assessing which activities appear to incur the most significant costs. It might be appropriate to analyse the activities using **Cooper's hierarchy of costs** into unit level, batch level, product level and facility level activities. This analysis highlights the decision level at which the cost of activities can be influenced.

Identifying cost drivers

Each of these activities' **cost drivers** should then be **identified,** perhaps by **interviewing a sample of the employees** carrying out the support services, asking them to identify what they believe drives the costs of the activities they are involved in. If a consistent view does not emerge, analysis of the activities and/or the work patterns of the employees concerned may be required. Compromise might be necessary: there is no guarantee that just one particular cost driver is suitable or that a suitable cost driver can be identified.

17   THE X, THE Y AND THE Z

> **Pass marks**. This question brings together standard costing and activity based costing. It involves a great many calculations so worksheets should be carefully designed to minimise repeating information.
>
> It was vital to grasp the fact that budget and actual overheads were split 80%/20% between fixed and variable. You were not required to calculate variances for individual products, as this just makes your calculations more complicated than necessary.

(a)   **Calculation of budgeted and standard hours produced**

	Products			
	X	*Y*	*Z*	*Total (where applicable)*
Standard direct labour hours per unit	4	2	3	
Budgeted output ('000 units)	30	45	8	
Budgeted hours ('000)	120	90	24	234
Actual output ('000 units)	25	60	9	
Standard hours produced ('000)	100	120	27	247

Calculation of budgeted and actual costs, and standard overhead rates

	Budgeted overhead £	*Actual overhead* £
Component receiving and handling	120,000	134,000
Setting up equipment for production runs	200,000	178,000
Consignment of orders to customers	75,000	82,000
Total	395,000	394,000
Fixed overhead (80%)	316,000	315,200
Variable overhead (20%)	79,000	78,800
Fixed overhead absorption rate per labour hour (FOAR)		
(o/hd ÷ 234,000)	£1.35	n.a.
Variable overhead absorption rate per labour hour (VOAR)		
(o/hd ÷ 234,000)	£0.34	n.a.

Variable overhead variance analysis

	£
247,000 standard hours should have cost (× £0.34)	83,980
but did cost	78,800
Total variance	5,180 (F)

	£
266,000 hours should have cost (× £0.34)	90,440
but did cost	78,800
Expenditure variance	11,640 (F)

Hours worked should have been	247,000 hrs
but were	266,000 hrs
Efficiency variance in hrs	19,000 hrs (A)
× VOAR	× £0.34
Efficiency variance	£6,460 (A)

Fixed overhead variance analysis

	£
247,000 standard hours should have cost (× £1.35)	333,450
but did cost	315,200
Total variance	18,250 (F)

Budgeted expenditure (234,000 × £1.35)	315,900
Actual expenditure	315,200
Expenditure variance	700 (F)

Budgeted hours	234,000 hrs
Actual hours	266,000 hrs
Capacity utilisation variance in hours	32,000 hrs (F)
× FOAR	× £1.35
Capacity utilisation variance	£43,200 (F)

Variable overhead efficiency variance in hrs	19,000 hrs (A)
× FOAR	× £1.35
Efficiency variance	£25,650 (A)

> **Pass marks.** The strict formula for the fixed overhead expenditure variance is (budgeted cost – actual cost). However, this produces a figure of £800 which, when added to the volume variances, is £100 more than the total variance. This is due to the **rounding of the FOAR used to calculate the volume variances**. The **modified expenditure variance formula** used above avoids the problem.

(b)

> **Pass marks.** You should use units of cost drivers for each activity cost, instead of labour hours. You then need to calculate the standard rate per cost driver unit. The Managing Director's comment in the question makes it clear that you are expected to treat the activity costs as if they are variable, so you should use the same approach as you employed to calculate the variable overhead variances in part (a) of the question.

Calculation of budgeted and standard number of cost driver units

Component receiving and handling – cost driver is number of component orders
Setting up equipment for production runs – cost driver is number of production runs
Consignment of orders to customers – cost driver is number of customer orders

	Products			
	X	Y	Z	Total
1. Budgeted output (000 units)	30	45	8	
2. Actual output (000 units)	25	60	9	
3. Standard component orders per 000 units	0.2	0.1	2.0	
4. Standard size of production run (000 units)	5.0	15.0	1.0	
5. Standard size of customer order	1.0	3.0	0.1	
6. Budgeted component orders (1 × 3)	6.0	4.5	16.0	26.5
7. Budgeted production runs (1 ÷ 4)	6.0	3.0	8.0	17.0
8. Budgeted customer orders (1 ÷ 5)	30.0	15.0	80.0	125.0
9. Standard component orders for actual output (2 × 3)	5.0	6.0	18.0	29.0
10. Standard production runs for actual output (2 ÷ 4)	5.0	4.0	9.0	18.0
11. Standard customer orders for actual output (2 ÷ 5)	25.0	20.0	90.0	135.0

Calculation of standard rate per unit of cost driver

Activity	Budgeted cost	Budgeted cost driver units	Standard cost per cost driver unit
Component receiving and handling	£120,000	26.5	£4,528
Setting up equipment for production runs	£200,000	17.0	£11,765
Consignment of orders to customers	£75,000	125.0	£600

Calculation of total variances

Activity	Standard cost driver units for actual output × standard cost	Actual cost	Total variance
Component receiving and handling	29 × £4,528	£134,000	£2,688 (A)
Setting up equipment for production runs	18 × £11,765	£178,000	£33,770 (F)
Consignment of orders to customers	135 × £600	£82,000	£1,000 (A)

Calculation of expenditure variances

Activity	Actual units × standard cost	Actual cost	Expenditure variance
Component receiving and handling	26 × £4,528	£134,000	£16,272 (A)
Setting up equipment for production runs	18 × £11,765	£178,000	£33,770 (F)
Consignment of orders to customers	145 × £600	£82,000	£5,000 (F)

XYZ Ltd – Activity based overhead cost variance analysis – Quarter 1, 20XX

Activity	Standard cost for actual output £	Actual cost £	Total variance £	Expend. variance £	Efficiency variance (bal) £
Component receiving & handling	131,312	134,000	2,688 (A)	16,272 (A)	13,584 (F)
Setting up equipment	211,770	178,000	33,770 (F)	33,770 (F)	0
Consignment of customer orders	81,000	82,000	1,000 (A)	5,000 (F)	6,000 (A)
Total	424,082	394,000	30,082 (F)	22,498 (F)	7,584 (F)

141

> **Pass marks.**
>
> (i) The **efficiency variances** in the above table were **obtained by deduction**. The calculation formula is [(standard cost driver units for actual output – actual cost driver units) × standard cost per cost driver unit].
>
> (ii) The CIMA suggested answer uses the terms 'price variance' and 'activity variance' in place of 'expenditure variance' and 'efficiency variance'.

(c) **Appraisal of the relative merits of the conventional and activity based approaches to overhead variance analysis**

The **conventional approach** to overhead variance reporting is based on the **assumption** that both fixed and variable **overheads are incurred in line with direct labour hours worked.** Not all overhead activities' costs will vary in line with labour activity, however, so the report is more about labour management than overhead control and is likely to **lead to fierce control of labour use and efficiency to the detriment of the effective use of overhead resources.** Moreover, given that XYZ Ltd's production operation has become increasingly automated and the majority of its production costs are overheads, direct labour hours are likely to be at a low level. The use of direct labour hours as a basis for absorbing overheads therefore seems inappropriate. Moreover, the conventional approach involves using an *arbitrary* breakdown between fixed and variable overheads. This can produce nothing but inaccurate variances.

An **activity-based approach** breaks down overheads into relevant control categories by establishing the **causes of the overheads** (the number of customer orders, production runs and so on). The variance report will **give some indication of areas for concern and may prompt action.** For instance, examination of the expenditure variances may encourage activity managers to control overhead spending while the monitoring of efficiency variances could encourage users of the activities to improve the efficiency with which they work.

Another possibility is that the calculation of activity-based standard **costs may highlight the cost of providing particular activities and so encourage managers to improve the efficiency with which they are provided and increase the economy with which they are consumed,** long before a variance report is produced. For instance, the analysis shows that the more component orders are made, the higher the overhead. By reducing the different number of components used, fewer orders will need to be made, with the result that the associated overhead will fall.

The activity-based approach therefore produces valuable management information whereas the conventional approach is of very little use.

> **Pass marks.** In practice the activity-based variance report at the end of part (b) could be made more useful by including non-financial indicators, such as the budgeted, actual and standard number of production runs, the number of units of Product X per production run (actual versus standard) and so on.

18   WCL LTD

> **Pass marks**. This was a fairly straightforward compulsory question (although it was rather long), especially as you had ample opportunity to reconcile and check your answer.
>
> You may have been unsure how to calculate the standard variable overhead cost for output achieved as you were given no detail about materials prices. But both the budgeted materials cost and the standard materials cost for output achieved were based on standard materials cost per unit, and so the difference between the two figures was entirely due to materials quantity usage, the basis for determining the level of variable overhead.
>
> You needed to relate your answer to (c) to the question scenario.

(a)   **Budget for manufacturing costs – November**

	Component X £	Component Y £	Component Z £	Total £
Labour (W1)	12,000	10,200	12,750	34,950
Materials (W2)	7,200	16,320	8,160	31,680
Variable overhead (given)				23,760
Fixed overhead (given)				40,000
Total				130,390

Standard cost for output achieved – November

	Component X £	Component Y £	Component Z £	Total £
Labour (W3)	13,200.0	9,150.0	12,250.0	34,600
Materials (W4)	7,920.0	14,640.0	7,840.0	30,400
Variable overhead (W5)	5,940.0	10,980.0	5,880.0	22,800
Fixed overhead (W6)	15,109.6	10,473.7	14,022.7	39,606
Total	42,169.6	45,243.7	39,992.7	127,406

Difference between manufacturing costs budget and standard cost for output achieved

The difference between the two totals is due to the **change in the quantities and mix of components manufactured.**

These changes mean that the **materials usage and labour hours figures differ** in the two calculations. (Both budget and standard totals are based on standard unit costs for materials and labour and so cost plays no part in the difference.)

	£	£
Budget		130,390
Difference due to discrepancy between budgeted labour		
hours and standard labour hours for actual output		
Effect on labour	(350)	
Effect on fixed overhead	(394)	
		(744)
Difference due to discrepancy between budgeted materials		
usage and standard materials usage for actual output		
Effect on materials	(1,280)	
Effect on variable overhead	(960)	
		(2,240)
Standard cost for output achieved		127,406

Workings

1		X	Y	Z	Total
	Quantity (units)	4,000	6,800	5,100	
	Std labour cost per unit	× £3.00	× £1.50	× £2.50	
	Total labour cost	£12,000	£10,200	£12,750	£34,950

2

	X	Y	Z	Total
Quantity (units)	4,000	6,800	5,100	
Std materials cost per unit	× £1.80	× £2.40	× £1.60	
Total materials cost	£7,200	£16,320	£8,160	£31,680

3

	X	Y	Z	Total
Quantity (units)	4,400	6,100	4,900	
Std labour cost per unit	× £3.00	× £1.50	× £2.50	
Total labour cost	£13,200	£9,150	£12,250	£34,600

4

	X	Y	Z	Total
Quantity (units)	4,400	6,100	4,900	
Std materials cost per unit	× £1.80	× £2.40	× £1.60	
Total materials cost	£7,920	£14,640	£7,840	30,400

5   Because the budgeted materials cost and the standard materials cost for actual output are both based on standard materials cost per unit, the difference between the two figures is due to materials quantity usage only, the basis for determining the level of variable overhead.

∴ Standard variable overhead rate

= budgeted overhead/budgeted materials cost

= £23,760/£31,680

= £0.75 per £ of material

X = £0.75 × £1.80 = £1.35 per unit; £1.35 × 4,400 = £5,940 in total
Y = £0.75 × £2.40 = £1.80 per unit; £1.80 × 6,100 = £10,980 in total
Z = £0.75 × £1.60 = £1.20 per unit; £1.20 × 4,900 = £5,880 in total

Total = standard materials cost × £0.75 = £30,400 × £0.75 = £22,800

6

	X	Y	Z	Total
Labour hours per unit	0.2	0.1	0.16667	
Quantity (units)	× 4,000	× 6,800	× 5,100	
Budgeted labour hours	800	680	850	2,330

	X	Y	Z	Total
Labour hours per unit	0.2	0.1	0.16667	
Quantity (units)	× 4,400	× 6,100	× 4,900	
Standard labour hours	880	610	816.7	2,306.7

Fixed overhead absorption rate per hour = £40,000/2,330

= £17.17

X = £17.17 × 880   = £15,109.6
Y = £17.17 × 610   = £10,473.7
Z = £17.17 × 816.7 = £14,022.7

Standard fixed overhead absorbed = standard direct labour hours × £17.17

= 2,306.7 × £17.17 = £39,606

(b) **Operating statement – November**

		£
Standard cost for output achieved (see (a))		127,406

Variances		(F) £	(A) £	
Labour	– rate (W1)		1,300.0	
	– efficiency (W2)	4,900.5		
Materials	– usage (W3)	456.0		
	– price (W4)		3,856.0	
Fixed overhead	– expenditure (W5)		800.0	
	– capacity (W6)		6,009.5	
	– efficiency (W7)	5,609.0		
Variable overhead	– efficiency (W8)	342.0		
	– expenditure (W9)		2,342.0	
		11,307.5	14,307.5	3,000 (A)
Rounding difference				(6)
Actual cost				130,400

Workings

1

	£
1,980 hours should have cost (× £15)	29,700
but did cost	31,000
Labour rate variance	1,300 (A)

2

Labour hours for actual output should have been (see (a) (W6))	2,306.7 hrs
but actual labour hours were	1,980.0 hrs
Variance in hours	326.7 hrs (F)
× standard rate per hour	× £15
Labour efficiency variance	£4,900.5 (F)

3 Materials usage variance

$= ((100 - 98.5)\% \text{ of standard materials usage}) \times \text{standard materials cost}$

$= 0.015 \times £30,400 \text{ (see (a)(W4))}$

$= £456 \text{ (F)}$

4

	£
Actual output should have cost (in terms of materials (see (a) (W4))	30,400
but did cost	33,800
Total materials variance	3,400 (A)
∴ Materials price variance = £(3,400 (A) – 456 (F))	£3,856 (A)

5

	£
Budgeted fixed overhead expenditure	40,000
Actual fixed overhead expenditure	40,800
Fixed overhead expenditure variance	800 (A)

6

Budgeted labour hours (see (a)(W6))	2,330 hrs
Actual labour hours	1,980 hrs
Variance in hours	350 hrs (A)
× overhead absorption rate per hour (see (a) (W6))	× £17.17
Fixed overhead capacity variance	£6,009.50 (A)

7

Labour efficiency variance in hours	326.7 hrs (F)
× overhead absorption rate per hour (see (a) (W6))	× £17.17
Fixed overhead efficiency variance	£5,609 (F)

8   Variable overhead efficiency variance

$$= (100 - 98.5)\% \times \text{standard variable overhead}$$
$$= 0.015 \times £22,800 \ (\text{see (a) (W5)})$$
$$= £342 \ (F)$$

9

	£
Actual output should have cost (in terms of variable overhead) (see (a) (W5))	22,800
but did cost	24,800
Total variable overhead variance	2,000 (A)

∴ Variable overhead expenditure variance = £(2,000 (A) – 342 (F)) = £2,342 (A)

(c)   It is now widely acknowledged that the **incidence of manufacturing overheads is determined by a wide range of factors** (or **cost drivers**). These include:

- The volume of output

- The mix of products manufactured

- The frequency and size of customer orders

- Purchasing policies

- Quality control procedures

- The way in which production is planned (number of set-ups, batch sizes, number of materials movements and so on)

Recognition of these relationships **has led to the development and widespread introduction of activity based costing (ABC). Manufacturing overheads at the factory** are attributed to products on the basis of **just two cost drivers**, however – material quantity usage for variable manufacturing overheads and direct labour hours worked for fixed manufacturing overheads. Such an approach would appear far too simplistic, failing to reflect the complex cost relationships in the modern manufacturing environment.

(i)   It is **unlikely that each overhead cost is either a fixed cost or a variable cost.** Costs may be **mixed**.

(ii)   It is **unlikely that all variable overheads are incurred in line with material quantity usage,** yet users of the statements may be persuaded that any savings in material usage will be amplified by savings in variable overheads.

(iii)   Likewise, it is **unlikely that all fixed overheads are incurred in line with the number of direct labour hours** worked.

It is therefore **unlikely that WCL's approach correctly allocates overheads to products** and so **product costs could be inaccurate**.

It is quite possible that **users** of WCL's operating statements may be **misled** by such a treatment of manufacturing overhead costs, with the following **repercussions**.

(i)   If users' attention is directed towards material usage and direct labour hours only, they may tend to ignore the scope for cost reduction available by addressing other causes of overhead costs.

(ii)   Manufacturing management will not be encouraged to economise on the consumption of overhead resources if the cost impact of such economies is not made clear.

(iii)   In order to achieve favourable fixed overhead variances, the company's manufacturing management may be persuaded to maximise output, whether or not sufficient demand exists for components X, Y and Z. At the very least extra inventory carrying costs would be incurred.

19   BENCHMARKING

> **Pass marks**. Part (a) was fairly straightforward. Your application skills were tested in part (b), however. All too often it is assumed that the introduction of AMT and new manufacturing management systems bring nothing but benefits to the organisation concerned. Here you were asked to think about why standard costs might *increase* as a result of their introduction, however. Don't forget that the management team may have forgotten to take certain factors into account. Never assume that the mangers in the question are above making mistakes.

(a)   **Benchmarking – definitions**

(i)   The CIMA *Official Terminology* describes benchmarking and its aims as 'The establishment, through data gathering, of **targets** and comparators, through whose use relative levels of performance (and particularly areas of underperformance) can be identified. By the adoption of identified best practices it is hoped that performance will improve'.

(ii)   Smith's clearer description is 'the formalisation of the basic notion of comparing practices. It is a **systematic analysis of one's own performance against that of another organisation** ... the overall objective of benchmarking is to improve performance by learning from the experience of others'.

Benchmarking therefore aims to **achieve competitive advantage by learning from others' experiences and mistakes**, finding **best practice** and translating this best practice into **use in the organisation**.

Types of benchmarking

(i)   **External benchmarking**

External benchmarking involves comparing the performance of an organisation with that of a **direct competitor** – ideally one that is acknowledged to be the 'best in class' (**competitive benchmarking**) or comparing the performance of an internal function with those of the best **external practitioners of those functions**, regardless of the industry within which they operate (**functional benchmarking**). Given that the benchmark is the 'best' in a particular field, it provides a meaningful target towards which the organisation should aim.

(ii)   **Internal benchmarking**

This involves **comparing** the performance of **one unit or function with another in the same industry**.

Operation of benchmarking

(i)   **Breakdown activities**

The **chosen activity needs to be broken down into specific processes or outputs that are capable of measurement**. External benchmarking might look at the percentage of rejects from a particular manufacturing process; internal benchmarking might consider the success of several bank branches' lending operations.

(ii)   **Internal measurement**

On the basis of the data collected from internal measurement, the **activity needs to be analysed** to see whether it is delivering what the customer wants.

(iii)   **Collect data**

'Best in class' organisations need to be identified and performance data collected.

147

Data from non-competitors

This might be fairly easy to obtain; **companies engaged in different industries might agree to collaborate** and exchange data on, for example, debt collection as this would not involve sharing potentially-damaging confidential information but would facilitate an assessment of internal processes that are essentially the same.

Obtaining data from competitors

To do this for the purposes of **competitive benchmarking** might be more **difficult**. Customer and supplier interviews and any publicly available data (such as promotional material and advertising, inter-firm comparison reports and information from credit rating agencies) can be used. Benchmarking clubs exist, run by firms of management consultants, several trade associations and professional bodies.

(iv) **Analyse data**

Once the data has been collected, it needs to be **analysed**. Any **changes** suggested by the exercise should be **implemented** and their **success monitored**. The whole process should be monitored periodically to ensure that the benchmarking is still being carried out against the 'best in class'.

Limitations

(i) **External benchmarking**

(1) Deciding which activities to benchmark

(2) Identifying which organisation is the 'best in class' at an activity

(3) **Persuading that organisation to share information**

(4) There is little point in comparing performance with an organisation that is not 'best in class' since it will only lead to complacency.

(5) Practices that get good results in one organisation may not transfer successfully to another organisation: they may depend on the talents or knowledge of particular individuals or on a particular culture.

(ii) **Internal benchmarking**

(1) The amount of resources devoted to the units may differ.

(2) There may be local differences (use of different computer hardware or software packages).

(3) Inputs and outputs may be difficult to define.

(4) Comparisons will only be valid if the figures reported are utterly reliable, but this is highly unlikely in practice.

(5) The possibility of the manipulation of figures must be considered.

Despite these limitations, however, many benefits have been reported from the use of benchmarking, both internal and external.

(b) **Possible reasons for similar standard costs in plants with differing technology**

(i) **Long-term benefits** such as increased customer satisfaction **as opposed to immediate cost savings** may well have been the aim of introducing the new technology and systems. If cost savings could not be made in the short term, standard costs would be unlikely to fall immediately.

(ii)   The standard costs may have **incorporated one-off costs** associated with AMT, JIT and TQM. For example, additional technicians may have had to be employed to oversee the introduction of new machinery.

(iii)   The introduction of new technology is likely to involve some sort of **learning curve effect**. In the period immediately following investment and the introduction of new systems, the labour force will be learning how to work with the new machines, systems and processes, but as they become more familiar with them, they will become more efficient and work more quickly. Standards may have been set to take account of this learning curve effect and hence would be higher than those ultimately envisaged once the learning process has stopped.

(iv)   The standard costs may have revised to **incorporate actual costs associated with unexpected problems** surrounding the implementation of the new technology and systems. For example, stricter quality control standards introduced as part of the TQM exercise may have led to the number of raw materials consignments rejected being higher than anticipated. This may have led to a shortage of materials and hence the labour force were idle for significant lengths of time, thereby reducing their planned efficiency level.

(v)   The introduction of AMT may have succeeded in reducing the size of the labour force required and hence the standard labour cost, but other costs, especially **fixed costs** (depreciation and so on), may have **increased.**

(vi)   The introduction of AMT, JIT, TQM and so on is likely to lead to a **change in the fixed overhead cost structure** and hence require a change in the approach used to apportion overheads to products, which may not have been taken into account when the standards were set. For example, activity based costing may be more appropriate than absorption costing. Once an alternative approach is adopted, the standard cost may change.

(vii)   **New manufacturing strategies such as JIT and TQM do involve additional costs.** In a JIT environment, the responsibility for the quality of goods lies with the supplier. It is his responsibility to inspect the parts before delivery and to guarantee their quality. This may involve paying a premium for such supplies. Although TQM programmes seek to reduce the costs of producing poor quality products, there are a multitude of costs associated with the implementation of a TQM programme. Training in quality control needs to be provided, inspection procedures need to be set up and so on. Such costs need to be incorporated into the standard cost.

It is thus imperative that management take into account such factors before deciding on the success or otherwise of the new technology and systems.

Appropriate benchmarking measures

Because of the different levels of technology used in the various plants, it could be **dangerous to benchmark product costs** (and the labour, material and overhead components of those costs), whether standard or actual.

Investment in new technology and new manufacturing systems should lead to reliable, quality products, a flexible approach to customer requirements, increased customer satisfaction, lower levels of stocks and shorter lead times. Of more relevance, therefore, are **benchmarks which assess how well the plants are satisfying customers, whether they be external or internal customers.**

(i) **Quality benchmarks**

These assess the effectiveness of TQM might include the proportion of items rejected, the costs of a customer service section as a proportion of turnover, losses from faults/defects in items sold as a proportion of turnover and the number of customer complaints as a proportion of items sold.

(ii) **Other customer satisfaction-orientated benchmarks**

These might include the **proportion of orders completed on time and the proportion of turnover attributable to recurring business.**

(iii) **Other benchmarks**

Benchmarks covering **stock levels** as a proportion of cost of sales (raw materials) or turnover (finished goods) could be used to assess the effectiveness of JIT systems.

Benchmarking could also cover **labour productivity levels, machine productivity levels, material wastage rates and lead times** (from placing of an order to delivery to the customer and from the start to finish of production).

Overall, the measures should be **relevant to the objectives of the organisation** and should allow the group to **gain competitive advantage.**

20 OBJECTIVE TEST QUESTIONS: BUDGETS

1 B Strategic (or corporate) planning covers periods longer than one year. Operation planning is planning on a very short-term or day-to-day basis. Budgetary or tactical planning involves preparing detailed plans which generally cover one year.

2 D A functional budget is a budget of income and/or expenditure for a particular department or process. A cash budget does not relate to a function.

3 C

	£
40% of May sales for cash (40% × £55,000)	22,000
70% of April credit sales less 2% discount (70% × 60% × £70,000 × 98%)	28,812
27% of March credit sales (27% × 60% × £60,000)	9,720
	60,532

If you chose **option A**, you forgot to include May's cash sales.

If you chose **option B**, you forgot to take account of May's cash sales and the 2% discount.

If you chose **option D**, you forgot to take account of the 2% discount.

4 A

	£
April customers: £21,000 × 0.05 × 0.98	1,029
March customers: £24,000 × 0.95 × 0.60	13,680
February customers: £22,000 × 0.95 × 0.25	5,225
January customers: £18,000 × 0.95 × 0.08	1,368
	21,302

If you selected **answer B**, you forgot to allow for the two per cent discount granted to customers who pay during April.

If you selected **answer C**, you forgot that the stated payment pattern was for the *remaining* customers, ie only 95 per cent of each month's sales.

If you selected **answer D**, you got muddled up and calculated that 2% of April customers took a 5% discount.

5 B

6 C

		£
August sales 70% × £90,000 × 97%		61,110
July sales 20% × £60,000		12,000
June sales 8% × £52,500		4,200
		77,310

If you chose **option A,** you forgot to take account of the 3% settlement discount.

If you chose **option B**, you reduced all receipts by the bad debt percentage.

If you chose **option D,** you deducted the 3% settlement discount from every month's receipts. It only applies for payment the month after sale.

7 B

8 D

	Units
Budgeted sales	18,000
Less budgeted reduction in finished goods stock	(3,600)
Budgeted production of completed units	14,400
Allowance for defective units (10% of output = 1/9 of input)	1,600
Production budget	16,000

	kg
Raw materials usage budget (16,000 × 6kg)	96,000
Budgeted increase in raw materials stock	3,400
Raw materials purchases budget	99,400

If you selected **option A** you did not make any allowance for defective units.

If you selected **option B** you calculated the correct figure for raw materials usage, but you forgot to adjust at the end for the budgeted increase in raw materials stock.

If you selected **option C** you calculated the allowance for defective units as 10% of satisfactory units, ie 1,440 units, rather than 10% of all units produced.

21   BUDGET PLANNING

> **Pass marks.** This question could have been answered in a variety of ways so don't be disheartened if your answer differs from ours. Perhaps you were able to incorporate your own experience into your solution.

REPORT

To:	Group finance director	
From:	Management accountant	Date: XX.XX.XX
Subject:	**Proposed changes to the budget preparation timetable**	

1   Introduction

1.1 This report suggests and explains the reasons for changes in budget preparation and planning for next year and considers how specific problems and anticipated difficulties could be dealt with.

2 Reasons for the proposed changes

2.1 Current approach

Our **current budget preparation timetable** requires that budgets are prepared after the third quarter's results are known and the fourth quarter forecast is prepared. The budgets are therefore based on information which is as **up-to-date** and accurate as possible, which is particularly important for the managerial **performance evaluation, resource allocation** and **control** functions of the budget: targets must be realistic if they are to motivate; budgets must accurate if they are to be used as the basis for optimal plans when resources are scarce; control will be useless if actual results are not compared with achievable expected results.

2.2 Disadvantages of current approach

With such an approach, there is often **insufficient time** between the beginning of the preparation process and the new budget period for key processes.

(a) An evaluation of the current position of the organisation in terms of both its internal resources and the external environment

(b) Planning by senior management

(c) Gathering of data

(d) Lower-level managers' involvement in the budgeting process

(e) Discussions on resource allocation issues

(f) Budget negotiation process

(g) Final agreement of budgets

2.3 Implications

There is a very real danger that operational managers in particular conclude that our budget preparation process as a whole is too rushed, that it is really nothing more than a planning exercise for senior management. **Negative attitudes** towards the budget can form and its **positive motivational impact fall**.

2.4 Advantages of proposal

A budget preparation timetable that begins after the half-year results for the current financial year are known gives management time, at both the senior level and operational level, **to research, discuss and prepare** the budgets. Operational-level managers will be able to **participate** in the process, improving motivation and morale and increasing acceptance of and commitment to the organisation's goals and objectives.

3 Specific problems – Division A

3.1 The problems

Because the appointment of a new managing director could take several months, it is likely that the divisional finance director, acting as managing director, will be in charge of the budget preparation process if the timetable changes are adopted.

3.2

There are thus two potential problems: the **new managing director** will inherit and have to **implement a budget over which he has had no input** and with which he might disagree strongly; there may be a **conflict of interest** as the finance director/acting managing director has no one to whom he should report.

3.3 The solution

Given this, it might be advisable to leave budget preparation until as late as possible, at least until a new managing director is appointed.

3.4 But it is possible to work to the suggested revised timetable, however. The division's **budget** for next year could be **based on this year's budget plus long-term divisional plans,** ignoring the poor performance in the first quarter.

3.5 A contingency plan would need to be drawn up, however, to cover the possibility of poor performance during the remainder of the year. Regular reviews would need to be made of divisional results to assess whether the contingency plan needed to be implemented.

3.6 If the **new managing director** is not appointed until after the final agreement of the budget, he should **not be held accountable** for any failure to achieve targets.

4 **Specific problems – Division B**

4.1 **The problem**

As the division's **new product range** was only launched in the first three months of this year, its **success can not yet be gauged.** In order that the proposed budget timetable can be adopted in the division, however, divisional management's knowledge and experience needs to be used to incorporate the anticipated results into the division's budget if the results are likely to have a significant impact on divisional and/or group profits.

4.2 **The solution**

Budgets based on worst possible/most likely/best possible outcomes could be drawn up, for example, or a **budget based on the probabilities of outcomes** could be used.

4.3 Even if management's estimates of the success or otherwise of the range are inaccurate, the budget will still be effective: the budget results can be **flexed** to reflect the actual level of activity for control purposes; a system of **planning and operational variances** can be used and the difference between the original standard activity level and the revised standard activity level set later this year be classified as a planning variance.

5 **Specific problems – Division C**

5.1 **The problem**

It is currently anticipated that the **new plant** will be operational in the third quarter but given the doubts over the likely quality of the output, it **could be the fourth quarter** or even next year before production can begin.

5.2 The expected **materiality** of the impact of the new machine in terms of the division's and the group's results affects the course of action which the division should adopt towards budget preparation.

5.3 **The solution**

If the impact is expected to be significant, the preparation of a realistic and accurate budget after the half-year results have been completed will be difficult. Following discussions with group management, the division's management could adopt the approach suggested for division B and prepare **optimistic/pessimistic/most likely budgets** or a **budget based on probabilities.**

6 **Other anticipated difficulties**

6.1 The change implies that **operational managers** will have to **devote more time and effort** to the budget preparation process. This, coupled with the fact that they might feel that the current approach is perfectly acceptable, may mean that they have to be **convinced of its shortcomings and the benefits of the proposal.**

6.2 Many managers' **bonuses** are based on their success in achieving budget targets and they may consider targets based on what could be out-of-date information to be far more difficult to achieve than the more realistic ones drawn up under the current system. This problem could be overcome by introducing a broader range of performance measures, perhaps incorporating **some non-financial indicators** such as reject rates, on-time deliveries and so on, which do not rely on the budget.

I hope this information is of use. If you have any questions please do not hesitate to contact me.

Signed: Management accountant

22   ZED PLC

> **Pass marks**. You could have wasted quite a lot of time in part (b)(i) if you did not think very carefully about what you were doing in advance. You were given demand information in terms of Product A and Product B but capacity information in terms of product A only so you had to convert all the information into machine hours.
>
> In part (b)(iii), to determine how many of each product you could produce, you had to look at how many sets of one unit of each product (which uses six machine hours) could be produced in the available time

(a) **What is the principal budget factor?**

Known as the **key budget factor** or **limiting budget factor**, this is the factor which, at any given time, effectively **limits the activities of an organisation**. The principal budget factor is **usually sales demand**: a company is usually restricted from making and selling more of its products because there would be no sales demand for the increased output at a price which would be acceptable/profitable for the company. The principal budget factor may also be machine capacity, distribution and selling resources, the availability of key raw materials or the availability of cash.

Its importance

Once this factor is identified **then the rest of the budget can be prepared.** For example, if sales are the principal budget factor then the production manager can only prepare his budget after the sales budget is complete.

Sales forecasting

There are two basic approaches to sales forecasting.

(i)   **Use of internal estimates**

In-house sales staff can forecast future sales using their experience and knowledge and by considering the following factors.

(1) Past sales patterns
(2) Economic environment
(3) Results of market research
(4) Anticipated advertising
(5) Competition
(6) Changing consumer taste
(7) New legislation
(8) Distribution and quality of sales outlets and personnel

(ii)   **Statistical techniques**

Such an approach is most appropriate if past sales patterns given some indication of future sales patterns (that is, extrapolation is valid). The techniques include **regression analysis by the least squares method in combination with moving averages analysis**.

Obviously both approaches can be **used in conjunction with each other**. Statistical forecasts can be considered and adjusted by sales personnel based on their knowledge and consideration of factors (1) to (8) listed above.

Use of microcomputers

Microcomputers are particularly useful for forecasting. They **facilitate complex calculations** within the statistical techniques, produce acceptably **accurate** estimates of future sales and are capable of performing 'what if' analysis, which shows management the effect of different sales levels on profit, cash flows and so on.

(b) (i)

	Demand	*Demand*	*Capacity*
	Units of A Units of B	Hrs*	Hrs
July	2,400 2,000	12,800	4,000
August	2,400 2,000	12,800	2,000
September	2,400 2,000	12,800	8,000
October–December	3,000 6,000	30,000	24,000
January – March	4,800 6,000	33,600	24,000
April – June	9,000 6,000	42,000	24,000
	24,000 24,000	144,000	86,000

There is a shortfall of 144,000 – 86,000 = 58,000 machine hours.

* $(2 \times$ demand for A in units$) + (4 \times$ demand for B in units$)$

(ii)   To prepare the budgets we produce the **maximum number of Product A** with the hours available and then use the **remaining hours to produce Product B**. In July, for example, we have 4,000 hours so we can produce only $4,000 \div 2 = 2,000$ units of Product A whereas in September we can produce 2,400 units of Product A, using 4,800 of the 8,000 hours. The remaining 3,200 can be used to make $3,200 \div 4$ hrs = 800 units of Product B. Likewise, in October, November and December, the demand for Product A can be met, leaving $8,000 - 2,000 = 6,000$ hours to produce $6,000 \div 4 = 1,500$ units of product B.

Production and sales budgets
July – December 20X8

	Product A	*Product B*
	Units	Units
July	2,000	–
August	1,000	–
September	2,400	800
October	1,000	1,500
November	1,000	1,500
December	1,000	1,500
	8,400	5,300

(iii) We have to sell **equal quantities** of each product and so for each Product A we have to produce one unit of Product B, which takes six hours in total. We therefore need to **divide up the available hours into groups of six hours** to determine what we can produce. In July, for example, the available capacity is 4,000 hours and so we can produce $(4,000 \div 6)$ 666 groups of products, where the products in each group take six hours in total (and where the products are one Product A and one Product B). We can't produce 667 groups because that would take 4,002 hours.

	Product A				Product B			
	Stock b/f	*Production*	*Sales (W4)*	*Stock c/f*	*Stock b/f*	*Production*	*Sales (W4)*	*Stock c/f*
	Units	Units	Units	Units	Units	Units	Units	Units
July	-	666 (W1)	666	-	-	666 (W1)	666	-
Aug	-	333 (W2)	333	-	-	333 (W2)	333	-
Sept	-	1,333 (W3)	1,333	-	-	1,333 (W3)	1,333	-
Oct	-	1,333 (W3)	1,000	333	-	1,333 (W3)	1,000	333
Nov	333	1,333 (W3)	1,000	666	333	1,333 (W3)	1,000	666
Dec	666	1,333 (W3)	1,000	999	999	1,333 (W3)	1,000	999
			5,332				5,332	

Workings

1 $4,000 \div 6 = 666$

2 $2,000 \div 6 = 333$

3 $8,000 \div 6 = 1,333$

4 Limited by demand each month

(iv) **Contribution July – December 20X8**
Sales mix (b)

	£	£
Sales of Product A (8,400 × £4.50 (W1))	37,800	
Sales of Product B (5,300 × £0.40 (W2))	2,120	
		39,920

Contribution July – December 20X8
Sales mix (c)

	£	£
Sales of Product A (5,332 × £4.50 (W1))	23,994	
Sales of Product B (5,332 × £0.40 (W2))	2,133	
		26,127

By adopting the sales mix proposed in (c), profit will decrease by £(39,920 – 26,127) = £13,793.

Workings

1 Contribution per unit of A = £(10 – 5.5) = £4.50

2 Contribution per unit B = £(8 – 7.60) = £0.40

23 **LMN LTD**

> **Pass marks.** A systematic approach is needed here to ensure that you take account of all the information given. One of the most important initial workings is to calculate the required production for each month, which means that you will need to interpret correctly the company policy concerning finished goods stocks. When you are preparing the cash budget, do not fall for the two cash budget traps.
>
> (a) Depreciation is not a cash flow and must not be included in the cash budget.
>
> (b) Bad debts are not a cash expense. They will never be received in cash and therefore they simply do not appear in the cash budget. (But you must remember to include them as an expense in the profit and loss account!)

Workings

1 **Finished goods stock policy**

Finished goods stock, 31 December 20X0	= 1,200 units
Budgeted unit sales in January 20X1	= 1,000 units
∴ Ratio of stock to unit sales for following months	= 1.2:1

2   **Monthly production and materials requirements**

	December Units	January Units	February Units	March Units
Required closing stock (1.2 × following month's sales)	1,200	1,680	1,920	2,160
Expected sales for month	1,300	1,000	1,400	1,600
Total requirements in month	2,500	2,680	3,320	3,760
Less opening stock	1,560*	1,200	1,680	1,920
Required production	940	1,480	1,640	1,840
Materials cost of production (× £12)		£17,760	£19,680	£22,080

The materials will be purchased in the month before production and paid for in the month following delivery. They are therefore paid for in the month in which they are used in production, as above.

* December opening stock = 1.2 × December sales = 1.2 × 1,300 units

3   **Overtime premium**

	January Units	February Units	March Units	Jan-March Total Units
Required production	1,480	1,640	1,840	4,960
Normal capacity	1,500	1,500	1,500	
Units produced in overtime	–	140	340	
× £24 per unit premium		£3,360	£8,160	£11,520

(a)   **BUDGETED PROFIT AND LOSS ACCOUNT FOR THE QUARTER JANUARY TO MARCH 20X1**

	£	£	£
Sales (4,000 × £90)			360,000
Less cost of sales			
Opening stock		66,500	
Variable production costs (4,960 × £44)	218,240		
Overtime premium (W3)	11,520		
Fixed production overhead (3 × £15,000)	45,000		
		274,760	
		341,260	
Less closing stock at actual cost			
$(2,160 \times \dfrac{£274,760}{4,960})$		119,654	
		221,606	
Gross profit			138,394
Administration overhead (3 × £23,000)		69,000	
Bad debts (3% × £360,000)		10,800	
			79,800
Net profit			58,594

BPP
PROFESSIONAL EDUCATION

(b)   **CASH BUDGET FOR THE QUARTER JANUARY TO MARCH 20X1**

	January £	February £	March £	Total £
Receipts				
Current month's sales (30%)	27,000	37,800	43,200	
Previous month's sales (67%)	78,390	60,300	84,420	
	105,390	98,100	127,620	331,110
Payments				
Materials (W2)	17,760	19,680	22,080	
Labour: basic rate	35,520	39,360	44,160	
overtime premium (W3)	-	3,360	8,160	
Variable overhead (production × £8)	11,840	13,120	14,720	
Fixed overhead (excl depreciation)	11,500	11,500	11,500	
Administration overhead	23,000	23,000	23,000	
	99,620	110,020	123,620	333,260
Net cash inflow/(outflow)	5,770	(11,920)	4,000	(2,150)

Note. We are not given the budgeted opening cash balance for January, and so it is not possible to calculate the closing cash balance for each month.

(c)   **Reconciliation of the net cash movement to the budgeted profit for the quarter**

	£	£
Budgeted net profit		58,594
Add back depreciation (3 × £3,500)		10,500
		69,094
Adjust for the increase in stock		
Opening stock	66,500	
Closing stock	119,654	
		(53,154)
Adjust for the increase in debtors		
Opening debtors (67% × December sales)	78,390	
Closing debtors (67% × March sales)	96,480	
		(18,090)
Net cash movement for the quarter		(2,150)

24   **AZ LTD**

> **Pass marks**. The first stage in this question should be to set out the budget proforma, and insert the figures that require little or no calculation (sales receipts, fixed costs, and capital expenditure). The key working is the calculation of the variable costs of production; the split of these gives the labour payments figures and further workings on material and variable overheads produce the payments figures for those costs. An advantage of setting out the workings in this way is that the considerable detail given in the question can be handled in clear stages, and confusion avoided. Remember that if the answer is wrong and there are no workings, then no marks can be awarded. Paper 8 budgeting questions could be more complex than this, but attempt this one – it is useful revision.

Cash budget

May, June, July 20X7	May £	June £	July £
Sales	401,700	450,280	425,880
Payments			
Materials (W1, W2)	161,640	172,440	166,320
Labour (W1)	86,040	86,400	79,920
Variable overheads (W1, W3)	26,592	28,728	27,936
Fixed costs (W4)	75,000	75,000	75,000
Capital expenditure	–	190,000	–
	349,272	552,568	349,176
Net cash flow	52,428	(102,288)	76,704
Opening cash balance	40,000	92,428	(9,860)
Closing cash balance	92,428	(9,860)	66,844

Workings

1 Costs of production

	April £	May £	June £	July £	August £
Sales	400,000	450,000	520,000	420,000	480,000
Cost of sales 60%	240,000	270,000	312,000	252,000	288,000
Cost of production:					
60% this month COS	144,000	162,000	187,200	151,200	-
40% next month COS	108,000	124,800	100,800	115,200	-
	252,000	286,800	288,000	266,400	
Split					
Materials 60%	151,200	172,080	172,800	159,840	
Labour 30% (to budget)	75,600	86,040	86,400	79,920	
Variable overheads 10%	25,200	28,680	28,800	26,640	

2 Material purchases

	April £	May £	June £
For this month's production (50%)	75,600	86,040	86,400
For next month's production (50%)	86,040	86,400	79,920
	161,640	172,440	166,320

Remember material suppliers are paid in the month after purchase.

3 Payments for variable overheads

	May £	June £	July £
Payment – for this month's costs (40%)	11,472	11,520	10,656
– for last month's costs (60%)	15,120	17,208	17,280
	26,592	28,728	27,936

4 Fixed costs

$$\text{Payments per month} = \frac{£(1,200,000 - 300,000)}{12} = £75,000$$

25 LIST PRICE

Pass marks. You will produce much better answers to parts (b) and (c) if you use your answer to part (a) to illustrate the points that you make. The question prompts you to do this in part (b) but it is a good technique to use even if you are not specifically instructed to refer back to earlier parts. Again, budget preparation in Paper 8 might be more complex than that required here but you should attempt this question for revision purposes.

(a) **Cash flow forecast**

	Sept £'000	Oct £'000	Nov £'000	Dec £'000	Jan £'000	Feb £'000
Receipts						
Credit sales (60% of last month's sales)	30.00	28.80	24.00	27.00	26.40	25.20
Cash sales (38% (40% × 0.95) of this month's sales)	18.24	15.20	17.10	16.72	15.96	19.00
Fixed asset disposal	-	8.00	-	-	-	-
	48.24	52.00	41.10	43.72	42.36	44.20
Payments						
Purchases (W1)	18.80	19.60	17.60	17.00	19.80	17.20
Wages (W2)	6.80	6.00	6.50	6.40	6.20	7.00
Fixed costs (less depn.)	6.00	6.00	6.00	6.00	6.00	6.00
Capital expenditure	15.00	-	10.00	-	–	4.00
Corporation tax	-	-	44.00	-	–	-
	46.60	31.60	84.10	29.40	32.00	34.20
Net cash flow	1.64	20.40	(43.00)	14.32	10.36	10.00
Opening balance	5.00	6.64	27.04	(15.96)	(1.64)	8.72
Closing balance	6.64	27.04	(15.96)	(1.64)	8.72	18.72

Workings

1   **Purchases payment month**

	Jul £'000	Aug £'000	Sept £'000	Oct £'000	Nov £'000	Dec £'000
Closing stock required (following month sales × 0.5 × 0.4)	10.0	9.6	8.0	9.0	8.8	8.4
(additional safety stock)	-	-	-	-	2.0	2.0
Sales at cost (× 40%)	17.6	20.0	19.2	16.0	18.0	17.6
	27.6	29.6	27.2	25.0	28.8	28.0
Less opening stock	8.8	10.0	9.6	8.0	9.0	10.8
Purchases	18.8	19.6	17.6	17.0	19.8	17.2
Payment month	Sept	Oct	Nov	Dec	Jan	Feb

2   **Wages**

	Sept £'000	Oct £'000	Nov £'000	Dec £'000	Jan £'000	Feb £'000
Fixed sum	2.0	2.0	2.0	2.0	2.0	2.0
10% of sales	4.8	4.0	4.5	4.4	4.2	5.0
	6.8	6.0	6.5	6.4	6.2	7.0

(b) **Spreadsheets** can **assist cash forecast preparation** in a number of ways.

(i)   The basic **calculation** function is performed **automatically,** thus saving time in calculating and re-calculating. In (a) the percentages credit and cash sales would be calculated using a formula.

(ii)   In a spreadsheet, the model can be separated into **input areas** and **display areas**. The cash budget would pick up information from input areas that contain the underlying relationships. For example the monthly purchase would be calculated as in (a) and the figure inserted into the cash budget as a cash payment two months later.

(iii)   The model would **display** the results of the calculations as shown in (a). This could be in whatever level of detail was required by the user. **Graphics** would also be used to aid presentation.

(iv) **Changes** to a cash flow forecast could also be **made easily** on a spreadsheet. Use of a spreadsheet would mean changes in data such as additional capital expenditure could be incorporated and all totals changed automatically. Likewise extra rows or columns could be incorporated, if further types of expenditure had to be added, or the model extended over additional months (if for instance a rolling budget was being used).

(v) Spreadsheets can also be used to **forecast** cash movements, in '**what if' analysis situations.** Management can enter different assumptions or situations, for example adding safety stock, or assessing the effect of an increase in sales, and the spreadsheet be adjusted easily.

(vi) Further columns can be added to the spreadsheet to **compare actual results with forecast**. Alternatively as actual results are known, the spreadsheet can be amended to incorporate these, and hence **revised forecasts** made of cash balances in the periods to come.

(vii) Once the basic model has been set up, it can be used with suitable amendments for **fresh forecasts in future periods.**

(c) **Feedforward control**

Feedforward control occurs when mangers **forecast likely outcomes** and then **compare these with the desired outcomes. Action can be taken in advance** to correct any adverse situations or to take full advantage of favourable situations.

For example, the cash forecast in part (a) shows that XYZ Ltd is likely to have a negative cash position in November and December. Managers can therefore take action now to avoid the situation if necessary. They could, for example, postpone the capital expenditure or perhaps arrange to pay for the asset(s) in instalments.

Feedforward control means that mangers are **forewarned** of any situation, whether it be good or bad, before it occurs.

Feedback control

Feedback control involves **recording actual results and then comparing them with forecast or budgeted results**. For example, a cash forecast can act as a feedback control mechanism if the actual cash flows for, say sales receipts, are compared with the forecast cash flows.

Reasons for differences can be identified and efforts made to ensure that **favourable differences continue to be exploited** and **adverse differences do not occur in the future.**

26   Q PLC

> **Pass marks.** Think about how you would tackle this question using a spreadsheet – the format and steps should then appear reasonably automatic. It is useful examination practice to occasionally do such problems using a spread sheet.
>
> The profit and loss account is reproduced here for clarity but you would not need to do this in the examination.
>
> A Paper 8 cash budgeting question could be more complex, perhaps incorporating other topics. But attempt this question for revision purposes.

(a) **Cash budget of Q plc for the months January to March 20X9**

	January £	February £	March £
Receipts			
Cash from customers	69,600	56,944	56,470
Interest receivable (W5)	0	0	37
	69,600	56,944	56,507
Payments			
Direct materials creditors (W3)	21,000	17,500	16,500
Direct labour (W2)	15,000	16,500	9,750
Production overheads (W4)	15,000	12,600	10,800
Administration & selling costs	15,000	-	-
Capital equipment	-	-	30,000
Interest payable (W5)	-	64	-
	66,000	46,664	67,050
Net cash flow	3,600	10,280	(10,543)
Opening balance	(5,000)	(1,400)	8,880
Closing balance	(1,400)	8,880	(1,663)

Workings

1   Budgeted profit & loss account

	January £	February £	March £	April £
Sales	60,000	50,000	70,000	60,000
Production cost	50,000	55,000	32,500	50,000
Stock adjustment	(5,000)	(17,500)	20,000	(5,000)
Cost of sales	45,000	37,500	52,500	45,000
Gross profit	15,000	12,500	17,500	15,000
Admin/selling overhead	8,000	7,500	8,500	8,000
Net profit before interest	7,000	5,000	9,000	7,000

2   Analysis of W1

	January £	February £	March £	April £
Direct materials				
(40% of production cost – see W1)	20,000	22,000	13,000	20,000
Direct labour (30% of production cost– see W1)	15,000	16,500	9,750	15,000
Production overhead (balance of production cost – see W1)	15,000	16,500	9,750	15,000
	50,000	55,000	32,500	50,000
Fixed production overhead	5,000	5,000	5,000	5,000
Depreciation	3,000	3,000	3,000	3,000
Other fixed production overheads	2,000	2,000	2,000	2,000
Variable production overhead	10,000	11,500	4,750	10,000

3   Calculation of payments to materials creditors

	January £	February £	March £
Opening materials creditors	10,000	11,000	6,500
Add purchases in month (Subsequent month in W1)	22,000	13,000	20,000
Less closing materials creditors (50% of purchases)	(11,000)	(6,500)	(10,000)
Payments to materials creditors	21,000	17,500	16,500

4   Calculation of payments to production overhead creditors

	January £	February £	March £
Opening production overhead creditors	11,000	8,000	8,900
Add fixed production overheads in month (W1)	2,000	2,000	2,000
Add variable production overhead in month (W1)	10,000	11,500	4,750
Less closing creditors (100% fixed, 60% variable)	(8,000)	(8,900)	(4,850)
Payments to production overhead creditors	15,000	12,600	10,800

5   Calculation of bank interest

	December £	January £	February £
Bank balance at beginning of month	5,000	(5,000)	(1,400)
Bank balance at end of month	(5,000)	(1,400)	8,880
Average	0	(3,200)	3,740
Interest payable at 2% per month		64	
Interest receivable at 1% per month			37

(b) **Feedforward control mechanisms**

Feed forward control occur when managers **forecast likely outcomes** and then **compare** these with the **desired outcomes. Action** can be taken **in advance** to correct any adverse situations or to take full advantage of favourable situations.

For example, Q plc could anticipate that it will need to obtain additional credit or collect as much cash as possible from debtors and delay payments to creditors in January and March (when cash balances are negative).

Q plc might also wish to defer the capital expenditure or perhaps arrange to make the payments in instalments. Similarly, if significant cash surpluses are budgeted (as in February) then managers could anticipate the opportunity to move some of the cash into short-term interest earning securities.

Feedforward control means that managers are **forewarned** of any situation, whether it be good or bad, before it occurs.

Feedback control mechanisms

Feedback control involves recording **actual results** and then **comparing** them with **forecast** or **budgeted results.**

The **cash budget** can also be used as a basis for feedback control in that **significant variances** may be **investigated** and either **action** taken to get **back on track** or steps taken to **revise the budget.** For instance if Q plc's payments to creditors are not in line with budget it would be necessary for the relevant budget holder to **explain any variances.**

Feedback control is therefore **reactive** and is not so useful as a control device.

27   PREPARATION QUESTION: BUDGETS ETC

> **Pass marks.** This preparation question covers a number of important budgeting topics and provides you with a useful revision opportunity.

BPP
PROFESSIONAL EDUCATION

(a) **Budgets for planning**

An organisation planning process can be divided into two sections, **long-term strategic planning** (also known as **corporate planning**) and **short-term planning**.

(i) **Long-term planning**

This involves selecting appropriate **strategies** so as to prepare a long-term plan to attain the organisation's **objectives**.

This long-term corporate plan serves as the long-term **framework** for the organisation as a whole but for **operational purposes** it is necessary to convert the corporate plan into a series of **short-term plans (or budgets),** usually covering one year, which relate to sections, functions or departments.

(ii) **Short-term planning**

The annual process of short-term planning (or **budgeting**) should be seen as **steps** in the progressive fulfilment of the corporate plan as each short-term plan steers the organisation towards its long-term objectives.

The short-term budgets for the various functions of the organisation are **coordinated** and **consolidated** by the budget committee into the **master budget,** which is a summary of organisation-wide plans for the coming period. The master budget is what is known as a **fixed budget.** This does not mean that the budget is kept unchanged. Revisions will be made to it if the situation so demands. It simply means that the budget is prepared on the basis of an estimated volume of production and sales, but no plans are made for the event that actual volumes differ from budgeted volumes.

Budgets for control

Having set the master budget, control processes need to be established. The basic control model involves **comparing actual results achieved with what results should have been under the circumstances.**

Every business is **dynamic,** however, and actual volumes of output cannot be expected to conform exactly to the fixed master budget. Comparing actual results directly with the fixed master budget results is meaningless. For useful control information, it is necessary to compare actual results at the actual level of activity achieved with the results that should have been expected at this level of activity, which is shown by a **flexible budget.**

(b) **Incremental budgeting – what is it?**

Incremental budgeting is the **traditional** approach to budgeting and involves basing the budget on the **current year's results plus an extra amount** for estimated growth or inflation next year. The approach is concerned mainly with the increments in costs and revenues which will occur in the coming period. As such they are fairly **easy** and **cheap** to prepare.

When to use it

It is a **reasonable procedure if current operations are as effective, efficient and economical as they can be.** It is also appropriate for budgeting for costs such as **staff salaries,** which may be estimated on the basis of current salaries plus an increment for inflation and are hence administratively easy to prepare.

Disadvantages

In general, however, it is an **inefficient** form of budgeting as it encourages **slack** and **wasteful spending** to creep into budgets. Past inefficiencies are perpetuated since the relationship between costs, benefits and objectives is rarely subjected to close scrutiny.

Zero base budgeting (ZBB) – what is it?

This starts from the **premise** that the **budget for next year is zero**, and **every part** of every process and cost has to be fully **justified** in order to be included in this budget, as if it were being **included for the first time**. This existing activities have to be justified in exactly the same way as new proposals.

Advantages

(i)   It helps to identify and remove inefficient or obsolete operations.

(ii)   It forces staff to avoid wasteful expenditure.

(iii)   It can increase motivation.

(iv)   It provides management with a budgeting and planning tool which responds to changes in the business environment: 'obsolescent' items of expenditure are identified and dropped.

(v)   The documentation required provides all management with a coordinated, in-depth appraisal of an organisation's operations.

(vi)   It challenges the status quo and forces an organisation to examine alternative activities and existing expenditure levels.

In summary, ZBB should result in a more efficient allocation of resources to an organisation's activities and departments.

Disadvantages

The major disadvantage of zero base budgeting is the **volume of extra paperwork** created. The assumptions about costs and benefits in each package must be continually updated and new packages developed as soon as new activities emerge. The following problems might also occur.

(i)   Short-term benefits might be emphasised to the detriment of long-term benefits.

(ii)   The false idea that all decisions have to be made in the budget might be encouraged. Management might feel restricted from carrying out new ideas simply because they were not approved by the ZBB process.

(iii)   It may call for management skills that the organisation does not possess, for example in the ranking process.

(iv)   It may be difficult to sell ZBB to managers as a useful technique because the processes can be difficult and/or because employees resent change.

(v)   The organisation's information systems may not be capable of dealing with the analysis required.

(vi)   The ranking process can be difficult.

In **summary**, the most serious drawback to ZBB is that it requires a lot of **management time and paperwork**.

(c)   **Rolling budgets – what are they?**

A rolling budget is a budget which is **continuously updated by adding a further period**, such as a month or quarter, and **deducting the earliest period**. At the end of each month or quarter, actual results are compared with budgeted results. If there is a large divergence between the two as a result of unexpected changes within the operating environment, the **budget for the remaining months/quarters can be amended to take account of any permanent changes** and a budget for an additional month/quarter prepared.

Advantages

Because budgets are up-to-date in the light of current events and expectations, **planning and control** are thus **improved** because they are based on a **recent plan** which is more **realistic** than a fixed annual budget that might have been prepared many months ago. And the fact that the plan is more realistic means that it should be more achievable. Rolling budgets should provide a **more appropriate yardstick for control purposes**, and the comparison of actual results against a realistic and achievable target should provide **more relevant feedback** and allow for **better feedforward control action.**

Budgetary slack – what is it?

In the process of preparing budgets, managers may **deliberately overestimate costs so that they will not be blamed in the future for overspending**. In controlling operations managers must then **ensure that their spending rises to meet their budget**, otherwise they will be 'blamed' for careless budgeting. Budgetary slack is the **difference between the minimum necessary costs and the costs managers build into their budgets or actually incur.**

Typical situation

A manager may waste money on non-essential expenses so that he uses all of his budget allowances. The reason behind such action is the fear that unless the allowance is fully spent it will be reduced in future periods thus making the manager's job more difficult in the future as the reduced budgets will not be so easy to attain. As inefficiency and slack are allowed for in budgets, achieving a budget target means only that costs have remained within the accepted levels of inefficient spending.

Budgetary slack and rolling budgets

Because rolling budgets **provide a continuously updated target, managers may not feel it is necessary to incorporate slack into their budgets**; if unexpected circumstances occur which require additional expenditure, the budget target can be amended to take this into consideration. On the other hand, however, the **continuous improvement ethic** inherent in a system of rolling budgets could be seen as one more **reason why a certain level of slack is required.**

28   **H PLC**

Pass marks. Mention of activity based budgeting may have made you panic but the calculation parts of this question were actually very straightforward. The statements in (a)(i) are derived simply by applying the relevant percentage to the relevant total cost. For example, in the first statement, budgeted salaries are 60% of £1,000,000 and actual salaries are 63% of £1,060,000. The variance is calculated as actual figure minus budget figure.

For part (a)(ii), a wide range of answers is possible. Award yourself marks if you identified four valid points, but only if you referred to information from the question in your answer.

(a) (i)   **Expense-based analysis**

PPD DEPARTMENT
BUDGET CONTROL STATEMENT – PERIOD ENDED 30 NOVEMBER 20X6
TRADITIONAL EXPENSE-BASED ANALYSIS

Expense type	Budget £'000	Actual £'000	Variance £'000	
Salaries	600	667.8	67.8	(A)
Supplies	60	53.0	7.0	(F)
Travel cost	120	127.2	7.2	(A)
Technology cost	100	74.2	25.8	(F)
Occupancy cost	120	137.8	17.8	(A)
	1,000	1,060.0	60.0	(A)

Activity based analysis

PPD DEPARTMENT
BUDGET CONTROL STATEMENT – PERIOD ENDED 30 NOVEMBER 20X6
ACTIVITY-BASED ANALYSIS

Activity	Budget £'000	Actual £'000	Variance £'000	
Routing/scheduling – new products	200	169.6	30.4	(F)
Routing/scheduling – existing products	400	360.4	39.6	(F)
Remedial re-routing/scheduling	50	127.2	77.2	(A)
Special studies – specific orders	100	84.8	15.2	(F)
Training	100	159.0	59.0	(A)
Management and administration	150	159.0	9.0	(A)
	1,000	1,060.0	60.0	(A)

(ii)   **Advantages of activity based budgeting (ABB)** include the following.

(1)   ABB **focuses on what the organisation actually does** (its **objectives**) rather than on the resources it buys to do it. For instance, the real activities and objectives of H plc might be to design and construct products, not to employ people and buy materials. With ABB the level of activity is used to decide how much resource should be allocated, how well it is being managed and to explain variances from budget.

(2)   ABB **concentrates on the whole of an activity**, not just its separate parts, and this means that there is more likelihood of getting it right first time. There is an activity called 'remedial re-routing/scheduling' in the production, planning and development department, recognising the need to co-ordinate labour, supplies and technology instead of regarding them as mere unrelated expenses.

(3)   ABB leads to the realisation that the **business as a whole needs to be managed with far more reference to the behaviour of its cost drivers and activities.** For example, traditional budgeting may make managers responsible for activities which are driven by factors beyond their control. In the production, planning and development department, training expenditure, for example, may be driven by demands from the personnel department. ABB may help to prioritise such demands.

(4)   ABB is **linked to other significant current management movements** such as customer service, business process re-engineering, total quality, employee empowerment, value added, waste elimination. All of these are ultimately intended to make organisations more competitive.

(5)   In H plc's case, the ABB study has **identified** a business process comprising three **value-added activities** (activities 1, 2 and 4), two **support activities** (training and management/administration) and one **non-value-added activity** (remedial re-routing/scheduling). Management efforts need to be devoted to improving the business process of getting goods into customers hands by eliminating the problems that lead to remedial re-routing/scheduling.

(iii)   **How to use the activity-based statement**

The **activity-based statement can be used in the same way as the conventional statement would be**. For example, it shows that the amounts spent on remedial re-routing/scheduling and training are significantly different from the amounts budgeted. These two variances may be **related**, and possibly the investment in training will lead to lower levels of remedial work in the future.

Savings have been made in all three principal areas, and again there may be **links** between economies in routing/scheduling and special studies cost and the level of reworking.

How to provide a clearer picture

Each of the variances could be further **broken down** into sub-variances to provide a clearer picture of why they have occurred. For instance, the favourable routing/scheduling variances may in reality include elements of salaries, supplies, technology cost and so on.

So far the pilot study seems to have merely divided up overall costs under different headings to the conventional ones, however.

Additional information

The **information that is needed for a more useful analysis is the identification of cost drivers for each of the activities**.

(1)   For instance, training costs may be driven by number of new employees, or number of unfamiliar procedures, and this would indicate that adverse variances in this area could be reduced by measures to improve staff retention or by the redesign of work processes on a more flexible basis so that they utilised existing skills rather than constantly requiring new skills to be acquired.

(2)   In other areas it may be possible to determine the most efficient level of a particular cost driver, such as the number of staff hours per individual route development for a new product. This can be compared with the actual hours and broken down on a per staff member basis so as to provide an indication of the efficiency of provision of the activity. The excess could be identified in a non-financial variance statement.

(b)

Activity	Cost driver	Total cost £'000	Units of cost driver '000	O/hd per CD unit £ (W2)	CD units per NPD Units (W3)	O/hd per NPD £ (W4)
Product design	Design hours	2,000	8	250	0.08	20.00
Purchasing	Purchase orders	200	4	50	0.02	1.00
Production	Machine hours	1,200 (W1)	12	100	0.75	75.00
Packing	Volume (m³)	400	20	20	0.40	8.00
Distribution	Weight (kgs)	600	120	5	3.00	15.00
Depreciation	(W5)					25.60
						144.60

Workings

1 **Production cost** = £1,500,000 less depreciation of £300,000 = £1,200,000

2 **Overhead cost per cost driver unit** = total cost ÷ units of cost driver

3 **Cost driver units per NPD:**

   Design hours. Total requirement for production of 5,000 units = 400 design hours. Design hours per unit = £400 ÷ 5,000 = 0.08

   Purchase orders. Each order covers 50 units and so each unit requires 1/50 of an order = 0.02 of an order

   Machine hours, volume (m³) and **weight** (kgs) provided in the question

4 **Overhead per NPD** = overhead per cost driver unit × cost driver units per NPD

5 3 months depreciation = £8,000

   Product life cycle = 4 yrs

   ∴ Cost = £8,000 × 4 yrs × 4 quarters per year = £128,000

   ∴ **Depreciation per NPD** = £128,000 ÷ 5,000 units = £25.60

29   OBJECTIVE TEST QUESTIONS: FORECASTING

1 B   Trend value   = 345.12 − (1.35 × 16) = 323.52
      Forecast sales = trend + seasonal component
               = 323.52 − 23.62
               = 299.9
               = 300 (to the nearest whole unit)

   If you selected **option A** you reduced the trend figure by 23.62 per cent, instead of subtracting 23.62 as an absolute figure.

   If you selected **option C** you forgot to adjust the trend for the seasonal variation.

   If you selected **option D** you added the seasonal component instead of subtracting it.

2 A   A regression equation is worthless unless a sufficiently large sample is used to determine it. In practice, samples of ten or more are acceptable.

   If you chose **option B**, you forgot that forecasting for values of x outside the range of original data leads to unreliable estimates because there is no evidence that the same regression relationship holds for such values.

   If you chose **option C**, you didn't realise that working to a high number of decimal places gives spurious accuracy.

If you chose **option D**, you obviously thought that a correlation coefficient close to 0 indicates a strong linear relationship between x and y. The coefficient must be close to +1 or –1 for such an indication, however.

3   D   Trend value = 7.112 + (3.949 × 19) = 82.143

Seasonally-adjusted trend value = 82.143 × 1.12 = 92

If you selected **option A** you forgot to adjust the tend value for the seasonal variation.

If you selected **option B** you added 1.12 to the trend value, instead of multiplying by 1.12.

If you selected **option C** you reduced the trend value by 12 per cent, instead of increasing it by that amount.

4   A   The correlation coefficient of 0.95 is close to 1 so there is a strong relationship.

5   C

	Units
Trend value for January 20X9	452
Increase to May 20X9: 4 × 16	64
Trend value for May 20X9	516

Predicted volume for May 20X9 = 516 × 103% = 531 units.

If you selected **option A** you reduced the trend by three per cent, instead of increasing it.

If you selected **option B** you forgot to adjust the trend for the seasonal variation.

If you selected **option D** you added five monthly increments to the trend value for January, instead of four.

6   C

		£
Total cost for 20,000 miles = 20,000 × £1.90	=	38,000
Total cost for 28,000 miles = 28,000 × £1.70	=	47,600
∴ Variable cost for 8,000 miles		9,600

		£
Variable cost per mile = £9,600/8,000	=	£1.20
Fixed cost = £38,000 – (20,000 × £1.20)	=	££14,000
Fixed cost per mile for 24,000 miles	=	£14,000/24,000
	=	£0.58
∴ Total cost per mile for 24,000 miles	=	£(1.20 + 0.58)
	=	£1.78

If you selected **option A** you calculated only the fixed cost per mile.

If you selected **option B** you calculated only the variable cost per mile

If you selected **option D** you calculated a simple average of the two unit costs supplied. This does not make allowance for the fact that the unit rate for fixed costs varies according to the number of miles travelled.

7   C   The four components of a time series are the trend, seasonal variations, cyclical variations and random variations. Totals must be divided by the appropriate figure to obtain the trend. The totals themselves are therefore not a component of the time series. They merely assist in the calculation of the trend.

8   C   Seasonal variations are short-term fluctuations in recorded values, due to different circumstances which affect results at different times of the year, on different days of the week and so on.

Option A describes the underlying trend.

Option B describes random variations.

Option D describes cyclical variations, which are medium-term changes caused by circumstances which repeat in cycles.

30   PMF PLC

> **Pass marks.** Parts (a), (b) and (c) were a gift and you should aim to get at least ten of the thirteen marks available.
>
> In (a), you would have earned four marks for determining the seasonal variation, two marks for calculating the trend value and one mark for the forecast.
>
> Common errors in part (a) were not using the trend equation provided (although this was set out in the question requirement), thereby wasting valuable time, and not using the multiplicative (proportional) model (although this was specified in the requirements).
>
> The examiner commented that candidates who could not answer part (b) should not have been sitting the paper (well – it was very easy!).
>
> To get full marks in (c), you needed to total the costs as required in the question.
>
> Effectiveness is one of what are known as the '3Es' – criteria often used to assess performance of non profit making organisations in particular.
>
> - **Economy** – spending money frugally
> - **Efficiency** – getting out as much as possible for what goes in
> - **Effectiveness** – getting done, by means of economy and effectiveness, what was supposed to be done

(a)   *Step 1.*   **Determine seasonal variations**

Trend figures are found using the trend equation $y = 10,000 + 4,200q$

Year	Quarter	Actual (Y)	Trend (T)	Seasonal variation (Y/T)
1	1	15,620	14,200	1.10
	2	15,640	18,400	0.85
	3	16,950	22,600	0.75
	4	34,840	26,800	1.30
2	1	34,100	31,000	1.10
	2	29,920	35,200	0.85
	3	29,550	39,400	0.75
	4	56,680	43,600	1.30

No averaging is necessary as the seasonal variations are the same in both years.

Step 2.   **Determine trend figure for the third quarter of year 3**

$y = 10,000 + 4,200q$

If $q = 11$, the trend figure for the number of passengers carried $= 10,000 + (4,200 \times 11) = 56,200$.

Step 3.   **Apply the appropriate seasonal variation to determine the expected number of passengers**

Seasonal variation for quarter 3 $= 0.75$

$\therefore$ Expected number of passengers $= 56,200 \times 0.75 = 42,150$

(b)   The equation for the Transit staff cost is in the form $y = 23,000 + 3x$ because the total cost per quarter is made up of a fixed cost of £32,000 and a variable cost per passenger carried of £3.

(c) The number of passengers to be carried in the third quarter of year 3 = 42,150 (from (a)).

$\therefore$ x in the cost equations = 42,150

Cost item	Relationship		Expected cost
			£
Premises costs	y = 260,000		260,000
Premises staff	y = 65,000 + 0.5x	£(65,000 + (0.5 × 42,150))	86,075
Power	y = 13,000 + 4x	£(13,000 + (4 × 42,150))	181,600
Transit staff	y = 32,000 + 3x	£(32,000 + (3 × 42,150))	158,450
Other	y = 9,100 + x	£(9,100 + 42,150))	51,250
Total cost			737,375

(d) **Reasons for differences between the actual data for the third quarter of year 3 and the predicted values**

(i) The **pattern of trend and seasonal variation** used to establish the estimated number of passengers **might not continue** in the future. For example, a competing transport operator might start to provide a link between the airport and the city centre at the beginning of year 3, with obvious effects on passenger numbers. Any inaccuracies in the number of passengers will obviously impact on the cost estimates, given that the number of passengers is a variable in the cost relationships.

(ii) **Random variations** may upset the pattern of trend and seasonal variations. For example, the event such as that which occurred in New York in September 2001 would have a significant impact on passenger numbers.

(iii) The **relationship** between passenger numbers and the time periods **may not be linear.**

(iv) As well as being affected by the period of time, the number of passengers travelling **could be affected by another variable.**

(v) An **additive model** might be **more appropriate** than a multiplicative model.

(vi) No account has been taken of **inflation**. Actual costs may therefore be higher than those estimated.

(vii) One or more of the **costs** might be **dependent on another factor** as well as the number of passengers.

(viii) Alternatively, the **relationship** between the **quarterly costs** and **passenger numbers might not be linear.**

(e) REPORT

To: Board of directors of PMF plc
From: Management accountant   Date: 2 November 20X1
Subject: **The effectiveness of the transport service**

1   Introduction

1.1 This report looks at the **reason why PMF plc should consider the use of non-financial performance** measures to measure the effectiveness of the transport service and suggests a **number of such measures** that could be used.

2   Effectiveness

2.1 Effectiveness is the relationship between an organisation's outputs (be they units of product X or a service such as carrying a passenger on a transit link) **and its**

objectives. In other words, it looks at the **degree to which objectives have been met.**

2.2   PMF plc might therefore be effective if, in carrying passengers, it has met am objective of 90% or more of arrivals being no more than three minutes late.

3   Non-financial performance measures

3.1   In today's competitive environment we are competing in terms of both the quality/reliability of the service we provide and customer satisfaction. Our **objectives** reflect this shift in emphasis **away from financial goals** such as providing a service at the lowest possible cost **towards those that focus on the way in which we can meet customer needs.**

3.2   Our **success in achieving these new objectives** cannot be measured by output from a traditional responsibility accounting system. It requires the use of a **range of measures** incorporating those that are financial as well as those which are non-financial.

4   Examples of non-financial performance measures to measure effectiveness

4.1   Number of trains running no more than 3 minutes late (for an objective concerned with punctuality)

4.2   Number of trains cancelled (for an objective concerned with punctuality)

4.3   Number of complaints received about staff (for an objective concerned with providing a courteous service)

4.4   % growth in passenger numbers (for an objective concerned with growth in customer numbers)

4.5   Training time per employee (for an objective concerned with providing staff with adequate training)

4.6   Number of injuries per thousand passengers carried (for an objective concerned with passenger safety)

5   I hope this information has proved useful but if you have any further questions please do not hesitate to contact me.

Signed: Management accountant

31   FGH HOLIDAYS

> **Pass marks**. Part (a) simply requires you to plug the numbers given into the appropriate formula but be careful when pressing the buttons on your calculator. Part (b) requires you to understand what it is you are calculating. This is a useful question if you had previously thought of linear regression as merely a form of torture devised by examiners. Don't forget that the linear regression equation of Y on X will be provided in the exam if necessary. Don't copy it down incorrectly. And don't calculate ΣX, ΣX^2 and so on yourself. They are provided!
>
> Make sure you don't come up with an 'impossible' answer: always check for reasonableness.

(a)   The **regression line equation is y = a + bx** where

$$b = \frac{n\Sigma XY - \Sigma X \Sigma Y}{n\Sigma X^2 - (\Sigma X)^2}$$

$$a = \overline{Y} - b\overline{X}$$

Using the figures given:

$$b = \frac{(10 \times 26{,}869) - (143 \times 1{,}411)}{(10 \times 2{,}881) - (143)^2} = \frac{66{,}917}{8{,}361} = 8.003, \text{ say } 8.$$

$$a = 1{,}411/10 - (8 \times 143/10) = 26.7$$

$$\therefore Y = 26.7 + 8X$$

This means that the number of holidays (Y) booked in, say, August will be 26.7 plus 8 times the number of brochures (in hundreds). If **no brochures were mailed** about 27 **holidays would still be booked**.

The **correlation coefficient** can be calculated using the formula:

$$r = \frac{n\Sigma XY - \Sigma X \Sigma Y}{\sqrt{\left(n\Sigma X^2 - (\Sigma X)^2\right)\left(n\Sigma Y^2 - (\Sigma Y)^2\right)}}$$

Using the numbers given:

$$r = \frac{(10 \times 26{,}869) - (143 \times 1{,}411)}{\sqrt{\left[(10 \times 2{,}881) - (143)^2\right]\left[(10 \times 257{,}229) - (1{,}411)^2\right]}}$$

$$= \frac{66{,}917}{\sqrt{8{,}361 \times 581{,}369}} = \frac{66{,}917}{69{,}720}$$

$$= 0.96$$

(b) The coefficient of determination in the **situation described** in (a) is $0.96^2 = 0.92$: this means that **92% of the variation in holidays can be explained by variation in brochures mailed**.

The coefficient of determination in the **second scenario** is only 0.46 (0.68^2) or **46%**. The regression line equation implies that **57 holidays would be booked even if no brochures were sent out**.

Common sense would suggest that holidaymakers are likely to **spend some time considering** which holiday to book. The delay may well be more than one month and it would be instructive to do some further calculations to see if there is a **stronger correlation between, say, holidays at time t and brochures at time t − 2**.

32   **MOC**

> **Pass marks**. This question is based on the multiplicative model for time series in which actual sales are estimated by trend × seasonal factor, where the average seasonal variation of, say, + 40% must first be converted into the seasonal factor 1.4.

(a)   Trend Y = 300 + 20X

For each new quarter, the trend increases by 20.

Hence trend forecasts for the remaining quarters of 20X7 are 520 + 20, 540 + 20, 560 + 20, ie 540, 560, 580.

(i)   If **average seasonal variations apply**, the sales forecasts are as follows.

Q_2: $540 \times 0.8 = 432$ units

Q_3: $560 \times 0.8 = 448$ units

Q_4: $580 \times 1.4 = 812$ units

(ii) **If seasonal variations are double the average,** ie -40%, -40%, $+80\%$ the sales forecasts are as follows.

Q_2: $540 \times 0.6 = 324$ units

Q_3: $560 \times 0.6 = 336$ units

Q_4: $580 \times 1.8 = 1{,}044$ units

(b) (i) **Total sales forecast** $= 2{,}212$ units

Forecast contribution $= £5 \times 2{,}212$

$= £11{,}060$

(ii) **Total sales forecast** $= 2{,}224$ units

Forecast contribution $= £5 \times 2{,}224$

$= £11{,}120$

The **marketing manager's views** on seasonal variability in 20X7 **do not greatly affect the forecasts of either total sales or total contribution.** They do however have quite a **marked effect** in **shifting demand and contribution** for about 200 units (ie about £1,000) **from the second and third to the fourth quarter.** This may create **cash flow problems** and **storage problems** if MOC produces holdalls according to the usual pattern of seasonality and then the marketing manager's views turn out to be correct. Despite the above warnings, it would be safest for MOC to **prepare for the usual pattern** of demand because **otherwise** there is a danger that they will **fail to meet demand** in the second and third quarters.

The **reliability** of both sets of forecasts depends upon the **continuation of the previous trend** as well as upon the **forecast seasonality**. It also assumes that there will be **no unforeseen events**.

(c) The **trend equation** could have been obtained using a **special package** which will **perform regression** and **correlation analysis** or, alternatively, the **formulae** for regression and correlation coefficients could have been inserted into a **spreadsheet**.

Regardless of the type of package being used, the data comprises corresponding X and Y values. The X value shows which quarter the Y value relates to, with X = 1 in the first quarter for which there is a Y value, X = 2 for the second quarter and so on.

We are told that the Y values are the **actual unit sales** but these are **very volatile** and so it would probably be better to calculate a **moving average trend** of the sales and use those figures as the Y values in the regression equation to forecast the trend. This could also be done on a **spreadsheet**. In any case, it is important to calculate the **correlation coefficient** for X and Y to check that there is a **linear relationship** between them and this will be much stronger if the Y values are **moving averages** rather than **actual sales figures**.

33 FURNITURE STORE

Pass marks. This question required quite a lot of computation, and the production of a neat graph, for 25 marks. When calculations are made under time pressure, errors are very likely. It is therefore essential that you show workings, so that credit can be given for method.

(a, b)

Furniture store
Graph of sales data and deseasonalised sales data

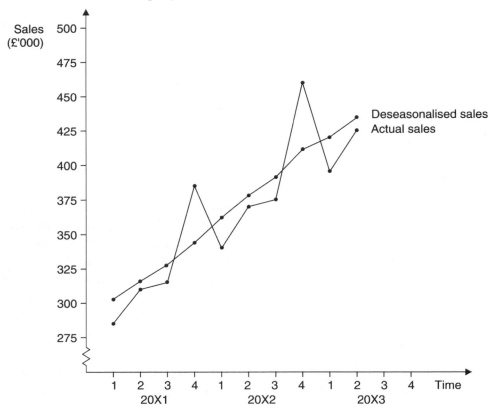

It is clear that the **trend** is a **rising** one. **Seasonal adjustments** expressed in terms of pounds of sales, as with the **additive model**, would therefore become **out of date**. Seasonal adjustments need to be expressed as **percentages** of current trend values, so that they **do not fall as proportions of trend** values. The multiplicative model is therefore more appropriate than the additive model.

The trend is found on removing the seasonal indices from the actual data ($Y = T \times S$ and so $Y/S = T$). This gives the following values, which are plotted on the graph above.

Year	Quarter	Deseasonalised sales data (actual ÷ seasonal indices) £'000
20X1	1	303
	2	316
	3	328
	4	344
20X2	1	362
	2	378
	3	391
	4	411
20X3	1	420
	2	434

(c) The trend line is to be found by applying least-squares regression to the trend data. **Time** is the **independent** variable and the **quarters** will be **numbered from 1 to 10.**

X	Y	X^2	XY
1	303	1	303
2	316	4	632
3	328	9	984
4	344	16	1,376
5	362	25	1,810
6	378	36	2,268
7	391	49	2,737
8	411	64	3,288
9	420	81	3,780
10	434	100	4,340
55	3,687	385	21,518

For a regression line **Y = a + bX**, we have

$$b = \frac{10 \times 21{,}518 - 55 \times 3{,}687}{10 \times 385 - 55^2} = \frac{12{,}395}{825} = 15.02$$

$$a = \frac{3{,}687}{10} - 15.02 \times \frac{55}{10} = 286.09.$$

The **trend line** is therefore Y = **15.02X + 286.09.** This means that sales of at least £286,090 will be made every quarter. Sales will increase by £15,020 every quarter.

Sales in £'000 = 286.09 + 15.02 × quarter number.

(d) The **estimated sales for the third quarter** of 20X3 are

$0.96 \times (286.09 + 15.02 \times 11)$ = 433.2576 = £433,257.60, say £433,000.

The **estimated sales for the fourth quarter** of 20X3 are

$1.12 \times (286.09 + 15.02 \times 12)$ = 522.2896 = £522,289.60, say £522,000.

(e) The estimates are likely to be **reasonably reliable,** as the period of extrapolation is only **two quarters into the future** and the **trend line** has been **computed** using data from **ten quarters.** However, there is always the possibility that the **trend** or the **pattern of seasonal variations** will **change suddenly** and unexpectedly. It is also possible that the **seasonal indices** used, being based on national averages, are **not entirely appropriate** for this particular business.

34 KDF LTD

> **Pass marks**. This question is a largely computational exercise and actually requires little specific technique. You simply need to perform lots and lots of calculations in part (a). The trick is to keep your workings neat and clear and look for patterns in the figures. Make sure that you own a calculator with a memory function and know how to use it.
>
> Take care with time allocation. Spend only 13 × 1.8 = 23 minutes on part (a). If you are unable to arrive at the profit-maximising rate of production, explain this at the beginning of part (b) and state that you are assuming that, say, the rate is 40,000 standard hours. You can then use this rate in your answer to (b) and you should only lose a minimum number of marks.

(a) Total demand over quarters 1 to 3 is 72,000 standard hours.

Production rate in quarters 1 to 3 must be the same.

∴ **Production rate in each of quarters 1 to 3** = 72,000/3 = **24,000 standard hours.**

We now need to **consider production rates at this minimum rate of 24,000 standard hours per quarter for quarters 1 to 3 and at four 4,000 standard hours increments. The production rate in quarter 4 will be the difference between 120,000 standard hours and the total for quarters 1 to 3.**

Rate for quarters 1 to 3 '000 std hours	Total for quarters 1 to 3 '000 std hours	Rate for quarter 4 '000 std hours
24	72	48
28	84	36
32	96	24
36	108	12
40	120	-

We can now start to **calculate the total costs at these production rates**.

Production rate quarters 1 to 3 '000 std hrs	Variable costs (W1) £'000	Holding costs (W5) £'000	Fixed costs £'000	Total cost £'000
24	1,728	36	1,200	2,964
28	1,536	108	1,200	2,844
32	1,536	180	1,200	2,916
36	1,632	252	1,200	3,084
40	1,944	324	1,200	3,468

Total costs are minimised at £2,844,000 and so the **profit-maximising quarterly production rate in quarters 1 to 3 is 28,000 standard hours.**

Workings

1   We begin by working out the **incremental variable costs** at the different output levels.

Output level Qs 1-3 Std hrs	Labour £per std hr	Material £per std hr	Combined cost £per std hr	Cost per '000 std hrs £'000	Total cost for the output range £'000
1 – 12,000	6	4	10	10	× 12 = 120
12,001 – 24,000	8	4	12	12	× 12 = 144
24,001 – 36,000	14	6	20	20	× 12 = 240
36,001 – 48,000	28	8	36	36	× 12 = 432

Now we can calculate the **variable costs**.

Production rate Qs 1-3 '000 std hrs	Incremental cost levels	Q1 costs £'000	Q2 costs £'000	Q3 costs £'000	Q4 costs £'000	Total £'000
24	1 – 12,000	120	120	120	120	
	12,001 – 24,000	144	144	144	144	
	24,001 – 36,000	–	–	–	240	
	36,001 – 48,000	–	–	–	432	
		264	264	264	936	1,728
28	1 – 12,000	120	120	120	120	
	12,001 – 24,000	144	144	144	144	
	24,001 – 36,000	80(W2)	80	80	240	
	36,001 – 48,000	–	–	–	–	
		344	344	344	504	1,536
32	1 – 12,000	120	120	120	120	
	12,001 – 24,000	144	144	144	144	
	24,001 – 36,000	160(W3)	160	160	–	
	36,001 – 48,000	–	–	–	–	
		424	424	424	264	1,536

Production rate Qs 1-3 '000 std hrs	Incremental cost levels	Q1 costs £'000	Q2 costs £'000	Q3 costs £'000	Q4 costs £'000	Total £'000
36	1 – 12,000	120	120	120	120	
	12,001 – 24,000	144	144	144	–	
	24,001 – 36,000	240	240	240	–	
	36,001 – 48,000	–	–	–	–	
		504	504	504	120	1,632
40	1 – 12,000	120	120	120	–	
	12,001 – 24,000	144	144	144	–	
	24,001 – 36,000	240	240	240	–	
	36,001 – 48,000	144(W4)	144	144	–	
		648	648	648	–	1,944

2   Cost of 4,000 units in 24,001 – 36,000 range = 4/12 × £240,000 = £80,000

3   Cost of 8,000 units in 24,001 – 36,000 range = 8/12 × £240,000 = £160,000

4   Cost of 4,000 units in 36,001 – 48,000 range = 4/12 × £432,000 = £144,000

5   **Q1 – Q3 production rate of 24,000 std hrs**

	Q1	Q2	Q3	Q4	Total
Cumulative production ('000 std hrs)	24	48	72	120	
Cumulative demand ('000 std hrs)	18	42	72	120	
Inventory at quarter end ('000 std hrs)	6	6	-	-	12

Holding cost = 12,000 × £3 = £36,000

Q1 – Q3 production rate of 28,000 std hrs

	Q1	Q2	Q3	Q4	Total
Cumulative production ('000 std hrs)	28	56	84	120	
Cumulative demand ('000 std hrs)	18	42	72	120	
Inventory at quarter end ('000 std hrs)	10	14	12	-	36

Holding cost = 36,000 × £3 = £108,000

Q1 – Q3 production rate of 32,000 std hrs

	Q1	Q2	Q3	Q4	Total
Cumulative production ('000 std hrs)	32	64	96	120	
Cumulative demand ('000 std hrs)	18	42	72	120	
Inventory at quarter end ('000 std hrs)	14	22	24	-	60

Holding cost = 60,000 × £3 = £180,000

Q1 – Q3 production rate of 36,000 std hrs

	Q1	Q2	Q3	Q4	Total
Cumulative production ('000 std hrs)	36	72	108	120	
Cumulative demand ('000 std hrs)	18	42	72	120	
Inventory at quarter end ('000 std hrs)	18	30	36	-	84

Holding cost = 84,000 × £3 = £252,000

Q1 – Q3 production rate of 40,000 std hrs

	Q1	Q2	Q3	Q4	Total
Cumulative production ('000 std hrs)	40	80	120	-	
Cumulative demand ('000 std hrs)	18	42	72	120	
Inventory at quarter end ('000 std hrs)	22	38	48	-	108

Holding cost = 108,000 × £3 = £324,000

(b) Profit at minimum Q1 – Q3 production rate (and a holding cost of £3 per std hr)

$$= (120{,}000 \times £28) - £2{,}964{,}000$$
$$= £396{,}000$$

Profit at profit-maximising Q1 – Q3 production rate (and a holding cost of £3 per std hr)

$$= (120{,}000 \times £28) - £2{,}844{,}000$$
$$= £516{,}000$$

Minimum Q1 – Q3 production rate

If holding cost is £0 per std hr, profit = £396,000 + holding cost = £396,000 + £36,000 = £432,000.

For every increase in holding cost per std hr by £3, profit will decrease by (inventory level × £3) = £36,000.

Holding cost £	Profit £'000
0	432
3	396
6	360
9	324

Profit-maximising Q1 – Q3 production rate

If holding cost is £0 per std hr, profit = £516,000 + holding cost = £516,000 + £108,000 = £624,000.

For every increase in holding cost per std hr by £3, profit will decrease by (inventory level × £3) = £108,000

Holding cost £	Profit £'000
0	624
3	516
6	408
9	300

We can now plot these holding cost/profit figures on a graph.

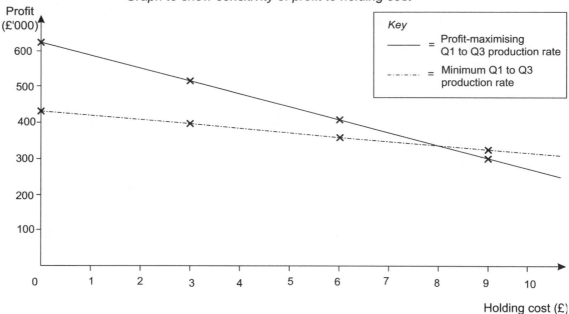

Graph to show sensitivity of profit to holding cost

It can be seen from the graph that both options give an equal profit when the holding cost is about £8 per standard hour.

(c)   **Budgeting and uncertainty**

Budgets use **estimates** of future volumes, capacities, costs, selling prices and so. The **actual** volumes, capacities, rates, costs and prices are **unlikely to be the same as those estimated**, however. It is therefore vital to **avoid giving managers the impression that a single point estimate** for budgeted profit is **cast in stone**. One way in which the mask of certainty can be stripped away is to use probabilities, another method is sensitivity analysis.

Sensitivity analysis

This involves determining by how much a particular variable can change before the original outcome becomes invalid. In other words, it involves calculation of the margin for error in the estimates.

Sensitivity analysis in this scenario

In the budgeting scenario in parts (a) and (b) above, **holding costs had to increase from £3 to £8 per standard hour** (that is, by £5 or 167%) before an alternative production rate became as profitable as the rate originally estimated as most profitable. The **margin for error in the estimate of holding costs was therefore quite high**. We could also have examined how sensitive our solution in part (a) was to a change in labour or material costs at particular production levels.

Sensitivity analysis and flexible budgets

The sensitivity of **budget estimates** to **changes in volume** can be examined **using flexible budgets.**

Sensitivity analysis and linear programming

Outputs from **computerised linear programming packages** (which might be used to determine the most profitable production mix for inclusion in the budget, say) usually include the **amount (or proportion) by which each figure in the formulation can change before an alternative optimum appears**, which is fundamentally a list of sensitivities.

Sensitivity analysis and spreadsheets

It is very easy to carry out sensitivity analysis on **spreadsheets**. All that is involved is the alteration of a particular variable within the model to the point where a new solution emerges. Figures produced from a sensitivity analysis may be **ranked** to identify the **most sensitive** variables in the model, that is the variable in which the smallest percentage change will lead to an alternative decision.

35   PQR AND PRODUCTS A, B, C

> **Pass marks.** The wording of the question suggests that direct material is a limiting factor. However, you should never assume this. Always use the available data to check first whether a limiting factor exists. If there is a limiting factor, you should select the products that earn the highest contribution per unit of limiting factor.

(a) **Initial workings**

	Product A	Product B	Product C	Total
Forecast 1				
Forecast sales quantity	500	800	2,200	
Materials – kg per unit	4	7	14	
Total materials required	2,000	5,600	30,800	38,400
Forecast 2				
Forecast sales quantity	350	700	1,000	
Materials – kg per unit	4	7	14	
Total material required	1,400	4,900	14,000	20,300

Materials supply is a limiting factor for forecast 1, but not for forecast 2.

Forecast 1

	Product A	Product B	Product C
	£	£	£
Sales price per unit	10.00	20.00	30.00
Variable cost per unit	6.50	11.00	18.10
	3.50	9.00	11.90
Contribution per kg of material	0.88	1.29	0.85
Ranking	2nd	1st	3rd

Optimum production plan for forecast 1

	Units	Kg of material	Contribution
			£
Product B	800	5,600	7,200
Product A	500	2,000	1,750
Product C	1,030	14,420 (balance)	12,257
		22,020	21,207

Forecast 2

	Product A	Product B	Product C	Total
	£ per unit	£ per unit	£ per unit	
Sales price	15.00	25.00	40.00	
Variable cost	6.50	11.00	18.10	
Contribution	8.50	14.00	21.90	
Sales volume (units)	350	700	1,000	
Total contribution	£2,975	£9,800	£21,900	£34,675

Forecast 2 should be adopted for the budget period. It produces a contribution of £34,675 which is £13,468 higher than the contribution for forecast 1.

The overall budgeted profit for forecast 2 will be as follows.

	£
Total contribution	34,675
General fixed costs	20,000
Profit	14,675

(b)
REPORT

To: Managing director
From: Management Accountant
Subject: **The budget preparation process**   Date: XX.XX.XX

1   Overview

1.1   As requested this report describes the **budget preparation process,** with particular reference to the principal budget factor, the budget manual and the role of the budget committee.

2   Principal budget factor

2.1   The **budget period** is the time period to which the budget relates. It is usually the same as the accounting year, subdivided into 12 or 13 control periods.

2.2   The **first step** in preparing the budget is to determine the **principal budget factor** for the budget period. This is the factor which **limits the organisation's activity**. The principal budget factor is often **sales volume** but it may be a factor of production such as machine capacity or the availability of material.

2.3   Once the principal budget factor has been identified the budget for it can be prepared, then **all other budgets must be co-ordinated to this**. For example, if sales is the principal budget factor or limiting factor, then the sales budget must be prepared first. This will then provide the basic data for the production budget, the material purchases budget and so on.

2.4   **If the principal budget factor is not identified** as the starting point then the resulting budgets may be **unachievable** and of **little use** for the purposes of planing and control.

3   Budget committee

3.1   The **co-ordination** and **administration** of the budgets is the responsibility of the **budget committee**.

3.2   **Every part of the organisation** should be **represented** on the committee, so there should be a representative from sales, production, marketing and so on.

3.3   The committee **meets on a regular basis** during the preparation of budgets, to ensure that **information** is **communicated** throughout the organisation and to clear up any **misunderstandings** or **misinterpretations** that may arise.

3.4   The multi-disciplinary and participative nature of the committee helps to ensure a **co-ordinated approach** to the budget preparation process. It also helps to **improve acceptance** of the budgets by those who are expected to work to achieve them.

4   Budget manual

4.1   The **budget manual** is usually issued by the budget committee.

4.2   It is a collection of **instructions** governing the **responsibilities** of persons and the **procedures, forms** and **records** relating to the preparation and use of budgetary data. It is effectively an **instruction/information manual** about the way budgeting operates in the organisation.

4.3   The **contents** of the budget manual would include the following.

- Explanation of the objectives of the budgeting process

- An organisation chart

- An outline of the principal budgets and the relationship between them

- A timetable for budget preparation

- Membership and terms of reference of the budget committee

- Specimen forms and instructions for completing them

- Account codes (a chart of accounts)

- The name of the person to whom queries should be addressed

- The assumptions to be used in budget preparation, eg the rate of inflation and key exchange rates

5   **Final stages of the budget preparation process**

5.1   Once the first set of budgets has been prepared and co-ordinated with each other, they are summarised into a **master budget** consisting of a **budgeted profit and loss account, budgeted balance sheet** and **cash budget**.

5.2   The **board of directors** will then **review** the budgeted results to see if they represent an acceptable plan for the organisation for the budget period.

5.3   If the plan is accepted then it becomes the planning and control document for the forthcoming period.

5.4   Often it will be **necessary to repeat** the whole process several times before a workable and acceptable budget is agreed for the whole organisation.

If you would like further information or would like me to expand on any of the points in this report please do not hesitate to contact me.

Signed: Management accountant

36   OBJECTIVE TEST QUESTIONS: OTHER ASPECTS OF BUDGETING

1   D   Imposed budgets are likely to be most effective in newly-formed organisations.

2   A

	Units	£
High activity	2,400	23,170
Low activity	1,650	20,770
	750	2,400

Variable cost per unit = £2,400/750   = £3.20 per unit

Fixed cost (substituting in high activity) = £23,170 − (2,400 × £3.20)

= £15,490

Budget cost allowance for 1980 units

	£
Variable cost (1,980 × £3.20)	6,336
Fixed cost	15,490
	21,826

If you chose **option B**, you divided the total cost for production of 1,650 units by 1,650 to get a 'cost per unit'. You then multiplied this cost by 1,980 to get the cost of 1,980 units. This is a valid approach only if you are dealing with variable costs.

If you chose **option C,** you divided the total cost for production of 2,400 units by 2,400 to get a 'cost per unit'. You then multiplied this cost by 1,980 to get the cost of 1,980 units. This is a valid approach only if you are dealing with variable costs.

If you chose **option D,** you selected the fixed cost.

3   B   A feedforward control system involves forecasting future outcomes, and comparing these with desired outcomes. Control action is then taken to minimise or remove any differences. **Models 1 and 3** are therefore feedforward control models.

Model 2 is a feedback control model, because it provides information on what has already happened, for comparison with a standard or plan (which in this case is the maximum or minimum stock level).

4   D   All of the measures would be appropriate for monitoring the innovation and learning perspective.

The higher the number of training days per employee (**measure (i)**), the more the organisation is focusing on learning, and improving the employees' skills.

The higher the percentage of revenue generated by new products and services (**measure (ii)**), the more innovative the organisation is being, rather than relying on established products and services.

It could be argued that the higher the labour turnover rate (**measure (iii)**), the more fresh ideas are being brought into the organisation as new employees join. This measure would need to be interpreted with care, however, as a high labour turnover rate may indicate dissatisfaction among employees, for example if they feel there is a lack of opportunity for training and further advancement.

5   A

6   A

7   D

8   B   Adjust price levels to a common basis, say index level 100.

	Volume Units	Total cost £	Cost at price level index = 100 £
High level	160,000	2,770,000 × (100/100)	2,770,000
Low level	110,000	2,092,800 × (100/109)	1,920,000
	50,000		850,000

∴ Variable cost per unit = £850,000/50,000 = £17

Now calculate the fixed costs.

	£
Total cost of 160,000 units (index 100)	2,770,000
Variable cost of 160,000 units (× £17)	2,720,000
Fixed costs (index 100)	50,000

Costs in year 3 at index 100

	£'000
Variable costs (120,000 × £17)	2,040
Fixed costs	50
	2,090

Costs in year 3 at index 112   = £2,090,000 × 112/100
                                = £2,340,800

Option A is the cost at index 100.

Option C is the answer if you rounded down instead of up.

Option D is the variable costs at index 100.

9   D   In the process of preparing budgets, managers might deliberately overestimate costs and/or understate sales, to avoid being blamed for overspending and poor results. This is known as building in budgetary slack.

Option A describes the increased budgeted cost allowance within a flexible budget.

Options B and C are incorrect because the budgetary plans are not finalised until they represent the optimum allocation of all available resources.

37 MPL LTD

> **Pass marks.** The key point to note in the scenario detail is that budgets are issued to the consultants, implying that an imposed system of budgeting is in place.

REPORT

(a) To: Board of directors of MPL Ltd
     From: Management accountant
     Subject: **Budgeting**   Date: 23 April 20X0

1   Overview

1.1 This report considers our present approach to budgeting, including the appropriateness of the format of the opening statement currently prepared.

2   Present approach to budgeting

2.1 Given that the budgets are **'issued to' consultants**, they clearly have very **little or no input to the budget process**. Budgets are **set centrally by senior management** and are **imposed** on consultants without consultants participating in their preparation.

3   Problems of present approach

3.1 Although there are advantages to such an approach (for example, strategic plans are likely to be incorporated into planned activities, there is little input from inexperienced or uninformed employees and the period of time taken to draw up the budgets is shorter), **dissatisfaction, defensiveness and low morale** amongst employees who must work with the budgets is often apparent.

3.2 The budget may be seen as a **punitive device** and **initiative may be stifled**.

3.3 More importantly, however, it is **difficult for people to be motivated to achieve targets that have been set by somebody else**.

  (i)   **Targets** that are **too difficult** will have a **demotivating** effect because **adverse efficiency variances** will always be reported.

  (ii) **Easy targets** are also **demotivating** because there is **no sense of achievement** in attaining them.

  (iii) **Targets set at the same levels as have been achieved in the past** will be too low and might **encourage budgetary slack**.

4   Alternative approach

4.1 Academics have argued that each individual has a **personal 'aspiration level'** which the individual undertakes for himself to reach, and so it may be more appropriate to adopt a **participative approach** to budgeting.

4.2 Budgets would be developed by the consultants and would be based on their perceptions of what is achievable and the associated necessary resources.

5   Advantages of alternative approach

5.1 Consultants are more likely to be **motivated** to achieve targets that they have set themselves and overall the budgets are likely to be more **realistic** (as senior management's overview of the business is mixed with operational level details and the expectations of both senior management and the consultants are considered).

6   Disadvantage of alternative approach

6.1   Allowing participation in the budget-setting process is **time consuming,** however, and can produce **budget bias.** It is generally assumed that the bias will operate in one direction only, consultants building **slack** into their budgets so targets are easy to achieve.

6.2   But **bias can work in two directions.** Optimistic forecasts may be made with the intention of pleasing senior management, despite the risk of displeasing them when optimistic targets are not met.

7   Format of the operating statement

7.1   The current format of the operating statement **classifies costs as either fixed or variable** in relation to the number of chargeable consultancy hours and **compares expected costs for the budgeted number of chargeable consultancy hours with actual costs incurred.**

8   Problem with current format

8.1   For **control purposes,** there is little point in comparing costs and revenues for the budgeted numbers of chargeable hours with actual costs and revenues if budgeted and actual hours differ.

9   Alternative format

9.1   An improved format would compare the **costs that should have been incurred given the actual number of chargeable consultancy hours** and **the actual costs incurred.**

9.2   Although fixed costs should be the same regardless of the hours charged, such a comparison requires **variable costs to be flexed** to the actual activity level.

9.3   More appropriate **variances** could then be calculated and denoted as either **adverse or favourable.**

9.4   The report should also **distinguish** between those **costs** which are **controllable** by consultants and those which are **uncontrollable.** Consultants' attention will then be focused on those variances for which they are responsible and which, if significant, require action.

I hope this information has proved useful. If you have any further questions, please do not hesitate to contact me.

Signed: Management accountant

(b) A spreadsheet model which requires only actual data to be input so that a flexed budget and variance calculations are produced would require **three separate areas.**

Output area

This would require four columns (original budget, flexed budget, actual costs and variances) and rows for chargeable consultancy hours, each cost classification (in total, not split into its fixed and variable components), total costs, fees charged and profit.

Input area

This would require cells containing the following details.

- Budget chargeable consultancy hours
- Actual consultancy hours
- Budget variable cost per consultancy hour for each cost classification
- Budget fixed cost for each cost classification

Calculation area

This would contain the formulae to do the following.

(i) **Produce the budget column.** For example, if the budget variable cost per chargeable consultancy hour for motor and travel costs was contained in cell B34, the budget fixed cost for motor and travel cost was contained in cell B35 and the budget chargeable hours in cell B27 (say), the formula would be B34*B27 + B35.

(ii) **Produce the flexed budget.** If the value for actual chargeable hours was contained in cell B28, the formula for the motor and travel costs would be B34*B28 + B35 (given that the budget fixed cost should be the same regardless of the number of chargeable hours).

(iii) **Produce the variances column.** The formulae would simply be the difference between the values in the flexed budget cells of the output area and those in the actual results cells. The formulae would need to be constructed in such a way that adverse and favourable variances were appropriately designated, brackets or minus signs perhaps signifying adverse variances.

(iv) **Produce the budget, flexed budget, actual and variance total costs and profit figures.**

Actual costs could then be **inserted** directly into the output area and the operating statement would be automatically prepared.

38   **TJ LTD**

> **Pass marks**. Profit may be expressed either as a percentage of cost of sales (**mark-up**) or as a percentage of sales (**margin**).
>
> - If profit is x% of sales (**margin**), then profit is also ($\frac{x}{100-x} \times 100\%$) of cost of sales (**mark-up**)
>
> - If profit is 16.67% of sales (**margin**), then profit is also 20% ($\frac{16.67}{100-16.67} \times 100\%$) of cost of sales (**mark-up**)

(a)   **Flexible budget statement for next year operating at 85% capacity**

	Workings		
Output	1	13,077 units	
		£	£
Sales revenue	9		5,911,484
Variable costs			
Direct materials	2	1,386,162	
Direct wages	3	2,357,129	
Variable production overhead	4	489,734	
Variable selling and distribution overhead	5	69,962	
			4,302,987
Contribution			1,608,497
Fixed costs			
Production overhead	6	330,000	
Selling and distribution overhead	7	161,250	
Administration overhead	8	132,000	
			623,250
Profit			985,247

Workings

1   65% of capacity = 10,000 units

∴ 100% of capacity = 10,000 ÷ 0.65 = 15,385 units

∴ 85% of capacity = (10,000 ÷ 0.65) × 0.85 = 13,077 units

∴ 75% of capacity = 11,538

∴ 55% of capacity = 8,462

2   Current direct material cost per unit   = £1,000,000 ÷ 10,000
                                             = £100 per unit

∴ Flexible budget allowance for next year   = £100 × 1.06 × 13,077
                                             = £1,386,162

3   Current direct wages cost per unit   = £1,750,000 ÷ 10,000
                                          = £175 per unit

∴ Flexible budget allowance for next year   = £175 × 1.03 × 13,077
                                             = £2,357,129

4   Production overhead increases by £53,830 for an increase in activity of (10,000 – 8,462) units

∴ Variable production overhead per unit = £35

∴ Variable overhead allowance for 85% capacity   = 13,077 × £35   = £457,695

Plus 7% increase   £32,039

Total allowance   £489,734

5   Selling overhead increases by £7,690 for an increase in activity of (10,000 – 8,462) units.

∴ Variable cost per unit = £5

∴ Variable overhead allowance for 85% capacity   = 13,077 × £5   = £65,385

Plus 7% increase   £4,577

Total allowance   £69,962

6   £
Total production overhead at 65% activity   650,000
Less variable overhead (10,000 × £35 (W4))   350,000
Fixed overhead this year   300,000
Plus 10% increase   30,000
Total allowance   330,000

7   £
Total selling overhead at 65% activity   200,000
Less variable overhead (10,000 × £5 (W5))   50,000
Fixed overhead this year   150,000
Plus 7.5% increase   11,250
Total allowance   161,250

8   Administration overhead = £120,000 × 1.1 = £132,000

9   The cost and selling price structure is as follows.

                                                    %
Sales price   100.00
Profit   16.67
Cost   83.33

∴ Profit as a percentage of cost = $\frac{16.67}{83.33} \times 100\% = 20\%$ of cost

		£
Total cost (£4,302,987 + £623,250)		4,926,237
Profit at 20% of cost		985,247
∴ Sales value		5,911,484

(b) Three **problems** which may **arise from the change in capacity level** are as follows.

   (i) There is likely to be a requirement for **additional cash for working capital,** for example stock levels and debtors will probably increase. This additional cash may not be available.

   (ii) It will probably be necessary to **recruit more direct labour.** The activities involved in advertising, interviewing and training may lead to increased costs.

   (iii) It may be necessary to **reduce the selling price** to sell the increased volume. This could have an **adverse effect on profits**.

(c) **Members of a budget committee**

   The budget committee would consist of a **representative from each function** in the organisation. It would usually be headed by the chief accountant or management accountant, and would also have a senior representative from each of the following functions.

   - Production
   - Sales and marketing
   - Personnel
   - Distribution
   - Purchasing

   Purposes of a budget committee

   (i) **Co-ordination** of the preparation of budgets. This includes drawing up timetables and distributing the budget manual.

   (ii) **Allocation** of responsibilities for the preparation of budgets.

   (iii) **Assisting** the preparation of budgets by providing information as required.

   (iv) **Control** of the budgetary process including highlighting and investigating the most significant variances.

   (v) **Reviewing** the usefulness of the budgetary process, and making appropriate improvements.

39   FIXED AND FLEXIBLE

> **Pass marks**. The key difference between fixed and flexible budgets which influences the answers to (a) and (b) is that actual costs are compared with expected costs at the expected level of activity under fixed budgeting, whereas under flexible budgeting actual costs are compared with actual costs at the actual level of activity. Note part (b) demands a discussion of the advantages and disadvantages of both fixed and flexible budgeting. An important point in (c) is that management requirements for output should govern the detail of input and the calculations made.

(a) These are important differences between fixed and flexible budgets at both the budget setting and performance review stages.

   (i) **Budget setting**

      (1) **Fixed budgets** are prepared on the basis that a certain volume of production and a certain volume of sales will be achieved (for example 10,000 units). **No alternatives are given to these levels.**

(2) A **flexible budget** is a budget which is designed to **change** as the **volume of activity changes**. A company may expect to sell 10,000 units. However it may prepare flexible budgets on the basis it produces and sells 8,000 units, or produces 10,000 units and sells 8,000 units.

Thus when preparing flexible budgets it will be essential to know **which costs vary with production**, and **which costs are fixed**. This information is not important with fixed budgeting because costs are only being budgeted at one level of production.

(ii) **Performance review**

(1) When a period is reviewed, a **fixed budget** would **not be adjusted** for the actual level of activity. Hence budgeted costs at the budgeted level of activity would be compared with actual costs at the actual level of activity; the actual level of activity may well differ from the budgeted level.

(2) **Flexible budgets** at the review stage would be set at the actual level of activity. Thus results at the actual level of activity can be compared with the results that should have been achieved at the **actual level of activity**.

(b) REPORT

To: The directors
From: The cost accountant   Date: 10 December 20X6
Subject: **Advantages and disadvantages of fixed and flexible budgets**

1   Fixed budgets – advantages

1.1 Preparing a fixed budget at one level will be **simpler** and **less time-consuming** than preparing flexible budgets at a number of levels.

1.2 A **number of costs will not vary** if actual output is different from expected output. These include plant costs and basic wage costs which are a significant proportion of our costs.

1.3 A fixed budget can provide a **focus for planning and co-ordination** of activities.

2   Fixed budgets – disadvantages

2.1 Preparing fixed budgets based on one activity level gives **no indication of what may happen** if actual sales and production do **differ** from expected levels. For example a fixed budget may not indicate at what level of activity cash flow or capacity problems might occur.

2.2 Fixed budgets will often **fail to provide a realistic target** against which performance can be judged. Certain costs will vary with production. It will be misleading to call managers to account for costs being greater than budgeted, if the reason for the difference is greater than expected activity levels, and not failure to control costs.

2.3 If managers know that they are being judged against a single pre-set standard, they will be more inclined to build unnecessary expenditure – **budgeting slack** – into their budgets to provide a cushion against unforeseen circumstances.

2.4 Managers may **spend up to budgetary limits even if** the expenditure is **unnecessary**, in order to justify the original allocation or to guard against the possibility of having a reduced budget in a future period.

3   Flexible budgets – advantages

3.1 Preparing flexible budgets at the **planning** stage may serve a number of purposes. Managers can assess what will be the **effect of activity falling short of**

target. As a result they may want to make plans for alternative uses of capacity. Alternatively, if **activity exceeds expectations**, managers can assess the **costs of extra resources** including overtime, sub-contracting work or extra machine hire.

3.2 Flexible budgets are helpful in **decision making**. Managers can set up 'what if' scenarios and assess the effects of various changes in the assumptions made.

3.3 Flexible budgets provide an appropriate **yardstick** for assessing how costs have been controlled. They enable comparisons to be made of results at the actual level of activity with results that would have been expected at that level of activity.

4   Flexible budgets – disadvantages

4.1 The **assumptions** on which flexible budgets are based may be **over-simplistic**. For example, variable costs per unit are assumed to be constant. In practice the availability for example of bulk discounts may mean that variable costs per unit vary at different levels of activity.

4.2 Managers may **not have the time** available to prepare flexible budgets to cover all possible scenarios.

4.3 Managers will have to make certain decisions at the start of the period for instance labour requirements, based on the **most likely activity level**. Hence this level **has to be identified** and highlighted.

4.4 Use of budgets generally may mean too much emphasis is placed on judging managers on how they control cost, and **not enough on market performance**.

5   Conclusion

5.1 Although flexible budgets should be used carefully, they do have significant advantages over fixed budgets, particularly as regards the assessment of actual performance.

Signed: Cost accountant

(c)   **Constructing a sales budget spreadsheet**

Step 1. **Input**

The input area will be used to enter the data such as sales volumes, prices, discounts etc.

The level of detail of input will be influenced by the desired output. Thus weekly estimates will be required if a weekly budget is being prepared; likewise details may also be required of expected sales by product or retail outlet.

Step 2. **Formulae**

The calculations area will be used to combine inputs to produce the desired outputs.

Formulae that will be used will include addition formulae, adding together sales for the year, or all sales for a particular region.

Percentage formulae may also be used. If for example gross profit is expected to be 40%, an appropriate calculation can be made.

Step 3. **Output**

The output section of the spreadsheet will collect together all the results of the calculations. There may be separate output sections for total sales budgets, and sales budgets by product or by outlet.

Advantages of spreadsheets

Using spreadsheets to prepare sales budgets has the following advantages.

(i)   **Format**. The format of rows and columns is a convenient way of presenting sales data.

(ii)   **Access**. Managers involved in budget preparation can have direct access to the spreadsheet model.

(iii) **Calculation**. A large number of calculations will be required when a sales budget is prepared, and use of a spreadsheet means managers will not need to perform these themselves. Hence time is saved.

(iv)   **Alteration**. Spreadsheets can be easily altered if expectations of forthcoming sales change. In addition they can be used for 'what if' analysis, with managers assessing the effects on revenue of changes in price and demand.

40   PDC LTD

> **Pass marks**. Remember that reports should always show the following.
>
> - Who the report is **to**
> - Who the report is **from**
> - The **subject** of the report
> - The **date** of the report
>
> Make sure that you don't provide a commentary on performance during March 20X7 rather than a commentary on the report itself.

(a)   REPORT

To: Management team
From: Cost accountant
Subject: **Format of monthly variance report**   Date: 17 April 20X7

1   Terms of reference and overview

1.1   Following my meeting with Mr Product Manager last week, I have undertaken a review of the format of the monthly variance report used throughout the organisation.

1.2   I have concluded that, because of the way in which the information is presented, the report could be **potentially misleading** for users. I therefore recommend that the format be adapted in a number of ways.

2   Former adaptions

2.1   **Information about volumes** (hrs, kgs and so on) should be reported **separately** in order to make the report **less confusing** and **easier to read** and **understand**. **All information** on the monthly variance report except that concerning sales and production volumes should be **monetary**.

2.2   The **volume variances** (those in hrs, kgs and so on) should be **converted** into **monetary amounts** in order that the financial implications of the variances are obvious.

2.3   Instead of calculating variances by comparing actual results and the original fixed budget results, **actual results should be compared with budget results flexed to the actual sales/production volumes**. The flexed results provide a far **more realistic** and **fair target** against which to measure actual results. For example, the direct labour (£) variance is currently calculated by comparing the

193

budgeted labour cost of producing 1,000 units with the actual labour cost of producing 9,905 units. A revised format should show a direct labour (£) variance calculated by comparing the actual direct labour cost with the budgeted direct labour cost of producing 9,905 units.

2.4 The report shows no flexed budget figures (the results which should have been expected at the actual production and sales levels achieved). A **flexed budget column** should therefore be included on the report.

2.5 Both **percentage** and **absolute variances** should be provided as the percentage figures currently provided draw attention away from the absolute financial impact of the variances.

2.6 The report does not provide a **narrative description** of any known reasons for the variances. Explanations would increase the report's user friendliness.

2.7 The report should use the **principles of exception reporting,** highlighting the most important variances in order to direct management attention to areas where action is most urgently required.

2.8 **Controllable fixed costs** (if they exist) should be included on the report and separately identified.

2.9 Information about **cumulative results to date** is needed. This will be particularly important when costs and revenues are subject to unpredictable monthly fluctuations. Management control is then more likely to concentrate on the cumulative trend in revenues, costs and variances.

3   Recommended layout

3.1 For the monthly variance report this is shown in the Appendix to this report. An identical format could be used for the presentation of cumulative results to date.

Signed: Cost accountant

APPENDIX

MONTHLY VARIANCE REPORT

	Original fixed budget Units	*Flexed budget* Units	*Actual results* Units	*Variances* *Quantity* £	*Price* £	*Total variance* £	%	*Notes*
Sales volume	X	X	X					
Production volume	X	X	X					
Sales revenue	X	X	X	X	X	X	X	
Costs								
Direct material	X	X	X	X	X	X	X	
Direct labour	X	X	X	X	X	X	X	
	X	X	X			X	X	
Contribution	X	X	X			X	X	
Controllable fixed costs	X	X	X		X	X	X	
Controllable profit	X	X	X			X	X	

The notes column could be used to provide an explanation of the reasons for various variances occurring and/or to highlight important variances.

(b) **Differences between budgetary control and standard costing**

(i) **Budgets are based on total costs and revenues**. The total budgeted material cost for producing product X might be drawn up, for example. Standard costs, on the other hand, are unit costs. For example, the standard cost of one unit of product X might be established.

(ii) **Budgetary control is based on controlling total expenditure;** it involves establishing targets or limits for a forthcoming period for a function or cost centre (such as a limit for the material cost of producing product X), comparing actual achievements or expenditures with the targets/limits and taking action to control any variances where necessary.

Standard costing also achieves control by comparison of actual results against a target but a standard cost is used to **control the efficiency with which resources are obtained and used.**

(iii) **The use of standard costing is limited** to situations where repetitive actions are performed and output can be measured. **Budgetary control** can be applied to **all functions**, even where output cannot be measured.

(iv) **A standard need not be expressed in monetary terms.** For example, a standard rate of output can be determined for control purposes without the need to put a financial value on it. In contrast, **budgets are expressed in financial terms.**

Many organisations find it useful to operate both of these control systems because **standard costing** can be used to control **production costs** (such as material and labour) whereas **budgetary control** can be used to control the **largely discretionary costs** of support departments such as administration and marketing.

(c) The **problems** of **extrapolating** past performance into the future stem from the **assumptions** made in such extrapolations.

(i) **Environmental conditions are assumed to remain unchanged**. This can render extrapolated data invalid. For example, fluctuations in exchange rates which were not present in the past may affect costs in the future.

(ii) **Operating conditions are assumed to remain constant.** For example, an extrapolation of costs may assume that fixed costs are constant. A change in the level of activity may cause a step in fixed costs, however, which would invalidate the extrapolation.

(iii) **The relationship between the variables is assumed to be linear.** For example, it may be assumed that if sales volume doubles then variable cost will also double. This may have been true for activity levels experienced in the past but it may not be valid to assume that the relationship will hold for activity levels in the future.

(iv) **It is assumed that all variables affecting past performance have been identified and that other conditions have remained constant.** The identified variables may not be the only factors affecting performance and the omission of other valid variables will affect the accuracy of the extrapolation.

These problems do not mean that the extrapolation of past performance into the future has no value. It is important that the resulting forecast is used with caution, however. Anyone relying on the forecast as the basis for decision making must be aware of its shortcomings and of any assumptions on which it is based.

41 **B LTD**

> **Pass marks.** The calculations in this question are fairly straightforward but there will also be marks awarded for presentation. Use a neat, tabular layout supported by detailed workings. In part (b) remember to check the unit cost rate at every level of activity in case the cost is semi variable.

(a) **Calculation of budgeted production (units)**

	Period 1	*Period 2*	*Period 3*	*Period 4*
Sales	15,000	20,000	16,500	21,000
Closing stock	2,500	3,300	2,500	3,000
	17,500	23,300	19,000	24,000
Less opening stock	4,000	2,500	3,300	2,500
Budgeted production	13,500	20,800	15,700	21,500

(b) **Direct labour**

Production in period 4 will be above 18,000 units so we need to know the bonus rate which applies above that level.

Direct labour rate below 18,000 units	= as periods 1 and 3
	= £270,000/13,500 or
	£314,000/15,700
	= £20 per unit
∴ Basic labour cost for period 2 production	= £20 × 20,800
	= £416,000
Actual labour cost	= £444,000
∴ Bonus paid for extra 2,800 units	= £(444,000 – 416,000) = £28,000
∴ Bonus per unit above 18,000 units	= £10

Direct materials

Constant rate per unit for all levels of output $= \dfrac{£108,000}{13,500} = £8$

Production overhead

The rate per unit is not constant for all levels of output so this is a semi-variable cost. Use the high-low method to determine the fixed cost and the variable cost per unit.

	Units	£
Period 2	20,800	154,000
Period 1	13,500	117,500
Change	7,300	36,500

∴ Variable cost per unit $= \dfrac{£36,500}{7,300} = £5$

∴ Fixed cost = £154,000 – (£5 × 20,800) = £50,000

Administration overhead

Let's use the high-low method again.

	Units	£
Period 2	20,800	106,600
Period 1	13,500	92,000
Change	7,300	14,600

∴ Variable cost per unit $= \dfrac{£14,600}{7,300} = £2$

∴ Fixed cost $= £106,600 - (£2 \times 20,800) = £65,000$

Selling overhead

Use the high-low method again, but this time based on sales volume.

	Units	£
Period 2	20,000	65,000
Period 1	15,000	60,000
Change	5,000	5,000

∴ Variable cost per unit   = £1

∴ Fixed cost   = £65,000 – (£1 × 20,000)
              = £45,000

COST BUDGET FOR PERIOD 4
PRODUCTION VOLUME 21,500 UNITS

		£'000	Budget cost £'000
Direct labour – basic rate	21,500 × £20	430.0	
– bonus	3,500 × £10	35.0	
			465.0
Direct materials	21,500 × £8		172.0
Production overhead – variable	21,500 × £5	107.5	
– fixed		50.0	
			157.5
Depreciation			40.0
Administration overhead – variable	21,500 × £2	43.0	
– fixed		65.0	
			108.0
Selling overhead – variable	21,000 × £1	21.0	
– fixed		45.0	
			66.0
Total budgeted cost			1,008.5

(c)   **VARIANCE REPORT FOR PERIOD 4**

	Budget £'000	Actual £'000	Variance £'000
Direct labour	465.0	458	7.0 Favourable
Direct material	172.0	176	4.0 Adverse
Production overhead	157.5	181	23.5 Adverse
Depreciation	40.0	40	-
Administration overhead	108.0	128	20.0 Adverse
Selling overhead	66.0	62	4.0 Favourable
	1,008.5	1,045	36.5 Adverse

(d)   **Criticisms of the assumptions on which the cost budgets have been prepared**

   (i)   **Volume may not be the only determinant of cost**. There could be many other factors to be taken into account such as inflation or changes in batch sizes.

   (ii)   **Variable costs may not be linear.** They may vary in a curvilinear fashion.

   (iii)   **Fixed costs may not be constant.** The planned range of activity is fairly wide and there may be a step in some of the fixed costs over this range.

   (iv)   The **variable elements of administration overhead may not all vary with production volume.** In addition to the comment at (i), it is possible that some costs will vary with sales volume, for example sales invoicing and credit control costs.

   (v)   **No allowance has been made for stock shrinkage,** in other words it has been assumed that all production will eventually be sold. No allowances are included for breakages, pilferage, deterioration and so on.

(vi) **Direct material costs may not be linear**. It may be possible to obtain bulk discounts at the higher levels of production.

(vii) **Depreciation** of production machinery **may not be constant** at all levels of output. It may be more appropriate to link depreciation to machine activity, perhaps by using a machine hour rate. The budgets would then give a better indication of the true cost of changes in activity levels.

42 RELUCTANCE

> **Pass marks.** Don't be tempted to write all you know about budgeting. You will simply produce irrelevant material which will gain no marks. Do not waste your valuable examination time in this way. Ensure that you continually refer back to the question to check that you answer is relevant to what is actually being asked.

Participative budgeting

This involves managers in **setting their own budgets**, in **contrast to** an authoritarian system of **imposed** budgets.

Reasons why managers may be reluctant to participate in the setting of budgets

(a) They may be **afraid** of undertaking tasks for which they have **not been trained**. They may have no financial knowledge and no clear understanding of how budgets are prepared and used.

(b) Managers may be reluctant to take on the **extra work** involved, especially if they cannot see how it will benefit them.

(c) They may mistrust their managers' motives for involving them in the budgetary process. They may feel that the participation is only a **cosmetic exercise** and that their views and input are not really valued.

(d) Managers may feel that they will be more open to **criticism** if variances arise against a budget which they have prepared themselves.

Overcoming these reservations

(a) All managers who are to be involved must be **fully trained** and conversant with the organisations' budgetary planning and control processes. In addition a well designed **budget manual** must be circulated, giving details of who is responsible for each budget, a timetable for their preparation, the name of the person to ask for help and advice and so on.

(b) The **advantages** of a participative planning system must be carefully **explained** to the mangers and it may be necessary to **reward** them for the extra work involved. Mangers can also be rewarded for achieving budget targets through the payment of bonuses and so on.

(c) The participation must be real and must **not be 'pseudo-participation'**. Managers' input must always be taken into account and if their decisions or proposals are overruled then the reasons must be clearly explained to them.

(d) Budgets must **not be used in a punitive way**. In other words managers must not be subject to severe criticism if they do not achieve budget targets. Adequate opportunity must be given in the control process for managers to explain the reasons for any variances which arise.

Benefits from participation

(a) **Morale** may **improve** as a result of the managers feeling more involved in the running of the organisation. Their jobs will be enriched and they may be motivated by feeling that their views are valued and sought by senior management.

(b) Managers who are involved in the day to day running of the organisation may be in a better position to provide a **realistic forecast** for future activities in their areas.

(c) If managers have been involved in setting a budget then they will be **more willing to commit themselves to achieving it**. The aspiration levels of the individuals and the departments involved would have been taken into account and the budget is more likely to be viewed as a realistic and achievable target.

(d) Managers who have been involved in the planning process will understand the data contained in the budgets and will more easily be able to **explain any variances** which arise.

(e) Involvement in the planning process will help managers to obtain a **wider view of the organisation** outside their own department. They will understand how their activities affect other parts of the organisation. There may be a reduction in dysfunctional behaviour and goal congruence should improve.

43   PREPARATION QUESTION: BALANCED SCORECARD

> **Pass marks**. This preparation question might be worth 10 or 12 marks if it were part of an examination question.

Traditional financial accounting measures such as return on investment and earnings per share have been criticised as giving misleading signals for continuous improvement and innovation – activities which today's competitive environment demands. The balanced scorecard is a way of measuring performance which **integrates traditional financial measures with operational, customer and staff issues** which are vital to the long-term competitiveness of an organisation.

The four perspectives

The balanced scorecard allows managers to look at their business from four important perspectives.

(a) **Customer perspective**. This section of the balanced scorecard requires customers themselves to identify a specific set of goals and performance measures relating to what actually matters to them, be it time, quality, performance of the product or service. In order to view the organisation's performance through customers' eyes, market researchers are hired to assess how the organisation is performing.

(b) **Internal business perspective**. Measures from the customer's perspective need to be translated into the actions the organisation must take to meet these expectations. The internal business perspective of the balanced scorecard identifies the business processes that have the greatest impact on customer satisfaction, such as quality and employee skills.

(c) **Innovation and learning perspective**. Whilst the customer and internal process perspectives identify the current parameters for competitive success, the organisation needs to learn, innovate and improve to satisfy future needs. It must produce new products, reduce costs and add value. Performance measures must emphasise continuous improvement in meeting customer needs. Examples of measures might be the length of time it takes to create new products or the percentage of revenue which comes from new products.

(d) **Financial perspective.** This includes traditional measures such as profitability and growth but the measures are set through talking to shareholders direct. The financial perspective looks at whether the other three perspectives will result in financial improvement.

The **success** of the balanced scorecard approach lies in **viewing all of the measure as a whole**.

Using the balanced scorecard

Once those factors that are important to the organisation's success have been established, performance measures and targets for improvement are set. The measures and targets must be clearly communicated to **all levels of management and employees** so that they understand how their efforts can impact upon the targets set. The balanced scorecard can then become the most important monthly management report.

44   SMALLTOWN COLLEGE I

> **Pass marks**. Any clear format will be acceptable for your budget. Note that you are asked to prepare a budget which maximises profits. This means that unsubsidised Social Sciences students must not be included because they produce a negative contribution. You must therefore restrict their numbers to those who will be subsidised.
>
> This was part of a question in the *Management Accounting Applications* exam and was worth only 11 marks. It is probably a bit more complex than a budget preparation question that you might encounter in Paper 8 but as we have given you 45 minutes you should be able to make a fair attempt at it.

UNW BUDGET FOR 20X7

	Note	Total	Business	Engineering	Social Sciences	Reprographics	Services
Number of students	(1)		760	460	100		
Expenditure		£'000	£'000	£'000	£'000	£'000	£'000
Variable costs	(3)	(5,970)	(3,040)	(2,300)	(300)	-	(330)
Fixed costs		(8,076)	(3,126)	(2,580)	(890)	(800)	(680)
Study manuals	(4)	(1,260)	-	-	-	(1,260)	-
Cross charges							
reprographics	(5)	-	(1,174)	(948)	(41)	2,163	-
services	(6)	-	(611)	(370)	(80)	–	ep 1,061
Income							
Tuition fees		8,080	4,560	3,220	300	-	-
Subsidy	(2)	4,980	2,100	2,380	500	-	-
Profit/(Loss)		(2,246)	(1,291)	(598)	(511)	103	51

Notes

1   **Numbers of students**

This will depend on teaching capacity, demand and available subsidies. Assuming that fixed costs cannot be saved, **students should be accepted only if their fees and subsidies cover their variable costs**.

	Business £'000 per student	Engineering £'000 per student	Social Sciences £'000 per student
Variable costs	4.00	5.00	3.00
Study manuals @ 0.03	(30) 0.90	(40) 1.20	(8) 0.24
Services	0.25	0.25	0.25
	5.15	6.45	3.49
Tuition fee	6.00	7.00	3.00

Tuition fees are greater than the variable cost of Business and Engineering students but the opposite is true for Social Sciences students.

∴ **Take the maximum number of Business and Engineering students** (subject to staff capacity and demand constraints respectively) **but only those Social Sciences students who are subsidised.**

	Business	Engineering	Social Sciences
Number of students	760	460	100

∴ The variable cost of, for example, Business students is $760 \times 4 = 3,040$

2 **Subsidies receivable**

£'000 per student	5	7	5
Maximum number subsidised	420	340	100
Total (£'000)	2,100	2,380	500

3 **Services variable cost** $= 0.25 \times (760 + 460 + 100) = £330,000$

4 **Study manual cost** $= (760 \times 0.90) + (460 \times 1.20) + (100 \times 0.24) = £1,260,000$

5 **Reprographics cross charges**

	Business	Engineering	Social Sciences	Total
Total number of manuals	22,800*	18,400	800	42,000
Cross charge pro rata (£'000)	1,174***	948	41	2,163**

*760 students × 30 manuals
**Full cost plus 5% = (800 + 1,260) × 1.05 = 2,163
*** 22,800/42,000 × 2,163

6 **Services cross charges**

	Business	Engineering	Social Sciences	Total
Number of students	760	460	100	1,320
Cross charge pro rata (£'000)	611**	370	80	1,061*

*Full cost plus 5% = (330 + 680) × 1.05 = 1,061
**760/1,320 × 1,061

45   SMALLTOWN COLLEGE II

> **Pass marks**. Did you regurgitate all you knew about the theory of budgeting without relating your answer to the precise requirements of the question? It takes a bit longer to make your answer relevant to the question asked but it is time well spent because you will end up earning more marks.

(a) **The relevance of the first statement**

Why does conflict arise?

In many organisations, especially large ones, conflict often arises from a lack of understanding; for example if one department does not fully understand why another department operates in the way that it does, or if individuals do not understand the goals of the organisation, problems may occur.

Using a committee to relieve conflict

UNW's former budgetary process was based on a **committee** of senior staff who prepared the budgets. Such a system may have gone some way to **relieving conflict** due to misunderstanding because there would have been some **discussion and exchange of views** at meetings of the committee. The **lack of involvement of junior staff may have caused problems,** however; if individuals are not involved in setting the budgets that they are expected to achieve, behavioural problems can occur. If they do not participate in the budgeting process, such individuals may be unaware of the organisation's goals and will be less likely to accept those goals as their own; this may lead to a lack of goal congruence.

Using budgets prepared on a departmental basis to relieve conflict

With UNW's **budgets arranged on a functional basis, clear goals** such as profit maximisation **would not have been evident** (especially given the fact that UNW is not a commercial organisation). **Individuals might therefore have adopted their own goals which may have conflicted with those of the organisation.** The **new arrangement should give a better understanding of the organisation's goal of maximising profit.** Preparing the **budgets on a departmental basis** may also help to encourage a **feeling of team spirit,** with each department working towards its own goal of maximising profit.

The new budgets should also give departments a **better understanding of the value of services provided by other departments.** However, if the **cross charges** are not handled carefully they **can cause inter-departmental conflict** and so UNW needs to ensure that there are **adequate facilities for negotiation and communication** within the departments.

The relevance of the second statement

The new budget system is being used as a means of communicating the new objective of profit maximisation and the method of recording performance by departments. The budgets are being prepared by UNW's finance officer but it is not clear whether they are being imposed on departments or whether departments are being invited to participate in the process. **If the budgets are imposed,** this could **lead to conflict** because of the lack of participation and eventually to poor goal congruence as discussed above.

It seems **likely that the basic data for the budgets have been obtained from managers within the departments.** If this is the case, the process is more participative, since more junior managers are involved than previously and hence they are more likely to feel that they 'own' the budget. In this way, **top management are therefore using the budgeting procedures as a means of conveying power.** A further advantage to the new system is that **managers who are operating at the 'grass roots'** of UNW may be in a **better position to provide reliable forecasts** on which to base the budgetary projections than the senior staff previously involved in the process.

(b) **What is zero based budgeting (ZBB)?**

Zero-based budgeting is a system whereby the **budgets for an organisation's activities are drawn up as if each activity were being performed for the first time. Existing activities must be justified in exactly the same way as new proposals.**

Steps in ZBB

The first step in the process is for mangers within the organisation to specify the **'decision units'** within their area of authority. A decision unit is a programme of work or capital expenditure programme or area of activity which can be individually evaluated.

The next step is for each of the separate activities or decision units to be described in a **'decision package'.** This is a document which identifies and describes the specific activity in such as way that management can evaluate it and rank it in order of priority against other activities.

Decision packages

Decision packages may take two forms.

(i)   **Mutually exclusive packages.** Each of these contains an alternative method of performing the same task. The best option among the packages must be selected by cost benefit analysis, the others being discarded.

(ii) **Incremental packages.** A given activity is divided into different levels of effort. The base package describes the minimum amount of work that must be done to carry out the activity, while the other packages describe what additional work could be done and the associated costs and benefits.

Applications of ZBB

ZBB has generally found to be most valuable when applied to **support expenses** such as marketing and finance.

Advantages of ZBB

The ranking process forces management to **define its priorities,** although ranking may become difficult when a large number of services are being evaluated, many of which are regarded as essential. If all levels of management and staff become involved in the creation and evaluation of the decision packages, this can help them to feel **more committed** to achieving organisational objectives and budget targets and hence can provide 'a means of reconciling the conflicts between the components of an organisation'. Moreover, changing to ZBB can convey **power to lower levels of management** because they are involved in the preparation of decision packages.

46   SMALLTOWN COLLEGE III

> **Pass marks.** You may have devised a very different budgetary control report which might have earned just as many marks as ours. The key points to bear in mind are that the control measures should be measurable and useful in the context of the given scenario (an educational establishment rather than the usual manufacturing environment).
>
> In answering part (c), beware of writing all you know about the merits of different methods of transfer pricing.

MEMORANDUM

(a)   To: Chief executive of UNW
      From: Finance officer   Date: xx.xx.xx
      Subject: **Budgetary control report**

1   Introduction

1.1   As a result of our meeting earlier this week, I set out below a design for a new budgetary control report for each department and performance indicators to be used in conjunction with it.

2   Budgetary control report

2.1   I believe that the budgetary control report should be prepared using a flexible budget system, the variance analysis being based on a budget cost allowance for the actual activity in the period.

2.2   A **sample departmental report** and accompanying notes are set out below.

BUDGETARY CONTROL REPORT
FOR THE MONTH ENDING XX.XX.XX

	Original budget £'000	Flexed budget £'000	Variance against flexed budget £'000	Variance description/analysis
Income				
Tuition fees	xxx	xxx (1)	xxx	= Tuition fee price variance
Subsidy	xxx	xxx (1)	xxx	= Subsidy rate variance (4)
Cross charges (2)	xxx	xxx (3)	xxx	
Expenditure				
Variable costs	xxx	xxx (1)	xxx (5)	= Variable cost expenditure variance + variable cost efficiency variance
Fixed costs	xxx	xxx (6)	xxx	= Fixed cost expenditure variance
Cross charges: (7)				
reprographics	xxx	xxx (8)	xxx	= Manual usage variance + manual price variance (9)
services	xxx	xxx (1)	xxx	= Service price variance (9)
Profit	xxx	xxx	xxx	

Notes

1   The budget cost allowance/revenue for these items would be **flexed according to student numbers**.

2   The classification of cross charges as income **applies only to support departments.**

3   Budgeted cross charge revenues are **flexed according to actual student numbers for the service department, and for the reprographics department according to the budgeted number of manuals for the actual number of students.**

4   The variance for cross charge revenues in the support departments would be analysed as follows.

   Reprographics: manual output variance (more or less manuals produced than standard for the number of students enrolled) and **manual price variance** (manual price charged was higher or lower than standard)

   Services: **service price variance** (price charged per student was higher or lower than standard)

5   Variable costs can be **further analysed** by expense type, such as staff costs, consumables, and so on. If there are any hourly paid teaching staff, the variance for their wages can be analysed into a staff rate variance and staff usage variance. The staff usage variance and the variable overhead efficiency variance would be based on student numbers according to the budgeted student/staff ratio.

6   For fixed costs, the flexed budget equals the original budget. This could also be **further analysed** by type of expenditure.

7   The classification of cross charges as expenditure applies only to teaching departments.

8   Reprographics would be flexed according to the *budgeted* number of manuals for the actual number of students.

9   These variances assume that the cross charge per manual/student is recalculated each month based on the support department's actual costs for that month.

10   This variance will highlight any under or over recruitment or higher than planned drop out rates.

3   Performance indicators

3.1   The main performance indicators to be used in conjunction with the budgetary control report would be as follows.

(i)   Actual profit per student

(ii)   Total cost per student (the main focus if the level of fees is outside the control of the department manager)

This can be further analysed as required to monitor staff costs per student, occupancy costs per student, and so on.

(iii) Staff/student ratio

(iv)   Students still attending/students originally enrolled (to monitor each teaching department's ability to control student drop out rates)

4   Summary

4.1   I hope that this provides a useful framework for the design of the new budgetary control report. If you would like to discuss any item further please do not hesitate to contact me.

Signed: Finance officer

(b) The lecturer is of the view that **financial controls** can in themselves affect the process that they are intended to control, that they **can have a behavioural impact** on the managers being monitored.

Rigid application of a few performance indicators

Performance indicators that are applied rigidly and punitively can result in managers **concentrating** on the achievement of an organisation's objectives and the **required performance in these areas to the detriment of all other factors** and other parts of the organisation.

(i)   For example, a manager **may cut staffing levels to the bare minimum in order to achieve a target staff-student ratio**. This may not be appropriate in the circumstances; the group of students may be less able than usual, for example. The result of such an action might be a lowering in educational standards and a potential knock-on adverse effect on UNW's reputation which may have repercussions for the demand for the university's courses in the longer term.

(ii)   Another short-term action which may affect UNW's long-term achievements is **cutting back staff training in order to achieve a strictly-applied expenditure budget**. The university depends on maintaining the quality of its teaching staff and excessive cutbacks on training could have an adverse impact on longer-term performance.

A **rigid approach to monitoring** the performance of only a few factors can therefore have an **adverse impact on a department's performance**, particularly in the longer term.

Use of a wide range of performance measures

The chief executive needs to **consider** the use of a **wide range of performance measures**, both financial and non-financial, which take account of controllable and non-controllable costs and which must be sympathetically applied. The **balanced scorecard approach**, involving a wide range of measures, might be appropriate. Due regard must also be given to measuring certain contentious aspects of performance such as the quality of education provided and student and staff morale.

47 OBJECTIVE TEST QUESTIONS: MODERN BUSINESS ENVIRONMENT AND COST REDUCTION

1　D

2　D　Profit maximisation is *not* a key success factor.

3　C

4　C　The four aspects of value to consider are cost, exchange, use and esteem.

5　D　**Issue I**　WCM aims to know what customer requirements are, to supply customers on time and to change products/develop new products as customer needs change.

　　　　Issue II　As above, WCM aims to change products/develop new products as customer needs change.

　　　　Issue III WCM incorporates the principles of TQM.

　　　　Issue IV This could lead to excess stocks, possibly of unwanted products, but JIT manufacturing is a key feature of WCM.

6　B　External failure costs are costs arising outside the manufacturing organisation of failure to achieve a specified quality (after transfer of ownership to the customer).

7　B　**Method I**　Even though they are more expensive, better quality materials might save costs because they are less likely to be faulty and/or might last longer.

　　　　Method II　This is a method of cost control rather than cost reduction.

　　　　Method III Costs can be reduced by improving productivity levels.

　　　　Method IV Cheaper materials may impair the suitability of goods or services for the use intended.

8　C　**I:** A TQM programme, in contrast to standard costing, aims to make all personnel aware of, and responsible for, the importance of supplying the customer with a quality product.

　　　　II: In a standard costing environment, processes or products must be standardised and repetitive so that standards can be established whereas in a TQM environment continual improvements are likely to alter prices, quantities of inputs and so on.

　　　　III: Attainable standards, which make some allowance for waste and inefficiencies, are more common. The use of such standards conflicts with the elimination of waste which is a vital ingredient of a TQM programme.

　　　　IV: Such an ethos is at odds with the philosophy of continuous improvement inherent in a TQM environment.

9   C   **I**   A stock-out in a hospital could be fatal.

        II   JIT, originated by Toyota, was designed at a time when all of Toyota's manufacturing was done within a 50 km radius of its headquarters.

        III   JIT is not suitable in all circumstances.

        IV   Because stocks are held at minimum level, there is very little risk that they might become obsolete.

10 B   **I**   JIT requires close integration of suppliers with the company's manufacturing process.

        II   In other words, JIT requires the use of machine cells.

        III   JIT recognises machinery set-ups as a non-value-adding activity.

        IV   Each component on a production line is produced only when needed for the next stage.

48   JIT

> **Pass marks.** In the exam you would probably only need to provide five (relevant) financial benefits in part (b) to gain the full five marks.

(a)   JIT production systems will include the following features.

Multiskilled workers

In a JIT production environment, production processes must be shortened and simplified. **Each product family is made in a workcell based on flowline principles.** The variety and complexity of work carried out in these work cells is increased (compared with more traditional processes), necessitating a group of dissimilar machines working within each work cell. **Workers must therefore be more flexible and adaptable, the cellular approach enabling each operative to operate several machines.** Operatives are trained to operate all machines on the line and **undertake routine preventative maintenance**.

Close relationships with suppliers

JIT production systems often go hand in hand with JIT purchasing systems. **JIT purchasing** seeks to **match the usage of materials with the delivery of materials** from external suppliers. This means that **material stocks can be kept at near-zero levels.** For JIT purchasing to be successful this requires the organisation to have confidence that the supplier will deliver on time and that the supplier will deliver materials of 100% quality, that there will be no rejects, returns and hence no consequent production delays. The **reliability of suppliers is of utmost importance** and hence the company must **build up close relationships** with their suppliers. This can be achieved by doing **more business with fewer suppliers** and placing **long-term orders** so that the supplier is assured of sales and can produce to meet the required demand.

Machine cells

With JIT production, factory layouts must change to reduce movement of workers and products. Traditionally machines were grouped by function (drilling, grinding and so on). A part therefore had to travel long distances, moving from one part of the factory to the other, often stopping along the way in a storage area. All these are non-value-added activities that have to be reduced or eliminated. **Material movements between operations are therefore minimised by eliminating space between work stations and grouping machines or workers by product or component** instead of by type of work performed. Products can flow from machine to machine without having to wait for the next stage of processing or returning to stores. **Lead times and work in progress are thus reduced.**

Quality

Production management within a JIT environment seeks to both **eliminate scrap and defective units during production and avoid the need for reworking of units.** Defects stop the production line, thus creating rework and possibly resulting in a failure to meet delivery dates. Quality, on the other hand, reduces costs. Quality is assured by **designing products and processes with quality in mind, introducing quality awareness programmes** and **statistical checks on output quality,** providing **continual worker training** and implementing **vendor quality assurance programmes** to ensure that the correct product is made to the appropriate quality level on the first pass through production.

Set-up time reduction

If an organisation is able to **reduce manufacturing lead time** it is in a better position to **respond quickly to changes in customer demand.** Reducing set-up time is one way in which this can be done. Machinery set-ups are non-value-added activities which should be reduced or even eliminated. **Reducing set-up time** (and hence set-up costs) also makes the manufacture of **smaller batches more economical and worthwhile;** managers do not feel the need to spread the set-up costs over as many units as possible (which then leads to high levels of stock). Set-up time can be reduced by the **use of one product or one product family machine cells,** by **training workers** or by the use **of computer integrated manufacturing (CIM).**

(b) JIT systems have a number of financial **benefits.**

- Increase in labour productivity due to labour being multiskilled and carrying out preventative maintenance

- Reduction of investment in plant space

- Reduction in costs of storing stock

- Reduction in risk of stock obsolescence

- Lower investment in stock

- Reduction in costs of handling stock

- Reduction in costs associated with scrap, defective units and reworking

- Higher revenue as a result of reduction in lost sales following failure to meet delivery dates (because of improved quality)

- Reduction in the costs of setting up production runs

- Higher revenues as a result of faster response to customer demands

49   WORLD CLASS MANUFACTURING

> **Pass mark.** This provides a good opportunity to demonstrate your knowledge of the modern business environment, but watch your time allocation. You are asked to describe briefly the principles because you then have to discuss the impact on budget preparation. Don't get carried away on the comparatively easy part: the second part of the question might be harder because you have to apply your knowledge but you would have to attempt it in the exam if you wanted to pass.

(a)   **Traditional incremental budgeting – what is it?**

The traditional approach to setting a budget is based on the **current year's results plus an extra amount (an 'increment') for estimated growth or inflation next year.** This is known as **incremental budgeting.**

What are its disadvantages?

It is an **inefficient** form of budgeting, although **administratively** it is **fairly easy** to prepare. It encourages **slack** and **wasteful spending** to creep into budgets and to become a normal feature of actual spending. If the increment makes the overall figures unacceptable, **elements in the new budget may be cut on an arbitrary basis** to make the overall total 'reasonable', whether or not this is desirable from a business point of view.

When can it be used?

Traditional incremental budgeting will be **sufficient only if current operations are as effective, efficient and economical as they can be,** without any alternative courses of action available to the organisation.

(b)   **Total quality ethos – what does it involve?**

A total quality ethos involves **focusing on quality in all resources, processes and relationships within the organisation.**

What are its principles?

One of the basic principles of a total quality ethos is that the **cost of preventing mistakes is less than the cost of correcting them once they occur.** The aim should therefore be to **get things right first time.** Total quality organisations operate a **zero defects policy.**

The second basic principle is dissatisfaction with the *status quo*: the belief that it is always possible to improve and so the aim should be to '**get it more right next time**'.

What is its impact on budget preparation?

These principles are at **odds with the incremental nature of traditional budgets,** which are based on the assumption that the existing budget model is still relevant, it simply needs adjusting to allow for planned changes in prices, activity and efficiency levels.

An organisation with a total quality ethos needs to accept that the only thing that matters is the **customer.** Budgets may therefore need to be **analysed according to customer or sales groupings.** Traditional budgets tend to be analysed departmentally or segmentally.

Within a total quality organisation, **employees are empowered**: they are allowed to decide how to do the necessary work, using the skills they possess and acquiring new skills as necessary to be an effective team member; they are made personally responsible for achieving targets and quality control. A far **greater level of employee involvement** is therefore required in the budget-setting process than required with a traditional system of budgeting.

A total quality ethos would incorporate the desire to **eliminate all non-value-added activities** such as moving from one part of a factory to another. It could prove difficult to incorporate the processes set up to achieve this into an incremental budget.

(c)   **Just-in-time philosophy – what is it?**

The just-in-time (JIT) philosophy has grown out of the criticisms of traditional responses to the problems of improving manufacturing capacity and reducing unit costs of production. It involves a **continuous commitment to the pursuit of excellence in all phases of manufacturing systems and design**. The **aims** of JIT are to **produce the required items, at the required quality and in the required quantities, at the precise time they are required**.

What are its key aspects?

There are seven **key aspects** of JIT.

(i) **JIT purchasing.** Small, frequent deliveries against bulk contracts when materials are needed by the production process and not before, requiring close integration of suppliers with the company's manufacturing process.

(ii) **Machine cells.** The groupings of machines or workers by product or component instead of by type of work performed.

(iii) **Set-up time reduction.** The recognition of machinery set-ups as non-value-adding activities which should be reduced or even eliminated.

(iv) **Uniform loading.** The operating of all parts of the productive process at a speed which matches the rate at which the customer demands the final product.

(v) **Pull system (Kanban).** The use of a Kanban, or signal, to ensure that products/components are only produced when needed by the next process. Nothing is produced in anticipation of need, to then remain in stock, consuming resources. Along with JIT purchasing, this ensures that stocks of raw materials, WIP and finished goods are kept to an absolute minimum.

(vi) **Total quality.** The design of products, processes and vendor quality assurance programmes to ensure that the product is of the appropriate quality level on the first pass through production.

(vii) **Employee involvement.** JIT involves major cultural change throughout an organisation. This can only be achieved if all employees are involved in the process of change and continuous improvement inherent in the JIT philosophy.

What is its impact on budget preparation?

Such fundamental changes to planning, stock holding policies, manufacturing systems and relationships with customers and suppliers will **affect the structure of the budget model which can be used and the budget preparation process**.

(d) **Activity based focus – what does it entail?**

A **focus on the activities that an organisation carries out,** as opposed to how its activities have traditionally been organised into separate functions, lies behind much modern thinking. For instance, it has been found to be more fruitful to think of what may have once been called the warehousing department (function) **in terms of what that department does,** such as inspection of goods, stock control and materials movement (activities).

This modern development entails finding new and better ways of doing existing things so as to **give greater satisfaction to customers at less cost to the business.** This is turn means that the business as a whole needs to be **managed with far more reference to the behaviour of activities and cost drivers identified by an activity based analysis** of the organisation and hence a **new approach to budgeting is required.**

What is its impact on budgeting?

Traditional budgeting may make managers responsible for activities which are driven by factors beyond their control: the personnel department cost of setting up new employee records is driven by the number of new employees required by managers other than the personnel manager.

Activity based budgeting (ABB), on the other hand, involves **defining the activities that underlie the financial figures in each function and using the level of activity to decide how much resource should be allocated, how well it is being managed and to explain variances from budget.**

ABB as a philosophy

Some writers treat ABB as **more of a philosophy** than a technique and attribute to it all the good features of strategic management accounting, zero base budgeting, total quality management, and other new and not so new ideas.

(i)   It is claimed that it will ensure that the organisation's overall strategy and any actual or likely changes in that strategy will be taken into account, because it attempts to **manage the business as the sum of its interrelated parts.**

(ii)   Concentration is focused on the whole of an activity, not just its separate parts, and so it is said that there is **more likelihood of getting it right first time.** For example, what is the use of being able to produce goods in time for their despatch date if the budget provides insufficient resources for the distribution manager who has to deliver them?

(iii)   Its focus on activities means that **activities will need to be classified as primary, secondary or support, value-adding or non-value-adding,** as part of the budget preparation process, linking it to the JIT philosophy we looked at above.

Summary

The planning process, of which the annual budget plays such a significant role, needs to take account of alternative options, and look for ways of improving performance, if it is to prove useful in the modern business environment in which a total quality ethos, a JIT philosophy and an activity based focus play a part. This is something that traditional incremental budgeting simply does not do.

50   PREPARATION QUESTION: QUALITY COSTS

> **Pass marks**. You would not be expected to reproduce CIMA *Official Terminology* definitions in the exam; any concise explanation in your own words would be more than sufficient. The tricky bit of this question is providing measures appropriate to the management accounting section. It is far easier to think of measures for manufacturing environments. Use your own experience, however, if you work in such an environment. You only need to provide one or two measures for each category of quality cost. We have included more.
>
> Don't provide a general essay on TQM (the question you think you should have been asked).

The cost of quality

The 2000 edition of the CIMA *Official Terminology* defines the **cost of quality** as 'The difference between the actual cost of producing, selling and supporting products or services and the equivalent costs if there were no failures during production or usage'. In other words it is the costs incurred by an organisation because the quality of its products or services is not perfect.

The costs of conformance and non-conformance

The *Official Terminology* goes on to split the cost of quality into the **cost of conformance** and the **cost of non-conformance**. The cost of conformance is 'The cost of achieving

211

specified quality standards' whereas the cost of non-conformance is 'The cost of failure to deliver the required standard of quality'.

Analysing the costs of conformance and non-conformance

The cost of conformance is further analysed into the **cost of prevention** and the **cost of appraisal** while the cost of non-conformance is analysed into the **cost of internal failure** and the cost of **external failure**.

These four categories of quality cost are defined in the *Official Terminology* as follows.

(a) **Prevention cost** is 'The costs incurred prior to or during production in order to prevent substandard or defective products or services from being produced'.

(b) **Appraisal cost** is 'The costs incurred in order to ensure that outputs produced meet required quality standards'.

(c) **Internal failure cost** is 'The costs arising from inadequate quality which are identified before the transfer of ownership from supplier to purchaser'.

(d) **External failure** cost is 'The cost arising from inadequate quality discovered after the transfer of ownership from supplier to purchaser'.

Examples of each category appropriate to a manufacturing environment

(a) Examples of **prevention cost** include the following.

  (i) Cost of training personnel in quality control

  (ii) Cost of designing, developing and maintaining quality control and inspection equipment

(b) Examples of **appraisal cost** include the following.

  (i) Cost of the inspection of finished products or services and other checking procedures and supplier vetting

  (ii) Cost of the inspection of goods inwards

(c) Examples of **internal failure** cost include the following.

  (i) Cost of material scrapped due to inefficiencies in goods receiving procedures and stores control

  (ii) Cost of material lost or wasted during production

  (iii) Cost of units rejected during inspection processes

  (iv) Losses due to lower selling prices for sub-quality goods

  (v) Cost of reviewing product specifications after failures

(d) Examples of **external failure cost** include the following.

  (i) Cost of product liability claims from customers
  (ii) Cost of repairing products returned from customers
  (iii) Cost of providing replacement items due to sub-standard products
  (iv) Cost of delivering returned units
  (v) Cost of administration of customer services section
  (vi) Cost of customer services section

Examples of each category appropriate to management accounting

(a) Examples of **prevention cost** include the following.

  (i) Cost of staff training programmes

  (ii) Cost of introducing computers to perform tasks previously performed manually

(b) Examples of **appraisal cost** include the following

    (i)   Cost of batch input controls to check the validity of processed data

    (ii)   Cost of performing computer audits to confirm the reliability of computer software

(c) Examples of **internal failure cost** include the following.

    (i)   Cost of reprocessing data input to the system incorrectly

    (ii)   Cost of reproducing incorrect reports

(d) Examples of **external failure cost** include the following.

    (i)   Cost to other functions in the organisation of incorrect decisions made on the basis of inaccurate or untimely information provided by the management accounting function (such as quoting uneconomical prices for jobs on the basis of incorrect information about labour, material and overhead)

    (ii)   Cost of dealing with external audit queries

51   ML PLC

> **Pass marks.** To provide balance, notice that we have briefly commented on the reasons why budget holders should not prepare budgets.
>
> You would have received marks for part (a) as follows.
>
> | | |
> |---|---|
> | • Report format | 1 mark |
> | • Explaining ZBB | 2 marks |
> | • Explaining ABB | 1 mark |
> | • Explaining similarities and differences between ZBB and ABB | 4 marks |
> | • Explaining participation in budgets | 2 marks |
> | • Explaining incremental budgeting | 2 marks |
> | • Explaining budget bias | 3 marks |
>
> The most common error in part (b) was not applying understanding of cost reduction and value analysis to the question scenario - six of the ten marks were awarded for this.

(a)
REPORT

To: Divisional manager
From: Management accountant   Date: 30 October 20X1
Subject: Financial planning and budgeting concepts

1   Introduction

1.1   This report explains a number of issues and concepts related to financial planning and control.

2   Zero based budgeting versus activity based budgeting

2.1 Zero based budgeting (ZBB)

2.1.2 ZBB **rejects** the **assumption** inherent in traditional incremental budgeting that the current period's activities will continue at the same level or volume next period, and that the **next period's budget can be based on the current period's costs plus an extra amount for inflation.**

2.1.3 It involves preparing a budget for each cost centre from a zero base. The expenditure for every activity and task therefore has to be **justified in its entirety** in order to be included in the next period's budget.

2.2 Activity based budgeting (ABB)

2.2.1 At its **simplest**, ABB is merely the **use of costs determined using activity based costing as a basis for preparing budgets.**

2.2.2 More **formally**, ABB involves defining the activities that underlie the financial figures in each function and **using the level of activity to decide how much resource should be allocated to that function, how well it is being managed and to explain variances from budget.**

2.3 Similarities between ZBB and ABB

2.3.1 Both ZBB and ABB require managers to perform a critical assessment of the various tasks and activities carried out within an organisation in order to determine whether or not they should be continued.

2.3.2 In **ABB, different activity levels** can be used to provide the **foundation for base and incremental decision packages** (descriptions of specific organisational activities), which are **used in ZBB to rank activities** in order of priority against other activities.

2.3.3 It is worth noting that some writers treat **ABB** as more of a **philosophy** than a technique and attribute to it all the good features of a number of 'new' or not so new ideas **including ZBB**.

2.4 Difference between ZBB and ABB

2.4.1 ABB considers all of an organisation's activities whereas ZBB tends to focus on discretionary costs such as advertising and training.

3 Who should prepare budgets?

3.1 When budget holders are **involved** in setting their own budgets, this is known as **participative** budgeting, which contrasts with an **authoritarian** system of **imposed** budgets.

3.2 Benefits of participative budgeting

3.2.1 Budget holders have **experience** of the day-to-day running of the business. Their **knowledge** can help to ensure that budget **targets** are **realistic**.

3.2.2 Having a detailed knowledge of day-to-day working practices and problems, budget holders are often best placed to **suggest innovations** to processes.

3.2.3 Input to target setting **encourages greater commitment** to budgets as the budgets are then perceived to be fair. This leads to **improved goal congruence**.

3.2.4 If budget holders are involved in the budget-setting process, they can be **groomed for top posts**. The consultation process involved in participative budgeting can be used to assess manager potential and helps provide training in the skills needed for higher-level management.

3.2.5 The budgeting process can be used to **communicate** important ideas such as the cost of various working practices and the success and direction of the organisation. As well as focussing budget holders' attention on cost control and corporate objectives, they may feel a **greater sense of belonging** to the organisation, which fosters loyalty, and a sense of purpose and **motivation**. They will understand how their activities affect other parts of the organisation and so there may be a **reduction in dysfunctional behaviour** and **goal congruence** should **improve**.

3.2.6 As well as communication, participation itself can **motivate** budget holders; they may feel their job is more important, which fosters self-esteem.

3.2.7 Budget holders may be **less resistant to change** since they have had a hand in the decision-making process.

3.3 Disadvantages of participative budgeting

3.3.1 It is important to note that there is a **range** of problems associated with participative budgeting. These include the setting of easily-achievable targets, slower decision making and the view that budget holder involvement is merely an attempt to cut costs or achieve greater productivity.

4 Incremental budgeting and budget bias

4.1 Incremental budgeting

4.1.2 This is the **traditional** approach to budgeting and involves setting a budget based on the current year's results plus an extra amount (an 'increment') for estimated growth or inflation next year. Existing activities and tasks are not subject to review or assessment but are assumed to continue.

4.1.3 Traditional incremental budgeting will be **sufficient only if current operations are as effective, efficient and economical as they can** be, without any alternative courses of action available to the organisation. The planning process should take account of alternative options, and look for ways of improving performance: this is something that incremental budgeting simply does not do.

4.1.4 Although from an administrative point of view incremental budgets are fairly **easy to prepare**, incremental budgeting is therefore an inefficient form of budgeting as it **encourages slack and wasteful spending** to creep into budgets.

4.2 Budget slack and budget bias

4.2.1 Slack is the **difference between the minimum necessary costs that are needed and the costs built into the budget or actually incurred.**

4.2.2 When preparing incremental budgets, **managers** are able to **deliberately overestimate costs or underestimate sales to create slack** and **bias their budgets** so that they will not be blamed for overspending and/or poor results.

4.2.3 A typical situation is for a manager to **pad** the budget and **waste** money on non-essential expenses so that he **uses all his budget allowances**. The reason behind his action is the fear that unless the allowance is fully spent it will be reduced in future periods thus making his job more difficult as the reduced budgets will not be so easy to attain. Achieving a budget target therefore simply means only that costs have remained within the accepted levels of inefficient spending.

4.2.4 Budget bias is therefore also typically found when **managers** are **rewarded for achieving their budget targets.**

4.3 It is obviously far **easier to introduce bias** within a system of **incremental budgeting** than if say ZBB or ABB were to be used (see section 2 above), because there is no effective control over budget limits and no questioning attitude of tasks, activities and related expenditure.

5 I hope this information has proved useful. If I can be of any further assistance please do not hesitate to contact me.

Signed: Management accountant

(b) **Cost reduction**

Cost reduction is a **planned** and **positive** approach to **reducing** the unit cost of goods/services **below current budgeted or standard** levels **without impairing** the **suitability for the used intended** for the goods produced/services provided by the organisation. It should not be confused with cost control, which is all about keeping costs within acceptable (standard or budgeted) limits.

Cost reduction in ML plc

A cost reduction programme in ML plc would therefore look at how to reduce, for example, the costs of designing a web site, or even a particular part of a web site, without the customer perceiving any fall in the value of the service the company is providing.

Value analysis

Conventional cost reduction techniques try to achieve the lowest unit cost for a specific product design/way of providing a service. Value analysis tries to **find the least-cost method of making a product or providing a service that achieves the desired function/outcome.**

Value analysis in ML plc

Value analysis within ML plc of, say, the design of web sites for customers, would involve the systematic investigation of both the costs connected with it and the way in which it is provided, with the **aim of getting rid of all unnecessary costs**. An unnecessary cost is an additional cost incurred **without adding to the following aspects of value.**

- **Use value** – the purpose fulfilled by the service
- **Exchange value** – the market value of the service
- **Esteem value** – the prestige the customer attaches to the service

Example

Given that ML plc has a multi-site operation with bases in the UK and overseas, cost reduction and value analysis techniques could investigate possible duplication of activities that occur as a result.

It is important that duplicated activities are not eliminated in an effort to reduce costs if value is adversely affected, however.

For example, given the nature of its services, specialist teams could be based anywhere in the world. Maintaining a physical presence in different parts of the world should improve customers' perceptions of the value of ML plc's services, however; customers would feel they were dealing with a local organisation.

52   **WYE HOTEL GROUP**

(a)

> **Pass marks.** We know that this answer is longer than anything you could produce in the exam but we have tried to cover a wide range of points given that the question was quite open and could have produced a great variety of answers.
>
> The examiner commented on the need to link the techniques (see our summary at the end of the solution).

(i)   **Cost reduction**

Cost reduction is a planned and positive approach to **reducing the unit cost** of goods/services below current budgeted or standard levels **without impairing their suitability for the use intended**. It should not be confused with cost control, which is all about keeping costs within acceptable (standard or budgeted) limits.

A cost reduction programme in the WYE hotel group would therefore look at how to reduce the cost of a guest staying a night in the hotel, a meal being served in the restaurant and so on, without the customer perceiving any fall in the value of the service provided.

How to reduce costs

The **improvement of efficiency levels** might be considered.

(1)   Improving materials usage (eg the use of food in restaurants or guest supplies in bedrooms)

(2)   Improving labour productivity (eg changing work methods to eliminate unnecessary procedures, perhaps in the work required to prepare rooms for new guests)

(3)   Improving efficiency of equipment usage (eg allowing members of the public to use the swimming pool at certain times of the day/year for payment of a fee)

A programme could also consider ways to **reduce the costs of resources**.

(1)   It might be possible to find cheaper suppliers for, say, wines and beers.

(2)   Increased automation of certain guest services, say the travel bureaux, would reduce labour costs.

Other aspects of a cost reduction programme might include **increased control over spending decisions**.

(ii)   **Value analysis**

Conventional cost reduction techniques try to achieve the lowest unit costs for a specific product design or specific way of providing a service. Value analysis tries to find the **least-cost method of making a product or providing a service that achieves the desired function/outcome.**

Value analysis of a particular service within the hotel group would involve the systematic investigation of both the costs connected with the service and the way in which it is provided, with the **aim of getting rid of all unnecessary costs**. An unnecessary cost is an **additional cost incurred without adding** to the following aspects of value.

- **Use value** – the purpose fulfilled by the service
- **Exchange value** – the market value of the service
- **Esteem value** – the prestige the guest attaches to the service

Applying value analysis

A value analysis of the guest entertainment provided might therefore pose the following questions.

(1)   **Are all parts of the entertainment programme necessary?** Could the cabaret show be removed from the programme without affecting guests' perception of the quality of the overall programme?

(2) **Could the programme be provided at a lower cost without affecting its value?** For example, could children's films be shown instead of using a live entertainer?

From the analysis a **variety of options** can be **devised** and **the least cost alternative which maintains or improves the value of the service to the guests can be selected.**

(iii) **Zero based budgeting (ZBB)**

The traditional approach to budgeting

Given that the hotel group has not implemented ZBB, we can assume that it uses the traditional incremental approach to budgeting that involves **adding an allowance for inflation to the current year's figures.** This is reasonable if operations are as effective, efficient and economical as they can be. In general, however, it tends to be an **inefficient** form of budgeting as it allows wasteful spending to be built into budgets on an ongoing basis.

The ZBB approach

ZBB, by contrast, starts from the premise that the **budget for next year is zero. Every part of every service** provided by the hotel and the associated costs have to be fully **justified** in order to be included in the budget, as if it were being included for the first time.

In reality, however, managers do not have to budget from zero, but can start from their current level of expenditure and work downwards, asking what would happen if any particular aspect of current expenditure and current operations were removed from the budget. In this way, every aspect of the budget is examined in terms of its cost and the benefits it provides.

The ranking process

Once **budgets** for individual services within the hotel (restaurant, bar and so on) have been stripped of unnecessary expenditure, they can be **compared** and the services **ranked. Resources** can then be **allocated** according to the funds available and the ranking of the services.

Questioning attitude

The most important aspect of the implementation of ZBB is the development of a questioning attitude by all those involved in the budgeting process. Existing practices and expenditures must be challenged and searching questions asked.

(1) **Does the service need to be carried out?** For example, the travel bureaux and shopping facilities are probably used by only a few guests but incur high fixed costs.

(2) **What would be the consequences if the service were not carried out?** If it were decided not to have swimming pools, the number of guests may drop. Closure of the shopping facilities would be less likely to have this effect.

(3) **Is the current level of provision adequate?**

(4) **Are there alternative ways of providing the service?**

(5) **How much should the service cost?**

(6) Is the expenditure worth the benefits received?

How ZBB might improve profitability

(1) Inefficient and obsolete activities/services could be identified and removed.

(2) Employees would be forced to avoid wasteful expenditure.

(3) Resources would be allocated more efficiently.

Summary

All three techniques can be used to **assess the efficiency of the hotels' operations**. Their application should improve profitability across the WYE hotel group because they **look for ways to reduce costs without having a detrimental effect on the value guests place on the service and hence without adversely affecting demand.**

(b)

> **Pass marks.** You would probably only have needed to make five appropriate points which were clearly related to the scenario to earn full marks.
>
> *Other points.* As well as the issues discussed below you might have mentioned the following.
>
> - Scrap allowance in a standard is at odds with the zero defects aim of TQM.
>
> - Standard costing focuses on quantity, but today quality is the issue.
>
> - Standard costing makes individual managers responsible for variances but a TQM programme aims to make all managers responsible for supplying a quality product.

Reason 1 – automation

M plc operates a **computer-controlled, automated processing** operation. Production will be **machine intensive** rather than labour intensive and hence **overheads are unlikely to be incurred in line with or be caused by labour hours worked.**

Reason 2 – JIT environment

Traditional **variance analysis** emphasises the need to avoid adverse efficiency variances, which means that managers should try **to prevent idle time** and should **maintain production**. M plc operates a **JIT** system, however, which aims for **small batch sizes** to meet specific customer requirements, and low levels of stock.

Reason 3 – cost is not the only issue

Variance analysis concentrates on only a narrow range of costs and so fails to give sufficient attention to issues such as **quality** and **customer satisfaction**, key issues in a modern manufacturing environment.

Reason 4 – long-term relationships with suppliers

In M plc's **JIT** environment, the keys issues in materials purchasing are supplier **reliability**, food **quality** and **delivery in small order quantities**. Purchasing managers **should not be shopping around every month looking for the cheapest price**. Many JIT systems depend **on long-term contractual links** with suppliers, which means that **material price variances** are **not relevant** for management control purposes.

Reason 5 – changing cost behaviour

Many **standard costing** variances **focus** on the control of short-term **variable costs**. In a **modern manufacturing environment** such as that in which M plc operates, the **majority of costs** tend to be **fixed** in the short term. In addition, the use of **standard absorption costing** to convert these fixed costs into unit costs provides **misleading** information.

Reason 6 – continuous improvement

Standard costing systems assume that **performance to standard** is **acceptable. Today's** business environment is more focused on **continuous improvement.**

Reason 7 – changing business environment and operations

Standard costing systems were developed when the business environment was more **stable** and less prone to change while **M plc's business environment** is more **dynamic.**

The use of **standard costing** relies on the existence of **repetitive operations** and relatively **homogeneous output.** Given **today's competitive environment,** however, M plc is likely to need to **continually respond to customers' changing requirements,** with the result that output and operations will not be so predictable.

Reason 8 – frequency of control information

Most standard costing systems produce control reports weekly or monthly. M plc's managers are likely to need much more frequent information in order to function efficiently in a dynamic business environment, however.

53   BWR PLC

> **Pass marks**. Notice how we mentioned British Rail at the end of our answer. Bring 'real-life' examples into your answer to show the examiner that you are aware of more than the theoretical aspects of management accounting.
>
> Don't forget to relate your answer to the specific requirements of the question. For example, in part (b), you should explore the implications for a transport operation.

(a) **Designing and implementing a cost reduction programme**

Cost reduction is a planned and positive approach to reducing expenditure. A cost reduction scheme aims to **reduce expenditure without affecting the performance of the product or service.** A carefully designed cost reduction programme would not be a set of hastily prepared crash measures to cut costs in the short term. Such measures often have detrimental long-term effects which are not immediately obvious in the short term.

A systematic cost reduction programme involves the continual assessment of BWR plc's services, operations, internal administration systems and so on. The exercise should be **planned campaign,** so that short-term cost reductions are not soon reversed and 'forgotten'.

Every aspect of BWR's internal and external operations should be investigated to seek opportunities for cost reduction. **Specific techniques** that could be applied include the following.

(i) **Work study or organisation and methods (O & M) programmes,** to look for cost savings from improved working methods

(ii) **Asset utilisation studies,** to identify assets or labour that are under utilised, or which are not being used effectively

(iii) **Value analysis,** to identify and eliminate any costs that do not add value to the final service provided to the customer

(iv) **Business process re-engineering,** to identify the activities undertaken within BWR and whether they could be undertaken more effectively

Features of BWR's operations which might produce problems

Particular difficulties which BWR could encounter stem from the **nature of the franchise operation**.

(i)   The fact that BWR has had to 'acquire the use' of freight depots, locomotives and so on is taken to mean that these assets and facilities are leased. It may therefore be difficult for BWR to control their quality and cost. However, it should be possible for the company to undertake studies to ensure their effective utilisation. Alternatively there may be opportunity for investment in assets and facilities now.

(ii)   The **fluctuating demand levels** will cause problems when attempting to ensure the optimum utilisation of resources. Seasonal peaks in demand may require the use of temporary workers or hired equipment to save costs.

(iii)   It is unlikely that, given the nature of container handling, technological advances will produce more efficient equipment for the industry. At freight depots, the loading docks designed to deal with category A goods will need to incorporate expensive safety systems and it is therefore vital that **demand** for the two types of good is **accurately forecast** so that the appropriate number of docks with advanced safety features can be established.

(b)   The **adoption of modern management practices** such as JIT and synchronous manufacturing **by its customers** is likely to have an **impact** on BWR plc's operations.

Changing pattern and nature of demand for BWR's services

The adoption by BWR's customers of modern management practices would affect the pattern and nature of their demand for BWR's services. JIT and related techniques tend to lead to **reduced batch sizes** and **more frequent orders**. BWR's customers would require set **delivery times** since their safety stock levels would be minimal in front of bottlenecks (according to synchronous manufacturing) or non-existent (according to JIT) and late delivery would halt production. BWR would probably be required to agree to more rigorous and reliable loading and delivery times, and would be likely to face penalty payments if the required service was not provided. Moreover, as such manufacturers will change production runs in response to fluctuating customer demand, the time period in which to arrange delivery of raw materials will be significantly reduced. BWR's operation must therefore be **flexible** enough to deal with unpredictable timings.

Increasing flexibility and reliability for customers

BWR operates a service and is therefore not able to hold a stock of goods to provide the necessary flexibility and reliability for customers. This **flexibility and reliability will have to be built into the system itself,** which will need to be capable of handling all arrivals without unnecessary queuing. There will be a need for **greater focus on preventive maintenance** to ensure the continuous availability of transport services for customers. It may also be necessary for BWR to undertake **further investment** in order to be able to deal with smaller loads and a greater mix of products.

Establishment of long-term commitments between suppliers and customers

JIT systems are often characterised by long-term commitments between suppliers and customers. The extra investment is therefore likely to reap rewards, particularly if it is part of a programme of joint commitment to continuous improvement by BWR and its customers.

Conclusion

To maintain a relationship with customers adopting practices such as JIT and synchronous manufacturing BWR must therefore offer the **most flexible, reliable and quick service possible,** something which British Rail in the UK failed to do, with the loss of their market to the road haulage business.

54 PREPARATION QUESTION: VALUE ANALYSIS

> **Pass marks**. Although the basic information for this question is contained in the BPP Study Text, you must remember to relate it to the scenario.

A value analysis report is prepared for management as a result of a value analysis exercise. Management can then act on the information in the report in order to reduce their organisation's costs.

Value analysis – definition and objective

Value analysis is a **planned, scientific approach to cost reduction,** which reviews the material composition of a product and production design to **identify modifications** and **improvements** which can be made **without reducing the value of the product** to the **customer.** The **objective** is to **maintain the same value of the product, or to improve its value, but at a reduced cost.**

Aspects of value

Four aspects of value should be considered in a value analysis report.

(a) **Cost value** is the cost of producing and selling a video recorder/player. Since value analysis seeks to reduce unit costs, this is the one aspect of value which the exercise aims to reduce.

(b) **Exchange value** is the market value of the video recorder/player.

(c) **Use value** is what the video recorder/player does, the purposes it fulfils. Value analysis attempts to provide the same (or a better) use value at a lower cost. Use value therefore involves consideration of the performance and reliability of the video recorder/player.

(d) **Esteem value** is the prestige the customer attaches to the video recorder/player. The value analysis exercise will attempt to maintain or enhance the prestige of the product at a lower cost. Esteem value also involves a consideration of aesthetics (what the recorder/player looks like).

Value analysis involves the systematic investigation of every source of cost and technique of production with the aim of **eliminating all unnecessary costs.** An unnecessary cost is an additional cost incurred without adding use, exchange or esteem value to the recorder/player.

There may be a **conflict** between reducing costs and maintaining another aspect of value, however, for example the esteem value of the recorder/player. The value analysis report should highlight the existence of such conflicts and seek clear direction from senior management about which is more important.

How benefits are achieved

A value analysis study can help an organisation to achieve **lower costs, better products** and **higher profits** in the following ways.

- Cost elimination/prevention
- Cost reduction

- Improving product quality and so selling greater quantities at the same price as before
- Improving product quality and so being able to increase the sales price

Additional benefits of a value analysis programme

These include the following.

- Improved product performance and reliability
- An increased product life (in terms of the marketable life and the useable life)
- Increased use of standardisation
- Encouraging employees to show innovation and come up with creative ideas

Preparation of a value analysis report

The preparation of a value analysis report requires the **full backing of senior management** as value analysis can be a **time-consuming** and **costly** exercise in itself. A **multi-disciplinary team** of experts which blends skill, experience and imagination must be formed. Within Clifton plc there must be representatives from production, maintenance, research and development and all other key functions.

Stages in a value analysis report

(a) **Collection and analysis of information about the video recorder/player**. Each aspect of the product should be analysed. During the exercise, questions such as the following need to be asked.

  (i) What does the recorder/player do?
  (ii) What does it cost?
  (iii) Are there alternative ways of making it?
  (iv) What would be the cost of these alternatives?
  (v) Can standardised parts be used?

  Any cost reductions must be achieved without the loss of use or esteem value. Or at least, cost savings must exceed any loss in value suffered, so that customers are compensated for the loss in use or esteem value in the form of a lower selling price.

(b) **Consideration of alternatives**. The report should detail a variety of options derived from the analysis. For example it may be possible to reduce costs in the assembly department by buying some components externally instead of relying on those manufactured in the circuit board and plastic mouldings departments.

(c) **Evaluation of alternatives.** The alternative options should be evaluated in terms of their effect on all four aspects of value.

(d) **Recommendation.** The report may make a final recommendation to the decision makers for approval.

55   **OBJECTIVE TEST QUESTIONS: COSTING SYSTEMS**

1   D

	£
Contribution ((1,220 + 150) × £47.90)	65,623
Fixed cost (£195,000/13)	15,000
Profit under marginal costing	50,623
Adjustment for stock decrease (150 × £8*)	1,200
Profit under absorption costing	49,423

  * £195,000/24,375 = £8

  Option A is the marginal costing profit.

  Option B is incorrect because the adjustment was added instead of deducted.

If you selected **option C,** you deducted the annual fixed costs rather than those allocated to one control period.

2   B   Closing stock valuation under absorption costing will always be higher than under marginal costing because of the absorption of fixed overheads into closing stock values.

The profit under absorption costing will be greater because the fixed overhead being carried forward in closing stock is greater than the fixed overhead being written off in opening stock.

3   D

4   A   We use the TA ratio as W Ltd uses throughput accounting.

$$\text{TA ratio} = \frac{\text{throughput contribution per factory hour}}{\text{conversion cost per factory hour}}$$

where throughput contribution per factory hour = (sales – material cost) per hour

	Alpha	Beta	Gamma	Delta
Throughput contribution per factory hour	£31.79	£56.20	£45.46	£55.03
Conversion cost per factory hour	£3.62	£21.10	£14.52	£29.53
TA ratio	8.78	2.66	3.13	1.86

5   C

	£
N revenue (£32.40 × (8,100 × 0.9))	236,196
Further processing costs (8,100 × £16.20)	131,220
Share of joint costs £210,600 × (8,100/(3,600 + 8,100 + 5,850))	97,200
	7,776

If you selected **option A** you deducted one third of the joint costs, not a share based on output volumes.

If you selected **option B,** you forgot to account for joint costs.

If you selected **option D,** you forget to account for the normal loss.

6   C   **(i)** and **(ii)** are not relevant because the common costs remain unaltered regardless of whether the joint products are processed further.

7   A   Using FIFO, only the work done to complete the opening stock must be included in the calculation of equivalent units.

	Total units				
		Equivalent costs			
		Materials		*Conversion*	
	Units	%	Units	%	Units
Opening stock completed	1,080	30	324	20	216
Completely processed this period	25,020	100	25,020	100	25,020
	26,100				
Normal loss	900	–	–	–	–
Closing stock	1,440	60	864	50	720
			26,208		25,956

Option B is the number of units finished during the period.

If you selected **option C,** you forgot to apply the percentages to opening stock.

If you selected **option D,** you included equivalent units for normal loss.

8   D   Total loss = opening WIP + input – (output + closing stock)
               = 3,500 + 29,120 – (21,950 + 2,220)
               = 8,450

Abnormal loss = total loss – normal loss
= 8,450 – (5% × 29,120)*
= 6,994

	Total units	Material		Conversion costs	
	Units	%	Units	%	Units
Opening WIP completed	3,500	100	3,500	100	3,500
Fully worked units	18,450	100	18,450	100	18,450
Output to next process	21,950		21,950		21,950
Normal loss*	1,456	–	0	–	0
Closing WIP	2,220	10	222	15	333
	25,626		22,172		22,283

Equivalent units (Material and Conversion costs columns)

Option A is based on including units of normal loss. Normal loss is always zero equivalent units.

Option B is based on using the FIFO method of valuation.

Option C is simply the number of units output to the next process.

9 B The main process account is debited with an abnormal gain, representing the normal production costs of the 'extra' units actually produced. This entry has the effect of cancelling out part of the normal loss entry. The corresponding credit is to the abnormal gain account.

56 MARGINAL AND ABSORPTION RECONCILIATION

Pass marks. Use of a columnar format in (a) would have saved time. The key information when splitting fixed and variable production overheads was the over and under absorption in each period. In (b) you should remember that it is the net effect of the change in stock levels that is used when reconciling absorption and marginal costing profits. Note in (c) the change in distribution costs has to be taken into account separately when reconciling the absorption costing profits of two periods. Under marginal costing the change would be reflected by a change in total contribution.

(a)

	January – June		*July – December*	
	£'000	£'000	£'000	£'000
Sales		540		360
Opening stock (£18 (W1) × 5,000/8,000 (W4))	90		144	
Production costs				
Direct materials	108		36	
Direct labour	162		54	
Variable overhead (£3 (W1) × 18,000/6,000)	54		18	
	414		252	
Closing stock (£18 (W1) × 8,000/4,000 (W4))	(144)		(72)	
		270		180
		270		180
Variable distribution costs (£1 (W5) × 15,000/10,000)		15		10
Contribution		255		170
Fixed costs				
Production overhead (W2)	24		24	
Selling costs	50		50	
Distribution costs (W5)	30		30	
Administration costs	80		80	
		184		184
Budgeted profit/(loss) under marginal costing		71		(14)

Workings

1 Fixed and variable costs per unit

	£
Direct materials (£108,000 ÷ 18,000)	6
Direct labour (£162,000 ÷ 18,000)	9
Variable overhead (W2)	3
Variable costs per unit	18
Fixed cost per unit (W3)	2
Total cost per unit	20

2 Fixed and variable overheads

	January – June £'000	*July – December* £'000
Overhead absorbed	90	30
(Over)/under absorption	(12)	12
Actual overhead	78	42

Using the high-low method, we can determine the fixed and variable elements of the production overheads.

	Production Units	*Production overheads* £
High	18,000	78,000
Low	6,000	42,000
	12,000	36,000

$$\text{Variable production overhead cost per unit} = \frac{£36,000}{12,000} = £3 \text{ per unit}$$

∴ When 18,000 units are produced, total variable production overheads = 18,000 × £3 = £54,000.

$$
\begin{aligned}
\text{Since total costs} &= \text{fixed costs} + \text{variable costs} \\
£78,000 &= \text{fixed costs} + £54,000 \\
∴ \text{Fixed costs} &= £78,000 - £54,000 \\
&= £24,000
\end{aligned}
$$

3 Total overhead cost per unit

January – June, total overheads = £90,000

January – June, production units = 18,000

$$∴ \text{Total overhead cost per unit} = \frac{£90,000}{18,000} = £5 \text{ per unit}$$

In (W2) we established that the variable overhead cost per unit = £3. Therefore the fixed overhead cost per unit = £5 – £3 = £2.

4 Opening and closing stock levels

	January – June units		*July – December* units
Opening stock				
(£100,000 ÷ £20 (W1))	5,000	(£160,000 ÷ £20 (W1))	8,000
Closing stock				
(£160,000 ÷ £20 (W1))	8,000	(£80,000 ÷ £20 (W1))	4,000

5   **Distribution costs**

	Sales units	Distribution costs
		£
High	15,000	45,000
Low	10,000	40,000
	5,000	5,000

$$\text{Variable distribution cost per unit} = \frac{£5,000}{5,000} = £1 \text{ per unit}$$

$$
\begin{aligned}
\text{Fixed costs} &= £45,000 - (15,000 \times £1) \\
&= £45,000 - £15,000 \\
&= £30,000
\end{aligned}
$$

(b)   From (W1) in part (a), it can be seen that the cost of stock under marginal costing = £18 per unit and the cost of stock under absorption costing = £20 per unit.

	January – June	July – December
	£'000	£'000
Absorption costing profit	77	(22)
Fixed overheads b/f in opening stock		
(£2 (W3) × 5,000/8,000)	10	16
Fixed overhead c/f in closing stock		
(£2 (W3) × 8,000/4,000)	(16)	(8)
Marginal costing profit (see (a))	71	(14)

(c)

	£'000
Profit January – June 20X7	77
Decrease in sales volume (5,000 × £16 (see below))	(80)
Difference in overhead recovery	(24)
Decrease in distribution costs	5
Loss July – December 20X7	(22)

Profit per unit under absorption costing

$$
\begin{aligned}
&= \text{sales price per unit } (£540,000 \div 15,000) - \text{cost per unit} \\
&= £(36 - 20) \\
&= £16
\end{aligned}
$$

(d)   **Fixed costs**

$$
\begin{aligned}
&= £184,000 \times 2 \\
&= £368,000
\end{aligned}
$$

Contribution per unit = Selling price – variable production costs – variable distribution costs

$$
\begin{aligned}
&= £36 - £18 \text{ (W1)} - £1 \text{ (W5)} \\
&= £17
\end{aligned}
$$

$$\therefore \textbf{Break-even point} = \frac{368,000}{17}$$

$$= 21,647 \text{ units}$$

(e)   The **advantages** of using **marginal costing** are as follows.

(i)   Marginal costing is **based on cost behaviour patterns,** the key principle being that contribution will vary in proportion to the units sold. Hence marginal costing demonstrates clearly how **cash flows and profits** will be **affected** by **changes in sales volume.**

(ii)   Using marginal costing means that **fixed costs** that relate to a period of a time are **matched** against the period by being charged against the period's **revenues.**

(iii)   Marginal costing situations can be shown easily and clearly on graphs.

(iv) Use of marginal costing will help in **short-term pricing decisions** concerning incremental profits. It will also help in **setting a buffer stock level**. Buffer stock must be valued at marginal cost, since fixed costs have not been incurred to produce a marginal quantity of finished goods that are unsold at the end of the period.

57 CA PLC

> **Pass marks.** Students often get in a muddle about whether absorption or marginal costing shows the higher profit when the fixed overhead included in closing stock is lower (for example) than that in opening stock. Remember that if the fixed overhead in closing stock is lower than that in opening stock then actual fixed overhead *plus* a bit more has been included in cost of sales if absorption costing is used, whereas with marginal costing just actual fixed overhead would have been deducted from profit. Marginal costing would therefore show the higher profit.

(a) The first step is to **calculate the fixed overhead absorption rates for each period on the basis of budgeted figures**.

	Period 1	Period 2	Period 3
Budgeted fixed overhead	£10,400	£19,170	£17,360
Budgeted production in units	8,000	14,200	12,400
Fixed overhead absorption rate per unit	£1.30	£1.35	£1.40

These can now be used to determine the amount of fixed overhead absorbed each period (fixed overhead absorption rate × actual number of units produced). By **comparing the fixed overhead absorbed with the actual overhead, the under or over recovery of overhead can be calculated**.

	Period 1	Period 2	Period 3
Fixed overhead absorbed	(8,400 × £1.30) 10,920	(13,600 × £1.35) 18,360	(9,200 × £1.40) 12,880
Actual fixed overhead	11,200	18,320	16,740
(Under-)/over-recovered overhead	(280)	40	(3,860)
Effect on profit	Reduce	Increase	Reduce

(b) In marginal costing, stocks are valued at variable production cost whereas in absorption costing they are valued at their full production cost (in other words, including fixed overhead). Consequently **if the amount of fixed overhead included in opening and closing stock values differ, the reported profits under the two systems will also differ. If the fixed overhead included in closing stock is less than that in opening stock** then more overhead than that actually incurred will be included in the profit calculation and hence **profit under absorption costing will be lower than that under marginal costing** (in marginal costing only overheads incurred being included in the profit calculation). If the fixed overhead included in closing stock is higher than that in opening stock then absorption costing will report the higher profit.

An assessment of the effect on profit of using absorption or marginal costing by CA plc can be made as follows.

	Period 0 Units	Period 1 Units	Period 2 Units	Period 3 Units
Opening stock		2,600	1,400	2,600
Production		8,400	13,600	9,200
Sales		(9,600)	(12,400)	(10,200)
Closing stock	2,600	1,400	2,600	1,600

	£	£	£	£
Fixed o/hd absorbed per unit		1.30	1.35	1.40
Fixed o/hd absorbed in closing stock	3,315	1,820	3,510	2,240
Fixed o/hd absorbed in opening stock		3,315	1,820	3,510
Fixed o/hd absorbed taken to P&L a/c		1,495	(1,690)	1,270

The fixed overhead absorbed in opening stock is higher than that absorbed in closing stock in periods 1 and 3. Absorption costing will therefore show a lower profit than marginal costing in periods 1 and 3 but a higher profit in period 2.

(c)   The **aim of absorption costing is to produce a product cost which ensures that overheads incurred during a period are recovered** via the inclusion of a share of overhead in each unit of output. Its principal aim is not, therefore, to produce accurate product costs.

The determination of absorption costing product costs **depends on a great deal of subjective judgement and hence, due to the requirement of accurate product costs for decision making, it is totally unsuitable for decision making. Areas of absorption costing requiring subjective judgement** include the following.

(i)   **Costs directly allocated to cost centres are only estimates** made during the budgeting process and the overhead absorbed into products will depend on these estimates.

(ii)   There is often **more than one method for apportioning an overhead** to a cost centre, the choice of method being at the discretion of, for example, the management accountant. The cost of the stores function could be apportioned to production departments on the basis of the number of issues made to departments or on the level of stock held for each department.

(iii)   The **choice of recovery rate** (labour hours, percentage of prime cost and so on) will affect the amount of overhead absorbed per product and hence the product cost.

(iv)   The **denominator of the absorption rate** (direct labour hours, machine hours and so on) **is a budgeted figure**.

(v)   In some absorption costing systems the **full cost of areas such as research and development**, administration and marketing and selling **may be absorbed into product costs. In other systems** the costs **may be written off** directly to the profit and loss account.

(vi)   **All of the costs (and activity levels)** included in the calculation of the amount of overhead to be included in each product **are based on estimates.** Such estimates are based on assumptions about the environment in which the organisation operates.

Due to the high degree of subjectivity involved in its operation, absorption costing can result in inaccurate and hence misleading information for decision making and should not therefore be used for that purpose.

It is not just the inaccuracy of the resulting product cost which makes absorption costing information unsuitable for decision making, however. Consider the following example.

Suppose that a sales manager has **an item of product** which he is having difficulty in selling. Its **historical full cost is £80**, made up of **variable costs of £50 and fixed costs of £30. A customer offers £60** for it.

(i)   **If there is no other customer** for the product, £60 would be better than nothing and the **product should be sold to improve income and profit** by this amount.

(ii)   If the company has **spare production capacity** which would otherwise not be used, it would be **profitable to continue making more** of the same product, if customers are willing to pay £60 for each extra unit made. This is because the additional costs are only £50 so that the profit would be increased marginally by £10 per unit produced.

(iii) **In absorption costing terms, the product makes a loss of £20, which would discourage the sales manager from accepting a price of £60 from the customer. His decision would be a bad one.**

    (1)   If the product is not sold for £60, it will presumably be scrapped eventually, so the **choice is really between making a loss in absorption costing terms of £20, or a loss of £80 when the stock is written off**, whenever this happens.

    (2)   If there is demand for some extra units at £60 each, the absorption costing loss would be £20 per unit, but at the end of the year there would be an additional **contribution to overheads and profit of £10 per unit**. In terms of absorption costing the **under-absorbed overhead would be reduced by £30 for each extra unit made and sold.**

Thus, for **once-only decisions or decisions affecting the use of marginal spare capacity, absorption costing information about unit profits is** *irrelevant*. On the other hand, since total contribution must be sufficient to cover the fixed costs of the business, **marginal costing would be unsuitable as a basis for establishing** *long-term* **prices for all output.**

58   PROCESS AND P&L

> **Pass marks.** Always adopt the following four-step approach when tackling process costing questions.
>
> - Determine output and losses
> - Calculate cost per unit of output, losses and WIP
> - Calculate total cost of output, losses and WIP
> - Complete accounts
>
> Common errors in this type of question include:
>
> - Including the normal loss units when calculating the number of equivalent units
>
> - Including the abnormal gain as a positive value when calculating the number of equivalent units
>
> - Ignoring the opening work in progress costs when calculating the cost per equivalent unit

Process 1

Step 1. **Determine output and losses**

Normal loss = $10\% \times 4,000 = 400$

Total loss = $4,000 + 3,000 - 2,400 - 3,400 = 1,200$

Therefore, abnormal loss = 800

	Equivalent kgs	
	Material costs	Conversion costs
Process 2	2,400	2,400
Abnormal loss	800	800
Closing WIP	3,400	1,360 ★
	6,600	4,560

★ 3,400 × 40%

Step 2. Calculate cost per unit of output, losses and WIP

$$\frac{\text{Costs incurred}}{\text{Equivalent units}} = \text{Cost per equivalent unit}$$

∴ Materials cost per equivalent unit $\quad = \quad \dfrac{£4,400 + £22,000}{6,600}$

$$= \quad \frac{£26,400}{6,600} \quad = \quad £4$$

∴ Conversion costs per equivalent unit $\quad = \quad \dfrac{£3,744 + £12,000 + £18,000}{4,560}$

$$= \quad \frac{£33,744}{4,560} \quad = \quad £7.40$$

Step 3. Calculate total cost of output, losses and WIP

	Materials	Conversion costs	Total
	£	£	£
Transfers to process 2	9,600	17,760	27,360
Abnormal loss	3,200	5,920	9,120
Closing WIP	13,600	10,064	23,664
	26,400	33,744	60,144

Step 4. Complete account

PROCESS 1 ACCOUNT

	Kg	£		Kg	£
WIP materials	3,000	4,400	Process 2	2,400	27,360
WIP conversion costs	–	3,744	Normal loss	400	–
Materials	4,000	22,000	Abnormal loss	800	9,120
Labour	–	12,000	WIP materials	3,400	13,600
Overhead	–	18,000	WIP conversion costs	–	10,064
	7,000	60,144		7,000	60,144

Process 2

Step 1. Determine output and losses

Opening WIP + transfers from process 1 = finished goods + normal loss + abnormal loss/gain + closing stock

∴ 2,250 + 2,400 = 2,500 + (10% × 2,400) + abnormal loss/gain + 2,600
∴ Abnormal gain = 690 kgs

	Equivalent kgs	
	Process 1	Conversion costs
Finished goods	2,500	2,500
Abnormal gain	(690)	(690)
Closing WIP	2,600	1,040 ★
	4,410	2,850

★ 2,600 × 40%

Step 2. **Calculate cost per unit of output, losses and WIP**

$$\text{Process 1} = \frac{£4,431 + £27,360 - £480^\star}{4,410} = £7.10$$

$$\text{Conversion costs} = \frac{£5,250 + £15,000 + £22,500}{2,850} = £15.00$$

$\star$ £2 × 240 units of normal loss (scrap value)

Step 3. **Calculate total cost of output, losses and WIP**

	Process 1 £	Conversion costs £	Total £
Finished goods	17,750	37,500	55,250
Abnormal gain	4,899	10,350	15,249
Closing WIP	18,460	15,600	34,060
	41,109	63,450	104,559

Step 4. **Complete account**

PROCESS 2 ACCOUNT

	Kg	£		Kg	£
WIP Process 1	2,250	4,431	Finished goods	2,500	55,250
WIP conversion costs	-	5,250	Normal loss	240	480
Process 1	2,400	27,360	WIP Process 2	2,600	18,460
Labour	-	15,000	WIP conversion costs	-	15,600
Overhead	-	22,500			
Abnormal gain	690	15,249			
	5,340	89,790		5,340	89,790

Other workings

1   ABNORMAL LOSS ACCOUNT

	£		£
Balance b/f	1,400	P&L	10,520
Process 1	9,120		
	10,520		10,520

2   ABNORMAL GAIN ACCOUNT

	£		£
Scrap recovery lost (690 × £2)	1,380	Balance b/d	300
P&L	14,169	Process 2	15,249
	15,549		15,549

Pass marks. The lost revenue from sales of scrap which results from an abnormal gain (ie lower than normal loses) is debited to the abnormal gain account so reducing its value.

---

3   £(585,000 + 52,000)

4   Cost of sales for September = opening finished goods stock + transfers of finished goods from Process 2 – closing finished goods stock = £(65,000 + 55,250 – 60,000) = £60,250

5   Annual cost of sales   = opening balance + balance for September
                          = £(442,500 + 60,250)
                          = £502,750

6   Overhead under or over absorbed = balance b/f + overheads charged to process 1 + overheads charged to process 2 – overheads incurred = £(250 + 18,000 + 22,500 – 54,000) = £13,250 under absorbed

ABC PLC PROFIT AND LOSS ACCOUNT
FOR THE YEAR ENDED 30 SEPTEMBER 20X8

	£	£
Sales (W3)		637,000
Cost of sales (W5)		502,750
Gross profit		134,250
Under-absorbed overhead (W6)	13,250	
Abnormal loss (W1)	10,520	
Abnormal gain (W2)	(14,169)	
		9,601
Net profit		124,649

59   P AND Q

> **Pass marks**. There is no work in process in process 1 and the losses were 100% complete, so there was no need to prepare an equivalent units calculation. In process 2 there was some closing work in process, however, and so an equivalent units calculation was necessary.
>
> The net realisable value of by-product R should not have been included in the apportionment of the common costs but included as an incidental source of revenue.
>
> In part (b), because the question asks for the toxic waste accounts we have prepared an account for normal, as well as abnormal, toxic waste.
>
> The trickiest part of the question was perhaps dealing with the disposal cost of the waste. The cost of disposing of the normal waste is included as a cost in the process account, whereas the cost of disposing of the abnormal waste does not affect the process account. Instead, the units of abnormal waste are valued at the full equivalent cost per kg in the process account.
>
> It was vital that you noted the word *and* which linked the two factors to be considered in the decision making part of the question (part (d)).

(a)   *Step 1*. **Determine output and losses**

Normal level of waste = $50/1,000 \times 10,000 = 500$ kg

$\therefore$ Abnormal waste = $(600 - 500)$ kg = 100 kg

Input (10,000 kg) = output of P (4,800 kg) + output of Q (3,600 kg) + output of by-product R (1,000 kg) + abnormal waste (100 kg) + normal waste (500 kg)

Step 2. **Determine cost per unit of output and abnormal loss**

Cost per kg of output

$$= \frac{\text{costs incurred (including cost of normal loss diposal)} - \text{by-product income}}{\text{expected kg of output}}$$

$$= \frac{£(15,000 + 10,000 + 4,000 + 6,000 + (500 \times £1.50) - (1,000 \times £1.75)}{4,800 + 3,600 + (600 - 500)}$$

$$= £4$$

Step 3. **Determine total cost of output and abnormal loss**

The rate of £4 per kg is used to value the abnormal waste. The total cost to be absorbed by products P and Q [(4,800 + 3,600) × £4 = £33,600] must be apportioned using the final sales value method.

The disposal cost of the normal waste only is entered in the process account (500 × £1.50).

The by-product does not carry any process costs. It is valued at its selling price of £1.75 per kg.

	P	Q	Total
Final sales value (£ per kg)	5	7	
Kg output	4,800	3,600	
Total sales value	£24,000	£25,200	£49,200
Joint cost apportioned pro rata	£16,390	£17,210	£33,600

MAIN PROCESS ACCOUNT – PROCESS 1

	kg	£		kg	£
Materials input	10,000	15,000	Finished goods – P	4,800	16,390
Direct labour		10,000	Process 2 – Q	3,600	17,210
Variable overhead		4,000	By-product stock – R	1,000	1,750
Fixed overhead		6,000	Normal waste	500	–
Normal waste disposal (2)		750	Abnormal waste	100	400
	10,000	35,750		10,000	35,750

(b)

NORMAL TOXIC WASTE ACCOUNT

	£		£
Bank – disposal cost	750	Main process	750

ABNORMAL TOXIC WASTE ACCOUNT

	£		£
Main process	400	Profit and loss account	550
Bank – disposal cost	150		
	550		550

Process 2: initial workings

Step 1. Determine output and losses

			Equivalent kgs
	Output	*Materials*	*Conversion costs*
	Kg	Kg	Kg
Product Q2	3,300	3,300	3,300
Closing WIP	300	300	150
	3,600	3,600	3,450

Step 2. Determine cost per unit of output

Costs	£	£
Main process input (from (a))	17,210	
Conversion fixed		6,000
variable (3,450 × £1.50)		5,175
	17,210	11,175
Cost per equivalent unit	£4.78	£3.24

Step 3. Determine total cost of output

	Equivalent units	*Cost per unit*	*Value*	
	£	£	£	£
Product Q2	3,300	8.02 (£(4.78 + 3.24))		26,465*
Closing WIP				
Materials	300	4.78	1,434	
Conversion costs	150	3.24	486	
				1,920

* There is a slight difference here due to rounding of the costs per equivalent unit in Step 2.

Step 4. **Complete account**

PROCESS 2 ACCOUNT

	kg	£		kg	£
Main process – Q	3,600	17,210	Finished goods – Q2	3,300	26,465
Fixed costs		6,000	Closing work in progress	300	1,920
Variable costs		5,175			
	3,600	28,385		3,600	28,385

(c) **Any method** of attributing pre-separation costs to joint products is **arbitrary**. The use of **sales value** as the basis for apportionment **assumes** that **all products** earn the same **profit margin** – if **sales value at the separation point** is used.

In this case the **final sales value of product** Q2 is used, however. This method does **not take into account the further processing costs** in process 2 and therefore the relative **apparent profit margin** for each product will be **distorted**.

Whatever method is used, the **resulting product unit costs** are only really **useful** for **stock valuation** in the financial accounts. They must **not** be used as the basis for any **management decisions**.

(d)

	£ per kg
Incremental revenue (£7 – £4.30)	2.70
Variable cost	1.50
Incremental contribution	1.20

This incremental contribution goes towards the **avoidable fixed costs** of operating process 2. There will be a breakeven throughput volume below which it would not be worthwhile operating process 2.

$$\textbf{Breakeven costs} = \frac{\text{avoidable fixed costs}}{\text{incremental contribution per kg}}$$

$$= \frac{£6,000 \times 60\%}{£1.20} = 3,000 \text{ kg per week}$$

At the current output of 3,300 kg of product Q2 per week it is therefore worthwhile operating process 2 on purely financial grounds. There is, however, a margin of safety of only 300 kg, or 9% of output. If output falls below 3,000 kg per week it would not be worthwhile processing product Q into product Q2.

60   NUMBER OF PROCESSES

> **Pass marks**. It is difficult to restrict the answer to part (a) of this question to the length of time available for 20 marks. Ensure that you focus on identifying the problems of process costing rather than going into too much detail on the range of possible solutions available.

REPORT

(a)   To: The board of directors

From: The management accountant

Date: 5 May 20X7

Subject: The problems associated with process costing

In an attempt to assess the problems associated with process costing it is important to understand the features of process costing which make it different from other costing methods.

(i)   The **continuous nature of production** in many processes means that there will usually be **closing work in process** which must be valued. In process costing it

235

is not possible to build up cost records of the cost per unit of output or the cost per unit of closing stock because production in process is an indistinguishable homogeneous mass.

(ii)   There is often a **loss in process** due to spoilage, wastage, evaporation and so on.

(iii)   Output from production may be a single product, but there may also be **a by-product (or by-products) and/or joint product(s)**.

It is these features which can lead to the problems associated with process costing.

The treatment of overheads

The problems faced in the treatment of overheads are essentially similar to those encountered with any costing method. The **choice of treatment is between marginal and absorption costing**. Absorption costing attempts to include all overheads into the process cost. Those which are of a non-specific nature are apportioned between processes on an arbitrary basis such as floor area. Overheads are then charged to production using, for example, a direct labour hour or a machine hour rate. The judgement involved in such a process means that product costs derived using absorption costing are only accurate up to the point of their marginal cost. Marginal costing product costs only include those overheads which vary directly with the production process, such as power, and hence provide a much more accurate basis for performance evaluation and decision making. Activity based costing could be considered as an alternative method of dealing with overheads.

Valuing work in process (WIP) and finished goods

Where there is closing WIP within the process costing system, the cost and management accountant faces the difficulty of apportioning the costs incurred between finished goods and closing WIP. One approach is to **use the concept of equivalent units**. Equivalent units are whole units of complete work representing units of incomplete work. It is then possible to calculate an average cost per equivalent unit which can be used to build up the total costs of finished output and closing WIP. The precise methods of calculation will depend on whether the stock is to be valued on a **'first in first out' (FIFO) basis** or on a **weighted average cost basis**. An added difficulty to this area of process costing is that an **assessment of the degree of completion of WIP** must be made by production personnel adequately qualified to do so.

The method chosen to value materials issued to a process will also impact upon the valuation of WIP and finished goods. In times of rising prices for example, the FIFO (first in, first out) method of stock valuation would understate the material component of the process costs.

The treatment of the cost of work undertaken buy subcontractors will also affect valuations. It can be included as a direct cost of the next process or the finished product where there is no further processing. However, the principal concern when using subcontractors is that quality is maintained and that delivery schedules are kept to.

Valuing different types of output

Outputs from a single process may include the following.

(i)   **Scrap** (of very **little value**)

(ii)   **By-products** (**limited sale value**)

(iii)   **Joint products** (may be finished goods or alternatively may form an input to a further process)

The **problem is how to apportion the costs of the process to each of the given outputs** so that they can be appropriately valued. It may be possible to attribute part of the process cost to a specific output but in practice this is rarely possible. Various approaches are possible, one example being as follows.

(i)   Value scrap at nil.

(ii)   Value by-products at selling price. The effect of this is to reduce the process cost attributed to the main output(s).

(iii)   Apportion to joint products the remaining process costs on the basis of their ultimate sales value (less any further costs to completion) of the finished products.

Note that methods of sharing process costs between products are simply a way of dividing the costs and should not be regarded as producing accurate product costs.

Losses in process

The **average or expected loss** (due for example to evaporation of liquids) is referred to as the **normal loss**. It is generally accepted that **no value** should be attributed to the normal loss. When the **actual loss exceeds or is less than the normal loss, then abnormal losses or gains occur.** The treatment of such losses and gains is well established. **The problem relates to identifying what is normal and what is abnormal.** The cost and management accountant needs to consult appropriate production personnel and consider past experience and forecasts of future production to make a judgement.

Conclusion

The debate between absorption and marginal costing is universal. The distinguishing features of process costing do, however, cause a number of difficulties for the cost and management accountant which are peculiar to a process costing environment.

If you require further information concerning the contents of this report then please do not hesitate to contact me.

(b) (i)   Joint cost **apportionments** are carried out on an **arbitrary basis**, often using output volume or sales value as the basis of apportionment. The resulting unit costs can **differ** widely depending on which apportionment basis is selected.

Managers using the resulting unit costs for **planning purposes** may **not arrive at correct cost projections** if they assume that they are relevant for any volume of output of each product.

(ii)   **Cost control** is achieved by **comparing actual costs** with a **standard** or **budget cost**. The budget costs must be a **realistic target** for the actual output which was achieved. This means that budgeted costs must be **flexed** to allow for changes in output volume, and then actual costs should be compared with these flexed costs.

The apportioned joint costs must therefore be **separated** into their **fixed** and **variable** elements so that the total budget cost can be correctly **flexed** to allow for changes in activity.

If costs are **correctly analysed** into their fixed and variable components then **apportioned joint costs** can be **used** for the **control** of total costs.

However, **no extra control information** is obtained by carrying out the joint cost apportionment since such an apportionment is purely **arbitrary**.

(iii) **Apportioned joint costs are of little use for decision making and in fact they can produce information which would lead to incorrect decisions.**

Simply by changing the basis of cost apportionment it is possible to make an unprofitable product appear profitable, and vice versa.

Management should be encouraged to **concentrate attention** on the **incremental costs** over which they can exercise control. They can **only control the total amount of joint costs** and they may be misled by the product 'profits' or 'losses' which result from arbitrary apportionment of joint costs.

61 OBJECTIVE TEST QUESTIONS: ABC

1   C   Number of machine hours =

$$(60,000 \times 0.4) + (80,000 \times 0.5) + (90,000 \times 0.3) = 91,000$$

Absorption rate = £72,800/91,000 = £0.80 per machine hour

Option A is incorrect because the different newspapers require different labour hours and machine hours, they are not identical.

Option B is incorrect because a labour hour rate is not appropriate (given that production is more machine intensive than labour intensive).

2   A

Activity	Cost driver	Number of cost drivers	Cost £	Cost per cost driver unit £
Distribution	Outlets	45	22,500	500.00
Maintenance	Machine hours	91,000	24,570	0.27
Setting up	Set-ups	10	25,730	2,573.00

Total overhead attributable to *The Post*

(15 × £500) + (60,000 × 0.4 × £0.27) + (4 × £2,573) = £24,272

Overhead attributable to each *Post*

£24,272/60,000 = £0.40

If you chose **option B**, you selected the total overhead attributable to *The Post*.

If you chose **option C**, you selected the traditional overhead absorption rate of £0.80 per machine hour.

If you chose **option D**, you calculated a rate per publication (£72,800 ÷ 230,000).

3   B

4   D   **I:**   Short-term variable overhead costs vary with the volume of activity, and should be allocated to products accordingly.

II: This statement is not completely correct. Many overhead costs, traditionally regarded as fixed costs, vary in the long run with the volume of certain activities, although they do not vary immediately. The activities they vary with are principally related to the complexity and diversity of production, not to sheer volume of output. For example, set-up costs vary in the long run with the number of production runs scheduled, not the number of units produced.

III: For example, the number of credit investigations undertaken within the credit review department of a bank would be the cost driver of the department's costs.

IV: Following on from III above, a mortgage might require three credit investigations and hence the mortgage should bear the proportion of the departments' costs reflected by three credit investigations.

5   A   Set-up cost per production run $= \dfrac{£84,000}{14} = £6,000$

Cost per inspection $= \dfrac{£48,000}{24} = £2,000$

Total attributed to Product Y

		£
Set-up costs	$4 \times £6,000$	24,000
Inspection costs	$12 \times £2,000$	24,000
		48,000

Cost per unit $\dfrac{£48,000}{4,000} = £12$

Option B is the cost per unit using the number of production runs as a basis for absorbing overheads.

Option C is the cost per unit using the number of inspections as a basis for absorbing overheads.

Option D is the overhead cost per unit using machine hours as a basis for absorbing overheads.

6   C   **IV** is a feature of traditional absorption costing methods.

7   C   **Option C** is the correct description of a cost driver. It is the factor which causes the costs of an activity to increase or decrease. For example a cost driver for materials handling costs could be the number of production runs: the higher the number of production runs, the higher will be the cost of material handling.

Option A is a description of a cost pool.

Option B is a description of an attributable overhead cost.

Option D is a description of a common cost.

8   B   ABC is sometimes introduced because it is fashionable, not because it will be used by management to provide extra information, to alter the production mix or to control non-value-added activities.

I: ABC is particularly useful in an AMT environment where overhead costs are a significant proportion of total costs.

II: This provides a means of controlling the occurrence of the overhead cost.

IV: ABC recognises the complexity of manufacturing with its multiple cost drivers.

9   A

62   **PREPARATION QUESTION: ACTIVITY BASED COSTING**

> **Pass marks**. This question serves as a gentle introduction to ABC. The figurework is relatively straightforward but you must try to present workings and schedules to the standard which is expected from a management accountant. The examiners frequently complain about poor presentation and yours will be greatly improved if you spend a few minutes planning your answer before drawing up the working papers.

(a) We begin by identifying a **cost driver** for each of the overhead costs.

Overhead cost	£	Cost driver	Units of activity	Cost per unit of activity £
Overhead applicable to machine-orientated activity	37,424	Machine hours	12,475 (W)	3.00
Set-up costs	4,355	Set-ups	17	256.18
Materials ordering	1,920	Material orders	10	192.00
Materials handling	7,580	Times material handled	27	280.74
Spare parts administration	8,600	Spare parts	12	716.67

Working

Machine hours in the period

Product	Volume Units	Machine time per per unit Hours	Total machine hours
A	500	0.25	125
B	5,000	0.25	1,250
C	600	1.00	600
D	7,000	1.50	10,500
			12,475

Overheads can now be **traced to products according to their use of the support activities.**

			Product						
	Cost per unit	A		B		C		D	
Overhead cost	of activity	Activity		Activity		Activity		Activity	
	£		£		£		£		£
Machine-orientated costs	3.00	125	375.00	1,250	3,750.00	600	1,800.00	10,500	31,500.00
Set-up costs	256.18	1	256.18	6	1,537.08	2	512.36	8	2,049.44
Materials ordering	192.00	1	192.00	4	768.00	1	192.00	4	768.00
Materials handling	280.74	2	561.48	10	2,807.40	3	842.22	12	3,368.88
Spare parts admin	716.67	2	1,433.34	5	3,583.35	1	716.67	4	2,866.68
			2,818.00		12,445.83		4,063.25		40,553.00
Units produced			500		5,000		600		7,000
Overhead cost per unit			£5.64		£2.49		£6.77		£5.79

(b)

	A £ per unit	B £ per unit	C £ per unit	D £ per unit
Overhead costs				
traced by present system	1.20	1.20	4.80	7.20
traced by ABC	5.64	2.49	6.77	5.79
Increase/(decrease)	4.44	1.29	1.97	(1.41)

Almost 40% of the overhead cost is related to non-machine activity but the traditional system had not reflected this when absorbing overhead costs into products.

Product D had been **overcharged** using the traditional system because the overheads were not traced to the product according to the use made of the facilities. Since product D is a **high volume product** it carried more overheads when absorption was based on machine time. The analysis of the cost drivers showed that D **used proportionately less of the production support activities**, however.

The **remaining products** had been **undercharged** with overheads, particularly products A and C which are **low volume** products. They **used proportionately more of the production support facilities** in relation to their volume and this is adequately reflected when cost drivers are used to trace overheads to products.

63   EXE PLC

> **Pass marks.** According to the examiner, too many candidates did not recognise the fact that Exe plc was operating in the modern environment and therefore produced answers that were too general.
>
> Correct definitions of each of JIT, JIT production and JIT purchasing would have earned you two marks each – how easy is that?

(a)   **World Class Manufacturing**

To survive and grow in today's global competitive market, manufacturing companies such as Exe plc need to follow a philosophy of World Class Manufacturing (WCM).

WCM is a broad term but basically it describes **the manufacture at low cost of high-quality products reaching customers quickly to provide a high level of performance and customer satisfaction.**

A WCM manufacturer will therefore have a **clear manufacturing strategy** aimed at issues such as **quality and reliability, short lead times, flexibility and customer satisfaction.**

The value chain

To compete, the world class manufacturer must appreciate that it is **not just in manufacturing that he must excel**. A clear **understanding** of the relationship between all the factors that add value to an organisation's products (the **value chain**) is vital.

Customers and suppliers are therefore important to organisations such as Exe plc because the value chain **starts externally with suppliers,** links them to the internal functions of research and development, design, production, marketing, distribution, customer service and **ends externally with customers**.

To **improve quality, reduce costs and increase innovation** (and hence improve market share), Exe plc must ensure that the **functions within the value chain are co-ordinated** within the overall organisational framework. This requires the company to develop and maintain communications with customers and suppliers.

Two key elements of WCM

Element 1 – A new approach to product quality

Instead of a policy of trying to detect defects or poor quality in production as and when they occur, WCM sets out to **identify the root causes of poor quality**, eliminate them and achieve zero defects (**100% quality**).

Element 2 – Flexible approach to customer requirements

The WCM policy is to develop **close relationships** with customers in order to **know what their requirements** are, **supply them on time, with short delivery lead times and change the product mix quickly and develop new products or modify existing products** as customer needs change.

How Exe plc can achieve this

Exe plc's achievement of these elements hinges on the introduction of a system of **just-in-time (JIT)**.

JIT

The aim of a JIT system is **to produce products or obtain components as they are required by a customer or needed in production.** A JIT system is therefore a **'pull' system** in that it responds to demand (either from production or from customers) as opposed to a 'pull' system in which stock acts as buffers between the different elements of a system (purchasing, production, sales and so on).

JIT has two key elements.

Element 1 – JIT production

JIT production is driven by demand for finished products with the result that **components are only produced when needed for the next stage.**

Element 2 – JIT purchasing

JIT purchasing is based on ensuring that the **receipt and usage of materials coincide.**

JIT and communications with customers and suppliers

Communication links with customers and suppliers are therefore of vital importance to ensure that Exe plc's finished products are ready when its customers require them and that materials from Exe plc's suppliers are available only when required for Exe plc's production line. They are vital to the operation of JIT, a system that would allow Exe plc to implement WCM and improve its market position.

(b)

> **Pass marks.** The CIMA model answer tends to concentrate on the differences between absorption and activity based costing. We have mentioned in our answer some of the other benefits given by ABC, as the question appeared to have this wider requirement.

The current approach

Exe plc uses a total costing system for pricing, based on recovering overheads by a labour hour absorption rate. This approach to dealing with overheads was **developed at a time when most organisations produced only a narrow range of products** and **when overhead costs were only a very small fraction of total costs,** direct labour and direct material costs accounting for the largest proportion of total cost. **Errors** made **in attributing overheads** to products were therefore **not too significant.**

Unsuitability of the current approach in the modern manufacturing environment within which EXE plc now operates

(i)   **Overhead costs have become a greater proportion of total production costs** incurred in the manufacture of motor cars for a number of reasons.

   (1)   High capital investment costs

   (2)   Many production set-ups in response to demand for a wide range of customer-specific products

   (3)   More paperwork and progress expediting to ensure supply of material and prompt delivery of products

   In contrast the direct labour cost proportion has declined, as a result of multiskilling, automation and teamworking.

(ii)   Most of the overheads incurred by organisations such as Exe plc, operating within a heavily automated environment, tend to be the cost of support activities such as setting-up and production scheduling.

These **support activities** assist the efficient manufacture of a wide range of products and are not, in general, affected by changes in production volume. Instead, they tend to **vary in the long term according to the range and complexity of products** (in this case, cars) manufactured. The **absorption** of Exe plc's overhead costs on a **direct labour hour basis** is therefore **unlikely to recognise the cost relationships that exist within its manufacturing processes.**

(iii)   The **assumption** in the use of absorption costing that **all cars consume all resources in proportion to their production volumes** has two main **implications.**

(1)   It tends to allocate too great a proportion of the cost of Exe plc's support services to high volume product lines (which actually cause relatively little diversity and hence use fewer support services).

(2)   It tends to allocate too small a proportion of the cost to low volume products (which actually cause greater diversity and therefore use more support services).

How activity based costing overcomes these problems

Activity based costing (ABC) attempts to overcome these problems by **identifying the activities or transactions (cost drivers) which underlie Exe plc's activities, and which cause the incidence of the activity, and hence the cost of the activity, to increase.**

For **example**, the costs of the production scheduling activity may well be influenced by the number of production runs, and so the number of production runs is the cost driver for this activity.

Benefit – more accurate product costs

The current **absorption costing** approach used by Exe plc uses just one absorption base to charge overheads to products while **ABC uses many cost drivers** as absorption bases. Absorption rates under ABC are therefore argued to be **more closely linked to the causes of overhead costs,** producing (it is claimed) **more realistic product costs** for the cars the company manufactures.

Benefit – more accurate prices

If Exe plc continues to use a cost based approach to pricing, the use of ABC costs should provide a **more realistic view of product profitability,** highlighting for example those cars that appear to be highly profitable but are actually loss making. More accurate pricing should enable Exe plc to **increase demand** for its products, thereby **increasing market share.**

Other benefits of ABC

(i)   The modern business environment is characterised by high levels of competition. Management's need for an accurate indication of how much it costs to take on competitors cannot be met by traditional costing systems.

(ii)   Support department costs have a tendency to increase. By identifying the driver of these costs, the management of Exe plc can control the costs by controlling the incidence of the cost driver.

(iii)   ABC facilitates the provision of information about the profitability of customers and market segments, vital if Exe plc wishes to compete successfully in the modern manufacturing environment.

Disadvantages of ABC

There have been a number of criticisms made of ABC which Exe plc needs to consider. Possibly of most importance is the fact that the **cost** of implementing ABC can be considerable and so it should only be introduced if the value of the information it provides is greater than the cost of implementation.

64 KL I

Pass marks. When calculating the value of the cost pools you had to apportion all possible costs to maintenance and then apportion the maintenance costs to the other activities.

When attempting part (c), you may have been misled by the wording in the paragraph describing the requirements for the production of component Z. The detail given, for example 15 production runs, relates to just one quarter, not the two-year period.

(a) **Unit costs of components using the single factory labour hour OAR**

Plant-wide OAR = £310,000 ÷ 2,000 = £155

	Component r	Component s	Component t
	£	£	£
Direct material costs	1,200	2,900	1,800
Direct labour (at £12 per hour)	300	5,760	600
Production overhead (at £155 per direct labour hour)	3,875	74,400	7,750
Total cost	5,375	83,060	10,150
Quantity produced	560	12,800	2,400
Cost per unit	£9.60	£6.49	£4.23

(b) Using the information given, an **ABC system** would be developed as follows.

Step 1. Identification of major activities (which, for KL, are receiving component supplies, setting-up production runs, quality inspections and dispatching goods)

Step 2. Creation of cost pools for each activity (a cost pool being a collection of the costs (both directly allocated and apportioned) associated with each activity)

Step 3. Identification of cost drivers (causes of the costs) associated with each activity which, for KL, are as follows

(i) Number of component consignments received, for receiving component supplies activity

(ii) Number of production runs set up, for setting-up production runs activity

(iii) Number of quality inspections carried out, for quality inspection activity

(iv) Number of customer orders dispatched, for dispatching goods activity

Step 4. Calculation of the cost per unit of cost driver associated with each activity (by dividing the value of the cost pool by the total quantity of cost driver)

Step 5. Attribution of overheads to components (by multiplying the given quantities of cost driver consumed by the component by the cost per unit of cost driver)

Step 6. Calculation of an average overhead cost per unit (by dividing the result in Step 5 by the number of components produced)

Calculation of the unit costs of components r, s and t using the above ABC system

We can begin at **Step 2 (creation of cost pools).**

	Mainten-ance £	Receiving supplies £	Setting-up £	Quality inspections £	Dispatching £	Total £
Allocated wages		35,000			40,000	75,000
Apportioned wages (W1)	25,500		34,000	25,500		85,000
Equipment operation expenses (W2)		18,750	87,500		18,750	125,000
Equipment maintenance expenses	25,000					25,000
Apportion maintenance expenses (W3)	(50,500)	7,575	35,350		7,575	
	-	61,325	156,850	25,500	66,325	310,000

Step 3

Number of cost driver units		980	1,020	640	420

Step 4

Cost per unit of cost driver		£62.58	£153.77	£39.84	£157.92

Steps 5 and 6 can now be performed.

Costs for total output

	Component r £	Component s £	Component t £
Direct material	1,200.00	2,900.00	1,800.00
Direct labour	300.00	5,760.00	600.00
Receiving supplies (£62.58 × 42/24/28)	2,628.36	1,501.92	1,752.24
Setting-up (£153.77 × 16/18/12)	2,460.32	2,767.86	1,845.24
Quality inspections (£39.84 × 10/8/18)	398.40	318.72	717.12
Dispatching (£157.92 × 22/85/46)	3,474.24	13,423.20	7,264.32
Cost of total output	10,461.32	26,671.70	13,978.92
Quantity produced	560	12,800	2,400
Cost per unit	£18.68	£2.08	£5.82

Workings

1 Equipment maintenance: 30% × £85,000 = £25,500
Setting-up: 40% × £85,000 = £34,000
Quality inspections: 30% × £85,000 = £25,500

2 Receiving supplies: 15% × £125,000 = £18,750
(Setting-up) Manufacturing: 70% × £125,000 = £87,500
Dispatching: 15% × £125,000 = £18,750

3 Receiving supplies: 15% × £50,500 = £7,575
(Setting-up) Manufacturing: 70% × £50,500 = £35,350
Dispatching: 15% × £50,500 = £7,575

(c) **Quarterly cost of component z**

	£
Direct material	2,000.00
Direct labour (80 × £12)	960.00
Receiving supplies (20 × £62.58)	1,251.60
Setting-up (15 × £153.77)	2,306.55
Quality inspections (30 × £39.84)	1,195.20
Dispatching (4 × £157.92)	631.68
Design cost (£40,000 ÷ 8)	5,000.00
	13,345.03

Charge per quarter

	£
Quarterly cost	13,345.03
Profit mark up (25% × £13,345.03)	3,336.26
	16,681.29

Factors relating to this selling price to consider

(i) KL's management should consider **the short-term cost behaviour identified by RAPIER** Management Consultants. They found that **40% of overheads** are **fixed** when there are **relatively small changes in the level of output** during a **period of two years or less.**

(ii) **RAPIER** also found that, in the same circumstances, **30% of overheads varied in relation to direct labour hours worked**, giving a short-term variable overhead rate of (£310,000 × 30%) ÷ 2,000 = £46.50 per direct labour hour.

(iii) Similarly, **30% of overhead** was discovered to **vary in the short term with the number of inspections**, giving a rate per inspection of (£310,000 × 30%) ÷ 640 = £145.31.

Cost of the order on this basis

	£
Direct material	2,000.00
Direct labour	960.00
Labour-related overhead (£46.50 × 80)	3,720.00
Inspection-related overhead (£145.31 × 30)	4,359.30
Design cost	5,000.00
	16,039.30

Comment

This cost is actually greater than the selling price arrived at using the sales director's method and suggests that **such a price would not cover the actual marginal costs of the order.**

Further analysis is therefore necessary to determine the reasons for the differences between the two approaches and to add to management's understanding of the cost drivers identified.

Management should also **reconsider the pricing method adopted.** Even if costs are correctly determined, the use of cost plus pricing may lead to a price far less than customers are actually willing to pay. On the other hand, orders may be lost if the price is higher than those charged by competitors. KL's sales director should **commission research** into the market.

65   KLI II

> **Pass marks.** A fairly straightforward question if you kept to the point and referred to KL in parts (a) and (b).

(a) (i) **The ideas concerning cost behaviour which underpin ABC**

Basic principle

Activity based costing (**ABC**) is based on the principle that **overhead costs can be analysed into two groups**, those that **vary with the volume of production (short-term variable costs)** and those that **do not vary with the volume of production but vary with a different measure of activity (long-term variable costs).**

Behaviour of long-term variable costs

It has been suggested that **long-term variable overhead costs** are **driven by** the **complexity and diversity of production** rather than simple volume of output. For example, costs for **support services** such as setting-up production lines and stock handling do not increase with the volume of output. They are fixed in the shorter term but vary in the longer term according to the range and complexity of product items manufactured. The more there are different products or product variations manufactured, the more complex and diverse those support activities become.

ABC v traditional approaches

The idea behind ABC is therefore that each category of **long-term variable overhead cost is caused/increases/decreases in line with the incidence of a particular event or activity** rather than production volume. This is a **more sophisticated approach** than that adopted traditionally, the **straightforward division of costs into those that are fixed and those that are variable.**

(ii) **The appropriateness of ABC in the modern manufacturing environment**

Traditional methods of dealing with overhead costs

These were developed in a time when most **organisations produced only a narrow range of products** and when **overhead costs were only a very small fraction of total costs**, direct labour and direct material costs accounting for the largest proportion. Errors made in attributing overhead costs to products were therefore not too significant.

Reasons for the inappropriateness of traditional methods

(1) Nowadays with the **advent of advanced manufacturing technology**, **overhead costs** have become a **greater proportion of total production costs** (because of high capital investment costs, many production set-ups in response to demand for a wide range of customer-specific products, more paperwork and progress expediting to ensure supply of materials and prompt delivery of products) and the **direct labour cost proportion has declined,** in some cases to less than ten percent of the total cost, as a result of **automation, multiskilling and teamworking.**

(2) The accessibility of **information technology** now allows for **more sophisticated overhead allocation methods** than in the past.

(3) The **majority of the overhead costs** incurred within the modern manufacturing organisation are **fixed in the short term** rather than variable, **and so marginal costing is not a particularly appropriate costing convention to use.** Some method of absorption costing is therefore preferred by AMT organisations.

(4) The **absorption of overhead costs on a direct labour hour basis does not recognise the cost relationships within the modern environment.**

It is against this background that ABC has emerged.

The ABC method of dealing with overhead costs

The ABC approach of identifying the activities or events that cause overhead costs to occur/increase/decrease and the use of a product's need for these activities/events as the basis for apportioning overheads to products is seen by the proponents of ABC to be more appropriate to a manufacturing environment in which the level of overhead costs has increased while the level of direct costs has decreased.

(iii) **KL and ABC – background**

Traditional costing systems accurately allocate to products the costs of those resources that are used in proportion to the number of units produced of a particular product. But **many resources are used in non-volume-related support activities,** which have increased due to AMT. These support activities assist the efficient manufacture of a wide range of products and are **not,** in general, **affected by changes in production volume.** They tend to vary in the long term according to the range and complexity of the products manufactured rather than the volume of output. The **wider the range and the more complex the products, the more support services will be required.**

Traditional costing systems, which assume that all products consume all resources in proportion to their production volumes, **tend to allocate too great a proportion of overheads to high volume products (which cause relatively little diversity and hence use fewer support services) and too small a proportion of overheads to low volume products (which cause greater diversity and therefore use more support services).**

The impact of this on KL

KL produces three components, **r (a fairly complex, low volume product), s (a straightforward, high-volume product), and t (an intermediate product in terms of composition and volume).**

Using a **traditional approach** to dealing with overheads, **too small a proportion of overheads will be allocated to component r** and **too high a proportion of overheads to component s.** This will cause the **product costs to be inaccurate and will have repercussions on the prices charged to customers.**

(b) **Deficiencies of current approach**

The current plant-wide overhead absorption rate is £155 per direct labour hour, which is nearly 1,300% of direct labour cost per hour. **The use of a plant-wide overhead absorption rate** means that the **costs allocated and apportioned to individual products do not reflect the different amounts of support activities used by the products, simply their labour hour content.**

How to achieve more meaningful product costs

(i) **Split the manufacturing department(s) into cost centres and apportion overhead costs,** as far as is possible, **between these manufacturing cost centres.** A conventional cascade approach can be used, with plant-wide overhead costs being split between manufacturing and service cost centres, and service cost centre costs then being split between manufacturing cost centres.

(ii) **Use overhead absorption bases for each manufacturing cost centre which reflect the predominant cost driver for that cost centre,** be it machine time, labour content, power or materials consumption. As **KL is heavily automated** it is likely that the **substitution of machine hours** for direct labour hours as the overhead absorption basis would go some way towards producing more realistic product costs.

248

Overall superiority of ABC

The management of KL should bear in mind, however, that **an improved absorption costing system will still produce inferior results to those provided by ABC**. Given that RAPIER Management Consultants have done the majority of the work associated with the implementation of a system of ABC, it would be just as straightforward to introduce ABC.

(c) **Traditional techniques as aids to decision making**

The traditional product costing technique of **absorption costing** is known to be an **unreliable source of decision-making information. Marginal costing,** the other traditional technique, **can aid decision making in the short term** as the effects of minor volume changes are made explicit.

ABC as an aid to decision making

Many of **ABC's** supporters claim that it can **provide effective assistance with decision making** in a number of ways.

(i)   It provides **accurate and reliable cost information.**

(ii) It **establishes a long-run product cost.**

(iii) It **provides data which can be used to evaluate different possibilities of delivering business.**

It is therefore **particularly suited for pricing decisions, decisions about promoting or discontinuing products or parts of the business or decisions concerning the development and design of changed products, new products or new ways to do business.**

Limitations of ABC as an aid to decision making

The conventional **ABC model may not be appropriate for costing short-life products or minor volume changes** as these may have no discernible impact on many overhead costs. And an ABC cost is not a true cost, but simply an average cost because some costs such as depreciation are still arbitrarily allocated to products. An ABC cost is therefore **not a relevant cost for all decisions.**

What ABC's developers have failed to appreciate is that the **speed with which the manufacturing environment is changing** means that **even ABC product costs can no longer be considered reliable for decision making.** Many products have very short lives, whilst those products which have long lives often incur heavy long-term fixed costs as their manufacture may be almost entirely automated. Management therefore need to **use a mixture of ABC and marginal costing**, concentrating on the costs relevant to the decision.

Prime benefits of ABC

These are behavioural rather than related to an improvement in decision-making information. The key benefit of the technique is **better cost management** by both support service users and support service providers. Yet, ironically, this was not what ABC was developed for. Instead, it was designed to improve the accuracy of product costs and hence help managers to optimise the allocation of production capacity between products.

Summary

Managers of those organisations that have introduced ABC have gained a better understanding of cost behaviour, however. And this can lead to a more accurate identification of decision-relevant costs.

249

66   KL III

> **Pass marks.** You may have had trouble providing an answer to part (c) but the topic was covered in a *Management Accounting* article in the January 1999 edition. This illustrates the importance of reading journals, especially for questions on this area of the syllabus.

(a)   **Traditional approach stock control**

   (i)   Factories tried to produce at or near **maximum output** in order to minimise unit costs.

   (ii)   **Large stocks of materials** and **high levels of work in progress and finished goods** were carried.

      (1)   This enabled manufacturers to achieve **long production runs** and so reduce average unit costs.

      (2)   They provided a **buffer** against interruptions to production (caused by supply problems or faulty inputs from other processes) and therefore minimised unproductive idle time.

      (3)   The use of buffer stocks was also believed to **simplify production management**, which was of particular importance in the pre-computer era when production control was a clerical activity.

   (iii)   **Negotiations with materials suppliers concentrated on price** – maximising bulk discounts and so on – and organisations moved to alternative suppliers if they were cheaper. Reliability of delivery and levels of quality were secondary issues.

JIT

It is against this background that just-in-time (JIT) has become popular. The **aims of JIT** are to **produce the required items, at the required quality and in the required quantities, at the precise time they are required**. To achieve these aims, JIT has the following **essential elements**.

   (i)   **JIT purchasing.** Parts and raw materials should be purchased as near as possible to the time they are needed, using **small frequent deliveries against bulk contracts**.

   (ii)   **Supportive supplier relations.** In a JIT environment, the responsibility for the **quality of goods lies with the supplier**. A **long-term commitment** between supplier and customer should therefore be established: the supplier is guaranteed a demand for his products since he is the sole supplier and he is able to plan to meet the customer's production schedules. If an organisation has confidence that suppliers will deliver material of 100% quality, on time, so that there will be no rejects, returns and hence no consequent production delays, **usage of materials can be matched with delivery of materials and stocks can be kept at near zero levels**.

   (iii)   **Uniform loading.** All parts of the productive process should be operated at a speed which matches the rate at which the final product is demanded by the customer. Production runs will therefore be shorter and there will be smaller stocks of finished goods because output is being matched more closely to demand (and so storage costs will be reduced).

   (iv)   **Set-up time reduction.** Machinery set-ups are **non-value-added activities** which should be reduced or even eliminated.

(v) **Machine cells**. Machines or workers should be **grouped by product or component** instead of by the type of work performed. The **non-value-added activity of materials movement** between operations is therefore **minimised** by eliminating space between work stations. Products can flow from machine to machine without having to wait for the next stage of processing or returning to stores. **Lead times and work in progress are thus reduced**.

(vi) **Quality**. Production management should seek to **eliminate scrap and defective units** during production, and to avoid the need for reworking of units since this stops the flow of production and leads to late deliveries to customers.

(vii) **Pull system (Kanban)**. The use of a Kanban, or signal, to ensure that **products/components are only produced when needed by the next process**. Nothing is produced in anticipation of need, to then remain in stock, consuming resources.

(viii) **Preventative maintenance**. Production systems must be reliable and prompt, without unforeseen delays and breakdowns. Machinery must be kept fully maintained, and so preventative maintenance is an important aspect of production.

(ix) **Employee involvement**. Workers within each machine cell should be trained to operate each machine within that cell and be able to perform routine preventative maintenance on the cell machines (ie to be **multiskilled and flexible**).

TQM

The JIT approach involves a continuous commitment to the pursuit of excellence in all phases of manufacturing systems and design and so is **closely linked with Total Quality Management (TQM)**. TQM is the process of focusing on **quality in the management of all resources and relationships within an organisation, not just those connected with manufacturing**. The basic principle of TQM is that **the cost of preventing mistakes is less than the cost of correcting them once they occur**.

(i) The organisation should therefore **'get it right first time'** and **aim for zero defects**.

(ii) **Quality** should be the **primary concern of every employee** at every stage of producing a product. Workers must therefore be **empowered** and take **responsibility** for the quality of the product, stopping the production line if necessary.

(iii) Products and processes should be designed with quality in mind, and **quality awareness programmes** and **statistical checks** on output quality introduced.

(iv) **Supportive supplier relations** are vital to ensure that quality materials, components and so on are delivered. **Vendor quality assurance programmes** should therefore be implemented.

The relevance of JIT, TQM and supportive supplier relations to KL

KL manufactures a **wide range of products** of varying degrees of **complexity** in an **increasingly automated manufacturing environment**. It is an environment well **suited to the introduction of JIT**, which will only succeed **when combined with TQM and supportive supplier relations**.

The introduction of JIT, TQM and supportive supplier relations should bring about the following **improvements** in KL's performance.

(i)   A **more responsive manufacturing facility**, able to react rapidly to changes in demand

(ii)   A decrease in stock levels and hence a **reduction in holding costs**

(iii) **Minimisation of non-value-adding activities**

(iv)   **Improved product quality**

These improvements should ultimately make KL **more competitive.**

(b) **Small batch sizes**

Organisations generally manufacture more than one product but it is usually uneconomic to continuously produce every product. Manufacturing is therefore often done in **batches,** different products being produced on different production lines at different times. **Stocks of each product are usually held** and replenished by new production when levels are reduced by sales.

The cost of small batch sizes

Compared with manufacturing in large infrequent batches, **small batch production can cause the following to occur.**

(i)   An **increase in the opportunity cost of lost production** while production lines are reset

(ii)   An **increase in set-up costs**

(iii) A **reduction in bulk purchase discounts** on material purchases

(iv)   **Extra clerical costs** associated with tracking and controlling more complex production schedules

(v)   An **increase in labour costs** due to a reduction in labour efficiency as the learning curve phenomenon is not fully exploited

(vi)   **Extra materials handling costs** because of replacing materials, assemblies and so on used for one batch with those required for the next

(vii) An **increase in the cost of maintaining quality,** as more emphasis must be put into assuring quality every time a new batch is started

Some of these 'costs of small batch sizes' may not occur at KL, however. Automated production using robots can minimise changeover times, direct labour input is minimal and modern computer-based production control systems are able to handle complex production schedules at low clerical cost.

The cost of small batch sizes and KL's cost accounting system

Cost accounting systems should attribute production costs to products in a meaningful way but **KL's existing cost accounting system does not identify all of the costs of small batch sizes.** Direct costs are directly allocated to products. But **overhead costs are absorbed into product costs using a single factory-wide overhead absorption rate based on direct labour hours,** however. **Products manufactured in small batches therefore bear exactly the same level of overheads as those manufactured in large batches** (unless the direct labour hours per unit is greater for products manufactured in small batches – direct labour waiting time may increase, for example).

Benefits of full knowledge and understanding of this cost

(i)   The identification of batch size costs enables **the optimum production batch sizes** to be calculated.

(ii)   **Short-term decision making** (make or buy, product discontinuance, one-off order pricing and so on) should be **improved**.

(iii) The identification of **ways** in which the overhead **costs** associated with small batch sizes can be **reduced** (the better use of IT, systems and procedures, better-trained workforce and so on).

67   ABC AND ABB

> **Pass marks.** Common weaknesses in part (b) included producing little more than an answer plan, repetition of the same point (albeit in different words) and making comments which appeared to contradict statements made in part (a).

(a)   The usefulness of activity-based techniques will depend on the characteristics of an organisation, in particular its cost structure, product range and environment.

(i)   **Cost structure**

(1)   **Impact of proportion of overheads**

Activity-based techniques are particularly useful in organisations where **overheads account for a significant proportion of total costs**. The allocation of material costs and direct labour costs to cost objects is fairly straightforward but the traditional methods used to apportion and absorb overheads can often produce misleading product cost information. The higher the level of overheads, the less accurate the product costs are likely to be.

(2)   **Impact of new technology/changes to business structure**

If an organisation has **introduced new technology** (leading to a large reduction in direct labour and a significant increase in overheads) or **business process re-engineering,** for example, an investigation is required into whether or not the existing cost system still provides a reasonable estimate of product or service costs as its cost structure is likely to be affected. Activity-based techniques can be used to review the cost allocation process.

(ii)   **Product range and diversity**

(1)   **Impact of range of products**

If an organisation produces only a small number of products, product mix decisions for example can be made on a relevant cost basis. If a **vast number of products** are produced, however, the number of individual products and the number of combinations of products would make relevant cost analysis impossible. A general-purpose activity-based system is required that reports long-run product costs. The product costs reported are not designed to be used directly for decision making; instead they should provide attention-directing information and highlight problem areas that need more detailed analysis and the attention of management.

With the current focus on satisfying the customer, many organisations produce a **huge range of diverse products**. ABC is useful if increased product diversity means that an organisation produces **both high-volume standard products and low-volume variant products**. A more sophisticated costing system is required because, as the level of diversity increases, so does the level of distortion reported by absorption costing systems (which tend to allocate too high a proportion of overheads to high-volume products and too low a proportion of overheads to low-volume products).

(2) **Impact of customer base**

Likewise, if an organisation's **customer base is wide**, ABC can provide information for customer profitability analysis. Costs such as those associated with travelling to call on a customer, after-sales service and special delivery methods are revealed, thereby assisting with the identification of profit-making/loss-making customers.

(iii) **Environment**

Increased **competition** may occur if other organisations recognise a particular product or service's profit potential, if the product or service has become feasible in terms of cost to make or perform, or if an industry has been deregulated. Organisations operating in a more competitive environment have a greater need for the more accurate cost information produced by activity-based techniques, since competitors are more likely to take advantage of any errors arising from the use of distorted cost information.

(b) Despite the many advantages claimed by researchers and writers, there are a number of reasons why an organisation might decide **not to use,** or even to **abandon** the use of, activity-based techniques.

(i) The implementation of activity-based techniques is a **time-consuming** and **expensive** process. Activities and cost drivers have to be identified, involving data collection, interviews and observation. Management may feel that the possible benefits are outweighed by the associated costs.

(ii) The introduction of any new technique will be met with **resistance from those employees** who feel threatened by a change to the status quo or who feel that the current system is more than adequate. Such resistance can be reduced if employees are kept fully informed of the reasons for, and the process of, the techniques' introduction, however.

(iii) Any change to the established way of doing things is unlikely to succeed unless the change has a **powerful champion** within the organisation. The champion of any activity-based techniques is likely to be the finance director. If the finance director is not supportive of their introduction or he/she is replaced by another director who is not supportive, their introduction and implementation is likely to fail.

(iv) Even if overheads make up a significant proportion of an organisation's costs, if those **overheads cannot be traced easily to products and services** because cost driver identification is difficult (perhaps if the majority of them are administration costs), the introduction of activity-based techniques might not increase the accuracy of product cost information and hence will not be welcomed by management.

(v) If the techniques appear to be part of a **policy of overhead cost reduction,** employees may worry about possible redundancies and **resist** their introduction. It is therefore vital that a detailed explanation of the reasoning behind any decision to introduce ABC, ABB and so on is given to affected members of the workforce.

(vi) An organisation may decide not to used activity-based techniques if it becomes clear that they will not **provide additional information** for management planning and control decisions.

68 R PLC

> **Pass marks.** Materials costs were not included in the list of costs in the appendix but you were provided with unit costs of materials and had to include the figures in the budget in part (a).

(a) **Activity based budget for production line X**
Six-month period to 30 June 20X9

		Total cost £	Product A Total cost £	Product A Cost per unit of Product A £	Product B Total cost £	Product B Cost per unit of Product B £
Product unit-based activities						
Materials	(W1)	1,215,000	540,000		675,000	
Labour, power etc		294,000	144,000		150,000	
	(W2)	1,509,000	684,000	76.000	825,000	55.000
Batch-based activities						
Production scheduling		29,600				
WIP movement		36,400				
Purchasing and receipt of material		49,500				
	(W3)	115,500	63,000		52,500	
Machine set-ups	(W4)	40,000	15,000		25,000	
	(W5)	155,500	78,000	8.667	77,500	5.167
Product-sustaining activities						
Material scheduling	(W6)	18,000	9,000		9,000	
Design/testing	(W7)	16,000	9,600		6,400	
	(W8)	34,000	18,600	2.067	15,400	1.027
Production line-sustaining activities						
Product line development	(W9)	25,000	20,000		5,000	
Production line maintenance	(W10)	9,000	6,000		3,000	
	(W11)	34,000	26,000	2.889	8,000	0.533
Factory-sustaining activities						
General factory costs administration		125,000				
occupancy		67,000				
	(W12)	192,000	72,000	8.000	120,000	8.000
Total		1,924,500	878,600	97.623	1,045,900	69.727

Workings

1   A's material cost = £60 × 9,000 = £540,000
    B's material cost = £45 × 15,000 = £675,000

2   Cost per A = £684,000 ÷ 9,000 = £76
    Cost per B = £825,000 ÷ 15,000 = £55

3   Number of batches of A = 9,000 ÷ 100 = 90
    Number of batches of B = 15,000 ÷ 200 = 75
    Total number of batches = 165

    A's share of costs = 90/165 × £115,500 = £63,000
    B's share of costs = 75/165 × £115,500 = £52,500

4   Total set-ups = 15 + 25 = 40

    ∴ A's share of set-up costs = £40,000 × 15/40 = £15,000
       B's share of set-up costs = £40,000 × 25/40 = £25,000

255

5   Cost per A = £78,000 ÷ 9,000 = £8.667
Cost per B = £77,500 ÷ 15,000 = £5.167

6   Quantity of components purchased for A = 20 × 9,000 =   180,000
Quantity of components purchased for B = 12 × 15,000 = <u>180,000</u>
<u>360,000</u>

∴ A's share of material scheduling costs = £18,000 × 180/360 = £9,000
  B's share of material scheduling costs = £18,000 × 180/360 = £9,000

7   Total number of components = 12 + 8 = 20 (per question)

∴ A's share of design/testing costs = 12/20 × £16,000 = £9,600
  B's share of design/testing costs = 8/20 × £16,000 = £6,400

8   Cost per A = £18,600 ÷ 9,000 = £2.067
Cost per B = £15,400 ÷ 15,000 = £1.027

9   Product line development costs for A = 80% × £25,000 = £20,000
Product line development costs for B = 20% × £25,000 = £5,000

10   Total maintenance hours = 300 + 150 = 450
Production line maintenance costs for A = £9,000 × 300/450 = £6,000
Production line maintenance costs for B = £9,000 × 150/450 = £3,000

11   Cost per A = £26,000 ÷ 9,000 = £2.889
Cost per B = £8,000 ÷ 15,000 = £0.533

12   Share of administration for X = 25% × £500,000 = £125,000
Share of occupancy for X = 25% × £268,000 = £67,000
Total units = 9,000 + 15,000 = 24,000

A's share of general factory costs = 9,000/24,000 × £192,000 = £72,000
Cost per A = £72,000 ÷ 9,000 = £8

B's share of general factory costs = 15,000/24,000 × £192,000 = £120,000
Cost per B = £120,000 ÷ 15,000 = £8

(b) (i)   A **cost pool** is a **grouping of all cost elements associated with a particular activity**. Cost pools can therefore be established at R plc for, for example, production scheduling and design/testing routines. The costs in the cost pool can then be shared out to products using the cost driver (see (iii) below) applicable to the activity in question.

    (ii)   A **cost driver** is the **activity or transaction which underlies an activity and which causes the incidence of the activity, and hence the cost of the activity, to increase**. For example, the costs of the production scheduling, WIP movement and purchasing and receipt of materials activities at R plc are assumed to be influenced by the number of batches of product that are manufactured and so the number of batches is the cost driver of these activities. By reducing the incidence of a cost driver, the costs of the associated activity can be reduced.

(c) Set out below is a sequential set of **steps** which may be included in an **investigation of activities in order to improve company profitability**.

    (i)   Determine the activities undertaken within the organisation.

    (ii)   Assess which activities could be eliminated without affecting the effective operation of the business.

(iii)   Analyse necessary activities to determine how well they are being carried out (in terms of effectiveness, quality, to what standard and so on)

(iv)   Ascertain the associated cost drivers for each activity.

(v)   Ensure that link between the cost driver, the level of activity and the associated cost is well understood.

(vi)   Use the resulting information for cost reduction and budgeting purposes, for example.

69   OBJECTIVE TEST QUESTIONS: RELEVANT COSTS AND LIMITING FACTOR ANALYSIS

1   D

	Z1	Z2	Z3
	£	£	£
Selling price per unit	15	18	17.00
Variable costs per unit	7	11	12.70
Contribution per unit	8	7	4.30
Labour cost per unit	£2	£4	£1.80
Contribution per £1 of labour	£4	£1.75	£2.39
Rank order of production	1	3	2

If you chose **option A**, you ranked according to contribution per unit.

If you chose **option B**, you ranked according to variable cost per unit.

If you chose **option C**, you ranked according to labour cost per unit.

2   A   The purchase and trade-in values have already been contracted and so are not relevant.

The factory manager is paid a salary and so her time is not relevant.

		Annual cost
		£
Option 1	Recruit new staff (3 × £21,000)	63,000
Option 2	Training	18,290
	Recruits (4 × £11,100)	44,400
		62,690

Option B is incorrect because you should select the lowest annual cost.

Option C incorrectly includes the cost of the supervisor's time supervising the new maintenance staff.

Option D is option 2 without the training cost.

3   B   The products must be ranked in order of their contribution per kg of direct material.

	X	Y	Z
	£ per unit	£ per unit	£ per unit
Selling price	75	95	96
Variable cost	34	41	45
Contribution	41	54	51
Kg of material used per unit	2	1	3
Contribution per kg	£20.50	£54	£17
Ranking	2	1	3

If you chose **option A**, you ranked according to unit contribution.

If you chose **option C**, you ranked according to selling price.

If you chose **option D**, you ranked according to usage of material.

4   D

£

Skilled labour: The relevant cost of skilled labour is the variable cost
plus the contribution foregone from not being able to put the labour
to its alternative use: 20 hrs × (£12 + £15)   540

Semi-skilled labour: They are being paid anyway, so their wages are
not relevant. The incremental cost incurred will be the wages paid to
the unskilled labour taken on to replace them: 23 hrs × £5   115

Unskilled labour: There is no indication that there is any opportunity
cost associated with unskilled labour and so the relevant cost is the
wages: 12 × £5 $\underline{60}$

$\underline{715}$

If you selected **option A** you omitted the variable cost of £12 per hour for skilled
labour. **Option B** is based on the actual hourly rates for each type of labour,
which are not necessarily the relevant rates. **Option C** omits the opportunity cost
of skilled labour.

5   B   As the materials are used regularly, the replacement cost of 95% × £13.75 =
£13.06 is more relevant than the historical cost. Given the scarce supply and the
regularly use, the bulk discount would be taken. The write down to NRV is
irrelevant and in the light of the current market price it would seem to be wrong.

6   A   The company should concentrate on the product with the highest C/S ratio.

7   B

70   CIVIL ENGINEERING INDUSTRY

> **Pass marks**. One way of determining which is the more advantageous of the two contracts is
> to calculate the net cost or benefit of cancelling the north-east contract in favour of the work
> on the south cost. We are asked to present comparative statements, however, and so our
> approach will be to prepare statements of the relevant costs of each contract.
>
> Did you read note 3 properly? Rent receivable is *not* an expense. Make sure that the
> explanations you give in part (b) do not differ from the treatment of items in part (a).

(a) **Statements of the relevant costs of each contract**

	Note	North East £	South Coast £
Material X in stock (£21,600 × 90%)	1	19,440	
Material Y in stock (£24,800 × 2)	2		49,600
Material X on order (30,400 × 90%)	1	27,360	
Material X not yet ordered	3	60,000	
Material Z not yet ordered	3		71,200
Labour	4	86,000	110,000
Site management	5	–	–
Staff accommodation and travel	6	6,800	5,600
Plant for north-east contract	7	(6,000)	
Plant for south coast contract	8	–	–
Interest on capital	9	–	–
Headquarters' costs	10	–	–
Penalty payment	11		28,000
Total relevant costs		193,600	264,400
Contract price		288,000	352,000
Net benefit		94,400	87,600

The **north-east** contract is therefore the **more advantageous**, with a net benefit to the
company of £94,400.

(b) The **reasoning** behind the treatment of each cost item is given in the following notes.

Notes

1   The relevant cost of the material X in stock and on order is the **opportunity cost** of the saving which is forgone by not using X as a substitute material.

2   Ignoring the time value of money and the cost of storing the material, it would not be worth selling material Y and then repurchasing it next year. In fact the cost of borrowing is 8%, which is much less than the 15% cost of disposing of the material. The relevant cost of using material Y is the **replacement cost** which would have to be paid to obtain more material for next year's contracts.

3   Since this material has not yet been ordered, the **current cost** is the relevant cost of a decision to proceed with each contract.

4   The labour costs are the **incremental costs** which would have to be incurred if the contract goes ahead. They are therefore relevant costs of both contracts.

5   The statement that site management is treated as a fixed cost is assumed to mean that it is a **committed cost** which will be incurred irrespective of the decision concerning these contracts.

6   It is assumed that these are **incremental costs** which will only be incurred if the contracts go ahead.

7   If the north-east contract is undertaken, the **rental value received** will be £6,000. The **depreciation cost is not relevant** (see note 8).

8   It is assumed that the depreciation cost is an accounting book entry and that the **value of the plant will not be affected** by using it on either contract.

9   Although there would probably be some incremental **working capital financing costs** as a result of the contracts, we have **no way of knowing** how much they would be. They would be somewhat reduced by the effect of the progress payments received from the contractee.

10   It is assumed that the total amount of headquarter's costs **would not be affected** by the decision to undertake either contract. This is therefore not a relevant cost.

11   The penalty payment is a **relevant cost of cancelling the north-east contract in order to proceed with the south coast contract.**

71   ANOTHER PRODUCT

> **Pass marks.** Remember that when faced with two decision options, you only need to include those costs and revenues which differ between the two options. So in (a), maximum demand for products P1 and P2 is always met and so revenue is the same under both options.
>
> Part (b) is straightforward, although you need to be able to think up relevant examples.

(a) We need to compare the cost of subcontracting all production of P2 with the costs of in-house manufacture/subcontracting.

   (i)   **Revenue** is **not a relevant cash flow** as the same number of units will be sold whatever option is chosen.

       Advertising expenditure is a **non-relevant cost** as it will be the same under both options.

20X9

	Subcontract only £	Produce and Subcontract £
Subcontract cost		
(8,000 × £80)	640,000	–
(8,000 – (10,000 – 8,000)) × £80	–	480,000
Component cost (2,000 × £30)	–	60,000
Cost of computer software	–	100,000
Variable costs		
(8,000 × £15)	120,000	–
(2,000 × £40) + (6,000 × £15)	–	170,000
Cash outflow	760,000	810,000

EM Ltd should **subcontract all of P2.**

20Y0

	Subcontract only £	Produce and subcontract £
Subcontract cost		
(8,000 × £80)	640,000	-
((8,000 – (10,000 – 6,000)) × £80)	-	320,000
Component cost (4,000 × £30)	-	120,000
Cost of computer software	-	100,000
Variable costs	-	-
(8,000 × £15)	120,000	-
(4,000 × £40) + (4,000 × £15)	–	220,000
Cash outflow	760,000	760,000

EM Ltd will be **indifferent between subcontracting all production and subcontracting a proportion of production.**

20Y1

	Subcontract only £	Produce and subcontract £
Subcontract cost		
(6,000 × £80)	480,000	–
((6,000 – (10,000 – 4,000)) × £80)	–	–
Component cost (6,000 × £30)	–	180,000
Cost of computer software	–	100,000
Variable costs		
(6,000 × £15)	90,000	–
(6,000 × £40)	–	240,000
Cash outflow	570,000	520,000

EM Ltd should **produce all of P2 in-house.**

(ii) A number of **additional factors may influence the decision to subcontract all or part of the production of P2.**

(1) The effect on the **workforce** of a decision to subcontract production rather than manufacture in-house. Would part of the workforce need to be made redundant?

(2) The **problems associated with subcontracting and then manufacturing in-house** (if EM Ltd decide to look at the decision on a year-by-year basis). Would the in-house workforce be sufficiently skilled to manufacture P2 in 20Y1. If employees have been made redundant because of a decision to subcontract in 20X9, would sufficient employees be employed in 20Y0/Y1? Would the company have retained sufficient machinery to produce to maximum capacity in 20Y0/Y1?

(3) The **reliability and quality of work of the subcontractor**. Poor quality work and/or late delivery could impact on sales estimates.

(4) Use of the **spare production capacity** should EM Ltd decide to subcontract all production of P2. Could another product be developed and manufactured using the spare capacity?

(5) The **reliability of the estimates** used in the decision analysis.

(6) The possibility of the **subcontractor increasing his costs**.

(b) (i) **Acceptance of contracts**

(1) An **example of directly attributable fixed costs** relevant to a contract would be the salaries of administrative staff who would be deployed to deal exclusively with matters arising from the contract.

(2) **Opportunity costs** will be relevant to the decision, for example the income from another contract that would have to be rejected if another were accepted.

(3) **Sunk costs** will not be relevant. For example, the cost of a machine already purchased would not be relevant even if it were to be used in carrying out the contract.

(4) **Incremental costs** will be relevant. An example would be the wages of workers with specialist skills who would have to be taken on in order to fulfil the contract.

(ii) **Make or buy decisions**

(1) **Directly attributable fixed costs** are those directly identifiable with a particular course of action, for example rental of factory space specifically in order to make something rather then buying it.

(2) **Opportunity costs** are the benefits are foregone by choosing one opportunity instead of the next best alternative. For example, in a make or buy situation, if materials could either be used to make the item or else resold, the proceeds from selling them would be their opportunity cost and this cost should be used for the purpose of making the decision.

(3) **Sunk costs** are never relevant in decision-making situations. A sunk cost is the cost of an asset which has already been acquired and which can continue to serve its present purpose but which has no significant realisable value and no income value from any other alternative purpose. An example in a make or buy situation would be materials already in stock that could be used for the purpose but have no other use and no resale value.

(4) **Incremental costs** are the additional costs incurred as a consequence of decision, for example the cost of a machine that has to be acquired if something is to be made internally rather than bought externally.

72   **ICE RINK**

> **Pass marks.** If you have a very disciplined mind you may have been able to do the whole calculation in (a) in four lines, but the layout below is more likely to reflect your thought processes in an exam situation – and it's kinder to your non-accounting managers, who may not be up to speed on relevant costs. Note the exam techniques of using a 'Notes' column, to fulfil the question requirements for explanations and assumptions without cluttering up the page, and of combining workings within the notes.
>
> In part (b) you may well have been able to 'see' what to do, but not quite have got your head round the maths. Don't rush it: it's worth eight marks, and it's just simple breakeven analysis really, so keep your head and work patiently backwards to the required percentage. If you actually write down your thought processes, as we do in our answer, the markers will be able to see that you had the right idea, even if you get the maths wrong, or get lost.

(a) **Heat recovery proposal**

	Notes	**Don't** *proceed*	**Do** *proceed*	*Net (saving)/cost*
		£	£	£
Survey	1	30,000.00	30,000.00	0.00
Heat extraction	2	132,000.00	132,000.00	0.00
Pool heating	3	115,500.00	43,312.50	(72,187.50)
Equipment hire	4	0.00	75,000.00	75,000.00
Salary	5	0.00	17,500.00	17,500.00
		277,500.00	297,812.50	20,312.50

Recommendation

The **net cost** of proceeding with the proposal is £20,312.50. Unless non-financial factors are judged to be more important, the proposal **should not proceed**.

Notes

1   The cost of the **survey** is a **sunk** cost: it has already been incurred, whether or not the proposal goes ahead. (This line is strictly unnecessary in the calculation, and could be omitted, but it is included for the benefit of non-accounting managers.)

2   **Heat extraction** costs are **not incremental** costs: they will be incurred whether or not the proposal goes ahead, and so again this line is strictly unnecessary and could be omitted.

   The cost is calculated as £120,000 × 110% = £132,000.

3   **Pool heating** costs of £150,000 will rise by 10%, but only **70%** of this amount is **relevant** to the decision: the **remainder** is a **notional share of general fixed overhead,** and we must **assume** that this **percentage will not change** whatever decision is taken.

   Pool heating with the **existing** system = £150,000 × 110% × 70% = £115,500.

   If the **proposal goes ahead** the cost of **pool heating** can be calculated as follows.

Heat extracted from the ice rink (units)	500,000
Recovery level	25%
Recovered units	125,000
Heat required to heat the swimming pool (units)	200,000
Balance to be recovered from the existing system (units)	75,000

   In the absence of other information the **cost** of the balance can be **assumed** to be 75,000/200,000 × the existing heating cost of £115,500 (see above) = £43,312.50.

Cost

$\dfrac{75}{200} \times 115,500$

$= 43312.50$

4   **Equipment hire** is an **incremental** cost: it will only be incurred if the proposal goes ahead.

5   The **supervisor** will retire, and will not be replaced if the proposal does not go ahead, so his **salary** is **only relevant** if he is retained to manage the **proposed** new equipment.

(b)   From part (a) (and note 3) we can deduce that **pool heating** costs need to be **less than or equal to £115,500** if we are to be **indifferent** between the two options.

The proposed system would incur the **equipment** hire cost (£75,000) and the fixed **salary** cost (£17,500) in any circumstance, plus a **variable amount** depending upon how much heat can be recovered.

	£
Breakeven amount	115,500
Less: Equipment hire	(75,000)
Less: Salary	(17,500)
Required variable cost	23,000

The **variable cost must not exceed £23,000**, so we need to know what percentage of heat has to be recovered and re-used from the heat extraction process to achieve a cost of **£23,000**.

200,000 units of heat are required to heat the pool. Using the existing system these will cost **£115,500 in total** , or £115,500/200,000 = **£0.5775 per unit**.

Therefore:

(i)   breakeven point will occur if no more than £23,000/£0.5775 = **39,826.84 units** are used from the existing system; and so

(ii)   200,000 – 39,826.84 = **160,173.16 units** from the total units extracted from the ice rink (**500,000 units**) must be recovered.

Percentage level of heat recovery = (160,173.16 / 500,000.00) × 100% = **32.03%**

73   PR PLC

(a)

> **Pass marks**. Part (a) is very straightforward and gave you the opportunity to earn eight very easy marks. According to the examiner a number of candidates were clearly unprepared for this topic.
>
> A common error in part (a)(ii), according to the examiner, was to apportion the fixed overhead between the services on an arbitrary basis to provide a 'profit per service'. This was not required.
>
> Part (b)(ii) was far more difficult than part (i), although throughput accounting is covered in the BPP Study Text. The first part of the question was so straightforward, however, that even if you fell down on part (ii) you should have been able to get about one quarter of the marks for the question on part (i) alone.
>
> Our answer to part (ii) describing throughput accounting is far longer than you could have produced in the time available but we think you will find the additional information useful for revision purposes.

(i)   *Step 1.* **Establish limiting factor.**

To meet full demand, the number of consultant's days required =

(150 × £900/£300) + (800 × £750/£300) + (200 × £1,500/£300) = 450 + 2,000 + 1,000 = 3,450

But only 2,400 days are available.

Consultants' time is therefore a limiting factor, there being a shortfall of 3,450 – 2,400 = 1,050 days per annum.

Step 2. **Calculate contribution per unit of limiting factor.**

> **Pass marks**. Remember to always rank on the basis of contribution per unit of limiting factor (not profit per service or contribution per service).

	A	B	C
	£	£	£
Fee income	2,500	2,000	3,200
Consultant	900	750	1,500
Specialist's report	400	200	500
Variable overhead	200	160	300
	1,000	890	900
Units of limiting factor required*	3 days	2.5 days	5 days
Contribution per unit of limiting factor	£333	£356	£180
Ranking	2	1	3

*Consultant cost ÷ £300

Step 3. **Determine optimum production plan.**

Service	Demand fulfilled	Days per service	Days used	Days remaining
				2,400
B	800	2.5	2,000	400
A	133*	3.0	399	1
			2,399	

*400 ÷ 3

Optimum production plan

	Number of services
B	800
A	133
C	–

(ii) **Budgeted profit statement for year ending 31 December 20X2**

		£'000	£'000
Income	B (£2,000 × 800)	1,600.0	
	A (£2,500 × 133)	332.5	
			1,932.5
Costs			
Consultants (2,399 days × £300)			(719.7)
Specialist's report	B (£200 × 800)	160.0	
	A (£400 × 133)	53.2	
			(213.2)
Variable overhead	B (£160 × 800)	128.0	
	A (200 × 133)	26.6	
			(154.6)
Fixed costs			(600.0)
			245.0

> **Pass marks**. Alternatively you could have presented the statement in columnar format with a separate column for each service and for the total.

(b) (i) A limiting factor or key factor in a business situation is anything that acts as a constraint on, or limits, activity because it is in short supply or it cannot be expanded or enlarged upon. It might be a resource such as labour or a certain type of material, or it may a one critical process in a chain of processes.

An organisation might be faced with **one limiting factor** (other than maximum sales demand) but there might also be **several scarce resources**, with two or more of them putting an effective limit on the level of activity that can be achieved.

Annual budgets should **recognise** limiting factors as they should be based on what is achievable given the available resources. The product or service mix adopted should **maximise profit by maximising the return earned by each product per unit of scarce resource.**

Examples of limiting factors are as follows.

(1) **Sales.** There may be a limit to sales demand or the sales force may be ineffective. The physical distribution system may be unable to increase the volume it deals with.

(2) **Labour.** The limit may be either in terms of total quantity or particular skills. Either way, there will be insufficient labour to produce enough to satisfy sales demand.

(3) **Materials**. There may be insufficient available materials, due to restrictions on supply, to produce enough units to satisfy sales demand.

(4) **Manufacturing capacity.** There may not be sufficient machine capacity for the production required to meet sales demand.

(5) **Financial resources.** There may not be enough cash to pay for the necessary production. The organisation may not be able to borrow the funds necessary for further expansion.

(6) **Working capital.** There may be insufficient working capital to finance the necessary stocks of finished goods or the required debtor levels.

Limiting factors are **usually short-term** constraints which can be overcome by investment, training, marketing and so on.

Limiting factors and WDL

Shortage of **finance** is the most likely limiting factor for WDL. This likelihood will increase if WDL has a high gearing ratio. Scarcity of **suitable land** for development may also prove to be a limiting factor, and its identification may also prove to be a limiting factor if WDL has a lack of skilled personnel.

Other potential limiting factors include the demand for housing, apartments and shops (which will be dependant on the state of the economy), the availability of builders (which may be problematic in boom times), the availability of architects and other professionals and the time taken in the local authority planning approval process.

(ii) **Throughput accounting (TA)** is a system of cost and management accounting which is primarily designed for use in a JIT **manufacturing environment.** **Throughput** is defined as **sales revenue less direct material cost** and the **aim** of throughput accounting is to **maximise this measure.**

The system is based on **three concepts.**

(1) In the short run, most factory costs, other than materials, are fixed.

(2) In a JIT environment, stockholding is discouraged and zero inventory is a business target. Accordingly, there should be no incentive for production managers to manufacture for stock simply to keep idle plant or labour occupied.

(3) Profitability is determined by the rate at which revenue is generated which, because there are no significant stocks, depends on how quickly goods can be produced to meet customer orders.

Throughput is therefore maximised by minimising material costs, maximising prices and maximising saleable output.

The aim of modern manufacturing approaches is to match production resources with the demand for them. This implies that there are no constraints, termed **bottleneck resources** in throughput accounting, within an organisation. The throughput philosophy entails the **identification and elimination** of these bottleneck resources. Where it cannot be eliminated, the bottleneck resource should be used to 100% of its availability. To avoid the build-up of work in progress, production must be limited to the capacity of the bottleneck resource. If a rearrangement of existing resources or buying-in resources does not alleviate the bottleneck, investment in new equipment may be necessary. The elimination of one bottleneck is likely to result in another occurring, however, albeit at a higher throughput level and possibly at a previously satisfactory location. Attention will then be concentrated on the new bottleneck, and so on. As a result, TA encourages a policy of **continuous improvement**.

The **factors which limit throughput** may include constraints other than a lack of production resources (bottlenecks).

(1) The existence of an uncompetitive selling price
(2) The need to deliver on time to particular customers
(3) Poor product quality and reliability
(4) The lack of reliable material suppliers

One criticism of TA is that it pays too little attention to overhead costs. This problem can be alleviated, however, by simultaneously operating an **activity based costing system**. In fact, the two systems are complementary.

TA and limiting factor analysis

There is a close similarity between TA measures and the idea of contribution per unit of limiting factor used in limiting factor analysis. There is a difference in concept, however; **TA uses value added** (sales revenue less material costs) as its output measure whereas **limiting factor analysis uses contribution**. There is also a difference in practice; **TA is a dynamic day-to-day management system** designed to concentrate management's minds on removing bottlenecks and continuous improvement, whilst **limiting factor analysis is a passive planning model** which simply provides solutions to optimise the use of a bottleneck resource. There is therefore a **similarity in concept but not in operation**.

TA and WDL

MDL does not operate within a manufacturing environment. Moreover, for TA to be effective it is necessary for there to be an operational environment in which the bottlenecks are identifiable in advance and are capable of being eliminated in the long term while production is manipulated in the short term so as to maximise throughput. Although bottlenecks may exist on WDL's developments (shortage of labour, material, equipment and cash are all possible), there is **not sufficient flexibility to move resources around between alternative 'products'** in the short term as there is in a factory environment. Although limiting factor analysis may be appropriate at the planning stage of WDL's developments, there is therefore **no case for attempting to use TA for the day-to-day management of a development.**

74   ABC LTD

> **Pass marks**. An analysis by behaviour (part (i)) means analysing the costs into those that are fixed and those that are variable. For each of the six options in part (ii) one factory is closed, one factory operates to 100% capacity and so the third factory produces the balance of the units.

(a)   (i)

	North £'000	Central £'000	South £'000
Variable costs			
Direct materials	500	1,000	750.0
Direct wages	800	1,600	1,200.0
Indirect materials	300*	600	450.5
Indirect wages	50	150	150.0
Indirect expenses	350	600	300.0
	2,000	3,950	2,850.5
Fixed costs			
Indirect materials	75**	200	79.5
Indirect wages	200	850	600.0
Indirect expenses	650	1,400	450.0
Administration (W)	100	150	50.0
	1,025	2,600	1,179.5
Total costs	3,025	6,550	4,030
Variable production cost per unit	£20.00	£19.75	£19.00
Transport cost per unit ***	£5.00	£4.00	£5.00

* Sample working: $375 \times 80\%$
** Sample working: $375 \times (100 - 80)\%$
*** Sample working: £500,000/100,000 = £5

Workings

Head-office cost per unit produced   = £900,000/(100,000 + 200,000 + 150,000)
                                                            = £2

For North:

Head office costs = 100,000 × £2 = £200,000

∴ Specific fixed costs = £(300,000 – 200,000) = £100,000

For Central:

Head office costs = 200,000 × £2 = £400,000

∴ Specific fixed costs = £(550,000 – 400,000) = £150,000

For South:

Head office costs = 150,000 × £2 = £300,000

∴ Specific fixed costs = £(350,000 – 300,000) = £50,000

(ii)   There are **six possible options**. Each option requires the closure of one factory and the relocation of that factory's production so that production is at maximum capacity in one of the remaining factories. Demand in 20X3 = 70% × 20X1 demand = 70% × 450,000 = 315,000 units.

		North		Central		South	
Option		'000 units	% of annual capacity	'000 units	% of annual capacity	'000 units	% of annual capacity
1		Close	0	250	100	65	36
2		Close	0	135	54	180	100
3		160	100	Close	0	155	86
4		135*	84	Close	0	180	100
5		160	100	155	62	Close	0
6		65	41	250	100	Close	0

* Sample working: $(135,000/160,000) \times 100\%$

Costs of each option

Variable cost = production cost + transport cost per unit

Option		North £'000	Central £'000	South £'000	Total £'000
1	Variable	- ₂50	5,937.50 65	1,560.0	
	Fixed	-	5,200.00	1,179.5	
		-	11,137.50 (W1)	2,739.5 (W2)	13,877
2	Variable	-	3,206.25	4,320.0	
	Fixed	-	2,600.00	2,359.0	
		-	5,806.25 (W3)	6,679.0 (W4)	12,485.25
3	Variable	4,000	-	3,720.0	
	Fixed	2,050	-	1,651.3	
		6,050 (W5)	-	5,371.3 (W6)	11,421.3
4	Variable	3,375	-	4,320.0	
	Fixed	1,025	-	2,359.0	
		4,400 (W7)	-	6,679.0 (W4)	11,079
5	Variable	4,000	3,681.25	-	
	Fixed	2,050	2,600.00	-	
		6,050 (W5)	6,281.25 (W8)	-	12,331.25
6	Variable	1,625	5,937.50	-	
	Fixed	1,025	5,200.00	-	
		2,650 (W9)	11,137.50 (W1)	-	13,787.5

Workings

1   **100% capacity**
Variable costs = $250,000 \times £(19.75 + 4.00)$
Fixed costs = $£2,600,000 \times 2$

2   **36% capacity**
Variable costs = $65,000 \times £(19 + 5)$
Fixed costs = $£1,179,500$

3   **54% capacity**
Variable costs = $135,000 \times £(19.75 + 4)$
Fixed costs = $£2,600,000$

4   **100% capacity**
Variable costs = $180,000 \times £(19 + 5)$
Fixed costs = $£1,179,500 \times 2$

5   **100% capacity**
     Variable costs = 160,000 × £(20 + 5)
     Fixed costs = £1,025,000 × 2

6   **86% capacity**
     Variable costs = 155,000 × £(19 + 5)
     Fixed costs = £1,179,500 × 140%

7   **84% capacity**
     Variable costs = 135,000 × £(20 + 5)
     Fixed costs = £1,025,000

8   **62% capacity**
     Variable costs = 155,000 × £(19.75 + 4)
     Fixed costs = £2,600,000

9   **41% capacity**
     Variable costs = 65,000 × £(20 + 5)
     Fixed costs = £1,025,000

The lowest cost option is Option 4. To maximise profits the Central factory should be closed, South factory should produce to full capacity and North factory should produce 135,000 units.

(b)   MEMO

To: Production controller
From: Management accountant
Subject: **Production scheduling**   Date: 17 March 20X2

Further to our meeting on Tuesday, I can confirm that, on the basis of the cost and output information available, the **Central factory should be closed, South factory should produce to full capacity** and **North should produce 135,000 units** if we wish to maximise profits. The following **factors** should also be taken into account, however, before a final decision is made.

(i)   Employees at the Central factory would either need to be transferred to the other two factories or made redundant. **Transfers** are known to cause dissatisfaction to employees. **Redundancy** costs could be high.

(ii)   There may be **other costs** associated with the closure of the Central factory such as machinery decommissioning costs.

(iii)   If employees from the Central factory are not willing to transfer, **additional staff** will need to be recruited for the North and South factory.

(iv)   The South factory would be required to operate at **maximum capacity**. This may cause **administrative burdens** for management and pressures of work might **reduce efficiency and effectiveness**.

(v)   If **demand** were to increase in the future we may be **unable to satisfy it** with the capacity available from the North and South factories alone. *How permanent is this drop*

(vi)   Employee **morale** in the organisation as a whole may suffer if we appear to be motivated by profit alone.

(vii)   The closure of the factory and the possible redundancies may tarnish the organisation's **public image** and this might have repercussions on sales demand.

(viii) Demand **forecasts** may be **inaccurate**. *How accurate are the sales forecast*

Are you sure the factory
Give me a call if you have any further questions. *very hard to open*

269   **BPP**
      PROFESSIONAL EDUCATION

75   **X LTD**

> **Pass marks**. The ranking of the products in part (a) is relatively straightforward, provided you adopt a systematic approach. The information provided in part (b) changes the ranking, and so you will need to recalculate the production plan. Don't forget that the minimum quantity of D has to be produced.

(a)

	A	B	C	D
	£/litre	£/litre	£/litre	£/litre
Selling price	100	110	120	120
Variable cost	54	55	59	66
Contribution	46	55	61	54
Labour hours used per litre	3	2.5	4	4.5
Contribution per labour hour	£15.33	£22	£15.25	£12
Ranking	2	1	3	4

The available **labour hours** should be allocated **first** to the **contract already made** with Y Ltd. The **remaining hours** should then be allocated to **products according to this ranking**, and **subject to the maximum demand**.

	Product	*Litres*		*Hours used*	*Cumulative hours used*
Y Ltd	A, B, C, D	20 each	(× 14)	280	280
Ranking	B	130	(× 2.5)	325	605
	A	180	(× 3)	540	1,145
	C	50	(× 4)	200	1,345

Summary of recommended production for next three months

Product	*Litres*
A	200
B	150
C	70
D	20

Calculation of profit for next three months

Product	*Litres*	*Contribution*	
		£ per litre	£
A	200	46	9,200
B	150	55	8,250
C	70	61	4,270
D	20	54	1,080
Total contribution			22,800
Fixed overhead (see working)			12,800
Profit			10,000

Working

Calculation of fixed overhead per quarter

Using product A, fixed overhead per hour = £24/3 = £8 per hour

∴ Budgeted fixed overhead = 1,600 hours × £8 = £12,800

Note. The calculation of the hourly rate of £8 per hour could have been based on any of the four products.

(b) Products **C and D** can both be **sold** for a **higher price than that offered by the overseas supplier**. The **unsatisfied demand** should therefore be **met** by using the **overseas supplier** next quarter.

	C	D
	£ per litre	£ per litre
External supplier's price	105	100
Internal variable cost of manufacture	59	66
Saving through internal manufacture	46	34
Labour hours used per litre	4	4.5
Saving per labour hour	£11.50	£7.56

Even when the extra cost of the pollution controls for product D is ignored, **it is therefore preferable to manufacture product C internally and purchase D from the overseas supplier**.

The capacity which would have been used to manufacture 20 litres of product D can now be allocated to product C (20 litres × 4.5 hours = 90 hours).

Summary of revised recommended production for the next three months

Product		*Hours*	*Litres*	*Litres*
A	Internal manufacture	600		200
B	Internal manufacture	375		150
C	Internal manufacture	370	92.5	
C	External purchase		7.5	100
D	External purchase			120
		1,345		570

Calculation of revised profit for next three months

Product	*Litres*		*Contribution*	
			£ per litre	£
A	200.0		46	9,200.00
B	150.0		55	8,250.00
C	92.5		61	5,642.50
	7.5	(120 – 105)	15	112.50
D	120.0	(120 – 100)	20	2,400.00
				25,605.00
Fixed overhead				12,800.00
Revised profit				12,805.00

Reasons that profit will increase by £2,805 per quarter are as follows.

(i) Production of product D is subcontracted and the time saved is used on production of product C.

(ii) The additional fixed cost is not incurred because Product D production is subcontracted.

(iii) Maximum demand for products C and D can be met.

A number of factors should be considered, however, including the following.

(i) The reliability of the supplier, which is particularly important in the case of an overseas supplier

(ii) The quality of supply

(iii) Any other sources of sub-contract supply

76   PQR LTD

> **Pass marks**. We had to make a number of assumptions in this question. Don't worry if this happens in an exam – it doesn't mean you don't understand the question. Simply state what you are assuming and you will get marks even if your assumptions are incorrect.

(a)   ***Step 1*. Determine the limiting factor**

Drilling time

	Demand Units	Demand Hrs	Requirement Hrs
Product C	250	3	750
Product D	500	4	2,000
Component A	50	2	100
Component B	100	1	100
Total requirement for drilling hours			2,950
Hours available			1,650
Shortfall			1,300

Grinding

	Demand Units	Demand Hrs	Requirement Hrs
Product C	250	1	250
Product D	500	3	1,500
Component A	50	2	100
Component B	100	4	400
Total requirement for grinding hours			2,250
Hours available			2,500

Grinding hours are not a limiting factor but drilling hours are.

We need to deal with this problem by determining the contribution per unit of limiting factor. We are given no details as to the contribution provided by the **products using A and B** and so we **assume** that they must be **produced up to their maximum demand**.

***Step 2*. Determine contribution per unit of limiting factor for each product**

	Product	
	C	D
	£	£
Selling price	127	161
Direct materials	33	38
Direct wages	20	25
Variable overhead	13	24
Total variable cost	66	87
Contribution	61	74
Drilling hours required per unit	3	4
Contribution per drilling hour	£20.33	£18.50
Order of production	1st	2nd

***Step 3*. Establish a production plan**

We need to allocate 1,650 – 200 = 1,450 hours to products C and D, leaving 200 hours for the production of components A and B.

Product	Demand Units	Hours per unit	Drilling hours required	Total hours
C	250	3	750	750
D	175	4	700	700
				1,450

Step 4. **Determine profit yielded by production plan**

	£
Contribution $((250 \times £61) + (175 \times £74))$	28,200
Fixed costs $((1,650 \times £6) + (2,500 \times £5))$	22,400
Weekly profit	5,800

We have assumed that all of the fixed costs have been borne by products C and D. Had **fixed overheads** been **allocated** on the **basis of hours,** products C and D would have borne the following overheads.

	C	*D*	*Total*
			£
Drilling	$(750 \times £6)$	$(700 \times £6)$	8,700
Grinding	$(250 \times £5)$	$(175 \times 3 \times £5)$	3,875
			12,575

New profit would be £(28,200 – 12,575) = £15,625

(b) (i)

	Components	
	A	*B*
Variable cost of manufacture	£32	£78
Variable cost of purchase	£50	£96
Extra variable cost of purchase	£18	£18
Drilling hours per unit	2	1
Extra cost per drilling hour	£9	£18

PQR Limited can increase contribution, and hence profit, by allocating the 200 hours of drilling time previously used for components A and B to product D since the **contribution per drilling hour from making one unit of product D is greater than the cost per drilling hour of purchasing the components.**

Revised production plan

Produce   250 units of product C
Produce   175 + (200hrs ÷ 4 hrs per unit) = 225 units of product D
Buy in   50 units of component A and 100 of component B

Net benefit caused by change

	£	£
Additional contribution from production of 50 extra units of product D $(50 \times £74)$		3,700
Less: Extra variable cost of purchase of components		
A – £18 × 50 units	900	
B – £18 × 100 units	1,800	
		(2,700)
Additional contribution		1,000

Note that the **fixed costs do not come into the net benefit calculation** since they will remain the same whatever the production plan.

(ii)   In situations involving just **one limiting factor,** the method is to calculate the contribution per unit of limiting factor for each product and **rank production according to the contribution per unit of limiting factor,** thus maximising contribution and hence profit.

When there is **more than one limiting factor,** the possible number of production plans which use all resources increases but only one will maximise profit. It is therefore no longer possible to rank items in order of contribution per unit of limiting factor in order to determine the profit-maximising output. Instead the graphical approach to **linear programming** can be used.

The **steps** involved in this technique are as follows.

(1) **Formulate the problem**

- Define the variables
- Establish the constraints
- Identify the objective function

Then model the constraints and objective function as equations.

(2) **Graph the equations representing the constraints.**

(3) **Establish the feasible area.**

(4) **Add an iso-profit/contribution line** and move it out across the feasible region until the point where it ceases to lie in the feasible area.

(5) Find the coordinates of this point, which represents the **optimal solution.**

77 FULLY AUTOMATED

> **Tutor's hint**. Initially, you may have thought that you needed to apply linear programming for parts (a) and (b) but that is not the case. Only one type of lampstand can be made and so it is a matter of working out the maximum production of each type of lampstand given the available resources and then finding which type offers the most contribution.

(a) *Step 1.* **Determine the contribution per unit**

	Model T £	Model M £
Selling price	45.00	40.00
Timber (2m × £2.50)	5.00	5.00
Machine X time (£25 × 0.25; £25 × 0.15)	6.25	3.75
Machine Y time (£30 × 0.20; £30 × 0.225)	6.00	6.75
Costs	17.25	15.50
Contribution	27.75	24.50

Step 2. **Identify the maximum units available from the limiting factors**

The limiting factors are machine hours and materials. These must be analysed in turn.

		Model T	Model M
Machine X	Maximum hours	1,700 hrs	1,700 hrs
	Machine time/hr	0.25 hrs	0.15 hrs
	∴ Maximum production	6,800 units	11,333 units
Machine Y	Maximum hours	1,920 hrs	1,920 hrs
	Machine time/hr	0.2 hrs	0.225 hrs
	∴ Maximum hours	9,600 units	8,533 units
Timber	Total available	17,000 metres	17,000 metres
	Usage per product	2 metres	2 metres
	∴ Maximum production	8,500 units	8,500 units
Maximum sales		7,400 units	10,000 units

T Ltd can produce a **maximum of 6,800 Model T or 8,500 Model M** lampstands.

Contribution from T = £27.75 × 6,800   £188,700
Contribution from M = £24.50 × 8,500   £208,250

M lampstands should therefore be made.

(b)

	Model T		Model M
Maximum production (units)	6,800		8,500
	£		£
Total contribution	188,700		208,250
Revenue from spare hrs of machine X	nil	$(1,700 - (8,500 \times 0.15)) \times £20$	8,500
Revenue from spare hrs of machine Y			
$(1,920 - (6,800 \times 0.2)) \times £30)$	16,800	$(1,920 - (8,500 \times 0.225)) \times £30$	225
	205,500		216,975

Thus it is **still preferable to make M lampstands**.

(c)

	Model T	Model M	Total
Units produced and sold	4,250	4,250	
Machine hours			
X $(4,250 \times 0.25 : 4,250 \times 0.15)$	1,062.50 hrs	637.50 hrs	1,700.00 hrs
Y $(4,250 \times 0.20; 4,250 \times 0.225)$	850.00 hrs	956.25 hrs	1,806.25 hrs
Timber (2m)	8,500 m	8,500 m	17,000 m
Contribution (£27.75/24.50)	£117,937.50	£104,125.00	£222,062.50
Additional sales outlets			
X $(1,700 - 1,700) \times £20$			–
Y $(1,920 - 1,806.25) \times £30$			£3,412.50
Total budgeted contribution			£225,475.00

(d) T Ltd can obviously sell more than it produces. The capacity constraints can be tackled in the following ways.

Machines X and Y

Reduce the amount of time per unit, although the increased speed might result in greater wear and tear and poorer quality. The workforce might also require a **bonus** for increased productivity.

Alternatively, **purchasing more machinery** might generate sufficient contribution, by enabling more production, to justify the increase in fixed costs.

It is possible that **machinery** might be **hired**. In the long term this might not be cost effective: it might be cheaper to buy the machinery.

Production could be **subcontracted** to other companies, but this might impair quality and there would be extra supervision costs.

Timber

More could be **purchased** perhaps, at a **higher price**, or from **further afield**.

78 **OBJECTIVE TEST QUESTIONS: LINEAR PROGRAMMING AND MULTI-PRODUCT CVP ANALYSIS**

1   D   This inequality states that X must be at most 2Y, as required.

The inequality in **option A** states that X must be at least 2Y, whereas 2Y is meant to be the very maximum value of X.

The inequality in **option B** states that Y must be at most 2X, whereas X is meant to be at most 2Y.

The inequality in **option C** states that Y must be at least 2X, whereas X is meant to be at most 2Y.

2   D   The region to the left of X = 41 satisfies X ≤ 41 while that above Y = 19 satisfies Y ≥ 19.

Option A is incorrect because the region you have described is bounded by $X \leq 41$, but $Y \leq 19$ instead of $Y \geq 19$.

Option B is incorrect because the region you have described is bounded by $X \geq 41$ and $Y \leq 19$ instead of by $X \leq 41$ and $Y \geq 19$.

Option C is incorrect because the region you have described is bounded by $Y \geq 19$ but by $X \geq 41$ instead of $X \leq 41$.

3 B Evaluating contribution at the vertices gives 40,000 at (0, 160), 37,000 at (40, 140), 34,000 at (80, 120) and 7,000 at (140, 0) and so (0, 160) represents the optimal solution.

Option A. In selecting (140, 0) it seems that you were minimising contribution rather than maximising it.

Option C. In selecting (40, 140) you were opting for the vertex that often represents the optimal solution in linear programming exam questions but, as you see, it need not be so.

Option D. Did you select (80, 120) because the X and Y co-ordinates total more than those for the other vertices?

4 D Contribution is 500 at P, 600 at Q and 600 at R. This means that the outcomes represented by Q and R and all points on the straight line joining them will all lead to the optimal contribution of 600.

For **option A,** you have chosen the vertex which gives minimum contribution.

For **option B,** it is not sufficient to claim that Q is optimal since this is not the full solution.

For **option C,** it is not sufficient to claim that R is optimal since this is not the full solution.

5 C

	Aye	*Bee*	*Cee*	*Total*
C/S ratio	0.4	0.5	*0.54	
Market share	$\times \frac{1}{3}$	$\times \frac{1}{3}$	$\times \frac{1}{3}$	
	0.133	0.167	0.18	0.48

* balancing figure

With revised proportions:

	Aye	*Bee*	*Cee*	*Total*
C/S ratio	0.40	0.500	0.540	
Market share	0.40	0.250	0.350	
	0.16	0.125	0.189	0.474

If you chose **option A,** you have selected the C/S ratio of the Aye.

If you chose **option B,** you have selected the C/S ratio of the Cee.

If you chose **option D,** you incorrectly calculated Cee's C/S ratio as 0.1 (possibly because you thought the sum of the C/S ratios should be 1.0).

6 B

7 D **Contribution per unit**

O £(12 – 7.90)   = £4.10
H £(17 – 11.20)   = £5.80

Contribution per mix

(£4.10 × 4) + (£5.80 × 3) = £33.80

Breakeven point in terms of mixes

Fixed costs/contribution per mix = £131,820/£33.80 = 3,900 mixes

Breakeven point in units

O	3,900 × 4	= 15,600
H	3,900 × 3	= 11,700

Breakeven point in revenue

			£
O	15,600 × £12	=	187,200
H	11,700 × £17	=	198,900
			386,100

Margin of safety

Budgeted sales – breakeven sales = £(398,500 – 386,100) = £12,400

If you chose **option A,** you selected the breakeven revenue.

If you chose **option B**, you deducted fixed costs from breakeven revenue.

If you chose **option C,** you deduced fixed costs from budgeted revenue.

8   B   **Contribution per unit**

A	£22
B	£19
C	£17

Contribution per mix

(£22 × 1) + (£19 × 1) + (£17 × 4) = £109

Required number of mixes

(Fixed costs + required profit)/contribution per mix

= £(55,100 + 43,000)/£109

= 900 mixes

Required sales of A

900 × 1 = 900 units

900 × £47 = £42,300 revenue

Option A is the variable cost of the required volume of product A.

Option C is the required sales value of product C.

Option D is the required sales volume (with a £ in front of it!).

79   **DP PLC**

> **Pass marks.** You should have had no problems with parts (a) and (b). In fact, the examiner commented that candidates who could not answer part (a) should not have been sitting the paper. Hopefully you remembered the rules for drawing graphs (although the examiner's report makes it clear that many candidates had no idea how to present a graph)!
>
> Part (c) was a bit more tricky and you may have wondered about the meaning of the figures for the constraints. If you had worked out the usage of S1 given the optimum product mix you would have discovered that the figure 23,875 was the number of minutes remaining. This should have indicated that the figures in the second column had to be shadow prices. You would have been awarded one mark for using a report format and giving an introduction, five marks for correct explanation of the slack variables and one mark for a conclusion.
>
> In part (d) read the requirements carefully, and do not determine a revised product mix. You do need to illustrate your answer, however, not simply regurgitate text book facts.

(a)   **Contribution per unit calculation**

		X		Y
		£ per unit		£ per unit
Selling price		800		1200
Costs				
Components		150		310
Assembly	(80 × £180/60)	240	(130 × £180/60)	390
Testing	(120 × £60/60)	120	(180 × £60/60)	180
Packaging	(60 × £20/60)	20	(30 × £20/60)	10
		530		890
Contribution		270		310

(b)   *Step 1.*   **Define variables**

Let x = number of X produced in the six months to 30 June 20X2

Let y = number of Y produced in the six months to 30 June 20X2

Step 2.   **Establish objective function**

Maximise contribution (C) = 270x + 310y

Step 3.   **Establish constraints**

Assembly time in minutes (S1) $1,000 × 60 ≥ 80x + 130y$

Testing time in minutes (S2) $875 × 60 ≥ 120x + 180y$

Maximum demand for X (S4) $x ≤ 300$

Maximum demand for Y (S5) $y ≤ 800$

Step 4.   **Graph the solution**

S1   If x = 0, y = 461.5
      If y = 0, x = 750

S2   If x = 0, y = 292
      If y = 0, x = 437.5

S4   x = 300

S5   y = 800

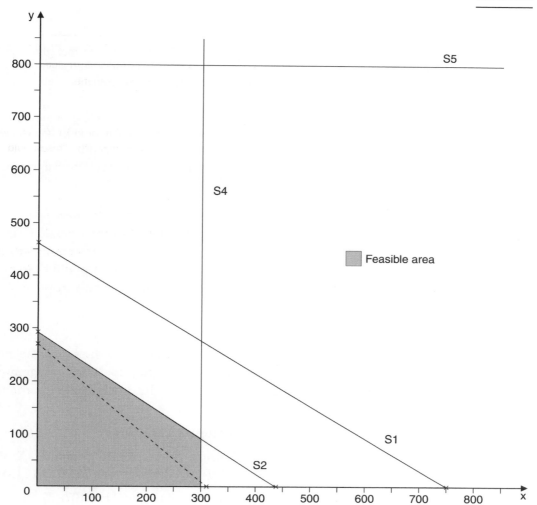

Step 5. **Define feasible area**

This is indicated on the graph.

Step 6. **Determine optimal solution**

Suppose C = 83,700

∴ If x = 0, y = 270

If y = 0, x = 310

These points can be used to plot an iso-contribution line. Putting a ruler on this line and then sliding the ruler across the paper, the optimal solution is found to be at the intersection of S2 and S4.

∴ The optimal solution is where x = 300 where (875 × 60) = 120x + 180y

∴ The optimal solution is at x = 300, y = 91.67

The profit-maximising product mix is therefore to produce 300 units of X and 91.67 units of Y.

Contribution earned = £270 × 300 + £310 × 91.67 = £109,418

(c)   REPORT

To: Management team
From: Management accountant
Date: 17 October 20X1
Subject: Sales mix for the six months ending 30 June 20X2

BPP
PROFESSIONAL EDUCATION

1 Introduction

1.1 This report sets out the most profitable assembly mix of computers for the six months ending 30 June 20X2 given available resources and provides recommendations for appropriate action given these results.

2 Background

2.1 Part of the planning process for the six months ending 30 June 20X2 has been an exercise to determine the most profitable assembly mix given the expected availability of resources (assembly time, testing time, packaging time) and expected maximum levels of demand.

3 Position given a shortage of assembly and testing time

3.1 Our initial analysis was based on the assumption that there would be no shortage of packaging time. The graphical approach to linear programming was applied to the problem and this indicated that the optimal solution would be to assemble to maximum demand for computer X (300) but assemble only 91.67 (ie 92) units of computer Y, resulting in contribution of £109,418.

4 Position given a shortage of all resources

4.1 It later became apparent that there may also be a limit on the number of packaging hours available. A computer package for linear programming was applied to the information available, the results of which are interpreted in the following section.

5 Interpretation of linear programming package output

5.1 To maximise contribution and hence profit, 268.75 computer X should be assembled and 112.5 computer Y. Effectively this means 269X and 113Y.

5.2 With this product mix, the optimal contribution will be £107,437.50.

5.3 31.25 units of demand for computer X and 687.5 units of demand for computer Y will not be met.

5.4 23,875 minutes of assembly time will not be used in the optimal solution, but all testing time and packaging time will be used up.

5.5 If one extra minute of testing time became available at its normal variable cost, contribution would increase by £1.46.

5.6 If one extra minute of packaging time became available at its normal variable cost, contribution would increase by £4.75.

6 Recommendations

6.1 Given that contribution falls by approximately £2,000 if there is a limit on the packaging hours available, it would be in the organisation's interests to attempt to employ local residents to make-up any shortfall in packaging hours. In fact, for every additional minute of packaging time available over and above the anticipated limit at its normal variable cost, contribution would increase by £4.75.

6.2 Our organisation is unable to meet maximum demand of either product. We should therefore be prepared to pay up to £1.46 per minute over and above the normal variable cost per minute for additional testing time and up to £4.75 per minute over and above the normal variable cost per minute for additional packaging time.

6.3   Given that there will be a surplus of 23,875 minutes of assembly time, **an alternate use for assembly workers** needs to be found. With appropriate training they could possibly be **used for testing and packaging** our products, thereby utilising the spare resource and eliminating our capacity problems.

7   I hope this information has proved useful. If I can be of any further assistance please do not hesitate to contact me.

Signed: Management accountant

(d)   (i)   **Budgeting.** If scarce resources are ignored when a budget is prepared, the budget is unattainable and is of little use for planning and control. When there is more than one scarce resource, linear programming can be used to identify the most profitable use of resources.

(ii)   **Calculation of relevant costs.** The calculation of relevant costs is essential for decision making. The **relevant cost of a scarce resource** is calculated as **acquisition cost of the resource plus opportunity cost**. When **more than one scarce resource** exists, the **opportunity cost** (or **shadow price**) should be established using linear programming techniques.

(iii)   **Selling different products.** Suppose that an organisation faced with resource constraints manufactures products X and Y and linear programming has been used to determine the shadow prices of the scarce resources. If the organisation now wishes to manufacture and sell a modified version of product X (Z), requiring inputs of the scarce resources, the relevant costs of these scarce resources can be determined (see above) to ascertain whether the production of X and Y should be restricted in order to produce Z.

(iv)   **Control.** Opportunity costs are important for cost control: standard costing can be improved by incorporating opportunity costs into variance calculations. For example, adverse material usage variances can be an indication of material wastage. Such variances should be valued at the standard cost of the material plus the opportunity cost of the loss of one scarce unit of material. Such an approach highlights the true cost of the inefficient use of scarce resources and encourages managers of responsibility centres to pay special attention to the control of scarce factors of production.

(v)   **Capital budgeting.** Linear programming can be used to determine the combination of investment proposals that should be selected if investment funds are restricted in more than one period.

80   RAB CONSULTING LTD

> **Pass marks.** This is a straightforward linear programming question. The examiner stated that he would keep new topics such as linear programming in the optional sections of the paper for the first couple of sittings – so watch out for a compulsory question in 2002.

(a) (i)

		Type A £ per project		Type B £ per project
Revenue		1,700		1,500
Variable costs				
Labour				
– qualified researchers	(20 hrs × £30)	600	(12 hrs × £30)	360
– junior researchers	(8 hrs × £14)	112	(15 hrs × £14)	210
Direct project expenses		408		310
		1,120		880
Contribution		580		620

(ii) **Define variables**

Let a = number of type A projects
Let b = number of type B projects

Establish objective function

Maximise contribution (C) = 580a + 620b, subject to the constraints below.

Establish constraints

Qualified researchers time:	$20a + 12b \leq 1,344$
Junior researchers time:	$8a + 15b \leq 1,120$
Agreement for type A:	$a \geq 20$
Maximum for type B:	$b \leq 60$
Non-negativity:	$a \geq 0, b \geq 0$

(iii) **Graphing the constraints**

Qualified researcher time:	if $a = 0$, $b = 112$
	if $b = 0$, $a = 67.2$
Junior researcher time:	if $a = 0$, $b = 74.67$
	if $b = 0$, $a = 140$
Agreement for type A:	graph the line $a = 20$
Maximum for type B:	graph the line $b = 60$

Iso-contribution line

580a + 620b = 35,960 (where 35,960 = 58 × 62 × 10) goes through the points (62, 0) and (0, 58)

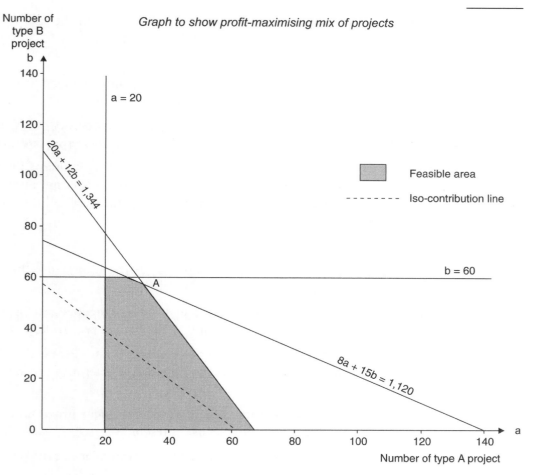

Graph to show profit-maximising mix of projects

Moving the iso-contribution line away from the origin, we see that it leaves the feasible area at the intersection of the two time constraints (point A).

Find the coordinates of A

20a + 12b	= 1,344	(1)
8a + 15b	= 1,120	(2)
20a + 37.5b	= 2,800	(3) (2) × 2.5
25.5b	= 1,456	(3) – (1)
b	= 57.09	
20a + 685.08	= 1,344	substitute into (1)
a	= 32.946	

The profit-maximising mix of projects is 33 of type A and 57 of type B.

(b) **Profit for profit-maximising mix**

		£
Contribution from type A:	33 × £580	19,140
Contribution from type B 57 × £620		35,340
Total contribution		54,480
Less: fixed costs		(28,000)
		26,480

(c) **The importance of identifying scarce resources when preparing budgets**

Scarce resources restrict the activity level at which an organisation can operate. For example, a sales department might estimate that it could sell 1,000 units of product X, which would require 5,000 hours of grade A labour. If there are no units of product X in stock, and only 4,000 hours of grade A labour available in the period, the company would be unable to make and sell 1,000 units of X because of the shortage of labour hours. Management must choose one of the following options.

- Reduce budgeted sales by 20%.
- Increase the availability of grade A labour by recruitment or overtime working.
- Sub-contract some production to another manufacturer.

If the fact that grade A labour is a **scarce resource** is **ignored** when the **budget** is prepared, it will be **unattainable** and of **little relevance for planning and control**.

Most organisations are **restricted** from making and selling more of their products because there would be **no sales demand for the increased output** at an acceptable price. The organisation should therefore budget to produce and sell the volume of its product(s) demanded.

Possible scarce resources

The **scarce resource** might be machine capacity, distribution and selling resources, raw materials or cash.

(i)   If an organisation **produces just one product**, the **budget for the scarce resources is usually the starting point in the budget preparation process.**

(ii)   If an organisation **produces two or more products** and there is only **one scarce resource, limiting factor analysis** must be used to determine the most profitable use of the scarce resource.

(iii) When there is **more than one scarce resource, linear programming** must be used to identify the most profitable use of resources.

The use of linear programming to determine the optimum use of resources

Linear programming is a technique which **determines the most profitable production mix, taking into account resource constraints and limitations** faced by an organisation. **All costs are assumed to be either fixed or variable in relation to a single measure of activity (usually units of output).**

The **problem** is **formulated** in terms of an **objective function** and **constraints** are then **graphed**. This process **highlights all possible output combinations** given the resource constraints and limitations and allows for the **identification of the output combination which would maximise contribution (the optimal solution).**

If there are **more than two types of output,** the graphical approach is not possible and the **Simplex method** must be used instead.

81 HJK LTD

> **Pass marks**. In part (a) you had to remember that you were dealing with a minimisation problem instead of the usual maximisation problem and that therefore you had to find the point of the feasible area first encountered by the objective function as it moved across the paper away from the origin rather than the point at which the objective function left the feasible area. It is always best to tackle linear programming questions using the step by step approach we have adopted in our solution.
>
> You may have had problems with the constraint which dealt with the fact that 'the quantity of one type must not exceed twice that of the other'. This can be interpreted as follows: the quantity of one type (say X) must not exceed (must be less than or equal to) twice that of the other (2Y) (ie $X \leq 2Y$).

(a)   **Define variables**

Let x = the number of X produced

Let y = the number of Y produced

Establish objective function

The **objective** is to minimise total production costs (C). The production cost of X = £100 and the production cost of Y = £80 (given in the question). The objective is to minimise C = 100x + 80y.

Establish constraints

(i) $x + y \geq 100$ (minimum production requirement)

(ii) $y \leq 2x$ (production ratio constraint)

(iii) $x \leq 2y$ (production ratio constraint)

(iv) $3x + 2y \leq 420$ (plating resources constraint)

(v) $4x + 8y \leq 800$ (circuitry resources constraint)

(vi) $x/3 + 2y/15 \leq 34$ *or*
       $20x + 8y \leq 34 \times 60$ (assembly resources constraint)

Graph the problem

For each of the constraint equations, turn the inequality sign into an equals sign, set x and then y equal to 0 and solve the resulting equations to find the points at which the constraints cross the axes. However, if when plotted on a graph the constraint goes through the origin we can only set x or y equal to 0 (as in (ii) and (iii) below) and another x or y value must be chosen. Use the coordinates determined to plot the constraints.

(i)   x = 0   ∴ 0 + y = 100
                    ∴ y = 100

       y = 0   ∴ x + 0 = 100
                    ∴ x = 100

       We therefore plot points at (x, y) = (0, 100) and (100, 0)

(ii)   x = 0   ∴ 0 = y
       y = 100   ∴ 100 = 2x
                    ∴ 50 = x

       We therefore plot points at (x, y) = (0, 0) and (50, 100)

(iii) x = 0   ∴ y = 0
       y = 100   ∴ x = 200

       We therefore plot points at (x, y) = (0, 0) and (200, 100)

(iv)   x = 0   ∴ 2y = 420
                    ∴ y = 210

       y = 0   ∴ 3x = 420
                    ∴ x = 140

       We therefore plot points at (x, y) = (0, 210) and (140, 0)

(v)   x = 0   ∴ 8y = 800
                    ∴ y = 100

       y = 0   ∴ 4x = 800
                    ∴ x = 200

We therefore plot points at (x, y) = (0, 100) and (200, 0)

(vi) x = 0   ∴ 2y/15 = 34
                  ∴ y = 255

      y = 0   ∴ x/3 = 34
                  ∴ x = 102

We therefore plot points at (x, y) = (0, 255) and (102, 0)

From the workings above to determine how to plot the constraints, it can be seen that we need to allow for a maximum of 200 for x and 255 for y.

Plot the points, join them up and label each line with (i) to (vi) as appropriate.

Constraints on HJK Ltd's production of alarm systems

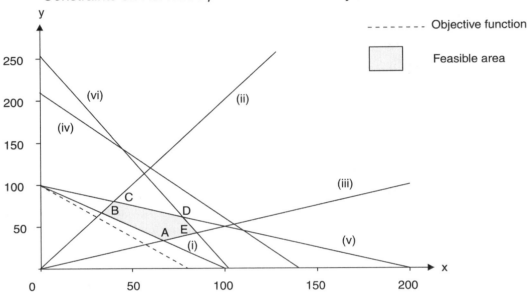

Define feasible area

Label the feasible area on the graph. You will probably make a mess if you try to shade it in, so don't do this. Our labelling gives a feasible area of ABCDE.

Determine optimal solution

We begin by establishing the slope of the objective function.

C = 100x + 80y
8,000 = 100x + 80y (say)

If x = 0, y = 100
If y = 0, x = 80

∴ Plot (0, 100) and (80, 0)

(**Pass mark**. A useful value of the objective function is often the product of the coefficients of the two variables (in this instance 100 × 80), as the coordinates are then whole numbers. Check that such coordinates fall within the range of your graph, however.)

We now find the optimal point.

The objective is to minimise costs. If we put a ruler on the objective function on the graph and slide it across the page, the first point of the feasible area it encounters (ie as close to the origin as possible) is the optimal solution. This can be seen to be point B, the intersection of constraints (i) and (ii).

At B: x + y = 100   (1)
        and y = 2x   (2)

Sub (2) into (1)   x + 2x = 100
                   ∴ 3x = 100
                   x = 33$\frac{1}{3}$
                   ∴ y = 2 × 33$\frac{1}{3}$ = 66$\frac{2}{3}$

The **optimal product mix** is therefore to produce 33$\frac{1}{3}$ type X alarms and 66$\frac{2}{3}$ type Y alarms.

(**Pass mark.** From your graph it may have been difficult to tell whether point A or point B represented the optimal solution. In such circumstances you need to determine the coordinates and value of the objective function at each point in order to assess which point represents the cost-minimising product mix.)

(b)   There are a number of **points** relating to this solution **which management should bear in mind.**

(i)   It is **impossible to produce fractional numbers of alarm systems.** Management should therefore regard the optimal product mix as 33 or 34 type X alarms and 66 or 67 type Y alarms each week.

(ii)   A number of **assumptions** have been made in arriving at this solution.

(1)   **All production can be sold.** At present, however, 75 units of each alarm system are produced and sold each week and so this assumption appears valid.

(2)   **The maximum amount of resources will be available each week.** The constraints upon production are not production resource constraints, however. Instead they relate to minimum production requirements and production ratios. The optimal product mix will therefore not require all of the weekly available resources (ie slack is available) and so this assumption appears valid.

Management could consider employing these slack resources elsewhere. The amounts available (when x = 33 and y = 67) are as follows.

Plating: 420 – ((3 × 33) + (2 × 67)) =   187 feet = 45% of total available
Circuitry: 800 – ((4 × 33) + (8 × 67)) = 132 units = 16.5% of total available
Assembly: 34 – (($\frac{1}{3}$ × 33) + ($\frac{2}{15}$ × 67)) = 14.07 hours = 41% of total available

The proportion available of the maximum resources is large (apart from possibly in circuitry) and so the second assumption appears valid.

82   WOODEN TABLES AND CHAIRS

> **Pass marks.** We have used an iso-profit line but it would be equally acceptable to evaluate contribution at each of the vertices A, B, C and D. For the purpose of the report it is useful, but not a requirement of the question, to calculate the contribution currently being made.

(a)   **Define the variables**

Let the number of chairs produced per day be X and the number of tables be Y.

Establish objective function

The objective function is to maximise contribution to profit given by 4X + 4Y

Establish constraints

Cutting

120 chairs take 8 hours so time per chair is $80 \times 60/120 = 4$ minutes

60 tables take 8 hours and so require 8 minutes each $(8 \times 60/60)$

Therefore $4X + 8Y \leq 8 \times 60$
$$X + 2Y \leq 120 \qquad (1)$$

Machining

Times required are $8 \times 60/96 = 5$ minutes

Therefore $5X + 5Y \leq 480$
$$X + Y \leq 96 \qquad (2)$$

Assembly

Times required are $8 \times 60/60 = 8$ minutes for chairs and

$8 \times 60/80 = 6$ minutes for tables

Therefore $8X + 6Y \leq 480$
$$4X + 3Y \leq 240 \qquad (3)$$

Finishing

Times required are $8 \times 60/56 = 60/7$ minutes for chairs and

$8 \times 60/96 = 5$ minutes for tables

Therefore $60/7X + 5Y \leq 480$

$$60X + 35Y \leq 3,360 \quad (4)$$

Non-negativity: $X, Y \geq 0$

Graph the problem

(1)   When $X = 0, Y = 120/2 = 60$
       When $Y = 0, X = 120$

(2)   When $X = 0, Y = 96$
       When $Y = 0, X = 96$

(3)   When $X = 0, Y = 240/3 = 80$
       When $Y = 0, X = 240/4 = 60$

(4)   When $X = 0, Y = 3,360/35 = 96$
       When $Y = 0, X = 3,360/60 = 56$

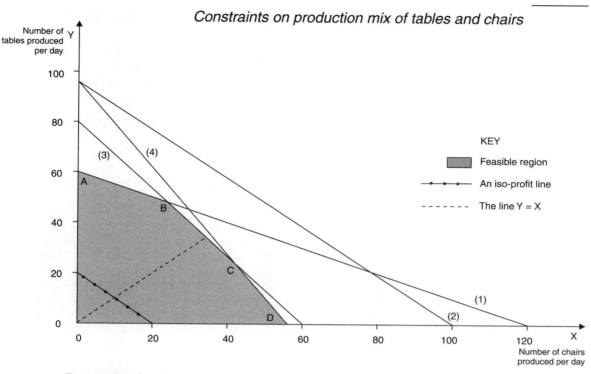

Constraints on production mix of tables and chairs

Determine feasible region

The feasible region is the shaded interior of OABCD as shown on the graph of constraints on production mix of tables and chairs.

Determine optimal solution

A typical iso-profit line is shown on the graph, linking points (0, 20) and (20, 0). Using it gives B as the optimal vertex, with $X = 24$ and $Y = 48$.

The maximum daily contribution to profit of $(4 \times 24) + (4 \times 48) = £288$ will therefore be achieved by producing 24 chairs and 48 tables.

On the graph, the **line Y = X** shows the **current practice** of producing equal numbers of chairs and tables. The optimal solution given this constraint is $X = Y = 34$ and daily contribution is £272.

(b)   REPORT

> To: Management
> From: Management accountant
> Subject: **Production of chairs and tables**   Date: xx.xx.xx

1   Introduction

1.1 The **factors influencing** the production of chairs and tables have been **analysed** in order to decide upon the **production mix** which will **maximise profit**.

2   Profit maximisation

2.1 The **maximum contribution to profit** of £288 per day will be achieved if 24 chairs and 48 tables are produced daily.

2.2 The **factors which limit** the maximum profit level are **cutting** and **assembly times** (finishing time is also very close to being a critical constraint). Machining time is considerably in excess of requirements.

2.3 The **current practice** of producing equal numbers of chairs and tables means that the **most profitable production level** is 34 of each at present, which gives a daily contribution of £272.

2.4 By **changing to the optimal production mix** described above FM Ltd would **increase contribution** by £16 per day or £4,000 per year.

3 Assumptions

3.1 This analysis is based on the **assumption** that contribution will remain the same for chairs and tables even though extra tables are produced and that maximum daily capacities in cutting, machining, assembly and finishing will also remain unchanged and can be achieved in practice.

Signed: Management accountant

83 G LTD

Pass marks. This question has all the hallmarks of a standard linear programming problem – the requirement is to select the product mix which will maximise profit subject to a series of constraints. The difficulty is that there are four products and so a graphical solution appears not to be possible. You therefore need to find a solution which enables the number of products to be cut down from four to two. Pixies and Elfs require totally different types of labour from Queens and Kings and so can be dealt with separately. Additionally, since Pixies and Elfs are subject to only one constraint, a full standard linear programming approach is not necessary for that part of the problem. Queens and Kings can then be dealt with using the standard graphical linear programming method.

(a) **Determine unit contribution**

	Pixie £	Elf £	Queen £	King £
Selling price	111	98	122	326
Direct materials	(25)	(35)	(22)	(25)
Variable overhead	(17)	(18)	(15)	(16)
Direct labour	(40)	(30)	(75)	(175)
Contribution	29	15	10	110

Deal with Pixies and Elfs

Pixie and Elf use only type 1 labour of which 8,000 hours are available. There is unlimited demand for these products and so we do not need to determine contribution per unit of limiting factor.

$$\text{Contribution if only Pixies are produced} = £29 \times \frac{8{,}000}{8} = £29{,}000$$

$$\text{Contribution if only Elfs are produced} = £15 \times \frac{8{,}000}{6} = £20{,}000$$

The company should therefore produce no Elfs and should produce 1,000 Pixies, giving a contribution of £29,000.

Deal with Queens and Kings

The decision regarding Queens and Kings requires linear programming.

Define variables

Let the number of Queens produced be x and the number of Kings be y.

Establish objective function

The objective function is to maximise contribution = 10x + 110y

Establish constraints

Type 2 labour	$10x + 10y \leq 20{,}000$	(1)	
Type 3 labour	$5x + 25y \leq 25{,}000$	(2)	
Non negativity and demand	$0 \leq x \leq 1{,}500$	(3)	
	$0 \leq y \leq 1{,}000$	(4)	

Graph the problem

Calculations needed to graph the constraints:

(1) when $x = 0$, $y = 2{,}000$
     when $y = 0$, $x = 2{,}000$
(2) when $x = 0$, $y = 1{,}000$
     when $y = 0$, $x = 5{,}000$

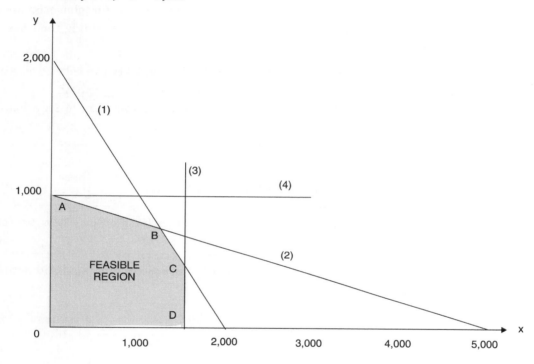

Define feasible region

The feasible region is shown as OABCD on the graph.

Determine the optimal solution

We will calculate the contribution at each vertex of the feasible region.

Vertex	*x*	*y*	*10x + 110y*
A	0	1,000	110,000
B	1,250	750	95,000
C	1,500	500	70,000
D	1,500	0	15,000

The **optimal solution** is therefore to produce **1,000 Kings** and **no Queens** giving a contribution of £110,000 and **1,000 Pixies** and **no Elfs** giving £29,000.

Profit resulting from this product mix is £29,000 + £110,000 – £15,000 = __£124,000__

(b) If **type 1 labour is paid at time and a half, labour costs** for Pixies and Elfs are 40×1.5 = £60 and 30×1.5 = £45 respectively. **Contributions** then become £9 and £0 respectively.

It is therefore **worthwhile paying type 1 labour for overtime** at time and a half to produce **more Pixies.**

Extra profit generated by 1,000 hours of overtime $= \dfrac{1,000}{8} \times £9 = \underline{\underline{£1,125}}$

The above **assumes** that fixed costs are not increased by such working.

(c)   The linear programming method **assumes linearity** of both **constraints** and the **objective function.** This will often not be valid in practice; for instance, if it takes eight hours to make one unit it will frequently not take twice that long to make two units. The method also **assumes** that **all the various constraints** in the formulation of the problem are **known** exactly and will **remain fixed.** In practice it is virtually impossible to say, for instance, that maximum demand will be exactly 1,000.

The validity of the production plan will be limited by the above but it may well continue to be useful to the company as broad guidance regarding their best course of action.

(d)   Solution using the **simplex** method could be very **quickly** carried out by a **computer.** The **limitations** of the **assumptions of linearity** would **remain** but the use of a **computer** does **enable changes** to be made in the **parameters** to see what effect this would have on the solution. Simplex packages also provide a lot of **other useful information** such as shadow prices.

84   PREPARATION QUESTION: BREAKEVEN POINT

> **Pass marks.** This preparation question provides you with the opportunity to practice basic CVP techniques and limiting factor analysis.

(a)   **Assumption.** The ratio of 4P to 3E relates to the ratio of units sold and not to the ratio of sales value.

	P	E
	£ per unit	£ per unit
Selling price	10	12
Variable costs	5	10
Contribution	5	2

Contribution per seven units sold $= (£5 \times 4) + (£2 \times 3) = £26$

Breakeven point $= \dfrac{£561,600}{£26}$ $= \textbf{21,600 sets of 7 units}$

The breakeven point is therefore as follows.

		Product P Units		Product E Units	Total
Breakeven point					
in units	$(21,600 \times 4)$	86,400	$(21,600 \times 3)$	64,800	
in £s	$(\times £10)$	£864,000	$(\times £12)$	£777,600	£1,641,600

(b)   **Contribution per eight units sold** $= (£5 \times 4) + (£2 \times 4) = £28$

Breakeven point $= \dfrac{£561,600}{£28}$ $= \textbf{20,057 sets of 8 units}$

The breakeven point is therefore as follows.

		Product P Units		Product E Units	Total
Breakeven point					
in units	$(20{,}057 \times 4)$	80,228	$(20{,}057 \times 4)$	80,228	
in £s	$(\times £10)$	£802,280	$(\times £12)$	£962,736	£1,765,016

(c) Ignoring commercial considerations, the sales mix in **(a)** is **preferred** to that in **(b)**. This is because it results in a **lower level of sales to break even** (because of the **higher average contribution per unit sold**). The average contribution per unit in (a) is £3.71 (£26/7). In (b) it is £3.50 (£28/8).

(d) The number of machine hours represents a limiting factor on production and sales since all output can be sold. PE Ltd should therefore manufacture the product which maximises the contribution per machine hour.

	P	E
Contribution per unit	£5	£2
Machine hours per unit	0.4	0.1
∴ Contribution per machine hour	£12.50	£20

Product E earns the higher contribution per hour and therefore this is the product which should be concentrated on. The contribution earned would be £640,000 (32,000 hours × £20) and the resulting profit £78,400.

	£'000
Contribution	640.0
Fixed costs	561.6
Profit	78.4

85   PREPARATION QUESTION: CVP ANALYSIS

Pass marks. Remember that on P/V charts for multiple products, products are shown individually from left to right, in order of decreasing size of C/S ratio.

(a)

	J £'000	K £'000	L £'000	M £'000	Total £'000
Sales	200	400	200	200	1,000
Variable costs	140	80	210	140	570
Contribution	60	320	(10)	60	430
Ranking	2nd	1st	4th	2nd	

(b)

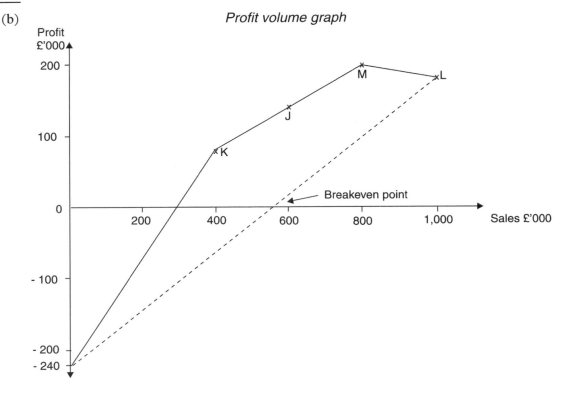

Profit volume graph

(c)

REPORT TO MANAGEMENT

To: Manager
From: Management accountant
Subject: **Analysis of budget**   Date: 1 January 20X1

1   Introduction

1.1   Following preparation of the annual budget, I have analysed the expected contribution towards fixed overheads and profit of products J, K, L and M.

2   Profit volume graph

2.1   The graph at appendix A shows the budgeted contributions made by each of the above products in order of descending contribution/sales ratio.

2.2   The **steepness of slope represents the relative amount of profit per pound generated by each product.** Thus product K generates 80p for every pound of sales, products J and M both generate 30p and product L generates a negative contribution of 5p in the pound.

3   Recommendation

3.1   Judging from the figures above it would seem **sensible not to produce product L**: on the face of it this could increase profit by £10,000. Product L **may be a loss-leader,** however, and sales of the other products may depend upon it.

4   Breakeven point

4.1   **Breakeven point** occurs at a point where sales have reached £558,140. This can be seen from the graph or may be calculated by dividing fixed costs (£240,000) by the average contribution/sales ratio (430,000/1,000,000).

Signed: Management accountant

86   POD LTD

(a) (i)

	Best possible			Worst possible		
	Sales units	*Cont'n per unit* £	*Total cont'n* £	*Sales units*	*Cont'n per unit* £	*Total cont'n* £
X	2,000	30	60,000	1,000	30	30,000
Y	2,000	40	80,000	1,000	40	40,000
Z	2,000	50	100,000	1,000	50	50,000
Total contribution			240,000			120,000
Fixed costs			160,000			160,000
Profit/(loss)			80,000			(40,000)

The company's **potential profitability ranges** from a profit of **£80,000 to a loss of £40,000 per month.**

(ii)

	£	£
Required (minimum) profit per month		25,000
Fixed costs per month		160,000
Required contribution per month		185,000
Contribution to be earned from:		
product X 1,500 × £30	45,000	
product Y 1,500 × £40	60,000	
		105,000
Contribution required from product Z		80,000

Contribution per unit of Z	£50
Minimum required sales of Z per month	1,600 units

(b) In 20X1 sales were 200,000 units. **The variable cost per unit** is therefore as follows.

	20X1 £	*20X2 prediction* £
Direct materials	4	4.40
Direct labour	2	2.30
Variable overhead	1	1.10
	7 per unit	7.80 per unit

Fixed costs

	£
20X1 total overhead (fixed plus variable)	600,000
Variable overhead in 20X1 (200,000 × £1)	200,000
Fixed overhead in 20X1	400,000
Add 20%	80,000
Estimated fixed overhead in 20X2	480,000

In 20X2, a **profit of £330,000 is required.**

	£
Required profit	330,000
Fixed costs	480,000
Required contribution	810,000

Contribution per unit in 20X2 (£10.50 – £7.80) = £2.70

Required sales $\dfrac{£810,000}{£2.70}$ = 300,000 units

This is an increase of 50% on 20X1 volumes. It is first of all **questionable** whether such a **large increase** could be **achieved** in one year. Secondly, given such an increase, it is likely that **output** will be **outside** the **relevant range** of output. Thirdly, **estimates of** fixed costs and variable costs are **unlikely to be reliable.**

(c) (i)

	Activity index	Cost £	Adjust for inflation	Cost at 20X5 price £
High activity 20X4	106	81,880	× 117/115	83,304
Low activity 20X1	98	73,080	× 117/105	81,432
Change	8			1,872

Variable cost per index point at 20X5 prices   = £1,872/8 = £234

Substituting in 20X4 figures, fixed cost   = £83,304 – (106 × £234)
= £58,500 at 20X5 prices

Forecast for 20X5

	£
Fixed cost (as above)	58,500
Variable cost (£234 × 110)	25,740
	84,240

(ii) **Data for breakeven chart**

	£
Sales value for 20X5 = £100,000 × 1.10 × 1.20 =	132,000
Variable cost (from (i))	25,740
Contribution	106,260

Contribution/sales ratio = £106,260/£132,000 = 0.805

Breakeven point = $\dfrac{\text{Fixed costs (£58,500)}}{0.805}$

= £72,671 sales value

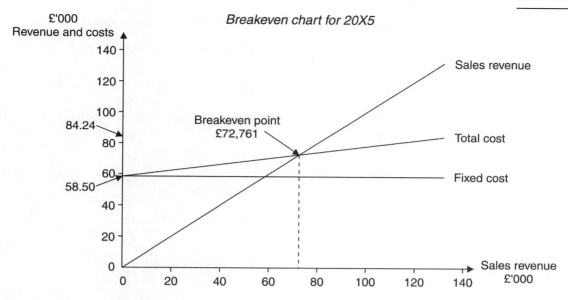

Breakeven chart for 20X5

87   **ZED LTD**

> **Pass marks.** If you do not know how to tackle part (b) of the question, read our list of steps and have another try before you look at the full solution. (Remember you covered ROCE in Paper 4 *Finance*.)
>
> Use the contribution per unit in part (c) as a short cut to calculating the resulting profit.

(a)   ZED LTD
   BIGTOWN BRANCH BUDGET FOR COMING YEAR

		(i)			
		External	*External*		
	Unit variable	*sales*	*sales*	*Newtown*	*Total*
	costs/prices	*22,000 units*	*22,000 units*	*2,000 units*	*24,000 units*
	£	*£'000*	*£'000*	*£'000*	*£'000*
Sales value	70/52	1,540	1,540	104	1,644
Variable costs					
Direct wages	20	440	440	40	480
Direct materials	15	330	330	30	360
Purchased components	4	88	88	8	96
Production overhead	8	176	176	16	192
Administration overhead	2	44	44	4	48
Selling and dist. overhead	6	132	132	–	132
Total variable cost		1,210	1,210	98	1,308
Contribution		330	330	6	336
Fixed costs					
Direct wages		20			20
Production overhead		30			30
Administration overhead		80			80
Selling and dist. overhead		10			10
Depreciation		60			60
		200			200
Net profit		130			136

(b)   Here is our suggested approach to this part of the question.

   Step 1.   Calculate the level of profit which will achieve a 10 per cent return on the capital employed.

Step 2. Add the fixed costs to this profit to determine the required contribution.

Step 3. Divide the required contribution by the contribution per unit to derive the number of units to be sold.

Step 4. Multiply by the sales value per unit.

(You could use the C/S ratio instead of steps 3 and 4 to produce a slightly different but equally acceptable answer.)

			£
Step 1. Required profit	= 10% × £400,000		40,000
Step 2. Add fixed costs			200,000
	∴ Required contribution		240,000
Step 3. Contribution per unit	= £70 – £55 variable cost		÷ 15
	∴ Required sales units		16,000
Step 4. Multiply by £70 selling price			× 70
	∴ Required sales value		£1,120,000

Using the contribution to sales ratio (C/S ratio) instead of steps 3 and 4

C/S ratio	= £15/£70 = 21.43%	
Required sales	= £240,000 ÷ 21.43% =	£1,119,925

The two answers would be exactly the same if the C/S ratio were stated to a greater number of decimal places.

(c)
	£
Revised contribution per unit = £68 – £55 variable cost =	13
Units to be sold (maximum output)	25,000

	£
Total contribution	325,000
Less fixed costs	200,000
Net profit if the sales manager's proposal is adopted	125,000

The net profit achievable in the original budget in part (a) exceeds the forecast under the sales manager's proposal. Sales cannot be expanded sufficiently to compensate for the proposed reduction in selling price. The proposal should not therefore be adopted.

(d) The best result in the original budget represents a return on capital of (£136,000/£400,000) × 100% = 34%, which far exceeds the target of 10% which is implied by the calculation in (b).

Breakeven point in (a)(i) for external sales only is £200,000/£15 = 13,334 units, giving a margin of safety of 8,666 units, 39.4% of forecast sales.

Breakeven point in (a)(ii) is (£200,000/£336,000) × £1,644,000 = £978,571 sales value in the given mix. The margin of safety is therefore £665,429, 40.5% of forecast sales.

Breakeven point for the sales manager's proposal is £200,000/£13 = 15,385 units, giving a margin of safety of 9,615 units, which is 38.5% of forecast sales. The sales manager's proposal is therefore not only less profitable but also slightly more risky than the original budgets in part (a).

88   STANDARD AND DELUXE

> **Pass marks.** You'll need to remember some of your Business Maths studies in part (c) as you have to calculate expected values.
>
> CIMA exams are cumulative and so the examiner could ask you to incorporate any topic from earlier studies.

(a)   **Data for breakeven charts**

	99,999 units £'000	172,000 units £'000
Standard quality		
Variable cost (× £4.50 per unit)	450	774
Fixed cost	200	350
	650	1,124
Sales value (× £7 per unit)	700	1,204
Deluxe quality		
Variable cost (× £6.50 per unit)	650	1,118
Fixed cost	250	400
	900	1,518
Sales value (× £10 per unit)	1,000	1,720

Breakeven chart for standard quality

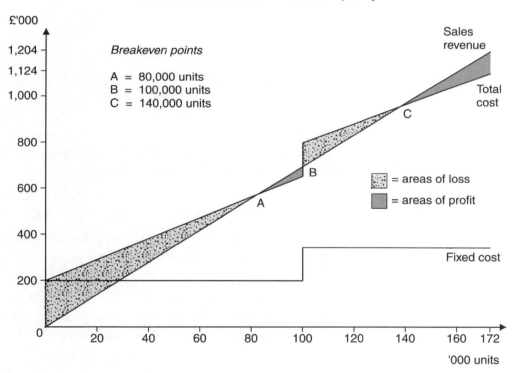

Breakeven points

A = 80,000 units
B = 100,000 units
C = 140,000 units

= areas of loss
= areas of profit

BPP PROFESSIONAL EDUCATION

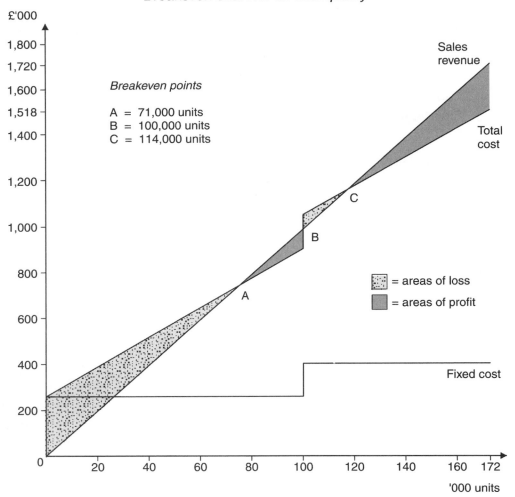

Breakeven chart for de luxe quality

Breakeven points

A = 71,000 units
B = 100,000 units
C = 114,000 units

= areas of loss
= areas of profit

Sales revenue

Total cost

Fixed cost

'000 units

(b) The charts show that the **step in fixed costs** at an output of 100,000 units results in **multiple breakeven points** for both qualities. Specifically, the charts reveal that the two qualities will **earn profits at the following output levels** (approximately).

(i)   **Standard.** Above 80,000 but below 100,000 units, and above 140,000 units.

(ii)   **De luxe.** Above 70,000 but below 100,000 units, and above 115,000 units.

Although the charts can provide **guidance to management regarding the sales levels which are required to break even,** they are **not sufficiently accurate to determine the breakeven point to the nearest unit.**

In addition, the charts **do not give any indication of the risk attached to the estimates used to prepare them, neither** do they show the cost and revenue patterns and therefore the **potential profitability outside the relevant range.**

(c)

	Quantity '000 units	Probability	'000 units
Standard	172	0.1	17.2
	160	0.7	112.0
	148	0.2	29.6
	Expected unit sales		158.8
De luxe	195.5	0.3	58.65
	156.5	0.5	78.25
	109.5	0.2	21.90
	Expected unit sales		158.80

300

Calculation of expected profits and margin of safety

	Standard	De luxe
Expected sales units	158,800	158,800
Contribution per unit	£2.50	£3.50
	£'000	£'000
Expected contribution	397	555.8
Fixed costs	350	400.0
Expected profit	47	155.8

Breakeven point $\left(\dfrac{£350,000}{£2.50}\right)$ 140,000 units $\left(\dfrac{£400,000}{£3.50}\right)$ 114,286 units

∴ Margin of safety   18,800 units   44,514 units

(× £7) = £131,600 sales value   (× £10) = 445,140 sales value

= 11.8% of expected sales   = 28.0% of expected sales

89   OBJECTIVE TEST QUESTIONS: MIXED BANK 1

1   C $y = 10x + 420$

$x = 33$

∴ $y = (10 \times 33) + 420 = 750$

Seasonally-adjusted sales units = 750

(**Pass marks.** Remember that seasonally-adjusted data (or deseasonalised data) is simply the trend.)

2   B

	£
20% of May sales = 20% × £48,000	9,600
50% of April credit sales = 50% × 80% × £55,000	22,000
25% of March credit sales = 25% × 80% × £60,000	12,000
20% of February credit sales = 20% × 80% × £45,000	7,200
	50,800

3   D

4   D

	Output Units		Total cost £
	8,000	(× £2.60)	20,800
	5,000	(× £2.78)	13,900
Variable cost of	3,000 units	=	6,900

∴ Variable cost per unit = £6,900/3,000 = £2.30

∴ Total variable cost of 6,250 units = 6,250 × £2.30 = £14,375

Total cost of 8,000 units = £20,800

Variable cost of 8,000 units = 8,000 × £2.30 = £18,400

∴ Fixed cost = £(20,800 − 18,400) = £2,400

∴ Total cost of 6,250 units   = total variable cost + fixed cost

= £(14,375 + 2,400) = £16,775

5   A

6   A

7   A

BPP
PROFESSIONAL EDUCATION

8   D   Average C/S ratio $= \dfrac{(2\times25\%)+(5\times35\%)}{7}$

$$= 32\%$$

Sales revenue at breakeven point $= \dfrac{\text{fixed costs}}{\text{C/S ratio}}$

$$= £90,000/0.32$$

$$= £281,250$$

If you chose **option A,** you calculated the average C/S ratio as (25% + 35%)/2. In other words, you forgot to take account of the sales ratio.

If you chose **option B,** you multiplied the fixed costs by the C/S ratio to get the breakeven sales revenue. You should have divided.

If you chose **option C,** you forgot to weight the components of the average C/S ratio by the sales ratio. You therefore calculated the C/S ratio as (25% + 35%)/7.

90   OBJECTIVE TEST QUESTIONS: MIXED BANK 2

1   B

	£
Revenue should have been (5,940 × £18)	106,920
but was (5,940 × £18.75)	111,375
Sales price variance	4,455 (F)

Budgeted volume	5,600 units
Actual volume	5,940 units
Variance in units	340 units (F)
× standard margin per unit	× £4.60
	£1,564 (F)

2   D   Y = 1.8x + 250

If x = 35, Y = (1.8 × 35) + 250 = 313

Expected sales = 313 × 110/100 = 344.3

3   C   Average C/S ratio $= \dfrac{(3\times27\%)+(2\times56\%)+(5\times38\%)}{(3+2+5)} = 38.3\%$

At breakeven point, contribution = fixed costs

$$\therefore \dfrac{£648,000}{\text{Breakeven sales revenue}} = 0.383$$

∴ Breakeven sales revenue = £1,691,906

4   C

5   C

6   B   Limiting factor is raw material.

	M	N	P
Contribution per kg of limiting factor			
£4.50/(£1.25 ÷ £0.50)	£1.80		
£4.80/(£1.50 ÷ £0.50)		£1.60	
£2.95/(£0.75 ÷ £0.50)			£1.97
Ranking	2	3	1

Usage of the 6,000 kg

	Kg
2,800 units of P ($\times$ (£0.75/£0.50))	4,200
720 units of M ($\times$ (£1.25/£0.50))	1,800
	6,000

Optimum production with additional 1,000 kg

	Kg
(1,000 – 720) units of M ($\times$ (£1.25/£0.50))	700
100 units of N ($\times$ (£1.50/£0.50))	300
	1,000

Contribution obtainable

	£
280 units of M ($\times$ £4.50)	1,260
100 units of N ($\times$ £4.80)	480
	1,740

This contribution is after charging £0.50 per kg.

$\therefore$ Contribution before material cost = £1,740 + (1,000 $\times$ £0.50) = £2,240.

7 C Need to determine the lowest sales to earn contribution of £700,000.

Minimum sales must be met.

		£
P	Contribution on sales of £100,000 ($\times$ 20%)	20,000
Q	Contribution on sales of £100,000 ($\times$ 25%)	25,000
R	Contribution on sales of £100,000 ($\times$ 30%)	30,000
		75,000

Include R next as it has the **highest C/S ratio** and hence earns the most contribution per £ of revenue

Contribution on difference between minimum and maximum sales =
30% $\times$ £1,400,000   420,000

Q has the **next highest C/S ratio.**

Contribution on difference between minimum and maximum sales =
25% $\times$ £900,000 = £225,000
Only require £(700,000 – 75,000 – 420,000) of contribution   205,000
$\therefore$ 700,000

Revenue from this sales mix

	£'000
Minimum sales	300
R	1,400
Q (205/225 $\times$ £900,000)	820
	2,520

8 B

Actual output should have taken	37,240 hrs
but did take	36,925 hrs
Variance in hrs	315 hrs (F)
$\times$ standard rate per hr (£266,000/38,000)	$\times$ £7
Variance in £	£2,205 (F)

9 A

Budgeted hrs of work	38,000 hrs
Actual hrs	36,925 hrs
Variance in hrs	1,075 hrs (A)
$\times$ standard rate per hr	$\times$ £7
	£7,525 (A)

91   OBJECTIVE TEST QUESTIONS: MIXED BANK 3

1	A		£
		Sales revenue should have been (521 × £300)	156,300
		but was (521 × £287)	149,527
		Sales price variance	6,773 (A)

2   A   Budgeted C/S ratio = 30%

∴ Budgeted contribution   = 30% × budgeted selling price
                                    = 30% × £300
                                    = £90

Sales volume should have been	500 units
but was	521 units
Sales volume variance in units	21 units (F)
× standard contribution per unit	× £90
Sales volume contribution variance	£1,890 (F)

3	A	Budgeted hours	8,000
		Actual hours	8,850
		Capacity variance in hours	850 (F)
		× standard absorption rate per hour★	× £15
		Capacity variance in £	£12,750 (F)

★ £120,000 ÷ 8,000 = £15

4	A	Output should have taken	8,215 hours
		but did take	8,850 hours
		Efficiency variance in hours	635 hours (A)
		× standard absorption rate per hour	× £15
		Efficiency variance in £	£9,525 (A)

5   D   Overhead recovery rate per purchase order   = £94,690 ÷ 2,785 purchase orders
                                                   = £34 per purchase order

	£
Overhead recovered (202 × £34)	6,868
Actual overhead	7,318
Under recovery	450

6   A   The calculation of breakeven sales value requires the average C/S ratio (from individual C/S ratios and the product mix ratio) and total fixed costs.

7   A   **I**   JIT features machine cells

      II   A pull system is the use of a Kanban, or signal, to ensure that products/ components are only produced when needed by the next process.

      III   Uniform loading is the operating of all parts of the productive process at a speed which matches the rate at which the final product is demanded by the customer.

      IV   JIT will only be successful if employees at all levels are involved in the process of change and continuous improvement that is inherent in the JIT philosophy.

8   D   In 20X9, x = 9 and hence the trend = 350 + 45/9 = 355. Multiplying by 0.93 to reduce the trend by 7% gives 330 units to the nearest whole number.

If you chose **option A,** you used a trend of 350 + (45 × x).

If you chose **option B,** you multiplied the trend by 1.07 so that you increased it by 7% instead of reducing it by 7%.

If you chose **option C,** you forgot to take account of the cyclical factor.

9   C

	£
Absorption costing profit	132,500
Marginal costing profit	167,460
Difference	34,960

Absorption rate per unit = £34,960/3,800 = £9.20.

Option A is incorrect because the closing stock level rather than the difference between the opening and closing stock levels was used on the denominator.

Option B is incorrect because the opening stock level rather than the difference between the opening and closing stock levels was used on the denominator.

Option D is the difference in profits.

10   A

	M1	M2	M3	M4
	£	£	£	£
Selling price	70	92	113	83
less: materials	(16)	(22)	(34)	(20)
conversion costs	(39)	(52)	(57)	(43)
plus: general fixed costs (W)	16	16	15	18
Contribution	31	34	37	38
Kg of material	4	5.5	8.5	5
Contribution per kg	£7.75	£6.18	£4.35	£7.60
Ranking	1	3	4	2

Working

M1	£24 × 40/60	= £16
M2	£24 × 40/60	= £16
M3	£24 × 37.5/60	= £15
M4	£24 × 45/60	= £18

Paper 8

May 2002 paper (amended)

Management Accounting – Performance Management

IMPM

INSTRUCTIONS TO CANDIDATES

You are allowed three hours to answer this question paper.
Answer the ONE question in section A (consisting of eight sub-questions). *Answer the ONE question in section B.* *Answer ONE question ONLY from section C.* *Answer ONE question ONLY from section D.*

**DO NOT OPEN THIS PAPER UNTIL YOU ARE READY
TO START UNDER EXAMINATION CONDITIONS**

SECTION A - 20 MARKS

ANSWER *ALL* EIGHT SUB-QUESTIONS

Each of the sub-questions numbered from 1.1 to 1.8 inclusive, given below, has only ONE *correct answer.*

REQUIREMENT:

On the SPECIAL ANSWER SHEET *provided at the end of this question, place a circle 'O' around the letter that gives the correct answer to each sub-question.*

If you wish to change your mind about an answer, block out your first answer completely and then circle another letter. You will not receive marks if more than one letter is circled.

Please note that you will not receive marks for any workings to these sub-questions.

1.1   Z plc provides a single service to its customers. An analysis of its budget for the year ending 31 December 20X2 shows that in period 4, when the budgeted activity was 5,220 service units with a sales value of £42 each, the margin of safety was 19.575%.

The budgeted contribution to sales ratio of the service is 40%.

Budgeted fixed costs in period 4 were nearest to

A   £1,700
B   £71,000
C   £88,000
D   £176,000   **2 Marks**

1.2   Which of the following statements is true?

(i)   A flexible budget can be used to control operational efficiency.

(ii)   Incremental budgeting is a system of budgetary planning and control that measures the additional costs of the extra units of activity.

(iii)   Participative budgeting is a method of centralised budgeting that uses a top-down approach and aspiration levels.

A   (i) and (ii) only
B   (ii) and (iii) only
C   (iii) only
D   (i) only   **2 Marks**

1.3   RT plc sells three products.

Product R has a contribution to sales ratio of 30%.

Product S has a contribution to sales ratio of 20%.

Product T has a contribution to sales ratio of 25%.

Monthly fixed costs are £100,000.

If the products are sold in the ratio:

R: 2   S: 5   T: 3

the monthly breakeven sales revenue, to the nearest £1, is

A   £400,000
B   £411,107
C   £425,532
D   Impossible to calculate without further information   **2 Marks**

1.4   The overhead costs of RP Limited have been found to be accurately represented by the formula

$$y = £10,000 + £0.25x$$

where y is the monthly cost and x represents the activity level measured in machine hours.

Monthly activity levels, in machine hours, may be estimated using a combined regression analysis and time series model:

$$a = 100,000 + 30b$$

where a represents the de-seasonalised monthly activity level and b represents the month number.

In month 240, when the seasonal index value is 108, the overhead cost (to the nearest £1,000) is expected to be

A   £35,000
B   £37,000
C   £39,000
D   £41,000   **3 Marks**

1.5   DRP Limited has recently introduced an Activity Based Costing system. It manufactures three products, details of which are set out below.

	Product D	Product R	Product P
Budgeted annual production (units)	100,000	100,000	50,000
Batch size (units)	100	50	25
Machine set-ups per batch	3	4	6
Purchase orders per batch	2	1	1
Processing time per unit (minutes)	2	3	3

Three cost pools have been identified. Their budgeted costs for the year ending 30 June 20X3 are as follows.

Machine set-up costs	£150,000
Purchasing of materials	£70,000
Processing	£80,000

The budgeted machine set-up cost per unit of product R is nearest to

A   £0.52
B   £0.60
C   £6.52
D   £26.09   **3 Marks**

1.6   The following data have been extracted from the budget working papers of WR Limited.

Activity	Overhead cost
Machine hours	£
10,000	13,468
12,000	14,162
16,000	15,549
18,000	16,242

In March 2002, the actual activity was 13,780 machine hours and the actual overhead cost incurred was £14,521.

The total overhead expenditure variance is nearest to

A   £1,750 (F)
B   £250 (F)
C   £250 (A)
D   £4,520 (A)   **4 Marks**

The following data is to be used to answer questions 1.7 and 1.8 below.

A division of PLR plc operates a small private aircraft that carries passengers and small parcels for other divisions.

In the year ended 31 March 20X2, it carried 1,024 passengers and 24,250 kgs of small parcels. It incurred costs of £924,400.

The division has found that 70% of its total costs are variable, and that 60% of these vary with the number of passengers and the remainder varies with the weight of the parcels.

The company is now preparing its budget for the three months ending 30 September 20X2 using an incremental budgeting approach. In this period its expects:

- All prices to be 3% higher than the average paid in the year ended 31 March 20X2
- Efficiency levels to be unchanged
- Activity levels to be 209 passengers and 7,200 kgs of small parcels

- -

1.7 The budgeted passenger related cost (to the nearest £100) for the **three months** ending 30 September 20X2 is

   A   £81,600
   B   £97,100
   C   £100,000
   D   £138,700

          2 Marks

1.8 The budgeted small parcel related cost (to the nearest £100) for the **three months** ending 30 September 20X2 is

   A   £64,700
   B   £66,600
   C   £79,200
   D   £95,213

          2 Marks

Total Marks = 20

MOCK EXAM 1

SPECIAL ANSWER SHEET FOR SECTION A

1.1	A	B	C	D
1.2	A	B	C	D
1.3	A	B	C	D
1.4	A	B	C	D
1.5	A	B	C	D
1.6	A	B	C	D
1.7	A	B	C	D
1.8	A	B	C	D

SECTION B – 30 MARKS

ANSWER THIS QUESTION

2   MF plc manufactures and sells two types of product to a number of customers. The company is currently preparing its budget for the year ending 31 December 20X3 which it divides into twelve equal periods.

The cost and resource details for each of the company's product types are as follows.

	Product type M £	Product type F £
Selling price per unit	200	210
Variable costs per unit		
Direct material P (£2.50 per litre)	20	25
Direct material Q (£4.00 per litre)	40	20
Direct labour (£7.00 per hour)	28	35
Overhead (£4.00 per hour)	16	20
Fixed production cost per unit	40	50
	Units	Units
Maximum sales demand in period 1	1,000	3,000

The fixed production cost per unit is based upon an absorption rate of £10 per direct labour hour and a total annual production activity of 180,000 direct labour hours. One-twelfth of the annual fixed production cost will be incurred in period 1.

In addition to the above costs, non-production overhead costs are expected to be £57,750 in period 1.

During period 1, the availability of material P is expected to be limited to 31,250 litres. Other materials and sufficient direct labour are expected to be available to meet demand.

It is MF plc's policy not to hold stocks of finished goods.

Required

(a)   Calculate the number of units of product types M and F that should be produced and sold in period 1 in order to maximise profit.   **4 Marks**

(b)   Using your answer to (a) above, prepare a columnar budgeted profit statement for period 1 in a marginal cost format.   **4 Marks**

After presenting your statement to the budget management meeting, the production manager has advised you that in period 1 the other resources will also be limited. The maximum resources available will be:

Material P   31,250 litres
Material Q   20,000 litres
Direct labour   17,500 hours

It has been agreed that these factors should be incorporated into a revised plan and that the objective should be to make as much profit as possible from the available resources.

Required

(c)   Use graphical linear programming to determine the revised production plan for period 1. State clearly the number of units of product types M and F that are to be produced.   **10 Marks**

(d)   Using your answer to part (c) above, calculate the profit that will be earned from the revised plan.   **3 Marks**

(e)   Calculate and explain the meaning of the shadow price for material Q.   **5 Marks**

(f)   Discuss the other factors that should be considered by MF plc in relation to the revised production plan.   **4 Marks**

Total Marks = 30

SECTION C – 25 MARKS

ANSWER *ONE* QUESTION ONLY

3   PH plc operates a modern factory that converts chemicals into fertiliser. Because the demand for its product is seasonal, the company expects that there will be an average level of idle time equivalent to 20% of hours paid. This is incorporated into the company's standard costs, and the standard labour rate of £6.00 per hour paid is then adjusted accordingly. Any difference between the expected and the actual amount of idle time is reported as the 'idle time variance' and is valued at the adjusted wage rate.

Data for each of the four months January to April 20X2 is as follows.

	January	*February*	*March*	*April*
Actual hours paid	10,000	14,000	17,000	30,000
Actual productive hours	7,200	10,304	12,784	23,040
Standards hours produced	6,984	9,789	11,889	20,966
Idle time variance	£6,000 (A)	£6,720 (A)	£6,120 (A)	?
Efficiency variance	£1,620 (A)	£3,863 (A)	£6,713 (A)	?

Required

(a)   Calculate the idle time variance and the efficiency variance for April.   **4 Marks**

(b)   (i)   Using the data provided and your answer to (a) above as appropriate, prepare a percentage variance chart that shows the trend of these variances. (Use graph paper and show both variances on the same chart.)

       (ii)   Comment on the usefulness of presenting the information in this format.
                                                                                       10 Marks

(c)   Comment briefly on the possible inter-relationships between the idle time variance and the efficiency variance.   **4 Marks**

(d)   Explain briefly the factors that should be considered before deciding to investigate a variance.
                                                                                       7 Marks

                                                                          Total Marks = 25

---

4   X plc manufactures three products in a modern manufacturing plant, using cell operations. Budgeted output for April 20X2 was as follows.

Product R	1,800 units in 36 batches
Product S	1,000 units in 10 batches
Product T	1,000 units in 40 batches

The product details are as follows.

	Product R	*Product S*	*Product T*
Standard labour hours per batch	25	30	15
Batch size (units)	50	100	25
Machine set-ups per batch	3	2	5
Power (kg) per batch	1.4	1.7	0.8
Purchase orders per batch	5	3	7
Machine hours per batch	10	7.5	12.5

During April 20X2, the actual output was as follows.

Product R	1,500 units in 30 batches
Product S	1,200 units in 12 batches
Product T	1,000 units in 40 batches

The following production overhead budgetary control statement has been prepared for April 20X2 on the basis that the variable production overhead varies in relation to standard labour hours produced.

Production overhead budgetary control report – April 20X2

	Original budget	Flexed budget	Actual	Variances	
Output (standard hours produced)	1,800	1,710	1,710		
	£'000	£'000	£'000	£'000	
Power	1,250	1,220	1,295	75	(A)
Stores	1,850	1,800	1,915	115	(A)
Maintenance	2,100	2,020	2,100	80	(A)
Machinery cleaning	800	760	870	110	(A)
Indirect labour	1,460	1,387	1,510	123	(A)
	7,460	7,187	7,690	503	(A)

After the above report had been produced, investigations revealed that every one of the individual costs could be classified as wholly variable in relation to the appropriate cost drivers.

Required

(a) Explain the factors that should be considered when selecting a cost driver.   **4 Marks**

(b) (i) Calculate the budgeted cost per driver for each of the overhead costs.   **10 marks**

(ii) Prepare a production overhead budgetary control report for April 20X1 using an activity based approach.   **6 Marks**

(c) Comment on the validity of an activity based approach to budgetary control for an organisation such as X plc.   **5 Marks**

Total Marks = 25

SECTION D – 25 MARKS

ANSWER *ONE* QUESTION ONLY

Amount of Divisions – Big Organisation

5   CM Limited was formed ten years ago to provide business equipment solutions to local businesses. It has separate divisions for research, marketing, product design, technology and communication services, and now manufactures and supplies a wide range of business equipment (copiers, scanners, printers, fax machines and similar items).

To date it has evaluated its performance using monthly financial reports that analyse profitability by type of equipment.

(a)   The managing director of CM Limited has recently returned from a course on which it had been suggested that the 'balanced scorecard' could be a useful way of measuring performance.

Required

Explain the 'balanced scorecard' and how it could be used by CM Limited to measure its performance.   **13 Marks**

(b)   While on the course, the managing director of CM Limited overheard someone mention how the performance of their company had improved after they introduced 'benchmarking'.

Required

Explain 'benchmarking' and how it could be used to improve the performance of CM Limited.

12 Marks

Total Marks = 25

---

6   (a)   SK plc is divided into five divisions that provide consultancy services to each other and to outside customers. The divisions are computing and information technology, human resources, legal, engineering, and finance.

It has been company policy for all budgets to be prepared centrally with each division being given sales and profit targets. However, the divisional managers feel that the targets are unrealistic, as they do not consider the individual circumstances of each division.

In response to the comments made by the divisional managers, SK plc has now asked the managers to prepare their own budgets for next year.

Required

(i)   State why organisations prepare budgets.   **3 Marks**

(ii)   Explain the arguments for and against the involvement of managers in the preparation of their budgets   **7 Marks**

(b)   SW Limited is a member of the SWAL group of companies. SW Limited manufactures cleaning liquid using chemicals that it buys from a number of different suppliers. In the past, SW Limited has used a periodic review stock control system with maximum, minimum and re-order levels to control the purchase of the chemicals and the economic order quantity to minimise its costs.

The managing director of SW Limited is thinking about changing to the use of a just-in-time (JIT) system.

Required

As management accountant, prepare a report to the managing director that explains how a JIT system differs from that presently being used and the extent to which its introduction would require a review of SW Limited's quality control procedures.   **15 Marks**

Total Marks = 25

ANSWERS

DO NOT TURN THIS PAGE UNTIL YOU
HAVE COMPLETED THE MOCK EXAM

PLAN OF ATTACK

We know you've been told to do it at least 100 times and we know if we asked you you'd know that you should do it. So why don't you do it in an exam? 'Do what in an exam?' you're probably thinking. Well, let's tell you for the 101st time. **Take a good look through the paper before diving in to answer questions**.

What you must do in the first five or ten minutes of the exam is look through the paper in detail, working out which questions to do and the order in which to attempt them. So turn back to the paper and let's sort out a **plan of attack.**

First things first

It's usually best to **start with the objective test questions**. You'll always be able to do at least a couple of them, even if you really haven't done as much preparation as you should have done. And answering even a couple of them will give you the confidence to attack the rest of the paper. **Don't even look at the other questions before doing Section A**. If you see something you don't recognise or which you don't think you can do, you'll only panic! Allow yourself **36 minutes** to do the objective test questions. No more. You can always come back to them at the end of the exam if you have some spare time.

The next step

You're probably either thinking that you don't even know where to begin or that you could answer all of the questions in two hours!

Option 1 (if you don't know where to begin)

If you're a bit **worried** about the paper, do the **questions in the order of how well you think you can answer them.**

- There is not much to choose between Questions 2 and 4 in terms of which might be the best first question. **Question 4** is a fairly straightforward question on ABC and budgetary control. Even if you have problems on the trickier areas, you'll still be able to pick up marks on the easier bits.

  If you can't think of a thing to write about part (a), don't panic. Part (b) does not depend on an answer to part (a) and so do part (a) at the end of the question – working through parts (b) and (c) might even give you some ideas and could deter you from producing a rote-learned list.

  Just sitting and drawing up a proforma budgetary control report required in part (b) will calm you down and give you confidence. Don't spend more than the allotted time on the calculations, however; there are a lot of them (although they are straightforward).

- **Question 2** is another straightforward question and, as it is compulsory, you might as well get it out of the way. The principal advantage of this question is that there is not too much follow-on between the parts of the question: part (c) can be answered without reference to answers to parts (a) and (b); you could get some marks for a definition of shadow price in (e) even if you couldn't do parts (c) and (d); part (f) can be answered to a great extent more or less independently of the rest of the question.

- **Question 6** might be a good one to do next. There are ten very easy marks on offer for part (a) and you don't even have to relate your answer to the scenario, so you can simply produce a list of points you have learned by heart.

Part (b) might appear a bit trickier but you could gain seven marks (ie just under half of the total for (b)) for using a report format, explaining the current system and describing JIT – which should cause you no problems.

- Although not on the most straightforward aspects of variance analysis, the majority of **question 3** should cause you little difficulty. The calculations in part (a) are not difficult because you can use the figures provided to check the basis of the calculations. And you should be able to earn near enough full marks for the written parts ((c) and (d)), even if you can't do the calculations, as the requirements are standard text book material.

- And that just leaves us with **question 5**. The parts are not dependent on each other and you should be able to write enough to gain half marks on each part provided you relate your answer to the scenario!

What you mustn't forget is that you have to **answer question 2, ONE question from Section C and ONE question from Section D**. Once you've decided on question 4, for example, it might be worth putting a line through question 3 so that you are not tempted to answer it!

Option 2 (if you're thinking 'I'll have done all six questions by 10.30')

It never pays to be over confident but if you're not quaking in your shoes about the exam then **turn straight to the compulsory question** in Section B. You've got to do it so you might as well get it over and done with.

Once you've done the compulsory question, choose one of the written questions in Section C and then do one of the calculation-based questions in Section D.

- If you prefer budgeting to variance analysis, try question 4. This question, although not difficult, requires budgeting *and* ABC knowledge, however, while the only bit of question 3 that might cause you problems is the chart.

- Question 6 might be a better option than Question 5 given that part (a) is **so** straightforward.

No matter how many times we remind you....

Always, always **allocate you time** according to the marks for the question in total and for the parts of the question. And always, **always follow the requirements** exactly. Question 5(a) asks for an explanation of the balanced scorecard and how it can be used by CM Limited. So don't simply explain the meaning of the balanced scorecard. You need to prepare a report in part (b) of question 6. So don't provide a memo.

You've got spare time at the end of the exam.....?

If you have allocated your time properly then you **shouldn't have time on your hands** at the end of the exam. If you find yourself with five or ten minutes spare, however, **go back to the objective test questions** that you couldn't do or **any parts of questions that you didn't finish** because you ran out of time.

Forget about it!

And don't worry if you found the paper difficult. More than likely other candidates would too. If this were the real thing you would need to **forget** the exam the minute you leave the exam hall and **think about the next one**. Or, if it's the last one, **celebrate**!

SECTION A

1.1   B   Budgeted revenue $= 5,220 \times £42 = £219,240$

Margin of safety $= 19.575\%$

$\therefore$ Breakeven revenue $= £219,240 \times (1 - 0.19575)$

$= £176,323.77$

C/S ratio $= 40\%$

$\therefore$ Contribution at breakeven point $= £176,323.77 \times 40\%$
$= £70,529.508$

At breakeven point, contribution $=$ fixed costs

$\therefore$ Fixed costs closest to £71,000

1.2   D

1.3   C   Average C/S ratio $= \dfrac{(2 \times 30\%) + (5 \times 20\%) + (3 \times 25\%)}{(2 + 5 + 3)} = 23.5\%$

At breakeven point, contribution $=$ fixed costs $= £100,000$

$\therefore$ Breakeven revenue $= £100,000/0.235 = £425,532$

1.4   C   Monthly activity level (deseasonalised) $= a = 100,000 + (30 \times 240) = 107,200$

$\therefore$ Incorporating seasonal variations, monthly activity level $= 107,200 \times 1.08 = 115,776$

$\therefore x = 115,776$

$\therefore y = £10,000 + (£0.25 \times 115,776) = £38,944$

1.5   A   **Budgeted number of batches**

D	100,000/100	$= 1,000$
R	100,000/50	$= 2,000$
P	50,000/25	$= 2,000$

Budgeted number of set-ups

D	$1,000 \times 3$	$= 3,000$
R	$2,000 \times 4$	$= 8,000$
P	$2,000 \times 6$	$= 12,000$
		$23,000$

$\therefore$ Cost per set-up $= £150,000/23,000 = £6.52$

$\therefore$ Cost per batch of R $= £6.52 \times 4 = £26.08$

$\therefore$ Cost per R $= £26.08/50 = £0.52$

1.6   B   **Determine fixed costs using high-low method**

	Hrs	£
Highest activity level	18,000	16,242
Lowest activity level	10,000	13,468
Difference	8,000	2,774

$\therefore$ Variable cost per hour $= £2,774/8,000 = £0.34675$

$\therefore$ Substituting in lowest activity level, fixed cost

$= £13,468 - (10,000 \times £0.34675) = £10,000.5$

	£	£
Expenditure should have been		
fixed	10,000.500	
variable (13,780 × £0.34675)	4,778.215	
		14,778.715
but was		14,521.000
Variance		257.715 (F)

1.7 A **In year to 31 March 20X0**, variable costs = £924,400 × 70% = £647,080

Proportion varying with passenger numbers = £647,080 × 60% = £388,248

∴ Cost per passenger = £388,248/1,024 = £379.15

In three months to 30 September 20X0, budgeted passenger-related cost

= £379.15 × 209 passengers × 1.03 = £81,619.62

∴ Cost to nearest £100 = £81,600

1.8 C **In year to 31 March 20X0** proportion of variable costs varying with parcel weight

= £(647,080 – 388,148) = £258,832

∴ Cost per kg = £258,832/24,250

In three months to 30 September 20X0, budgeted small parcel-related cost

= £258,832/24,250 × 7,200 kgs × 1.03 = £79,155

∴ Cost to nearest £100 = £79,200

SECTION B

2

(a)   *Step 1.* **Calculate contribution per unit**

	M	F
	£	£
Selling price per unit	200	210
Variable costs per unit	104	100
Contribution per unit	96	110

Step 2. **Calculate contribution per unit of limiting factor**

	M	F
Contribution	£96	£110
Litres of P required per unit		
£20/£2.50	8	
£25/£2.50		10
Contribution per litre of P	£12	£11

Step 3. **Rank products**

	M	F
Ranking	1	2

Step 4. **Production and sales budget**

Product	Demand Units	Litres required	Litres available		Production Units
M	1,000	8,000	8,000	(÷8)	1,000
F	3,000	30,000	23,250 (bal)	(÷ 10)	2,325
			31,250		

(b)

	Product type M £'000	Product type F £'000	Total £'000
Revenue			
(1,000 × £200)	200		
(2,325 × £210)		488.250	
			688.250
Variable costs			
Direct material P			
(1,000 × £20)	20		
(2,325 × £25)		58.125	
			78.125
Direct material Q			
(1,000 × £40)	40		
(2,325 × £20)		46.500	
			86.500
Direct labour			
(1,000 × £28)	28		
(2,325 × £35)		81.375	
			109.375
Overhead			
(1,000 × £16)	16		
(2,325 × £20)		46.500	
			62.500
	104	232.500	336.500
Contribution	96	255.750	351.750
Fixed costs			
Production (W)			150.000
Non-production			57.750
			207.750
Profit			144.000

Working

Total budgeted fixed cost = 180,000 hrs × £10 = £1,800,000
Budget for period 1 = £1,800,000/12 = £150,000

Pass marks. The contribution values for each product and in total were worth two marks, the fixed costs values in total another two marks.

(c) *Step 1.* **Define variables**

Let m be the number of product M produced
Let f be the number of product F produced

Step 2. **Establish objective function**

Maximise contribution (C) = 96m + 110f

where the unit contribution figures are as calculated in (a)

Step 3. **Establish constraints**

(1) **Material P:** $0 \le 8m + 10f \le 31{,}250$

(2) **Material Q:** $0 \le 10m + 5f \le 20{,}000$

(3) **Labour:** $0 \le 4m + 5f \le 17{,}500$

(4) **Maximum M demand:** $0 \le m \le 1{,}000$

(5) **Maximum F demand:** $0 \le f \le 3{,}000$

(6) **Non negativity:** $0 \le m$
                          $0 \le f$

Step 4. **Graph the problem**

Constraint (1)   If m = 0, f = 3,125
                  If f = 0, m = 3,906.25

Constraint (2)   If m = 0, f = 4,000
                  If f = 0, m = 2,000

Constraint (3)   If m = 0, f = 3,500
                  If f = 0, m = 4,375

Sample objective function:

$C = 96 \times 110 \times 20 = 211,200 = 96m + 110f$

$\therefore$ When m = 0, f = 1,920
   When f = 0, m = 2,200

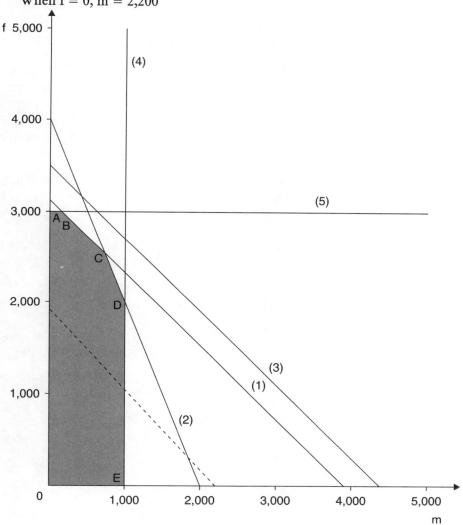

Step 5. **Define feasible area**

The feasible area is OABCDE

Step 6. **Determine optimal solution**

Using the sample contribution line, the optimal solution can be seen to be at point C, where constraints (1) and (2) are equal.

We can find the coordinates using simultaneous equations:

$$
\begin{aligned}
8m + 10f &= 31{,}250 &\quad&(1)\\
10m + 5f &= 20{,}000 &\quad&(2)\\
20m + 10f &= 40{,}000 &\quad&(3) \qquad (2)\times 2\\
12m &= 8{,}750 &\quad&(3)-(1)\\
\therefore m &= 729.17 &\quad&\\
\therefore f &= 2{,}541.67 &\quad&\text{Sub into (2)}
\end{aligned}
$$

The **optimal solution** is to produce 729 units of M and 2,541 units of F.

> **Passmarks**. A correct answer to the end of Step 3 was worth 5.5 marks, Step 4 was worth 3.5 marks, while the correct optimal mix was worth the final one mark.

(d)   Revised profit = (729 × unit contribution of M) + (2,541 × unit contribution of F)
                          – fixed costs (from (b))

$$
= (729 \times £96) + (2{,}541 \times £110) - £207{,}750
$$

$$
= £141{,}744
$$

> **Passmarks**. Each contribution value was worth 1 mark, as was the fixed costs value.

(e)   The shadow price of material Q is the amount by which contribution would fall if availability of material of Q were reduced by one litre.

To calculate the shadow price we need to compare contribution when availability is 20,000 litres with contribution when availability is 19,999 litres.

Availability = 20,000 litres

Using the actual figures determined in (c), and the objective function C = 96m + 110f, contribution would be [8,750/12 × £96] + *[(20,000 – (8,750 × 10)/12)/5 × £110] = £349,583.33

* Value of f determined by substitution of value of m into equation (2) in Step 6 of (c).

Availability = 19,999 litres

If one less litre were available constraint (2) would become $0 \le 10m + 5f \le 19{,}999$

We can now recalculate revised values for f and for m using simultaneous equations.

$$
\begin{aligned}
8m + 10f &= 31{,}250 &\quad&(1)\\
10m + 5f &= 19{,}999 &\quad&(2)\\
20m + 10f &= 39{,}998 &\quad&(3) \qquad (2)\times 2\\
12m &= 8{,}748 &\quad&(3)-(1)\\
\therefore m &= 729 &\quad&\\
\therefore f &= 2{,}541.8 &\quad&\text{Sub into (2)}
\end{aligned}
$$

$\therefore$ C = (729 × £96) + (2,541.8 × £110) = £349,582

Difference in contributions = £1.33 = shadow price of a litre of material Q.

> **Passmarks**. The explanation was worth one mark, the calculation four marks.

Alternative approach

The CIMA model solution takes an alternative approach. This involves comparing the profit achieved when material Q is not a binding constraint (answer (b)) with that achieved when it is (answer (d)). The difference is profits is the shadow price of the difference in litres of material Q used.

The value of the shadow price is largely affected by the accuracy of rounding carried out to determine the optimal solution in (c), however.

(f)   **Other factors to be considered by MF plc**

   (i)   The impact of unsatisfied demand for both products (as demand for M was met under the original production plan)

   (ii)   The possibility of finding alternative suppliers of materials P and Q (even if a premium has to be paid)

   (iii)   The possibility of using alternative materials

   (iv)   The problem in overcoming a shortage of labour if additional material could be sourced

   (v)   Subcontracting production

Passmarks. You would have got one mark for each reasonable point made, to a maximum of four.

SECTION C

3

> **Pass marks.** You may have been a bit unsure about the adjusted wage rates. A productive hour actually costs more than £6 as payment of £6 only results in 60 mins × 80% of productivity. A productive hour therefore costs £6/80%.
>
> A percentage variance chart shows variances as a percentage of the standard costs. So, for example, the labour efficiency variance is shown as a percentage of the standard time for actual output.

(a) **Adjusted wage rate**

£6 is the standard rate per hour
20% of time is deemed idle
∴ An hourly rate of £6 is equivalent to 80% productivity
∴ A productive hour would cost £6/80% = £7.50
∴ Adjusted wage rate = £7.50

Idle time

Average or standard level of idle time = 20% of hours paid

Actual idle time = actual hours paid minus actual productive hours

Idle time variance for April

Idle time should have been (20% × 30,000)	6,000 hrs
but was (30,000 – 23,040)	6,960 hrs
Idle time variance in hours	960 hrs (A)
× adjusted wage rate	× £7.50
Idle time variance in £	£7,200 (A)

Efficiency variance for April

Output should have taken	20,966 hrs
but did take	23,040 hrs
Efficiency variance in hrs	2,074 hrs (A)
× adjusted wage rate	× £7.50
Efficiency variance in £	£15,555 (A)

> **Passmarks.** The calculation of the adjusted wage rate was worth one mark, while the variances were worth three marks in total.

(b) (i) **Idle time**

Month	Standard level of expected idle time Hrs	Standard cost of expected level of idle time £	Variance £	%
January	2,000	15,000	6,000 (A)	40 (A)
February	2,800	21,000	6,720 (A)	32 (A)
March	3,400	25,500	6,120 (A)	24 (A)
April	6,000	45,000	7,200 (A)	16 (A)

Efficiency

Month	Standard hrs produced	Standard cost of std hrs produced	Variance	
	Hrs	£	£	%
January	6,984	52,380.00	1,620 (A)	3 (A)
February	9,789	73,417.50	3,863 (A)	5 (A)
March	11,889	89,167.50	6,713 (A)	8 (A)
April	20,966	157,245.00	15,555 (A)	10 (A)

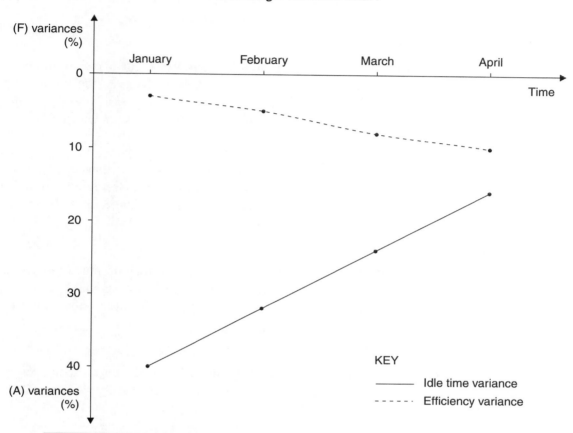

Percentage variance chart

> **Passmarks**. Four marks would have been awarded for the correct calculation of the percentage variance values, two marks for plotting these values on the graph and four marks for part (ii).

(ii)   **Usefulness of presentation format**

(1)   Non finance managers often find pictorial or graphical representation of data far easier to understand than tables of figures.

(2)   The trend in variances can be as important as their absolute value. Presenting the variances over time highlights this factor. For example, the percentage values of the efficiency variance are not high but the chart shows the worsening trend.

(3)   The use of percentages rather than monetary amounts or hourly figures removes the distorting effects of differences in activity levels and allows the monthly information to be compared on a like-for-like basis.

(c)   **Interrelationship between idle time variance and efficiency variance**

The idle time variance and the efficiency variance together make up the overall efficiency variance.

The interrelationship between the two is therefore not based on one being adverse and one being favourable, as with most other variance interrelationships. Instead as the chart in (b) shows, as one improves, the other worsens. In this instance, the idle time variance is seen to improve while the labour efficiency variance worsens, possibly because employees are deliberately being inefficient and taking longer to do their work, to avoid being idle.

> **Passmarks.** An explanation of the general relationship was worth one mark, the relationship in the question three marks.

(d) **Factors to consider before deciding to investigate a variance**

   (i) **Materiality**

Small variations in a single period are bound to occur and are unlikely to be significant. Finding an 'explanation' is likely to be time-consuming and the 'explanation' is likely to be chance, which is not particularly useful management information. For such variations further investigation is not worthwhile.

   (ii) **Controllability**

If the cause of a variance is beyond the control of management (such as a worldwide increase in raw material prices), there is little value in investigating the variance. Uncontrollable variances call for a change in the plan, not an investigation into the past.

   (iii) **Trend in variances**

A variance of £2,000 (A) might be worthy of investigation but if the variance is £2,000 (A) every month, it would appear that the standard has been set incorrectly. Variances should not therefore be considered in isolation but viewed over time.

   (iv) **Cost**

The likely cost of an investigation needs to be weighed against the cost to the organisation of allowing the variance to continue in future periods.

4   (a)

> **Pass marks.** A common error, according to the examiner, was providing an explanation of ABC without focusing on the context of the question.

Factors to consider when selecting a cost driver

Is there a cause and effect relationship?

The **most important** requirement of a cost driver is that there is a **cause and effect relationship between the cost and the proposed driver**.

For example, the cost of maintenance for X plc could realistically be driven by the number of hours for which the machines are used, given that the cost could well increase the more the machines are used. It is less likely that purchase orders could be the cost driver, however, as it is difficult to think of any possible correlation between the incidence of purchase orders and the cost of maintenance.

Can the cost driver be measured?

There is little point in establishing a cause and effect relationship if the incidence of the cost driver cannot be **measured in quantitative terms,** however. A driver such as complexity of the production process cannot be measured *per se*, but this could perhaps be **represented** by number of components used or number of individual processes.

Does a suitable cost driver exist?

It has been argued that it might not be activities that cause costs. Some people have suggested that **decisions cause costs** or **the passage of time causes costs,** or indeed that there is **no clear cause of cost.**

(b)

Pass marks. This part of the question involved six key steps.

Step 1. Identify the cost driver associated with each cost pool.

Step 2. Calculate the budgeted incidence of the cost drivers.

Step 3. Calculate the budgeted cost driver rates (budgeted cost/budgeted number of cost drivers).

Step 4. Determine the number of cost drivers that should have been incurred given the actual activity level. (2 marks awarded to here)

Step 5. Apply the cost driver rates to the results of step 4. (Another 2 marks awarded to here)

Step 6. Compare the results of step 5 with the actual results to determine the variances for the period. (Final 2 marks awarded to here)

(i)   **Suggested cost drivers of production overheads**

Overheads	Driver
Power	Power (kj) used
Stores	Number of purchase orders
Maintenance	Number of machine hours
Machinery cleaning	Number of machinery set-ups
Indirect labour	Number of standard labour hours

For each cost driver we need to calculate the incidence of the cost driver. We then divide the original budgeted figure by the number of cost drivers to find the budgeted cost per driver.

Power

		kjs
R	1.4 kjs × 36 batches =	50.4
S	1.7 kjs × 10 batches =	17.0
T	0.8 kjs × 40 batches =	32.0
		99.4

Budgeted cost per driver = £1,250,000 ÷ 99.4 = £12,575.45 per kj

Stores

		Purchase orders
R	5 purchase orders × 36 batches =	180
S	3 purchase orders × 10 batches =	30
T	7 purchase orders × 40 batches =	280
		490

Budgeted cost per driver = £1,850,000 ÷ 490 = £3,775.51 per purchase order

Maintenance

		Machine hours
R	10 hrs × 36 batches =	360
S	7.5 hrs × 10 batches =	75
T	12.5 hrs × 40 batches =	500
		935

Budgeted cost per driver = £2,100,000 ÷ 935 = £2,245.99 per machine hour

Machinery cleaning

			Set-ups
R	3 set-ups × 36 batches =		108
S	2 set-ups × 10 batches =		20
T	5 set-ups × 40 batches =		200
			328

Budgeted cost per driver = £800,000 ÷ 328 = £2,439.02 per set-up

Indirect labour

			Standard labour hrs
R	25 std labour hrs × 36 batches =		900
S	30 std labour hrs × 10 batches =		300
T	15 std labour hrs × 40 batches =		600
			1,800

Budgeted cost per driver = £1,460,000 ÷ 1,800 = £811.11 per standard labour hour

(ii) The flexed budget needs to be **flexed on the basis of the standard number of cost drivers for the actual output.**

Costs	*R*	*S*	*T*	*Total*
Power	(30 × 1.4)	(12 × 1.7)	(40 × 0.8)	94.4 kj
Stores	(30 × 5)	(12 × 3)	(40 × 7)	466 purchase orders
Maintenance	(30 × 10)	(12 × 7.5)	(40 × 12.5)	890 machine hours
Machinery cleaning	(30 × 3)	(12 × 2)	(40 × 5)	314 set-ups
Indirect labour	(30 × 25)	(12 × 30)	(40 × 15)	1,710 hrs (as per question)

Costs flexed on the basis of cost drivers

		£'000
Power	(94.4 × £12,575.45 per kj)	1,187
Stores	(466 × £3,775.51 per purchase order)	1,759
Maintenance	(890 × £2,245.99 per machine hr)	1,999
Machinery cleaning	(314 × £2,439.02 per set-up)	766
Indirect labour	(1,710 × £811.11 per std labour hr)	1,387

Budgetary control report for April 20X1

Costs	*Original budget* £'000	*Flexed budget* £'000	*Actual* £'000	*Variance* £'000
Power	1,250	1,187	1,295	108 (A)
Stores	1,850	1,759	1,915	156 (A)
Maintenance	2,100	1,999	2,100	101 (A)
Machinery cleaning	800	766	870	104 (A)
Indirect labour	1,460	1,387	1,510	123 (A)
	7,460	7,098	7,690	592 (A)

(c)

> **Pass marks.** Apparently candidates tended to comment on the use of activity based approaches for costing products and for pricing. This was not what was required.

The validity of an activity based approach to budgetary control for an organisation such as X plc

Traditional approach to budgetary control

A traditional approach to budgetary control tends to **flex costs on the basis of just one factor, usually production volume**. This implies that all costs vary in line with changes in production volume.

Cost behaviour in a modern manufacturing environment

In a modern manufacturing environment, however, many **costs tend to vary in line with, or be driven by, factors other than volume of output**. Many costs, particularly **support costs** which have increased dramatically with changes to production processes, are nowadays **related to the range of products and complexity of the manufacturing undertaken**.

For example, the costs of setting-up X plc's machines per batch is likely to be related to how complex a product is (more machine set-ups being required for more complex products). The number of set-ups will not vary with the size of the batch.

Activity based approach to budgetary control

An activity based approach to budgetary control recognises that to flex costs on the basis of production volume is inappropriate and instead **flexes** them on a **wide range of bases depending on the underlying driver** of that cost.

Advantages of such an approach

(i) By flexing different costs on different bases, the **flexed budget cost** is likely to be a **more accurate and realistic target**. Resulting **variances** will therefore be a **more reliable indicator for management action**. In particular, the variances for power, stores and maintenance are significantly different using the two approaches.

(ii) Given that the underlying causes of costs are highlighted (the cost drivers), it should be possible to **control and/or reduce the costs by control and/or reduction of the cost driver**. The link between cost and cause is far more apparent.

SECTION D

5

> **Pass marks.** A relatively straightforward question provided you were able to relate your answers to CM Limited.

(a) **Traditional approach to performance measurement**

Traditional management accounting views of performance measurement **focus solely on financial measures.** This has been compared to driving a car by looking in the rear view mirror, or flying an aeroplane by watching the altimeter alone. Such measures **focus on past performance** and **encourage management to take a short-term view** (profits now, not later), rather than adopt the long-term viewpoint that today's organisations require for success.

Much of the successful work done in organisations is **preparation to achieve financial goals**. For example, CM Limited might achieve process innovations, train workers or forge strong relationships with particular customers. The success or otherwise of such work is **best measured in non-financial or qualitative terms.** Financial results do not highlight such issues or demonstrate how they contribute to the realisation of an organisation's goals.

Moreover, **financial measures** are **inwards looking**. They do not look outside the organisation to take account of competitors' actions and industry best practice.

The balanced scorecard approach and its perspectives

The balanced scorecard consists of a variety of performance indicators, both **financial and non-financial,** and aims to overcome the problems identified above by focusing on not one, but four, different perspectives.

(i)   **Customer perspective**

This gives rise to targets that matter to customers. Examples of measures that CM Limited could adopt include:

- Price as compared with competitors

- Number of favourable reviews in the press

- 'Satisfaction' levels measured on the basis of customer feedback, number of complaints and product ratings

- Performance in relation to areas that customers might say are important, such as percentage of deliveries on time

(ii)   **Internal perspective**

This aims to improve internal processes and decision making. Examples of measures CM Limited could consider include:

- Number of quality control rejects
- Speed of producing management information

(iii)   **Innovation and learning perspective**

This considers an organisation's capacity to maintain its competitive position through the acquisition of new skills and the development of new products.

CM Limited might consider using measures such as:

- Level of long-term investment in new product development

- Average time taken to develop new products

- Sales revenue derived from new products compared with that from established ones

(iv)   **Financial perspective**

This covers traditional measures such as profitability, return on investment, cash flow and growth.

The implications of adopting the balanced scorecard

The scorecard is 'balanced' in the sense that managers are required to think in terms of all four perspectives, to **make sure that improvements in one area are not made at the expense of performance in another area.** For example, funding of the research division of CM Limited is less likely to be cut to boost short-term profitability. And the **financial effect** of changes in the three operational areas can be **seen immediately** because of the **linkage** between the three areas.

By improving performance in the three non-financial areas, measures in the **financial perspective** should also **improve.** If CM Limited were to reduce the number of customer complaints, for example, satisfied customers might increase their spending levels and so increase the company's profitability levels.

The contrast with CM Limited's current approach to performance measurement

The way in which the company **currently** evaluates performance **does not allow an organisational-wide assessment of performance.** Instead of focusing management attention on products, the **balanced scorecard** would provide an **overall view**, based around **key indicators** crucial for the achievement of organisational objectives. These indicators would provide a powerful message and provide a **forwards-looking, strategic focus** for **everyone** in the organisation.

> **Passmarks**. A good overview of the balanced scorecard was worth five marks, a general explanation of the perspectives four marks, while the application of each perspective to CM Limited was worth 4 marks.

(b) **Benchmarking**

Benchmarking can be described as a technique whereby an organisation tries to **emulate or exceed the standards achieved or processes adopted by another organisation,** generally a very successful one. Benchmarking exercises usually reveal improvements and benefits for both sides.

The 'model' organisation could be a direct competitor – ideally one that is acknowledged to be 'best in class' (**competitive benchmarking**). But this is not always the case. Indeed it might be difficult to persuade a direct competitor to part with any information which is useful for comparison purposes.

Functional benchmarking, whereby internal functions are compared with those of the **best external practitioners of those functions, regardless of the industry** they are in, does not always involve direct competitors. For instance a railway company may be identified as the 'best' in terms of on-board catering, and an airline company that operates on different routes could seek opportunities to improve by sharing information and comparing their own operations with those of the railway company.

CM Limited and benchmarking

CM Limited manufactures and sells business equipment and so could consider **benchmarking** its goods inwards, stores, production, stock holding, order taking and delivery **processes** with a **similar organisation** operating in a **different geographical market. Alternatively** it could benchmark against a manufacturer of **electrical white goods** operating in the same geographical market.

The benchmarking process should lead **to improved and more efficient processes** and **challenging but achievable** (because they have been already, by another organisation) **targets.** Improvements in internal processes would affect **the internal perspective** of the balanced scorecard; benchmarks which assess how well CM Limited is satisfying customers would impact on the **customer perspective**; any necessary staff training highlighted by the exercise would result in changes to the measures in the **innovation and learning perspective.**

In the **short term,** there may be an **adverse impact** on the **financial perspective** in terms of cash flow but, in the **medium to long term,** the effect of improvements will cause CM Limited's **financial position** to **improve.**

> **Passmarks**. The twelve marks for this part of the question were split equally between an explanation of the principles of benchmarking and application of benchmarkng to CM Limited.

6

> **Pass marks.** You really have no excuse for not providing first class answers to parts (a)(i) and (ii) as they simply require regurgitation of book knowledge.

(a) (i)   **Reasons why organisations prepare budgets**

(1)   To ensure that an organisation's objectives are achieved by drawing up quantified expressions of those objectives as targets

(2)   To compel formal and coordinated planning

(3)   To allow ideas and plans to be communicated to the appropriate personnel

(4)   To coordinate activities to ensure maximum integration of efforts towards common goals

(5)   To provide a framework for responsibility accounting

(6)   To establish a system of control, a budget being a yardstick against which actual performance is measured and assessed

(7)   To motivate employees to improve their performance with the incentive offered by a comparison of actual and budget performance

(ii) **Arguments for the involvement of managers in the preparation of their budgets include:**

(1)   Such budgets are based on information from employees most familiar with the division. Budgets should therefore be more realistic.

(2)   Knowledge spread among several levels of management is pulled together, again producing more realistic budgets.

(3)   Because managers are more aware of organisational goals, they should be more committed to achieving them.

(4)   Coordination and cooperation between those involved in budget preparation should improve.

(5)   Senior managers' overview of the business can be combined with operational-level details to produce better results.

(6)   Managers should feel that they 'own' the budget and will therefore be more committed to the targets and more motivated to achieve them.

(7)   Participation will broaden the experience of those involved and enable them to develop new skills.

Overall, participation in budget setting should give those involved a more positive attitude towards the organisation, which should lead to better performance.

Arguments against the involvement of managers in the preparation of their budgets include:

(1)   Managers may set easy budgets, or introduce budgetary slack or budget bias, given that they will recognise that the budget will be used as a target against which their performance will be measured.

(2)   The approach can encourage 'empire building', managers setting their budget to achieve a greater share of resources and hence increase their own importance.

(3)   The process can be time consuming and an earlier start to the budgeting process may be required.

(4)   Managers may become demotivated if participation is not real, with senior management overriding their decisions and introducing changes.

Passmarks. Part (i) was worth 3 marks, part (ii) 7 marks.

(b)   REPORT

To: Managing director of SW Limited
From: Management accountant   Date: 13 November 20X1
Subject: **Stock control systems**

1   Introduction

1.1   This report looks at the **differences between the stock control system currently being used within SW Limited and a just-in-time (JIT) system** and then considers the extent to which the **introduction of JIT would require a review of the organisation's control procedures.**

2   JIT

2.1   The **objective** of a JIT system is to **produce products or components as they are needed by the customer or by the production process, rather than for stock.**

2.2   A **JIT production system** therefore only **produces a component when needed in the next stage of production.**

2.3   In a **JIT purchasing system,** purchases of raw materials are contracted so that, as far as possible, the receipt and usage of material coincides.

3   Current stock control system versus a JIT system

3.1   A JIT stock control system for the purchase of chemicals would be fundamentally different to the one currently being used.

3.1.1 Raw materials would not **ordered** when a reorder level is reached but when they were actually need in production.

3.1.2 **Stock levels** would therefore be **reduced to near zero levels,** there would be no maximum and minimum levels.

3.1.3 **Supplies** would be **delivered** on a **long-term contract basis as soon as they were needed,** but in small **quantities**.

3.1.4 This would obviously increase ordering costs.

3.1.5 The costs of space for holding stocks of chemicals, and costs such as damage or deterioration in stores, stores administration and security would be minimal, however. In particular the interest cost and opportunity cost of tying up working capital in large inventories would be avoided.

3.1.6 The economic order quantity model would therefore not be relevant, not only because the exact quantity needed would be delivered, but because holding costs would be kept to a minimum while no direct effort would be made to minimise ordering costs.

4   JIT and the implications for quality control procedures

4.1   JIT purchasing

4.1.1 If raw material stocks were to be kept at near-zero levels, the company would have to have **confidence** that **suppliers** would **deliver on time** and that they would deliver chemicals of **100% quality**. There could be no rejects or returns; if there were, production would be delayed because no stocks are held.

4.1.2 The reliability of the organisation's suppliers would therefore be of the utmost importance and hence we would have to build **up close relationships** with them. This could be achieved by **doing more business with fewer suppliers** and placing **long-term orders** so that the supplier would be assured of sales and could produce to meet the required demand.

4.1.3 A **supplier quality assurance programme** (such as BS EN ISO 9000) should be introduced. The quality of the chemicals delivered would be guaranteed by suppliers and the onus would be on the supplier to carry out the necessary quality checks, or face cancellation of the contract.

4.2   JIT production

4.2.1 Because stocks of components would not be held, production management within a JIT environment would seek both **to eliminate scrap and defective chemicals during production and avoid the need for reworking**. Defects would stop the production line, thus creating rework and possibly resulting in a failure to meet delivery dates.

4.2.2 **Quality control procedures** would therefore have to be in place to **ensure that the correct cleaning liquid was made to the appropriate level of quality on the first pass through production**.

- Products would need to be designed with quality in mind.

- Controls would have to be put in place within processes to prevent the manufacture of defective output.

- Quality awareness programmes would need to be established.

- Statistical checks on output quality both during production and for finished goods would be required.

- Continual worker training would be necessary.

5   I hope this information has proved useful but if I can be of any further assistance please do not hesitate to contact me.

Signed: Management accountant

Pass marks. Marks would have been awarded for part (b) as follows.

- Report format - 1 mark

- Explanation of present system of stock control - 4 marks

- Explanation of JIT system - 2 marks

- Explanation of need for quality supplies of material - 4 marks

- Explanation of need for quality during processing - 4 marks

---

Paper 8

November 2002 paper (amended)

Management Accounting – Performance Management

IMPM

INSTRUCTIONS TO CANDIDATES

You are allowed three hours to answer this question paper.

Answer the ONE question in section A (consisting of nine sub-questions).

Answer the ONE question in section B.

Answer ONE question ONLY from section C.

Answer ONE question ONLY from section D.

**DO NOT OPEN THIS PAPER UNTIL YOU ARE READY
TO START UNDER EXAMINATION CONDITIONS**

SECTION A - 20 MARKS

ANSWER *ALL* NINE SUB-QUESTIONS

Each of the sub-questions numbered from 1.1 to 1.9 inclusive, given below, has only ONE correct answer.

REQUIREMENT:

On the SPECIAL ANSWER SHEET *provided at the end of this question, place a circle 'O' around the letter that gives the correct answer to each sub-question.*

If you wish to change your mind about an answer, block out your first answer completely and then circle another letter. You will not receive marks if more than one letter is circled.

Please note that you will not receive marks for any workings to these sub-questions.

1.1   KLQ plc sells three products. The ratio of their total sales values is K2:L3:Q5. The contribution to sales ratios of the products are:

K   30%

L   25%

Q   40%

If fixed costs for the period are expected to be £120,000, the revenue (to the nearest £1,000) needed to earn a marginal costing profit of £34,000 is:

A   £392,000
B   £413,000
C   £460,000
D   £486,000   **2 Marks**

The following data is to be used to answer questions 1.2 and 1.3 below.

SW plc manufactures a product known as the TRD100 by mixing two materials. The standard material cost per unit of the TRD100 is as follows:

		£
Material X	12 litres @ £2.50	30
Material Y	18 litres @ £3.00	54

In October 2002, the actual mix used was 984 litres of X and 1,230 litres of Y. The actual output was 72 units of TRD100.

- -

1.2   The total material mix variance reported was nearest to

A   £102 (F)
B   £49 (F)
C   £49 (A)
D   £151 (A)   **3 Marks**

1.3   The total material yield variance reported was nearest to

A   £102 (F)
B   £49 (F)
C   £49 (A)
D   £151 (A)   **2 Marks**

1.4 The following details relate to three services provided by JHN plc.

	Service J	Service H	Service N
	£	£	£
Fee charged to customers	84	122	145
Unit service costs:			
Direct materials	12	23	22
Direct labour	15	20	25
Variable overhead	12	16	20
Fixed overhead	20	42	40

All three services use the same type of direct labour which is paid £30 per hour.

The fixed overheads are general fixed overheads that have been absorbed on the basis of machine hours.

If direct labour is a scarce resource, the most and least profitable uses of it are:

	Most profitable	*Least profitable*
A	H	J
B	H	N
C	N	J
D	N	H

2 Marks

The following data is to be used to answer questions 1.5 and 1.6 below.

SD plc is a new company. The following information relates to its first period:

	Budget	Actual
Production (units)	8,000	9,400
Sales (units)	8,000	7,100
Breakeven point (units)	2,000	
Selling price per unit	£125	£125
Fixed costs	£100,000	£105,000

The actual unit variable cost was £12 less than budgeted because of efficient purchasing.

1.5 If SD plc had used standard absorption costing, the fixed overhead volume variance would have been.

   A   £15,638 (F)
   B   £17,500 (F)
   C   £25,691 (F)
   D   £28,750 (F)

2 Marks

1.6 If SD plc had used marginal costing, valuing finished goods stock at actual cost, the profit for the period would have been nearest to

   A   £335,200
   B   £337,600
   C   £340,200
   D   £450,400

3 Marks

The following data is to be used to answer questions 1.7, 1.8 and 1.9 below.

Q plc sells a single product. The standard cost and selling price details are as follows:

	£
Selling price per unit	200
Unit variable costs	124
Unit fixed costs	35

During October 20X2, a total of 4,500 units of the product were sold, compared to a sales and production budget of 4,400 units. The actual cost and selling price details were as follows:

	£
Selling price per unit	215
Unit variable costs	119
Unit fixed costs	40

- -

1.7 The budgeted margin of safety is closest to

- **A**   100 sales units
- **B**   £154,000 sales value
- **C**   £334,000 sales value
- **D**   £475,000 sales value

2 Marks

1.8 The sales volume contribution variance for October was

- **A**   £4,100 (F)
- **B**   £5,600 (F)
- **C**   £7,600 (F)
- **D**   £9,600 (F)

2 Marks

1.9 The sales price variance for October was

- **A**   £20,000 (F)
- **B**   £21,500 (F)
- **C**   £66,000 (F)
- **D**   £67,500 (F)

2 Marks

Total Marks = 20

MOCK EXAM 2

SPECIAL ANSWER SHEET FOR SECTION A

1.1	A	B	C	D
1.2	A	B	C	D
1.3	A	B	C	D
1.4	A	B	C	D
1.5	A	B	C	D
1.6	A	B	C	D
1.7	A	B	C	D
1.8	A	B	C	D
1.9	A	B	C	D

SECTION B – 30 MARKS

ANSWER THIS QUESTION, showing supporting calculations where appropriate

2   AHW plc is a food processing company that produces high-quality, part-cooked meals for the retail market. The five different types of meal that the company produces (products A to E) are made by subjecting ingredients to a series of processing activities. The meals are different, and therefore need differing amounts of processing activities.

Budget and actual information for October 20X2 is shown below:

Budgeted data

	Product A	Product B	Product C	Product D	Product E
Number of batches	20	30	15	40	25

Processing activities per batch

	Product A	Product B	Product C	Product D	Product E
Processing activity W	4	5	2	3	1
Processing activity X	3	2	5	1	4
Processing activity Y	3	3	2	4	2
Processing activity Z	4	6	8	2	3

Budgeted costs of processing activities

	£'000
Processing activity W	160
Processing activity X	130
Processing activity Y	80
Processing activity Z	200

All costs are expected to be variable in relation to the number of processing activities.

Actual data

Actual output during October 20X2 was as follows:

	Product A	Product B	Product C	Product D	Product E
Number of batches	18	33	16	35	28

Actual processing costs incurred during October 20X2 were:

	£'000
Processing activity W	158
Processing activity X	139
Processing activity Y	73
Processing activity Z	206

Required

(a)   Prepare a budgetary control statement (to the nearest £'000) that shows the original budget costs, flexible budget costs, the actual costs, and the total variances of each processing activity for October 20X2.   **15 Marks**

Your control statement has been issued to the managers responsible for each processing activity and the finance director has asked each of them to explain the reasons for the variances shown in your statement. The managers are not happy about this as they were not involved in setting the budgets and think that they should not be held responsible for achieving targets that were imposed upon them.

Required

(b)   Explain briefly the reasons why it might be preferable for Managers *not* to be involved in setting their own budgets.   **5 Marks**

(c)   (i)   Explain the difference between fixed and flexible budgets and how each may be used to control production costs and non-production costs (such as marketing costs) within AHW plc.   **4 Marks**

     (ii)   Give two examples of costs that are more appropriately controlled using a fixed budget, and explain why a flexible budget is less appropriate for the control of these costs.   **3 Marks**

Many organisations use linear regression analysis to predict costs at different activity levels. By analysing past data, a formula such as

$y = ax + b$

is derived and used to predict future cost levels.

Required

(d)   Explain the meaning of the terms **y, a, x** and **b** in the above equation.   **3 Marks**

Total Marks = 30

SECTION C – 25 MARKS

ANSWER **ONE** QUESTION ONLY, showing supporting calculations where appropriate

3   ZED plc sells two products, the Alpha and the Beta. These are made from three different raw materials that are bought from local suppliers using a Just-in-Time (JIT) purchasing policy. Products Alpha and Beta are made to customer order using a JIT manufacturing policy. Overhead costs are absorbed using direct labour hours as appropriate.

The following information relates to October 20X2:

	Alpha	Beta
Budgeted production (units)	2,400	1,800

Standard selling price

The standard selling price is determined by adding a 100% mark-up to the standard variable costs of each product.

Standard variable costs per unit

	Alpha	Beta
	£	£
Direct material X (£5 per metre)	10.00	12.50
Direct material Y (£8 per litre)	8.00	12.00
Direct material Z (£10 per kg)	5.00	10.00
Direct labour (£7 per hour)	14.00	10.50
Variable overhead costs	3.00	2.25

Actual data for October 20X2

Direct material X	10,150 metres	costing	£348,890
Direct material Y	5,290 litres	costing	£44,760
Direct material Z	2,790 kgs	costing	£29,850
Direct labour	9,140 hours paid	costing	£67,980
Direct labour	8,350 hours worked		
Variable overhead			£14,300
Fixed overhead			£72,000
Actual production	Alpha	3,000 units	
	Beta	1,500 units	

Sales variances

The following sales variances have been calculated:

	Absorption costing		Marginal costing	
	Alpha	Beta	Alpha	Beta
	£	£	£	£
Selling price	6,000 (A)	4,500 (F)	6,000 (A)	4,500 (F)
Sales volume	18,000 (F)	11,925 (A)	24,000 (F)	14,175 (A)

Required

(a)   Calculate the budgeted fixed overhead cost for October 20X2.   **3 Marks**

(b)   Calculate the budgeted profit for October 20X2.   **2 Marks**

(c)   Calculate the actual profit for October 20X2.   **2 Marks**

(d)   Prepare a statement, using absorption costing principles, that reconciles the budgeted and actual profits for October 20X2, showing the variances in as much detail as possible. Do not calculate material mix and yield variances.   **15 Marks**

(e)   Explain why it would be inappropriate to calculate material mix and yield variances in requirement (d) above.   **3 Marks**

Total Marks = 25

4   PM Holidays Ltd is a holiday company which offers a range of package holidays abroad. The management are examining the viability of three types of holiday for the coming season.

An analysis of costs and revenues of each of the holiday packages is shown below:

	Sports holiday		Culture holiday		Special interest holiday	
Maximum number of customers	100		100		100	
	£	£	£	£	£	£
Total revenue (100 customers)		42,000		48,000		30,000
Costs: (100 customers)						
Air travel	8,100		8,400		7,800	
Hotel and meals	16,800		19,800		7,200	
Local courier	1,500		1,500		1,750	
Other customer costs and office overheads	10,560		11,880		6,180	
Commission	6,300		4,800		6,000	
		43,260		46,380		28,930
Profit/(loss)		(1,260)		1,620		1,070

Past experience has shown that the average number of places taken up on the holidays, as a percentage of the maximum number of customers, will be 70% on sports, 80% on culture and 60% on special interest holidays.

The costs of the local couriers will not change irrespective of the number of customers. The costs of air travel are also fixed and are based on a block booking of seats for the season. The booking with the airline has already been confirmed. Contracts for the couriers have not yet been signed.

All accommodation costs are variable with the number of passengers. The commission is proportional to the price of the holiday.

The other customer costs and office overheads, in the table above, are allocated over all the company's different package holidays. They are semi-variable costs and an analysis of these costs for the last three years relating to all holidays is as follows:

	Total number of customers	Total customer costs and office overheads £
20X6	10,000	900,000
20X7	12,000	990,000
20X8	15,000	1,125,000

The effects of exchange rates and inflation may be ignored.

Required

(a)   Analyse the costs and revenues into a form more suitable to an assessment of the short-term viability of each holiday. Calculate one possible breakeven number of customers required for each holiday.

NB. Your analysis should be presented showing, where appropriate, costs and revenues per customer.   **10 Marks**

(b)   Identify clearly the shortcomings of the original analysis, explain your preferred analysis and interpret the results.   **10 Marks**

(c)   The limitations of breakeven analysis are often the subject of discussion. Provide a contrast to the criticisms by briefly describing three advantages of its use.   **5 Marks**

Total Marks = 25

SECTION D – 25 MARKS

ANSWER **ONE** QUESTION ONLY

5   SG plc is a long-established food manufacturer which produces semi-processed foods for fast food outlets. While for a number of years it has recognised the need to produce good quality products for its customers, it does not have a formalised quality management programme.

A director of the company has recently returned from a conference, where one of the speakers introduced the concept of Total Quality Management (TQM) and the need to recognise and classify quality costs.

Required

(a)   Explain what is meant by TQM and use examples to show how it may be introduced into different areas of SG plc's food production business.   **12 Marks**

(b)   Explain why the adoption of TQM is particularly important within a Just-in-Time (JIT) production environment.   **5 Marks**

(c)   Explain four quality cost classifications, using examples relevant to the business of SG plc.**8 Marks**

Total Marks = 25

6   PG plc manufactures gifts and souvenirs for both the tourist and commercial promotions markets. Many of the items are similar except that they are overprinted with different slogans, logos, and colours for the different customers and markets. For many years, it has been PG plc's policy to produce the basic items in bulk and then overprint them as required, but this policy has now been questioned by the company's new finance director.

She has also questioned the current policy of purchasing raw materials in bulk from suppliers whenever the periodic stock review system indicates that the re-order level has been reached.

She has said that it is most important in this modern environment to be as efficient as possible, and that bulk purchasing and production strategies are not necessarily the most efficient strategies to be adopted. She has suggested that the company must carefully consider its approaches to production, and the associated costs.

Required

(a)   Compare and contrast the current strategies of PG plc for raw materials purchasing and production with those that would be associated with a Just-in-Time (JIT) philosophy.   **15 Marks**

(b)   Explain what is meant by cost reduction.   **3 Marks**

(c)   Explain how PG plc might introduce a cost reduction programme without affecting its customers' perceptions of product values.   **7 Marks**

Total Marks = 25

ANSWERS

DO NOT TURN THIS PAGE UNTIL YOU
HAVE COMPLETED THE MOCK EXAM

A PLAN OF ATTACK

What's the worst thing you could be doing right now if this was the actual exam paper? Sharpening your pencil? Wondering how to celebrate the end of the exam in 2 hours 59 minutes time? Panicking, flapping and generally getting in a right old state?

Well, they're all pretty bad! But what you should be doing is spending a good **5 minutes looking through the paper in detail**, working out which questions to do and the order in which to attempt them. So turn back to the paper and let's sort out a **plan of attack**.

First things first

It's usually best to **start with the objective test questions**. You'll always be able to do at least a couple of them, even if you really haven't done as much preparation as you should have done. And answering even a couple of them will give you the confidence to attack the rest of the paper. **Don't even look at the other questions before doing Section A**. If you see something you don't recognise or which you don't think you can do, you'll only panic! Allow yourself **36 minutes** to do the objective test questions. No more. You can always come back to them at the end of the exam if you have some spare time.

The next step

You've got **two options** now.

Option 1 (if you're thinking 'Help!')

If you're a bit worried about the paper, do the questions in the order of how well you think you can answer them.

Question 3 might be the best one to start with. A lot of the techniques required (absorption costing, variance analysis) you will have encountered in your earlier studies and even those from the Paper 8 syllabus (more advanced variance analysis) do not have to be applied in a complex way. It is basically a 'working backwards' question, and you should be confident with such questions having done those included in the Kit! Even if you can't get your statement to reconcile in (d), you will earn the majority of the fifteen marks available for calculating the variances. Don't avoid part (e) just because it's on mix and yield variances – its actually very easy. Of course, if you are not happy with variance analysis you should avoid this question at all costs as it's not a technique that you can guess at how to apply to a question

As you've got to do it anyway, given that it's a compulsory question, it might be worth doing **question 2** next. This is a nice compulsory question because all parts of the question are independent of each other, so if you can't do one part, your ability to do the others will not be affected. It might be worthwhile attempting the part you feel most confident with first (flexible budgeting with ABC, behavioural issues, fixed v flexible budgets or forecasting). Obviously, don't avoid part (a), as it is worth half of the marks for the question and, once you have worked out how to flex the costs, it is straightforward. You should be able to earn at least three marks for part (b) as it simply requires regurgitation of book knowledge (notice the *not*), as does (c) (i). And you should be disappointed if you can't score near enough full marks for (d), which again is simply regurgitation of book knowledge.

Question 4 has replaced a question on transfer pricing, a topic no longer on the Paper 8 syllabus. Take note of the phrase 'a form more suitable' in (a), as that is where the principal problem with the question lies. You need to be able to draw up this more suitable form and you are not given much guidance. Vague requirements are to be avoided unless you have no alternative. The remainder of the question is straightforward, however, and you should be able to pick up enough marks on the second part of (a), and on (b) and (c), to easily pass the question.

By putting two questions that require written answers in Section D, the examiner has ensured that you have to do one fully written answer. There's not much to choose between **questions 5 and 6**. Both are divided into three distinct parts (so if you can't answer one part particularly well, this should not affect your performance on the other parts), both are on topics in Part C of the syllabus and both refer to JIT.

Your choice will obviously be affected ultimately by the topics covered, so think hard before you choose between them. Once you start a question you really have to keep going: you don't have enough time to give up on one and start the other. Choose question 5 if you know more about TQM, question 6 if you know more about cost reduction/value analysis.

What you mustn't forget is that you have to **answer question 2, ONE question from Section C and ONE question from Section D**. Once you've decided on question 4, for example, it might be worth putting a line through question 3 so that you are not tempted to answer it!

Option 2 (if you're thinking 'It's a doddle')

It never pays to be over confident but if you're not quaking in your shoes about the exam then **turn straight to the compulsory question** in Section B. You've got to do it so you might as well get it over and done with.

Once you've done the compulsory question, choose one of the questions in Section C and then do one of the questions in Section D.

- Unless you really have problems with variance analysis, question 3 is likely to be a better option than the vaguer question 4. You should have done lots of variance analysis questions and so shouldn't have to spend too much time thinking about how to approach the question.

- The structure of the paper means that you have to do a written question. The format of the two questions is so similar that your choice will have to be made on the basis of which topics you know most about. Our choice would be question 5: part (c) can to an extent be answered from book knowledge and is worth one third of the marks for the question.

No matter how many times we remind you....

Always, always **allocate your time** according to the marks for the question in total and then according to the parts of the question. And **always, always follow the requirements** exactly. Question 4 part (c), for example, asks for three advantages. So provide three. Not four. Not two. And you are not required to calculate mix and yield variances in question 3 part (d). So don't waste time calculating them.

You've got spare time at the end of the exam.....?

If you have allocated your time properly then you **shouldn't have time on your hands** at the end of the exam. But if you find yourself with five or ten minutes to spare, **go back to the objective test questions** that you couldn't do or to **any parts of questions that you didn't finish** because you ran out of time.

Forget about it!

And don't worry if you found the paper difficult. More than likely other candidates will too. If this were the real thing you would need to **forget** the exam the minute you leave the exam hall and **think about the next one**. Or, if it's the last one, **celebrate**!

SECTION A

1.1   C   Contribution – fixed costs = target profit

∴ Contribution = £(34,000 + 120,000) = £154,000

We now know contribution but need to find revenue.

We therefore need an average C/S ratio.

$$\text{Average C/S ratio} = \frac{(2 \times 30\%) + (3 \times 25\%) + (5 \times 40\%)}{(2 + 3 + 5)} = 33.5\%$$

∴ Contribution/sales = 0.335

$$\therefore \frac{£154,000}{0.335} = \text{sales revenue}$$

∴ £459,701 = sales revenue

1.2   B   **Standard mix of actual usage**

		Litres
X	12/30 × (984 + 1,230) =	885.6
Y	18/30 × (984 + 1,230) =	1,328.4
		2,214.0

Material	Actual input Litres	Standard mix of actual input Litres	Variance Litres	× std cost £	Variance £
X	984	885.6	98.4 (A)	2.50	246.0 (A)
Y	1,230	1,328.4	98.4 (F)	3.00	295.2 (F)
	2,214	2,214.0	–		49.2 (F)

Alternative approach

Standard weighted average price per litre calculation

X	12	litres costing	£30
Y	18	litres costing	£54
	30		£84

$$\therefore \text{Standard weighted average price} = \frac{£84}{30} = £2.80$$

Material	Difference Litres	× difference between w av price and standard price	Variance £
X	98.4	£(2.80 – 2.50) = £0.30	29.52 (F)
Y	(98.4)	£(2.80 – 3.00) = £(0.20)	19.68 (F)
	-		49.20 (F)

1.3   D

(984 + 1,230) litres should have yielded (÷ 30)	73.8 units
but did yield	72.0 units
Yield variance in units	1.8 units (A)
× standard cost per unit (£(30 + 54))	× £84
	£151.20 (A)

1.4   A

	Service J	Service H	Service N
Contribution per unit	£45	£63	£78
Labour hours required per unit	1/2	2/3	5/6
Contribution per labour hour	£90	£94.50	£93.60
Ranking	3	1	2

1.5   B   Absorption rate per unit $= \dfrac{£100,000}{8,000} = £12.50$

The fixed overhead volume variance is the under or over absorption of fixed overhead caused by a difference between budgeted and actual production volume

$= (8,000 - 9,400) \times £12.50 = £17,500$ over absorption
$ = £17,500 \,(F)$

1.6   A

	£
Sales (7,100 × £125)	887,500
Cost of sales (7,100 × £63 (W))	(447,300)
Fixed costs	(105,000)
Profit	335,200

Working

At breakeven point (2,000 units), fixed costs = contribution

∴ At breakeven point £100,000 = 2,000 × £(125 – variable cost per unit)

∴ Budgeted variable cost per unit = £75

∴ Actual variable cost per unit = £75 – £12 = £63

1.7   D   Budgeted margin of safety = budgeted sales – breakeven sales

Breakeven sales

Breakeven point occurs when fixed costs = total contribution

Budgeted fixed costs = 4,400 × £35 = £154,000

Budgeted unit contribution = £(200 – 124) = £76

∴ Breakeven volume $= \dfrac{£154,000}{£76} = 2,027$ units

∴ Margin of safety (units) = (4,400 – 2,027) units = 2,373 units

Margin of safety (revenue) = 2,373 × £200 = £474,600 revenue

1.8   C

Budgeted volume	4,400 units
Actual volume	4,500 units
Volume variance in units	100 units (F)
× standard margin per unit	× £76
	£7,600 (F)

1.9   D

	£
Revenue should have been (4,500 × £200)	900,000
but was (4,500 × £215)	967,500
Selling price variance	67,500 (F)

SECTION B

2

> **Pass marks**. What a nice the compulsory question! The only marks you might have lost should have been if you made an arithmetic error in part (a). The trick in part (a) was to work out a budgeted cost per individual processing activity.

(a)

	Original budget cost £'000	Flexed budget costs (W) £'000	Actual costs £'000	Variances £'000
Processing activity W	160	159	158	1 (F)
Processing activity X	130	135	139	4 (A)
Processing activity Y	80	78	73	5 (F)
Processing activity Z	200	206	206	–
	570	578	576	2 (F)

Working

Budgeted number of processing activities

Costs are expected to be variable in relation to the number of processing activities. We therefore need to calculate the budgeted number of activities for each process.

W $(20 \times 4) + (30 \times 5) + (15 \times 2) + (40 \times 3) + (25 \times 1) = 405$

X $(20 \times 3) + (30 \times 2) + (15 \times 5) + (40 \times 1) + (25 \times 4) = 335$

Y $(20 \times 3) + (30 \times 3) + (15 \times 2) + (40 \times 4) + (25 \times 2) = 390$

Z $(20 \times 4) + (30 \times 6) + (15 \times 8) + (40 \times 2) + (25 \times 3) = 535$

Budgeted cost per processing activity

W $\dfrac{£160,000}{405} = £395.06$

X $\dfrac{£130,000}{335} = £388.06$

Y $\dfrac{£80,000}{390} = £205.13$

Z $\dfrac{£200,000}{535} = £373.83$

Bgt Control Report

	Original	Flexed	Actual	Variance	
W	160	159	150	1	F
X	130	135	139	4	A
Y	80	78	73	5	F
Z	200	206	206	0	
	570	578	576	2	F

Actual number of processing activities

Units of Processing Activity

W $(18 \times 4) + (33 \times 5) + (16 \times 2) + (35 \times 3) + (28 \times 1) = 402$

X $(18 \times 3) + (33 \times 2) + (16 \times 5) + (35 \times 1) + (28 \times 4) = 347$

Y $(18 \times 3) + (33 \times 3) + (16 \times 2) + (35 \times 4) + (28 \times 2) = 381$

Z $(18 \times 4) + (33 \times 6) + (16 \times 8) + (35 \times 2) + (28 \times 3) = 552$

Budgeted cost for actual number of processing activities

W $£395.06 \times 402 = £158,814.12$

X $£388.06 \times 347 = £134,656,82$

Y $£205.13 \times 381 = £78,154.53$

Z $£373.83 \times 552 = £206,354.16$

(b) **Reasons for managers not to be involved in setting their own budgets**

  (i)   Participative budgeting consumes more time than a system of imposed budgeting and hence the budgeting process has to **start earlier.**

  (ii) There may be **dissatisfaction** if senior managers implement **changes** to budgets drawn up by lower levels of management.

  (iii) Budgets may be **unachievable** if managers drawing them up do not have the necessary skills, knowledge or expertise. For example, senior management have an awareness of total resource availability, lower level managers may not.

  (iv) Participative budgeting gives managers the opportunity to introduce **budgetary slack** and **budget bias.**

  (v)   A system of allowing managers to participate in the budgeting process can support '**empire building**'.

  (vi) **Strategic** plans are less likely to be successfully incorporated into planned activities.

(c) (i)   There are important **differences between fixed and flexible budgets** at both the budget-setting and performance review stages.

   (1) Budget setting

   - **Fixed budgets** are prepared on the basis that a certain volume of activity/production and a certain volume of sales will be achieved (such as 200 units). **No alternatives are given to these levels.**

   - A **flexible budget** is a budget which is designed to **change** as the **volume of activity changes**. A company may expect to sell 200 units. However it may prepare flexible budgets on the basis it produces and sells 180 units, or produces 200 units and sells 180 units.

   Thus when preparing flexible budgets it is essential to know **which costs vary with activity levels** and **which costs** are **fixed**. This information is not important when using fixed budgeting because costs are only being budgeted at one level of activity.

   (2) Performance review

   - When a period is reviewed, a **fixed budget** would **not be adjusted** for the actual level of activity. Hence budgeted costs at the budgeted level of activity would be compared with actual costs at the actual level of activity; the actual level of activity may well differ from the budgeted level.

   - **Flexible budgets** at the review stage would be set at the actual level of activity. Thus actual results at the actual level of activity can be compared with the results that should have been achieved at the **actual level of activity.**

   Control of production and non-production costs

   Production costs tend to be **variable** costs and hence **cannot be controlled using fixed budgets** as the budget allowance does not reflect the expected cost at the actual level of production. Control is better achieved using flexible budgets, as the budget cost allowance reflects the cost that should have been achievable given the actual level of production.

Non-production costs (such as marketing costs) tend to be **unaffected by changes in activity level** and hence can be **controlled by both fixed and flexible budgets.**

(ii) **Costs that are more appropriately controlled using a fixed budget**

Any fixed cost, and particularly non-production fixed costs, can be controlled using a pre-set expenditure limit, which is a form of fixed budget, because they should be unaffected by changes in activity level (within a certain range). Examples included research costs and advertising costs.

(d) In the linear regression equation y = ax + b, the terms have the following meanings.

(i) **y** is the **dependent variable,** in this instance the level of **total costs**. Its value is dependent upon the level of activity.

(ii) **x** is the **independent variable,** in this instance the **level of activity**. Its value is independent of the other variables in the equation.

(iii) **a** is the **level of fixed costs**. In other words, it is the value of y when x is zero (the cost when there is no level of activity).

(iv) **b** is the **variable cost per unit** of activity. In other words, it is the change in y (total cost) as a result of x (activity level) changing by one unit.

SECTION C

3

> **Pass marks**. It was important to realise that, although we are not given details of sales volumes, we are told that products are made to customer order and so production equals sales.

(a) The difference between absorption costing and marginal costing sales volume variances is the variance in units multiplied by the fixed overhead absorbed per unit. (The volume variance is higher using marginal costing because the marginal costing margin is higher than the absorption costing margin.)

Alpha

Difference in value of volume variances = variance in units × fixed overhead absorbed per unit

∴ £(24,000 – 18,000) = (3,000 – 2,400) × fixed overhead absorbed per unit

∴ Fixed overhead absorbed per unit = £10

Beta

Difference in value of volume variances = variance in units × fixed overhead absorbed per unit

∴ £(14,175 – 11,925) = (1,800 – 1,500) × fixed overhead absorbed per unit

∴ Fixed overhead absorbed per unit = £7.50

Budgeted fixed overhead cost = (2,400 × £10) + (1,800 × £7.50) = £37,500

Alternative approach

Alpha

Sales volume variance (absorption)

Budgeted sales volume	2,400 units
Actual sales volume	3,000 units
Variance in units	600 units (F)
× standard margin per unit	× £X
	£18,000 (F)

∴ Standard margin per unit of Alpha = £18,000/600 = £30

Standard margin = standard selling price – standard variable costs – standard fixed overhead absorbed per unit

Standard selling price = 2 × standard variable costs

∴ Standard margin = (2 × standard variable costs) – standard variable costs – standard fixed overhead absorbed per unit

∴ £30 = standard variable costs – standard fixed overhead absorbed per unit

∴ £30 = £40 (given) – standard fixed overhead absorbed per unit

∴ Standard fixed overhead absorbed per unit = £10

∴ Standard absorption rate per direct labour hour = £10/2 = £5

Beta

Sales volume variance (absorption)

Budgeted sales volume	1,800 units
Actual sales volume	1,500 units
Variance in units	300 units (A)
× standard margin per unit	× £X
	£11,925 (A)

∴ Standard margin per unit of Beta = £11,925/300 = £39.75

Using same approach as for Alpha:

£39.75 = £47.25 – standard fixed overhead absorbed per unit

∴ Standard fixed overhead absorbed per unit = £7.50

∴ Standard absorption rate per hour = £7.50/1.5 = £5

Budgeted fixed overhead cost

= (2,400 units of Alpha × 2 hours × £5) + (1,800 units of Beta × 1.5 hours × £5)

= £24,000 + £13,500 = £37,500

(b)   Standard selling price per unit = 2 × standard variable costs per unit

∴ Standard contribution per unit = standard variable cost per unit

Budgeted profit = budgeted total contribution – budgeted fixed costs

∴ Budgeted profit   = budgeted total variable costs – budgeted fixed costs

                        = [(2,400 × £40) + (1,800 × £47.25)] – £37,500

                        = £143,550

(c)   We need the actual sales revenue to able to determine the actual profit.

This can be determined from the selling price variances by 'working backwards'.

Alpha

	£
Revenue from 3,000 units should have been (3,000 × £80★)	240,000
but was	X
	6,000 (A)

∴ X = actual revenue = £234,000

Beta

	£
Revenue from 1,500 units should have been (1,500 × £94.50★)	141,750
but was	X
	4,500 (F)

∴ X = actual revenue = £146,250

★ 2 × standard variable costs per unit

Actual profit = actual revenue – actual variable cost – actual fixed costs

	£	£
Revenue [£(234,000 + 146,250)]		380,250
Variable costs		
direct material X	48,890	
direct material Y	44,760	
direct material Z	29,850	
direct labour	67,980	
variable overhead	14,300	
		(205,780)
Contribution		174,470
Fixed overhead		(72,000)
Actual profit		102,470

(d)

		£	£	£
Budgeted profit				143,550
Sales variances: price	Alpha	6,000 (A)		
	Beta	4,500 (F)		
			1,500 (A)	
volume	Alpha	18,000 (F)		
	Beta	11,925 (A)		
			6,075 (F)	
				4,575 (F)
Actual sales minus the standard cost of sales				148,125

Cost variances (W)

		£	£	
		(A)	(F)	
Direct material X	price		1,860	
	usage	2,000		
Direct material Y	price	2,440		
	usage	320		
Direct material Z	price	1,950		
	usage		2,100	
Direct labour	rate	4,000		
	efficiency	700		
	idle time	5,530		
Variable overhead	rate	1,775		
	efficiency	150		
Fixed overhead	expenditure	34,500		
	efficiency	500		
	capacity		4,250	
		53,865	8,210	45,655 (A)
Actual profit				102,470

Workings

Direct material X

	£
10,150m should have cost (× £5)	50,750
but did cost	48,890
Price variance	1,860 (F)

3,000 units of Alpha should have used (× 2m)	6,000m
1,500 units of Beta should have used (× 2.5m)	3,750m
	9,750m
but did use	10,150m
	400m (A)
× standard cost per m	× £5
Usage variance	£2,000 (A)

363

Direct material Y

	£
5,290 litres should have cost (× £8)	42,320
but did cost	44,760
Price variance	2,440 (A)

3,000 units of Alpha should have used (× 1 litres)	3,000 litres	
1,500 units of Beta should have used (× 1.5 litres)	2,250 litres	
		5,250 litres
but did use		5,290 litres
		40 litres (A)
× standard cost per litre		× £8
Usage variance		£320 (A)

Direct material Z

	£
2,790 kgs should have cost (× £10)	27,900
but did cost	29,850
Price variance	1,950 (A)

3,000 units of Alpha should have used (× 0.5 kg)	1,500 kgs	
1,500 units of Beta should have used (× 1 kg)	1,500 kgs	
		3,000 kgs
but did use		2,790 kgs
		210 kgs (F)
× standard cost per litre		× £10
Usage variance		£2,100 (F)

Direct labour

	£
9,140 hours should have cost (× £7)	63,980
but did cost	67,980
Rate variance	4,000 (A)

3,000 units of Alpha should have taken (× 2 hrs)	6,000 hrs	
1,500 units of Beta should have taken (× 1.5 hrs)	2,250 hrs	
		8,250 hrs
but did take		8,350 hrs
		100 hrs (A)
× standard rate per hr		× £7
Efficiency variance		£700 (A)

Hours worked	8,350 hrs
Hours paid for	9,140 hrs
Idle hours	790 hrs (A)
× standard rate per hour	× £7
Idle time variance	£5,530 (A)

Variable overhead

	£
8,350 hrs should have cost (× £1.50 per hr)	12,525
but did cost	14,300
Rate variance	1,775 (A)

Labour efficiency variance	100 hrs (A)
× standard rate per hour	× £1.50
Efficiency variance	£150 (A)

Fixed overhead

		£
Budgeted expenditure (from (a))		37,500
Actual expenditure		72,000
Expenditure variance		34,500 (A)

Labour efficiency variance		100 hrs (A)
× standard rate per hour (from (a))		× £5
Efficiency variance		£500 (A)

Budgeted hours of work *		7,500 hrs
Actual hours of work		8,350 hrs
		850 hrs (F)
× standard rate per hour		× £5
Capacity variance		£4,250 (F)

* (2,400 × 2) + (1,800 × 1.5) = 7,500

(e) Mix and yield variances should **only be calculated** when **proportions** of materials in a mix are **changeable** and **controllable** or when the **usage variance** of individual materials is of **limited value** because of variability of the mix.

Direct materials **X, Y and Z cannot be substituted** for each other because they are obviously **completely different**, being measured in units, litres and kgs respectively. It should therefore be impossible to substitute one kg of X, for example, for one litre of Y. The proportions in the mix are therefore not changeable.

4

> **Pass marks**. Presentation is important in your answer to (a), as well as clear explanations of any assumptions you make. In order to assess the viability of each holiday it is important to highlight the contribution from each, as well as the specific fixed costs. The question implies that the fixed element of 'other customer costs' is an arbitrary allocation of central costs which is not relevant when assessing the relative viability of the holidays. Since the question provides information concerning fixed costs which are sunk (air travel) and others which are avoidable (local couriers) we have taken this into account in calculating our breakeven point. Other breakeven calculations, for example including all fixed costs in the numerator, would have been equally acceptable.

(a)

	Sports holiday		Culture holiday		Special interest holiday	
	£ per customer	£ per customer	£ per customer	£ per customer	£ per customer	£ per customer
Sales revenue		420		480		300
Variable costs:						
hotel and meals	168		198		72	
other customer costs and o'heads (W)	45		45		45	
commission	63		48		60	
		276		291		177
Contribution		144		189		123

	Sports holiday £		Culture holiday £		Special interest holiday £	
Contribution per average hol	(× 70)	10,080	(× 80)	15,120	(× 60)	7,380
Less incremental fixed costs:						
local courier		1,500		1,500		1,750
Profit before sunk costs		8,580		13,620		5,630
Less sunk fixed costs:						
air travel		8,100		8,400		7,800
Profit/(loss) per average holiday		480		5,220		(2,170)

Working

Use **high-low method** to analyse other customer costs.

	Customers	Costs £
High 20X8	15,000	1,125,000
Low 20X6	10,000	900,000
Change	5,000	225,000

$$\text{Variable cost per customer} = \frac{£225,000}{5,000} = £45$$

Calculation of breakeven number of customers

Since some of the fixed costs are already **committed** and cannot now be avoided if the holidays do not proceed (the air travel costs), they will **not be included** in the calculation of the breakeven point. The resulting breakeven point will then be useful if managers are using it as the basis for a **proceed/cancel decision**.

$$\text{Breakeven point} = \frac{\text{avoidable fixed costs}}{\text{contribution per passenger}}$$

	Sports holiday	Culture holiday	Special interest holiday
Breakeven point	£1,500	£1,500	£1,750
	£144	£189	£123
	= 11 customers	= 8 customers	= 15 customers

(b) **Shortcomings of the original analysis**

(i)   The original analysis **did not distinguish between fixed and variable costs**. This made it impossible for managers to ascertain which costs would change if more or less customers booked a particular holiday.

(ii) The original analysis **did not highlight the contribution per customer** from each type of holiday. Managers were not able to see the rate at which profit would increase as additional customers booked each type of holiday.

(iii) The original analysis **allocated fixed office overheads** across each type of holiday on an apparently **arbitrary** basis. The resulting relative 'profit' figures were distorted.

(iv) The original analysis was **based on 100% capacity** and took no account of the fact that **past experience** shows that **take up ranges from 60%** on special interest holidays to **80%** on culture holidays.

(v)   The original analysis **did not distinguish** between those **fixed** costs which were **sunk** at the beginning of the season (air travel) and those which were **incremental** for each package (courier costs).

Explanation of the preferred analysis

(i)   The preferred analysis **separates the fixed and variable costs** and thus **highlights** the **contribution** from each type of holiday.

(ii)   It also **allocates** only the **specific fixed** costs to each type of holiday, and makes **no attempt** to **arbitrarily apportion** general office costs to the individual types of package.

(iii)   The **specific fixed costs** are analysed to indicate those which **are incremental and avoidable** in the short term, and those which are **sunk and unavoidable** in the short term.

Interpretation of the results

(i)   **Culture** holidays earn the **largest contribution per customer**. This means that profits will increase at the fastest rate if more customers are booked onto this type of holiday. The **lowest contribution per customer** is earned by **special interest** holidays.

(ii)   The **highest profits** are earned from **culture** holidays, after taking account of specific fixed overheads and the average number of places taken up.

(iii)   **Special interest holidays** generate a **loss** after taking account of specific fixed overheads. The average holiday does earn a contribution which is sufficient to cover the incremental fixed costs (the courier costs) which would arise if a specific holiday were offered once the season had begun, however. At this stage the air travel costs would be sunk and would not be relevant to a decision to continue to offer a particular holiday.

(iv)   The **highest profit** is generated by the average **culture** holiday.

(v)   The **breakeven point** is **lowest** for **culture** holidays, at eight customers. It increases to 11 customers for sports holidays and is highest at 15 customers for special interest holidays. This is the number of customers that must be attracted to each type of holiday once the season has begun, as it does not take account of the sunk air travel costs which are committed at the beginning of the season.

(c) **Advantages of the use of breakeven analysis**

(i)   **Graphical** representation of cost and revenue data can be more easily **understood** by non-financial managers.

(ii)   A breakeven model enables the **determination of the profit or loss at any level of activity** within the range for which the model is valid, and the **contribution to sales ratio** can **indicate relative profitability** for different products.

(iii)   Highlighting the breakeven point and the margin of safety gives managers some **indication of the level of risk** involved, and as such is an aid to production and sales.

SECTION D

5

> **Pass marks.** This was a fairly straightforward question. Part (c) in particular should have caused you very little problem – although it was vital to provide examples.

(a) Total Quality Management (TQM) is the process of focusing on quality in the management of all resources and relationships within the organisation. It has two basic principles.

    (i) **Getting things right first time**, on the basis that the cost of correcting mistakes is greater than the cost of preventing them from happening in the first place.

    (ii) **Continuous improvement**, which is the belief that it is always possible to improve, no matter how high quality may be already.

TQM and SG plc

TQM is a management technique, applicable to all of an organisation's activities, not just to production. It can therefore be applied to all of SG plc's activities, not just to food production.

    (i) **In relation to design.** Products and processes should be designed with quality in mind (so that faults are not incorporated from the outset). For example, SG plc would need to ensure that specifications for food were 100% correct.

    (ii) **In relation to food production.** The quality of output depends on the quality of input materials and so TQM would require procedures for acceptance and inspection of goods inwards and measurement of rejects. Inspection of output could take place at various key stages of the production process to provide a continual check that the production process is under control. Machines should be maintained so that quality production occurs.

    (iii) **In relation to sales.** Some sub-standard output will inevitably be produced. Customer complaints should be monitored in the form of letters of complaint, returned goods, penalty discounts and so on.

    (iv) **In relation to suppliers.** Supplier quality assurance schemes could be established so that suppliers would guarantee the quality of goods supplied. The onus would then be on the supplier to carry out the necessary quality checks or face cancellation of the contract.

    (v) **In relation to employees.** Quality should be the primary concern of every employee at every stage of production. Workers must therefore be empowered and take responsibility for the quality of SG plc's products, stopping the production line if necessary. Quality circles might be set up, perhaps with responsibility for implementing improvements identified by the circle members.

    (vi) **In relation to the information system.** The information system should be designed to get the required information to the right person at the right time.

(b) Just-in-time (JIT) systems incorporate:

    (i) **JIT production,** which is a system driven by demand for finished products so that work in progress is only processed through a stage of production when it is needed by the next stage. The result is **minimal** (or in some cases non-existent) **stocks of work in progress and finished goods.**

(ii)   **JIT purchasing**, which seeks to match the usage of materials with the delivery of materials from external suppliers. This means that **material stocks** can be kept at **near-zero levels.**

Production management within a JIT environment therefore needs to **eliminate scrap and defective units** during production and **avoid the need for reworking of units. Defects stop** the **production line**, creating **rework** and possibly resulting in a **failure to meet delivery dates** (as **buffer stocks** of work in progress and finished goods are **not held**). **TQM** should ensure that the **correct product** is made to the **appropriate level of quality** on the **first pass through production.**

For JIT purchasing to be successful, the organisation must have confidence that the **supplier** will **deliver on time** and will deliver **materials of 100% quality**, that there will be no rejects, returns and hence **no consequent production delays.** This confidence can be achieved by **adopting supplier quality assurance schemes** and stringent **procedures for acceptance and inspection of goods inwards**, which are integral parts of TQM.

(c)   Quality costs can be classified in four ways.

(i)   **Costs of internal failure** are costs arising within an organisation due to failure to achieve the quality specified. Examples relevant to the business of SG plc could include the cost of foods scrapped due to inefficiencies in goods inwards procedures, the cost of foods lost in process and the cost of foods rejected during any inspection process.

(ii)   **Costs of external failure** are costs arising outside the organisation of failure to achieve specified quality after transfer of ownership to the customer. SG plc examples could include the cost of a customer complaints section and the cost of replacing and delivering returned foods.

(iii)   **Costs of prevention** represent the cost of any action taken to investigate, prevent or reduce defects and failures. Examples for SG plc could include the cost of training personnel in TQM procedures and the cost of maintaining quality control/inspection equipment.

(iv)   **Costs of appraisal** are the costs of assessing the level of quality achieved. Examples applicable to SG plc could be the cost of any goods inwards checks and the costs of any supplier vetting.

6

> **Pass marks.** The CIMA model answer did not mention value analysis in part (c), but considered cost reduction in wider terms.

(a)   **Basis of PG plc's current strategy**

(i)   Production at or near maximum output in order to minimise unit costs

(ii)   Large stocks of materials and high levels of work in progress and finished goods

(1)   Facilitate long production runs and hence reduce average unit cost

(2)   Provide a buffer against interruptions to production (caused by supply problems or faulty inputs from other processes) and therefore minimise unproductive idle time

(iii)   Negotiations with materials suppliers focused on price – maximising bulk discounts and so on

(1)   Move to alternative suppliers only if they are cheaper

(2)   Level of quality is a secondary issue

(iv)   No attempt to predict demand for inputs or final products and difficulty in tailoring products to customers

(v)   Capacity to cope with disruptions in both materials supply and production

(vi)   Workforce likely to be highly skilled but inflexible

JIT

It is against this background that JIT has become popular. The aims of JIT are to produce the required items, at the required quality and in the required quantities, at the precise time they are required.

JIT purchasing

(i)   JIT purchasing seeks to match the usage of materials with the delivery of materials from external suppliers. This means raw materials are not ordered when a reorder level is reached but when they are actually needed in production. Stocks are kept at near zero levels, there are no maximum and minimum levels. Supplies are delivered on a long-term contract basis as soon as they are needed, but in small quantities.

(ii)   The organisation must therefore be 100% confident that suppliers will deliver material of 100% quality, on time, so that there will be no rejects, no returns and hence no production delays (because no buffer stock is held). Supportive supplier relations are vital and vendor quality assurance programmes should be implemented.

JIT production

JIT production systems are driven by demand for finished products, and so products/components are only produced when needed by the next process. Nothing is produced in anticipation of need, to then remain in stock, consuming resources. Production runs are therefore shorter, and so there are more of them, and stocks of finished goods are smaller because output is matched more closely with demand. Production can be tailored to individual customer demands.

Employees are trained to operate each machine within each machine cell and carry out routine preventative maintenance (ie to be multiskilled and flexible).

Effect of JIT on stock costs

JIT obviously increases ordering costs, but stock holding costs (including damage and deterioration in stores) are minimal. In particular the interest cost and opportunity cost of tying up working capital in large stock holdings is avoided.

(b)   Cost reduction should not be confused with cost control. Cost control is about regulating the costs of operating a business and keeping costs within acceptable limits.

Cost reduction, in contrast, is a **planned** and **positive** approach to reducing expenditure and **starts with the assumption** that **current cost levels,** or planned cost levels, are **too high,** even though cost control might be good and efficiency levels high.

So whereas cost control aims to reduce costs to budget or standard level, cost reduction aims to **reduce costs to below budget or standard level**, as budgets and standards do not necessarily reflect the costs and conditions which minimise costs.

(c) The first step in a cost reduction programme would be to identify the product characteristics valued by customers.

Product values

A product's values could be classified as follows.

(i) **Cost** value is the cost of producing and selling an item.

(ii) **Exchange** value is the market value of the product.

(iii) **Use** value is what the article does, the purpose it fulfils.

(iv) **Esteem** value is the prestige the customer attaches to the product.

Conventional cost reduction programmes aim to achieve the lowest production cost for a specific product design without considering the impact on exchange, use and esteem values.

Value analysis

Value analysis, on the other hand, is a particular approach to cost reduction which recognises these various types of value which a product provides, analyses these values, and then seeks ways of improving or maintaining aspects of these values but at a lower cost.

Value analysis at PG plc would involve the systematic investigation of every source of cost and technique of production with the aim of getting rid of all unnecessary costs. An unnecessary cost is an additional cost incurred without adding use, exchange or esteem value to the product.

Of course value analysis is not quite as simple as this in practice, as there might be a conflict between, say, reducing costs and maintaining the aesthetic (esteem) value of a product. Where cost cutting and aesthetics are incompatible, there should be clear direction from senior management about which is more important.

Introducing a value analysis

A value analysis of a product might pose the following questions.

(i) **Are all variants of the product necessary?** Could the product be produced in just three colours without affecting customers' perception of product quality.

(ii) **Could the product be provided at a lower cost without affecting its value?** For example could T-shirts be manufactured in a cheaper material?

From the analysis a variety of options can be derived and the least cost alternative which maintains or improves the value of the product to customers can be selected.

LOGARITHMS

	0	1	2	3	4	5	6	7	8	9	1	2	3	4	5	6	7	8	9
10	0000	0043	0086	0128	0170	0212	0253	0294	0334	0374	4	9	13	17	21	26	30	34	38
											4	8	12	16	20	24	28	32	37
11	0414	0453	0492	0531	0569	0607	0645	0682	0719	0755	4	8	12	15	19	23	27	31	35
											4	7	11	15	19	22	26	30	33
12	0792	0828	0864	0899	0934	0969	1004	1038	1072	1106	3	7	11	14	18	21	25	28	32
											3	7	10	14	17	20	24	27	31
13	1139	1173	1206	1239	1271	1303	1335	1367	1399	1430	3	7	10	13	16	20	23	26	30
											3	7	10	12	16	19	22	25	29
14	1461	1492	1523	1553	1584	1614	1644	1673	1703	1732	3	6	9	12	15	18	21	24	28
											3	6	9	12	15	17	20	23	26
15	1761	1790	1818	1847	1875	1903	1931	1959	1987	2014	3	6	9	11	14	17	20	23	26
											3	5	8	11	14	16	19	22	25
16	2041	2068	2095	2122	2148	2175	2201	2227	2253	2279	3	5	8	11	14	16	19	22	24
											3	5	8	10	13	15	18	21	23
17	2304	2330	2355	2380	2405	2430	2455	2480	2504	2529	3	5	8	10	13	15	18	20	23
											2	5	7	10	12	15	17	19	22
18	2553	2577	2601	2625	2648	2672	2695	2718	2742	2765	2	5	7	9	12	14	16	19	21
											2	5	7	9	11	14	16	18	21
19	2788	2810	2833	2856	2878	2900	2923	2945	2967	2989	2	4	7	9	11	13	16	18	20
											2	4	6	8	11	13	15	17	19
20	3010	3032	3054	3075	3096	3118	3139	3160	3181	3201	2	4	6	8	11	13	15	17	19
21	3222	3243	3263	3284	3304	3324	3345	3365	3385	3404	2	4	6	8	11	13	15	17	19
22	3424	3444	3464	3483	3502	3522	3541	3560	3579	3598	2	4	6	8	10	12	14	16	18
23	3617	3636	3655	3674	3692	3711	3729	3747	3766	3784	2	4	6	8	10	12	14	15	17
24	3802	3820	3838	3856	3874	3892	3909	3927	3945	3962	2	4	6	7	9	11	13	15	17
25	3979	3997	4014	4031	4048	4065	4082	4099	4116	4133	2	3	5	7	9	10	12	14	15
26	4150	4166	4183	4200	4216	4232	4249	4265	4281	4298	2	3	5	7	8	10	11	13	15
27	4314	4330	4346	4362	4378	4393	4409	4425	4440	4456	2	3	5	6	8	9	11	13	14
28	4472	4487	4502	4518	4533	4548	4564	4579	4594	4609	2	3	5	6	8	9	11	12	14
29	4624	4639	4654	4669	4683	4698	4713	4728	4742	4757	1	3	4	6	7	9	10	12	13
30	4771	4786	4800	4814	4829	4843	4857	4871	4886	4900	1	3	4	6	7	9	10	11	13
31	4914	4928	4942	4955	4969	4983	4997	5011	5024	5038	1	3	4	6	7	8	10	11	12
32	5051	5065	5079	5092	5105	5119	5132	5145	5159	5172	1	3	4	5	7	8	9	11	12
33	5185	5198	5211	5224	5237	5250	5263	5276	5289	5302	1	3	4	5	6	8	9	10	12
34	5315	5328	5340	5353	5366	5378	5391	5403	5416	5428	1	3	4	5	6	8	9	10	11
35	5441	5453	5465	5478	5490	5502	5514	5527	5539	5551	1	2	4	5	6	7	9	10	11
36	5563	5575	5587	5599	5611	5623	5635	5647	5658	5670	1	2	4	5	6	7	8	10	11
37	5682	5694	5705	5717	5729	5740	5752	5763	5775	5786	1	2	3	5	6	7	8	9	10
38	5798	5809	5821	5832	5843	5855	5866	5877	5888	5899	1	2	3	5	6	7	8	9	10
39	5911	5922	5933	5944	5955	5966	5977	5988	5999	6010	1	2	3	4	5	7	8	9	10
40	6021	6031	6042	6053	6064	6075	6085	6096	6107	6117	1	2	3	4	5	6	8	9	10
41	6128	6138	6149	6160	6170	6180	6191	6201	6212	6222	1	2	3	4	5	6	7	8	9
42	6232	6243	6253	6263	6274	6284	6294	6304	6314	6325	1	2	3	4	5	6	7	8	9
43	6335	6345	6355	6365	6375	6385	6395	6405	6415	6425	1	2	3	4	5	6	7	8	9
44	6435	6444	6454	6464	6474	6484	6493	6503	6513	6522	1	2	3	4	5	6	7	8	9
45	6532	6542	6551	6561	6571	6580	6590	6599	6609	6618	1	2	3	4	5	6	7	8	9
46	6628	6637	6646	6656	6665	6675	6684	6693	6702	6712	1	2	3	4	5	6	7	7	8
47	6721	6730	6739	6749	6758	6767	6776	6785	6794	6803	1	2	3	4	5	5	6	7	8
48	6812	6821	6830	6839	6848	6857	6866	6875	6884	6893	1	2	3	4	4	5	6	7	8
49	6902	6911	6920	6928	6937	6946	6955	6964	6972	6981	1	2	3	4	4	5	6	7	8

BPP
PROFESSIONAL EDUCATION

	0	1	2	3	4	5	6	7	8	9	1	2	3	4	5	6	7	8	9
50	6990	6998	7007	7016	7024	7033	7042	7050	7059	7067	1	2	3	3	4	5	6	7	8
51	7076	7084	7093	7101	7110	7118	7126	7135	7143	7152	1	2	3	3	4	5	6	7	8
52	7160	7168	7177	7185	7193	7202	7210	7218	7226	7235	1	2	2	3	4	5	6	7	7
53	7243	7251	7259	7267	7275	7284	7292	7300	7308	7316	1	2	2	3	4	5	6	6	7
54	7324	7332	7340	7348	7356	7364	7372	7380	7388	7396	1	2	2	3	4	5	6	6	7
55	7404	7412	7419	7427	7435	7443	7451	7459	7466	7474	1	2	2	3	4	5	5	6	7
56	7482	7490	7497	7505	7513	7520	7528	7536	7543	7551	1	2	2	3	4	5	5	6	7
57	7559	7566	7574	7582	7589	7597	7604	7612	7619	7627	1	2	2	3	4	5	5	6	7
58	7634	7642	7649	7657	7664	7672	7679	7686	7694	7701	1	1	2	3	4	4	5	6	7
59	7709	7716	7723	7731	7738	7745	7752	7760	7767	7774	1	1	2	3	4	4	5	6	7
60	7782	7789	7796	7803	7810	7818	7825	7832	7839	7846	1	1	2	3	4	4	5	6	6
61	7853	7860	7868	7875	7882	7889	7896	7903	7910	7917	1	1	2	3	4	4	5	6	6
62	7924	7931	7938	7945	7952	7959	7966	7973	7980	7987	1	1	2	3	3	4	5	6	6
63	7993	8000	8007	8014	8021	8028	8035	8041	8048	8055	1	1	2	3	3	4	5	5	6
64	8062	8069	8075	8082	8089	8096	8102	8109	8116	8122	1	1	2	3	3	4	5	5	6
65	8129	8136	8142	8149	8156	8162	8169	8176	8182	8189	1	1	2	3	3	4	5	5	6
66	8195	8202	8209	8215	8222	8228	8235	8241	8248	8254	1	1	2	3	3	4	5	5	6
67	8261	8267	8274	8280	8287	8293	8299	8306	8312	8319	1	1	2	3	3	4	5	5	6
68	8325	8331	8338	8344	8351	8357	8363	8370	8376	8382	1	1	2	3	3	4	4	5	6
69	8388	8395	8401	8407	8414	8420	8426	8432	8439	8445	1	1	2	2	3	4	4	5	6
70	8451	8457	8463	8470	8476	8482	8488	8494	8500	8506	1	1	2	2	3	4	4	5	6
71	8513	8519	8525	8531	8537	8543	8549	8555	8561	8567	1	1	2	2	3	4	4	5	5
72	8573	8579	8585	8591	8597	8603	8609	8615	8621	8627	1	1	2	2	3	4	4	5	5
73	8633	8639	8645	8651	8657	8663	8669	8675	8681	8686	1	1	2	2	3	4	4	5	5
74	8692	8698	8704	8710	8716	8722	8727	8733	8739	8745	1	1	2	2	3	4	4	5	5
75	8751	8756	8762	8768	8774	8779	8785	8791	8797	8802	1	1	2	2	3	3	4	5	5
76	8808	8814	8820	8825	8831	8837	8842	8848	8854	8859	1	1	2	2	3	3	4	5	5
77	8865	8871	8876	8882	8887	8893	8899	8904	8910	8915	1	1	2	2	3	3	4	4	5
78	8921	8927	8932	8938	8943	8949	8954	8960	8965	8971	1	1	2	2	3	3	4	4	5
79	8976	8982	8987	8993	8998	9004	9009	9015	9020	9025	1	1	2	2	3	3	4	4	5
80	9031	9036	9042	9047	9053	9058	9063	9069	9074	9079	1	1	2	2	3	3	4	4	5
81	9085	9090	9096	9101	9106	9112	9117	9122	9128	9133	1	1	2	2	3	3	4	4	5
82	9138	9143	9149	9154	9159	9165	9170	9175	9180	9186	1	1	2	2	3	3	4	4	5
83	9191	9196	9201	9206	9212	9217	9222	9227	9232	9238	1	1	2	2	3	3	4	4	5
84	9243	9248	9253	9258	9263	9269	9274	9279	9284	9289	1	1	2	2	3	3	4	4	5
85	9294	9299	9304	9309	9315	9320	9325	9330	9335	9340	1	1	2	2	3	3	4	4	5
86	9345	9350	9355	9360	9365	9370	9375	9380	9385	9390	1	1	2	2	3	3	4	4	5
87	9395	9400	9405	9410	9415	9420	9425	9430	9435	9440	0	1	1	2	2	3	3	4	4
88	9445	9450	9455	9460	9465	9469	9474	9479	9484	9489	0	1	1	2	2	3	3	4	4
89	9494	9499	9504	9509	9513	9518	9523	9528	9533	9538	0	1	1	2	2	3	3	4	4
90	9542	9547	9552	9557	9562	9566	9571	9576	9581	9586	0	1	1	2	2	3	3	4	4
91	9590	9595	9600	9605	9609	9614	9619	9624	9628	9633	0	1	1	2	2	3	3	4	4
92	9638	9643	9647	9652	9657	9661	9666	9671	9675	9680	0	1	1	2	2	3	3	4	4
93	9685	9689	9694	9699	9703	9708	9713	9717	9722	9727	0	1	1	2	2	3	3	4	4
94	9731	9736	9741	9745	9750	9754	9759	9763	9768	9773	0	1	1	2	2	3	3	4	4
95	9777	9782	9786	9791	9795	9800	9805	9809	9814	9818	0	1	1	2	2	3	3	4	4
96	9823	9827	9832	9836	9841	9845	9850	9854	9859	9863	0	1	1	2	2	3	3	4	4
97	9868	9872	9877	9881	9886	9890	9894	9899	9903	9908	0	1	1	2	2	3	3	4	4
98	9912	9917	9921	9926	9930	9934	9939	9943	9948	9952	0	1	1	2	2	3	3	4	4
99	9956	9961	9965	9969	9974	9978	9983	9987	9991	9996	0	1	1	2	2	3	3	3	4

Time series

Additive model: Series = Trend + Seasonal + Random

Multiplicative model: Series = Trend * Seasonal * Random

Regression analysis

The linear regression equation of Y on X is given by:

$Y = a + bX$ *or*

$Y - \overline{Y} = b(X - \overline{X})$, where

$$b = \frac{\text{Covariance (XY)}}{\text{Variance (X)}} = \frac{n\sum XY - (\sum X)(\sum Y)}{n\sum X^2 - (\sum X)^2}$$

and $a = \overline{Y} - b\overline{X}$,

or solve $\sum Y = na + b\sum X$

$\sum XY = a\sum X + b\sum X^2$

Exponential $Y = ab^x$

Geometric $Y = aX^b$

See overleaf for information on other
BPP products and how to order

CIMA Order

To BPP Professional Education, Aldine Place, London W12 8AW
Tel: 020 8740 2211. Fax: 020 8740 1184
www.bpp.com Email publishing@bpp.com
Order online www.bpp.com

Mr/Mrs/Ms (Full name)
Daytime delivery address
Postcode
Email
Daytime Tel
Date of exam (month/year)

	7/02 Texts	1/03 Kits	1/03 Passcards	Tapes	Videos	Virtual Campus	7/02 i-Pass	7/02 i-Learn	7/02 MCQ cards
FOUNDATION									
1 Financial Accounting Fundamentals	£20.95	£10.95	£6.95	£12.95	£25	£50	£24.95		£5.95
2 Management Accounting Fundamentals	£20.95	£10.95	£6.95	£12.95	£25	£50	£24.95		£5.95
3A Economics for Business	£20.95	£10.95	£6.95	£12.95	£25	£50	£24.95		£5.95
3B Business Law	£20.95	£10.95	£6.95	£12.95	£25	£50	£24.95		£5.95
3C Business Mathematics	£20.95	£10.95	£6.95	£12.95	£25	£50	£24.95		£5.95
INTERMEDIATE							i-Learn 7/02		
4 Finance	£20.95	£10.95	£6.95	£12.95	£25	£80	£24.95	£34.95	£5.95
5 Business Tax (FA 2002)	£20.95 (10/02)	£10.95	£6.95	£12.95	£25	£80	£24.95	£34.95	£5.95
6 Financial Accounting	£20.95	£10.95	£6.95	£12.95	£25	£80	£24.95	£34.95	£5.95
6i Financial Accounting International	£20.95	£10.95	£6.95	£12.95	£25	£80	£24.95	£34.95	£5.95
7 Financial Reporting	£20.95	£10.95	£6.95	£12.95	£25	£80	£24.95	£34.95	£5.95
7i Financial Reporting International	£20.95	£10.95	£6.95	£12.95	£25	£80	£24.95	£34.95	£5.95
8 Management Accounting - Performance Management	£20.95	£10.95	£6.95	£12.95	£25	£80	£24.95	£34.95	£5.95
9 Management Accounting - Decision Making	£20.95	£10.95	£6.95	£12.95	£25	£80	£24.95	£34.95	£5.95
10 Systems and Project Management	£20.95	£10.95	£6.95	£12.95	£25	£80	£24.95	£34.95	£5.95
11 Organisational Management	£20.95	£10.95	£6.95	£12.95	£25	£80	£24.95	£34.95	£5.95
FINAL									
12 Management Accounting - Business Strategy	£20.95	£10.95	£6.95	£12.95	£25				
13 Management Accounting - Financial Strategy	£20.95	£10.95	£6.95	£12.95	£25				
14 Management Accounting - Information Strategy	£20.95	£10.95	£6.95	£12.95	£25				
15 Case Study (1) Workbook	£19.95			£12.95	£25				
(2) Toolkit		£19.95 (For 5/03: available 3/03. For 11/03: available 9/03)							
Learning to Learn (7/02)	£9.95								

Total [ ]

POSTAGE & PACKING

Texts/Kits

	Mail Order First	Each extra	On-line per item
UK	£5.00	£2.00	£2.00
Europe*	£6.00	£4.00	£4.00
Rest of world	£20.00	£10.00	£10.00

£ [ ] / £ [ ] / £ [ ]

Passcards/MCQ Cards/Success Tapes/Videos/CDs

	Mail Order First	Each extra	On-line per-item
UK	£2.00	£1.00	£1.00
Europe*	£3.00	£2.00	£2.00
Rest of world	£8.00	£8.00	£8.00

£ [ ] / £ [ ] / £ [ ]

Grand Total (Cheques to *BPP Professional Education*)
I enclose a cheque for (incl.Postage) £ [ ]
Or charge to Access/Visa/Switch
Card Number [ ][ ][ ][ ][ ][ ][ ][ ][ ][ ][ ][ ][ ][ ][ ][ ]
Expiry date [ ]   Start Date [ ]
Issue Number (Switch Only) [ ]
Signature

We aim to deliver to all UK addresses inside 5 working days. A signature will be required. Orders to all EU addresses should be delivered within 8 working days. *Europe includes the Republic of Ireland and the Channel Islands.

REVIEW FORM & FREE PRIZE DRAW

All original review forms from the entire BPP range, completed with genuine comments, will be entered into one of two draws on 31 July 2003 and 31 January 2004. The names on the first four forms picked out on each occasion will be sent a cheque for £50.

Name: _____   Address: _____

_____

_____

How have you used this Kit?
(Tick one box only)

☐ Self study (book only)

☐ On a course: college (please state)_____

_____

☐ With 'correspondence' package

☐ Other _____

Why did you decide to purchase this Kit?
(Tick one box only)

☐ Have used the complementary Study Text

☐ Have used other BPP products in the past

☐ Recommendation by friend/colleague

☐ Recommendation by a lecturer at college

☐ Saw advertising in journals

☐ Saw website

☐ Other _____

During the past six months do you recall seeing/receiving any of the following?
(Tick as many boxes as are relevant)

☐ Our advertisement in *CIMA Insider*

☐ Our advertisement in *Financial Management*

☐ Our advertisement in *Pass*

☐ Our brochure with a letter through the post

☐ Our website

Which (if any) aspects of our advertising do you find useful?
(Tick as many boxes as are relevant)

☐ Prices and publication dates of new editions

☐ Information on product content

☐ Facility to order books off-the-page

☐ None of the above

When did you sit the exam? _____

Which of the following BPP products have you used for this paper?

☐ Study Text ☐ MCQ Cards ☑ Kit ☐ Passcards ☐ Success Tape ☐ Breakthrough Video ☐ i-Pass

Your ratings, comments and suggestions would be appreciated on the following areas of this Kit.

	Very useful	Useful	Not useful
Effective revision	☐	☐	☐
Exam guidance	☐	☐	☐
Background (Websites and mindmaps)	☐	☐	☐
Multiple choice questions	☐	☐	☐
Objective test questions	☐	☐	☐
Guidance in answers	☐	☐	☐
Content and structure of answers	☐	☐	☐
Mock assessments	☐	☐	☐
Mock assessment answers	☐	☐	☐

	Excellent	Good	Adequate	Poor
Overall opinion of this Kit	☐	☐	☐	☐

Do you intend to continue using BPP products?   ☐ Yes   ☐ No

Please note any further comments and suggestions/errors on the reverse of this page. The BPP author of this edition can be e-mailed at: alisonmchugh@bpp.com

Please return this form to: Nick Weller, CIMA range manager, BPP Professional Education, FREEPOST, London, W12 8BR

REVIEW FORM & FREE PRIZE DRAW (continued)

Please note any further comments and suggestions/errors below.

FREE PRIZE DRAW RULES

1   Closing date for 31 July 2003 draw is 30 June 2003. Closing date for 31 January 2004 draw is 31 December 2003.

2   Restricted to entries with UK and Eire addresses only. BPP employees, their families and business associates are excluded.

3   No purchase necessary. Entry forms are available upon request from BPP Professional Education. No more than one entry per title, per person. Draw restricted to persons aged 16 and over.

4   Winners will be notified by post and receive their cheques not later than 6 weeks after the relevant draw date.

5   The decision of the promoter in all matters is final and binding. No correspondence will be entered into.